1858

ABRAHAM LINCOLN, JEFFERSON DAVIS,

ROBERT E. LEE, ULYSSES S. GRANT

AND THE WAR THEY FAILED TO SEE

BRUCE CHADWICK

SOURCEBOOKS, INC.®
NAPERVILLE, ILLINOIS

Published by Sourcebooks, Inc.

P.O. Box 4410, Naperville, Illinois 60567-4410

(630) 961-3900

Fax: (630) 961-2168

www.sourcebooks.com

Library of Congress Cataloging-in-Publication Data

Chadwick, Bruce.
  1858 : Abraham Lincoln, Jefferson Davis, Robert E. Lee, Ulysses S. Grant, and the war they failed to see / Bruce Chadwick.
    p. cm.
  Includes bibliographical references.

  ISBN-13: 978-1-4022-0941-3 (hardcover)

  ISBN-10: 1-4022-0941-X (hardcover)

  1. United States--History--Civil War, 1861-1865--Causes. 2. United States--Politics and government--1857-1861. 3. Politicians--United States--Biography. 4. Generals--United States--Biography. 5. Politicians--Southern States--Biography. 6. Generals--Southern States--Biography. 7. Secession--Southern States. 8. Southern States--Politics and government--1775-1865. I. Title. II. Title: Eighteen fifty-eight.

E458.C425 2008

973.7'11--dc22

2007039254

Printed and bound in the United States of America.

BG 10 9 8 7 6 5 4 3 2 1

For

Margie

and Rory

CONTENTS

ACKNOWLEDGMENTS

T he gratification in writing about history is not the publication of the book, but the journey to that moment. My journey on this book was long and complicated because I found myself writing biographies in one long story about one of the most critical twelve-month periods in American history. I realized that I needed plenty of help to tell the story of *1858* and I received it.

I want to thank many people for their assistance in my work on *1858*, but first I want to thank Hillel Black, my editor and the executive editor of Sourcebooks. Hillel, a lover of history, helped me to make an entire story out of seven fragmented tales in this work and has, over the years, encouraged me in all of my work about history. Also at Sourcebooks, I must thank Tara Van Timmeren, who also edited the book, and Heather Moore, the hard-working director of publicity.

My tracking of the year 1858 took me to numerous libraries, archives, and museums. Many thanks to the gracious people at the Virginia State Library, the Abraham Lincoln Presidential Library, Princeton University's Firestone Library, Rutgers University's Alexander Library, the David Library of the American Revolution, Cindy Van Horn at the Lincoln Museum, Ronald Baumann at Oberlin College, Lisa Keys at the Kansas State Historical Society, Elizabeth Hogan at the University of Notre Dame Archives, Mary Troy and historian Frank Cucurrulo at Arlington House, the Robert E. Lee Memorial, Heather Milne at the Museum of the Confederacy, Mike Coker at the South Carolina Historical Society, Peter Wisbey at the William Seward House Museum, and Jim Gerswenc at Dickinson

College Library. Dr. Michael Birkner at Gettysburg College was kind enough to read through the Buchanan chapters of the book and offer suggestions. Thanks, too, to Fred Smith, at New Jersey City University's Guarini Library, and to Jo Bruno at New Jersey City University for their encouragement.

I want to thank my agents at McIntosh and Otis, Elizabeth Winick and Jonathan Lyons, plus Rebecca Strauss, for their support in this project and my other work.

And, as always, thanks to my wife Marjorie for her never-ending assistance and for sharing my hopes and dreams.

AUTHOR TO READER

The Civil War began in April 1861, when Confederate forces in Charleston, South Carolina, bombarded Fort Sumter, ensconced on an island in the city's harbor. The terrible conflict has resulted in hundreds of books about the war, its battles, causes, and aftermath. This book explores the events and personalities of a single year to show what happened in those twelve months that would set the nation, North and South, on a collision course that culminated in the war that ripped the country apart and brought about the deaths of more than 630,000 young men.

The record of that year is told within seven separate stories that stand alone as complete sagas, and together explain what happened throughout the nation that year, a year in which slavery came to dominate every election and discussion from the gold fields of California to the mansions of Boston to the campaign trail in Illinois. The stories of events of that critical year include: Mississippi senator and Mexican War hero Jefferson Davis, who later became the president of the Confederacy, nearly died, but recovered to become the nation's secessionist spokesman. A disgruntled Colonel Robert E. Lee, who later led the Confederate Army, had to decide whether he would resign from the military, disappear from public life and return to his beloved Virginia to run his wife's family plantation. William Tecumseh Sherman, one of the great Union generals in the Civil War, left the army to make his wife happy. He had failed at a number of jobs, and by the fall of 1858 he was reduced to running a roadside food stand in Kansas.

In autumn of that year, two dozen residents of Oberlin, Ohio, freed a slave that had been apprehended by slave catchers from Kentucky; their arrest and well-publicized trial set off a firestorm of debate across America. During that same autumn, in the middle of the elections, New York Senator William Seward seemed to solidify his hold on the 1860 Republican presidential nomination with a fiery speech in Rochester, New York, in which he told the country that all Americans were engaged in an "irresistible conflict" over slavery that might end in Civil War. That winter, abolitionist fanatic John Brown, who later attacked Harper's Ferry, freed several slaves in a daring raid in Missouri, marching them eleven hundred miles to Canada in a trek involving chases and gunfights that the nation's newspapers covered from coast to coast. And, of course, 1858 was the year in which the famous U.S. Senator Stephen Douglas, certain to be the Democratic presidential nominee in 1860, engaged in seven historic debates with little-known Abraham Lincoln in their Illinois senate race.

At the same time that all of these events transpired, at the White House President James Buchanan ignored slavery, engaged in questionable imperialist schemes, divided his own party during the elections, started feuds with dozens of important people, and exhibited a distinct lack of leadership at a time when the nation desperately needed some. The stories of his meanness and ineptitude will hold the seven main stories together to offer a comprehensive account of a nation of angry people, North and South, drifting toward one of the tragic conflicts of history.

I thought that evoking the events of that critical year with seven dramatic stories, linked by the chronology of James Buchanan's presidency and his insistent fumbling, would be more beneficial than writing a straight history of those crucial twelve months. Within this format, event by event and person by person, I think I can explain how the country reluctantly, and perhaps inevitably, stumbled toward that moment in April 1861, when the guns in Charleston opened up on Fort Sumter.

Chapter One

THE WHITE HOUSE

NEW YEAR'S DAY 1858

The year 1858 could not have started in a grander fashion than it did on January 1 in Washington, DC. The New Year arrived on a cold but sunny day. It was welcomed with parties and receptions all over the nation's capital. The Republicans and Democrats who had fought so bitterly throughout 1857 over the slavery issue put aside their differences and mingled with each other at the homes of the country's political leaders. One of the most well-attended receptions took place at the home of Vice President John Breckinridge, a thirty-seven-year-old former Kentucky slaveholder and rising political star. Another party was hosted by the Speaker of the House of Representatives, James Orr. Several cabinet members flung open the doors of their homes for guests invited to similar receptions. Senators and congressmen, such as Jefferson Davis of Mississippi, Thomas Hart Benton of Missouri, John Slidell of Louisiana, William Bigler of Pennsylvania, and George Pugh of Ohio, held lavish soirées. The most important public figures in public life attended these parties, wearing their best suits and hats. They were accompanied by their wives, dressed in fashionable gowns and adorned in expensive jewelry.

Continuing a tradition, President James Buchanan, in office just under a year, hosted a three-hour reception at the White House for members of the diplomatic corps, Democratic members of the Senate and House, and political friends on the morning of New Year's Day. Guests arrived at the White House just before eleven o'clock in the morning and remained until the middle of the afternoon. There were several hundred of them and they came in a continuous parade of elegant carriages. At noon, the front doors of the White House were opened to the public to meet the president. Thousands of ordinary people walked into the executive mansion, many for the very first time, all impressed with its size. After a lengthy wait in a receiving line, they met President Buchanan, who wished them all a Happy New Year.[1]

The atmosphere at the president's New Year's reception was jovial and most of the conversation between the fifteenth president and his guests did not involve the issue of slavery that seemed about to overwhelm America. Everyone was grateful for that. The year 1857 had been difficult. A recession that sent financial markets reeling in the past year still crippled the dollar, weakened the banks, and hurt the import/export trade. Unemployment was up, factories shut their doors, the federal government ran a deficit, the public staged runs on banks, and financially pressed banks could not meet their specie payments.[2] Hinton Helper's book, *The Impending Crisis of the South,* highly critical of Southerners and slavery that was published during the previous year, was still the central topic of many conversations. At the end of the year, politicians in the Kansas Territory, eager to bring it into the Union as a state, had sent Congress not one, but two state constitutions, one recognizing slavery and one not, for a decision. Three congressmen were forced to resign during the year following a corruption scandal connected to the 1856 campaign.

In addition, Buchanan sent an army of twenty-five hundred men on an ill-advised expedition to Utah to put down what he described as an uprising of Mormons; the result was a debacle that included an attack by Indians on the troopers, the burning of army supply wagon trains, destruction of crops and homes to deny the army food, and lengthy journeys through snow-bound mountain passes by the army across what one trooper described as "the most desolate country I have ever beheld."[3] The expedition was a humiliation of the army and the administration.[4]

An illegal slave ship jammed with six hundred captives, possibly headed for America, was intercepted off the coast of Africa in a well-publicized seizure at the end of November, and its capture was followed by reports of other slave vessels that had secretly made it to the United States.[5]

An American adventurer, William Walker, led a coup against the government of Nicaragua and seized control of the country, only to be deposed by the forces of neighboring nations.[6]

And all across the nation, controversy still raged over the Supreme Court's *Dred Scott* decision, handed down in March of 1857, in which the high court upheld the Fugitive Slave Act, reappealed the Missouri Compromise of 1850, decided that Congress could not declare any territory free, and ruled that slaves were not people, but property. And, on top of all that, the population of America continued to explode, increasing by nearly 25 percent over the last decade.

No one was happier to move forward and put 1857 behind him than President James Buchanan. The president was an odd-looking man. He was tall and heavy-set, with a mop of curly white hair. He had had throat and nasal growths surgically removed, but the operations, primitive in the era, left large and ugly scars on his neck. He also suffered from myopic vision that forced him to bend his head severely to the left and forward in order to read, further exposing the huge scars he tried to hide with very high shirt collars. His vision caused him to squint severely whenever he read something or tried to look out over a crowded room, further adding to his unusual appearance. One of his eyes was brown and the other hazel. His forward-leaning head also misled many into thinking he agreed with what they said. He was a big man, but oddly had tiny feet that he bragged about to everyone he met.

Buchanan had arrived in Washington as the victor in a close presidential race in 1856 in which he was the nominee of a disorganized and overly confident Democratic Party that found itself fighting for its life at the polls against the fiery new Republicans, who had replaced the defunct Whigs, and the zealots of the American Party, who mounted a strong third-party challenge. Buchanan had carried nineteen of the forty-one states and won the election with 59 percent of the electoral vote, but the Republicans surprised everyone. Their presidential nominee, explorer John C. Fremont, won eleven states. Fremont had earned the nickname "the Pathfinder" following his five well-publicized expeditions through the Rocky Mountains and the Great Plains over the previous decade. A third-party candidate, former president Millard Fillmore, a sectional candidate running on the ticket of the American Party (an anti-Catholic and anti-immigrant group formerly called the "Know-Nothings"), captured one state.

Buchanan earned 45 percent of the popular vote, giving up 30 percent to Fremont and 25 percent to Fillmore. If Fillmore had carried several Southern states and denied Buchanan the election, or forced it into the House of Representatives, Fremont would have come close to winning the election outright. Buchanan won his home state, Pennsylvania, by just 577 votes out of nearly 500,000 cast, and Indiana by less than 2,000 out of 235,000. He only earned 105,528 votes in Illinois, 44.1 percent, against 130,306 cast against him, but was awarded the state's eleven electoral votes because his two opponents split that larger ballot. Even Buchanan was forced to admit that the loss of just two states would have given Fremont the White House.[7]

Buchanan, sixty-five, appeared to be one of the most qualified men to ever take the oath of office. He had served two terms in the Pennsylvania state legislature, five terms in the U.S. House of Representatives, two years as minister to Russia, two terms in the U.S. Senate, four years as President James Polk's secretary of state, and was the minister to Great Britain under President Pierce—more than four decades in public service.

Looking back, he may have been one of the most ill-prepared men ever elected president. While applauded for a long life in public service, he was denounced by others, who jokingly called him the "Old Public Functionary." He had been in politics a long time but did not seem to understand that his own party had changed dramatically during his lifetime. A Jacksonian Democrat, the president-elect was hopelessly stuck in the past and unaware of the deep divisions the slavery issue had created in the party that he now led. At a time when the national political stage was crowded with colorful, vivid personalities—Stephen Douglas of Illinois, Senator William Seward of New York, up-and-coming state legislator Abraham Lincoln of Illinois, Jefferson Davis of Mississippi, and Governor Salmon Chase of Ohio—the president was a reserved man who had little personal warmth. Henry Foote, a Mississippi senator who knew Buchanan for years, told friends that he had never once heard him tell a joke.[8]

Even those who gave Buchanan important jobs later lamented their decision to do so. President Andrew Jackson, when asked why he selected Buchanan as his minister to Russia, scoffed that, "It was as far as I could send him out of my sight; and where he could do the least harm. I would have sent him to the North Pole if we had kept a minister there."[9]

Buchanan was not an aggressive man and throughout his career friends had complained that he never fought for his principles. He was always detached from whatever political crisis was at hand, standing back as a cold and disinterested observer to watch others argue issues with great passion. He was so detached from life, some asserted, that he even wrote his memoirs in the third person.

The Pennsylvanian had always wanted to become president in what seemed a fitting final chapter to his long years of service to the country, yet he could never bring himself to actively seek the office. In 1841, Pennsylvania political leaders told him that he could win the Democratic presidential nomination over Martin Van Buren. He might have, too, but he would not fight for it. Buchanan would not fight for anything. He haughtily dismissed the invitation and said he would only do so if he had assurances that every single one of Pennsylvania's delegates would support him. "If the Democrats of [Pennsylvania] would sustain me with an unbroken front I think my chances are fully equal if not superior to his [Van Buren]…should there be even the appearance of a serious division in [Pennsylvania], I shall make my bow and retire."[10]

He was a leader without defined goals, a serious flaw in a president, and now, in 1858, his tentative leadership would make him partially responsible for the continued deterioration of the unity of the United States.[11]

The president became an immediate target for not only the Republicans, but the Southern Democrats, who feared that the Northern wing of their party, led by Buchanan, would abandon them. The Southerners insisted that Buchanan pledge that he would not support any legislation that weakened slavery or their regional power. Robert Rhett, the editor of the Charleston, South Carolina, newspaper *Mercury*, even demanded that Buchanan form a group to rewrite the Constitution of the United States with strong proslavery language in it.

At the same time, the Northern Democrats told the president that he could not let these Southern radicals hold him a political prisoner. Buchanan, never an adept political infighter, stumbled toward a compromise between the warring wings of his party and pleased neither. He also paid little attention to the consequences of any of his actions. In an outrageous incident of tampering, Buchanan wrote to a Pennsylvanian on the U.S. Supreme Court and tried to convince him to vote against Dred Scott in the 1857 case so that the final *Dred Scott* decision looked more national in scope than Southern (most of the other anti–*Dred Scott* votes were from Southern justices). Never for a moment did Buchanan think that interference and his subsequent support of the ruling would anger Northerners. That casual attitude would pervade his administration.[12]

One Southerner, Edmund Ruffin, wrote prophetically in his diary of the new president that he had "very little of the respect or the confidence of the men from the South by whose support alone he was sustained and elected. I anticipate for him a reign that will bring him but little of either pleasure or honor."[13]

Buchanan encountered nothing but problems during his first year in office. It started in the worst possible way when he left his estate at Wheatland, Pennsylvania, for the carriage ride to the capital for the March 4 inaugural. A cold wave had moved in and it had snowed all night; the small crowd that turned out in the freezing weather offered few cheers and the musicians refused to play because their fingers would freeze on their instruments. Following the arrival of his train in Washington, Buchanan was placed in a carriage. The horse suddenly bolted and the president was saved from being dumped on the roadway by an alert coachman who jumped down on top of the horse to calm her.[14]

Ignoring talent, he selected a "unity" cabinet, with someone for every-one.[15] The president named people who had no business running the coun-try, such as the obese, seventy-four-year-old former Democratic presidential nominee Lewis Cass, the secretary of state, who suffered from frequent attacks of vertigo and was often too sick to run his department. Buchanan was told by many that Cass was not healthy and was practically senile. The president even insinuated that to Cass, but was still delighted to give him the most powerful job in the country. He wrote Cass that he had checked with the old man's friends and that "I am happy, however, to learn from the most authentic sources that you are now as capable of mental labor and physical exertion as you were ten years ago." Secretary of War John Floyd was a hap-less administrator.[16]

The president became embroiled in feuds with anyone who expressed the slightest displeasure with his cabinet. Some of his critics were among the most powerful men in the country, allies he would need in the years to come. Henry Wise, the governor of Virginia, worried that Buchanan would listen to the men proposed for his centrist cabinet and not make decisions himself. Buchanan might have dismissed the governor's concerns, but instead snapped at Wise in a long and harsh letter. He wrote him, "Do you in your heart believe that if any one of these gentlemen should be a member of my cabinet I would suffer them to checkmate my best mind? Or have you so little confidence in my nerve to imagine I should submit to such injustice?"[17]

The cabinet secretaries who were going to steer the country were worked hard by the president, who for several months insisted on exhausting daily cabinet meetings. The secretaries' view of the chief soon became rather like that of his former aides in other offices. They accused him of harboring a "cold and unimpassioned nature," of being inflexible and unable to see any point of view but his own.[18] They thought him imperious and nicknamed him "the Squire." They also had no idea what his policies were. Attorney General Jeremiah Black summed it up best when he wrote that, "He is a stubborn old gentleman, very fond of having his own way—and I don't know what his way is."[19]

The tidal wave of forces at work in the 1850s had dramatically changed the nature of national politics. Buchanan was so oblivious to that change that he still believed that a president's prestige did not depend on domestic accomplishments, but far-off international achievements. Instead of arbitrating the constant battles over slavery, he embarked on a series of questionable foreign policy adventures—the annexation of Cuba, a threatened war in Paraguay—that sometimes took his attention far away from the issue of slavery. He often appeared to be more concerned about Central America than central Kansas, more worried about Nicaragua than New England.

The new president was a bachelor in a city filled with political couples. He had disdained all thoughts of matrimony after an early engagement to Anne Coleman had ended disastrously—she died following a quarrel with him.[20] He never showed any interest in marriage after that and spent his time in Washington with bachelors, mostly Southerners. In private life, his single status mattered little, but on the political stage a bachelor chief executive seemed out of place on the Washington social scene. His niece, the gracious and attractive Harriet Lane, lived in the White House with him and served as his hostess, but it was not the same as having a First Lady to entertain public figures and foreign dignitaries.

The president did date many women, bringing them to the White House for state functions or taking them to the homes of friends for dinner parties. He spent lengthy periods of time dressing for these dates, so fastidious in the way he looked that an aide once derisively called him "a masculine Miss Fribble." At official functions and visits to friends, Buchanan passed himself off as a connoisseur of fine wines, but he was not. An aide joked that all he drank was "his nutty old Madeira."[21]

Unsure of himself on the national stage and unwilling to trust many people, he became a hopeless micromanager, spending long hours every night reading paperwork that any other executive would have passed on to underlings. In the spring of 1858, exhausted from it all, he wrote Britain's Lord Clarendon that he had no time for himself, that he was too busy with work. He told Clarendon that he intended to correspond with him, "but my numerous and pressing engagements have hitherto rendered this almost impossible. I have now scarcely time to say my prayers." He added that he knew that the chores of the president were time-consuming, but the way he conducted them "the business has increased ten, I may say twentyfold and is now so onerous that no man can very long bear the burden."[22] He told friend Arnold Plumer that he was forced to write him on Sunday, what should have been the president's day off. "Although I do not write letters on the Sabbath, I have no time to write them on any other day."[23]

There was an iron regimen to his workday, too. The president arrived at his office at the White House precisely at 9:00 a.m., never before, and worked until precisely 4:00 p.m. He then took an hour-long walk around the White House grounds, regardless of the weather, dined at exactly 5:00 p.m., except when there was a state dinner, and returned to his office and worked all night. "He often worked just for work's sake," insisted niece Annie Buchanan.[24]

He was a religious man who said his prayers every day, went to church every Sunday, read his Bible often, and refused to permit any dancing in White House events on Sunday or religious holidays.

He was also nosy and pried into the personal lives of his cabinet members, boldly asking one, Howell Cobb, how much money he earned. Buchanan had an acute sense of hearing and claimed that he could hear whispers coming from another room; he often strained to listen to conversations, certain those involved were talking about him. He was even more curious about the love life of his niece Harriet, constantly opening her mail, infuriating her each time he did so.

Buchanan was always ill at ease with people because his unusual physical appearance invariably drew stares. With his neck craned to one side, continual eye squinting, excessively high shirt collars flowing up to his ears, and his tangle of white hair, he looked like an oversized white carrot that had been pulled sideways out of the ground.

He wound up feuding with people who could have helped him over petty disagreements. For years, he snubbed his own vice president, John Breckinridge, whose support he needed, just because Breckinridge socialized with John Forney, an old friend with whom Buchanan had split over a patronage squabble.[25]

And on top of all that, contaminated water at the opulent, five-story National Hotel, where he lived during the weeks prior to his inauguration, gave him a severe case of stomach disorders. The attacks could not be cured with the primitive elixirs of the day; the diarrhea made him ill and irritable during the crucial first several months of his presidency.[26]

Just before returning to the United States from England to actively campaign for the presidency in the winter of 1856, Buchanan wrote political operative William Marcy that being president would be "the trial of his life." He was right.[27]

The new president was determined to put the slavery question behind him right away, restore harmony to the country, and then move on with his dreams of manifest destiny and an American presence in places such as Paraguay, Venezuela, Tahiti, Mexico, Nicaragua, Alaska, and the annexation of Cuba.

Many Americans believed it might be possible for Buchanan to cool the heated and seemingly endless debates over slavery. He was a Pennsylvanian who sided with the South on the legitimacy of slavery and the right of residents in the new territories to determine whether or not they wanted it. He had always felt that way and never hid his feelings, telling those who greeted him just after his election that "the Southern people still cherish a love for the Union; but what to them is even our blessed confederacy, the wisest and the best form of government ever devised by man, if they cannot enjoy its blessing and its benefits without being in constant alarm for their wives and children…[from] the storm of abolition."[28]

The electoral votes of the Southern states had carried him into the White House. Buchanan was thankful for that because, he reminded his followers, he received no similar help in the North. He wrote, "The preachers and fanatics of New England had excited the people to such a degree on the slavery question that they generally prayed and preached against me from their pulpits."[29] The Southern firebrands who had threatened to leave the Union if John Fremont was elected seemed placated. Just before the election, the murderous wars over slavery in Kansas had died down following the installation of a new government there.

Buchanan told a crowd of well-wishers gathered at his estate in 1857 that the defeat of both the radical Republicans and the American Party at the polls, along with apparent order in Kansas and the *Dred Scott* ruling that shattered the Republican claims that Congress could prohibit slavery in new territories, meant that the slavery issue had been pretty much defused. "The night is departing, and the roseate and propitious morn now breaking upon us promises a long day of peace and prosperity for our country," he whimsically informed the cheering crowd. He also assured the throng that peace was at hand in the territories. "We shall hear no more of bleeding Kansas."[30] Others were not so certain.

Buchanan's Inaugural Ball was one of the liveliest in Washington history. Handsomely attired men and women in elegant dresses dined on a sumptuous feast and drank until the late hours of the evening. Hundreds of the invited guests whirled about on the dance floor. One of them was the minister from Russia, Baron de Soeckl, with Madame Sartiges, the wife of the French minister, in his arms. He told her that the situation in the United States reminded him of the days just before the French Revolution in 1830. At a party in Paris, France's prime minister Talleyrand watched dancers float about the ballroom, too. He pulled King Louis aside and whispered to him ominously, "Sire, we are dancing on a volcano."[31]

KANSAS AND THE LECOMPTON CONSTITUTION

Buchanan was badgered on all sides over the slavery issue and Kansas's proposed proslavery Lecompton Constitution, so named because it was passed at the town of Lecompton, the territorial capital of Kansas. The strife in Kansas was all anyone talked about. Entire copies of the controversial Lecompton Constitution were printed in the pages of most large daily newspapers and they were filled with letters about it for weeks.[32]

There was no rest from news about Kansas; newspapers even published stories about the woes of that territory on Christmas Day.[33] Feelings on Kansas were so volatile in the nation's capital, in fact, that the *National Intelligencer*, one of Washington's leading newspapers, pleaded with its readers on December 28, 1857, to suspend all argument on the subject during the holiday week.[34] Instead of trying to broker a compromise on Lecompton and stake out a successful national policy on slavery, President Buchanan dismissed the issue just about every time it came up in conversation. His New Year's Day reception capped a week of violence between the proslavery and antislavery forces in Kansas that was reported in every major American newspaper, and yet the president never commented on the battles in public. The president did everything he could to swat away the issue, like one would swat away annoying flies in the hot Washington summer.[35]

Buchanan had no great opposition to the Southerners' belief that they had a right to protect slavery.[36] "I am decidedly in favor of its [Kansas's] admission and thus terminating the Kansas question," he wrote in a lengthy message urging congressional approval.[37] Defeat of the bill, he argued, "would alarm the fears of the country for the union, reduce the value of property, and injuriously interfere with our reviving trade."[38]

Some key Southerners trusted him completely. Senator Alexander Stephens of Georgia wrote a friend that if Buchanan was elected in 1856, "I do verily believe…there will never be another sectional or slavery struggle in the United States at least in our day."[39]

The Lecompton Constitution had a tangled history. Nearly two-thirds of Kansas's territorial residents were against slavery, but proslavery forces managed to elect a majority of the state legislature; that body authorized a special convention that drew up a constitution that authorized slavery for Kansas. In a referendum in which both sides charged poll fraud, the proslavery constitution passed handily. Buchanan sent the constitution to the House and Senate in December, supported it, and asked the body to ratify it right away to put it out of his mind.[40]

His presumption that both the Senate and House of Representatives would pass the bill without much debate was typical of his thinking. To him, passage of a bill or the ruling of a court ended a matter once and for all and any further discussion was a waste of time. He had said much the same thing about the controversial Fugitive Slave Act. "All slaves in free states or territories can be brought back and protected by the Constitution and federal government," he said simply, never understanding why there was such an intense national debate over that bill.[41] He assured people that all was well with Kansas, even though his own governor there, James Denver, wrote on the final day of 1857 that events in Kansas "must lead to bloodshed, anarchy, and confusion."[42]

Buchanan was determined to get his way on the Kansas slavery constitution, using all of his presidential clout to shove slavery to the political back burner and move on. That not only included traditional behind-the-scenes political arm twisting, but firing people working for senators and congressmen who were going to vote against Lecompton and awarding jobs, domestic and foreign, to those who would. "I'll carry Lecompton or die," he vowed.[43]

At the same time Buchanan sent the Kansas constitution to Congress, he told friends and political brokers that he did not understand why slavery in Kansas caused such a public uproar. The president, in fact, wondered "whether the peace and quiet of the whole country are not of greater importance than the mere temporary triumph of either of the political parties in Kansas."[44] He thought most Americans agreed with him. "The public is tired...ad nauseum on the Kansas agitation."[45] And in his annual message, in which he discussed Kansas, he told Congress that "Kansas has for some years occupied too much of the public attention. It is high time this should be directed to far more important issues."[46]

Few agreed with the president. The Kansas question had become a litmus test for politicians, North and South. Northern Republicans were furious with the president for trying to force slavery upon the territory's residents. "Poor Kansas!" wailed Massachusetts Republican Senator Charles Sumner. "I am pained by the trials and sorrows of this territory and my indignation overflows when I see the president and cabinet lending themselves to the cruel work."[47] Sumner added that advocating slavery in the territory was "unutterably wicked." Even state political leaders criticized Buchanan's plan. Illinois's Republican leader Abraham Lincoln called it "the most exquisite farce ever enacted."[48]

To the Republicans, the slaveholders in Kansas were the secondary villains in the dispute. The primary villain was President Buchanan. The radical Republicans flayed him. "[Buchanan] is the meanest man that has ever occupied the presidential chair, in having violated all of the pledges he has ever made, and that he is the greatest despot we have ever had," said Republican Congressman Thaddeus Stevens of Buchanan's home state of Pennsylvania.[49]

Republican governors, too, pounded the president over Kansas. "I will never consent to the doctrine that a majority can enslave a minority rightfully and that it is no objection to the admission of a state into the union that her fundamental acts, her Constitution, provides for such enslavement," said Ohio's governor Salmon Chase.[50]

The Democrats that Buchanan had to count on to carry the Kansas Constitution in the vote in both houses of Congress were not as numerous as they had been. The success of the Republicans in the elections of 1855, 1856, and 1857 had decreased the number of Democrats in the House from ninety-three to fifty-three, and twenty-two of them were from Northern states and were reluctant to approve a slave constitution. The Democratic margin in the Senate was also slender.[51]

Buchanan not only ignored his critics, but, incredibly, stopped reading the newspapers to avoid them, telling a friend on January 11, 1858, that "I do not read the press, simply because it distresses me."[52]

And so, on the first day of 1858, the year that would become one of the most critical in American history and put America on the road to a Civil War, a happy President James Buchanan nursed his glass of champagne and greeted his many important guests at the White House, leaning a little to the side, squinting a bit as he peered at them, trying very hard to smile, and every once in a while pulling his shirt collar ever higher.

THE DEATH OF JEFFERSON DAVIS

On February 8, 1858, Jefferson Davis, the immaculately dressed, slender, well-spoken senator from Mississippi, stood in the chamber of the United States Senate and rose to his full height of six feet one to applaud the proslavery Lecompton Constitution. The constitution would admit the Kansas Territory as a new slave state. Davis told his attentive audience in the Senate and in the public galleries above the chamber that it was an example of a constitution that recognized the right of the people to authorize slavery if they so desired. He denounced the Northerners trying to vote it down, and said with passionate conviction that their heated arguments were not "the means by which fraternity is to be preserved, or this Union rendered perpetual."[53]

The Lecompton Constitution had become the most heated political issue in the country and had a complicated history. Voters in that territory elected delegates to a constitutional convention in the summer of 1857, but only people who had lived in Kansas for three months and paid their taxes could vote for delegates. Thousands who did not want to pay taxes saw it as a trap and did not cast their ballots; thousands more lied about residency. Voter fraud was rampant. Census takers reported eleven families in Oxford County, but 1,828 proslavery votes were cast there; McGee County, with fourteen residents, cast 1,226 votes. The entire Republican Party boycotted the election and denounced the proslavery delegates who were chosen.

The proslavery constitution was passed, but the territorial governor insisted that it be voted on in a referendum by all the people of Kansas with both proslavery and antislavery clauses. The antislavery clause, however, also provided that slaves already in Kansas could remain. Many feared that owners would sneak in many more slaves before the constitution could take effect, making them legal too. The constitution also barred any changes in the slavery law for at least seven years. President Buchanan said the referendum was a good idea. The proslavery clause carried by the lopsided margin of 6,143 to 599, with charges of voter fraud by the antislavery forces.

The Kansas voters' choice in the Lecompton referendum:

1. Proslavery: slavery permitted, barred the emancipation of any slaves now in Kansas, no amendment to the law for seven years and then only by a vote of two-thirds of both houses of the legislature, tough enforcement of the Fugitive Slave Act, twenty years' residency requirement for any Kansas governor, freed blacks to be ejected from Kansas and no future freed blacks permitted.

    Also, the current governor would be ousted and a provisional government appointed, headed by John Calhoun, surveyor general of Kansas. He would call for new elections to replace the entire territorial legislature, he would appoint election commissioners to oversee the balloting and personally count all of the votes.
2. Antislavery: No new slaves would be permitted in Kansas, current slaves and their families would remain in bondage, any slaves who arrived in the territory before the referendum took effect would remain in bondage.[54]

The territorial governor quit in disgust, criticizing the president for interference, and the newly elected Kansas legislature then ordered another public referendum on the constitution in early January 1858. Its leaders insisted that this referendum, sponsored by the territorial legislature, would override the constitutional convention referendum. This time residents could vote yes or no on the entire constitution and also on a proslavery clause. In this referendum, most of the piqued proslavery people stayed home and the antislavery people defeated the whole package, 10,226 against the constitution to just 138 for it with slavery and only 24 for it without slavery. The proslavery forces argued that it did not count because they boycotted it. As an example, the heavy antislavery vote included counties such as Marshall, Franklin, Anderson, and Calhoun, where not a single vote was cast for the slavery version at all.[55]

Ignoring the January vote, Buchanan insisted that Congress had to approve the proslavery constitution that he had formally submitted in his annual message at the end of December. Republicans argued that they could vote it down in favor of the January legislative referendum. Tension over the divided territory was everywhere. Members of the territorial legislature issued a joint statement in which they "believed the peace of [Kansas] is in imminent danger." Members of the constitutional convention charged that the legislators were not "true Kansans" and that their actions would tear apart Kansas and the Union. They soon had proof of that when a man was killed in yet another dispute at Fort Scott, Kansas, during the last week of 1857. On the last day of the year, Acting Governor Denver begged both sides to stop the violence and resolve the issue peacefully.[56]

The people who resided in Kansas and were just trying to make a living there were angry at everybody. William Tecumseh Sherman, a former army officer who was struggling to make ends meet as a farmer in Kansas—and doing badly at it—lamented that "Kansas has been settled by the lawyers and politicians, instead of farmers and mechanics."[57]

The debate over the new Kansas constitution, on and off the floors of the House and Senate underneath the half-finished dome of the Capitol building, was long and bitter, as many had predicted.[58] Stephen Douglas, the "Little Giant," the short, rotund, loquacious Illinois senator whose 1854 Kansas-Nebraska Act had permitted slavery in the territory pending resident approval, now opposed the proslavery constitution, as did other Northern Democrats and the Republicans, especially New York Senator William Seward, the champion of the Republican antislavery radicals. The Southern Democrats, led by Davis, favored it. Arguments had raged throughout the winter. The nation's newspapers covered all of them. Northern papers generally denounced the slavery constitution while most of the Southern papers, particularly the most vociferous states' rights journals, such as Robert Rhett's *Charleston Mercury*, favored it.

Northerners saw the Kansas constitution as a test over "slave power," a term used often by senators and congressmen, North and South, to describe the legislative stranglehold that Southerners who supported slavery always seemed to have over bills in Congress. In the debates, Senator James

Hammond of South Carolina even taunted the Republicans that the Southerners held the upper hand on any and all issues concerning slavery.[59]

The fashionably dressed, handsome Jefferson Davis cut quite a figure in the Senate in the early days of the Lecompton debates, just as he had in Congress since his arrival in 1846. He was a refined, well-read man who impressed all. A friend wrote that the sophisticated senator "carried himself with such an air of conscious strength and ease and purpose...to cause a stranger to turn and look at him."[60]

Davis scoffed at the idea that Kansas would be overrun with slaves because the soil and climate did not lend themselves to the production of cotton or any other crop that had been successfully raised on warm-weather Southern plantations requiring slave labor. He pointed out that in 1858 Kansas actually only had six official slaves and even the total number of rumored slaves was barely over one hundred. The state had no need for slaves and the congressional argument over the issue was pointless. This was, he insisted, yet one more case of the North stepping into the business of the South and its slaves—uninvited—with no purpose other than to cause trouble.[61]

Throughout the debates in the Senate over the Kansas constitution, no senator argued the side of the states' rights, proslavery faction with more force than Jefferson Davis of Mississippi. Once more, as he had so often in the past, he laid all the blame for the earlier warfare in Kansas and its current troubles on meddling out-of-state abolitionists and Northern politicians. He said, yet again, that this was one more attack by the Northerners on the Southerners, and not just a slavery issue. "You have made it a political war," he said to the Northerners in the Senate. "We are on the defensive."[62] He told the legislators that the Senate chamber looked ready for war, not debate, and in numerous passionate speeches, he argued that the Northerners were trying to wreck the Union that he loved.

Few men in the nation's capital had grown more in stature as an effective public figure than Jefferson Davis. Over the years, he had become one of the country's most eloquent speakers, whether in senatorial debates, at public appearances, or on the stump for himself or fellow Democrats. Friends said that he had a rich voice that contained much fluctuation. He was not a rousing "Fourth of July" speaker, noted one newspaper editor. "He seldom stormed, he seldom spoke loudly or impetuously; but he often filled the hearts of his hearers with unspeakable passion, and captured their entire sympathies by that evidently forced moderation of tone and language."[63]

"I never saw him worsted in a debate. He was an off hand speaker and debater and always thoroughly up on every question that he discussed," wrote friend Lucius Lamar, later a U.S. Supreme Court justice.[64]

When he campaigned for Congress in 1843, James Ryan, the editor of the *Vicksburg Daily Sentinel* wrote that people "anticipate for him a proud and honorable career, should a sphere for the display of his talents once be presented." The editor of the *Macon (Mississippi) Jeffersonian* wrote that "he is dignified, with a bold and noble countenance, commanding great attention, using chaste and beautiful language, giving no just ground for offense, even to his opponents who are, at the same time, withering under his sarcasm at every sentence."[65]

He had not only become the South's states' rights champion, replacing the venerated John C. Calhoun, but by the winter of 1858 he was seen in that capacity by Northern senators and congressmen and even influential Northern newspaper editors such as Horace Greeley of the *New York Herald Tribune*.

The flamboyant Greeley, with his long, snow-white beard, floppy hats, loose clothing, and ambling walk, saw Davis as one of the most important men in American government. The editor, whose newspaper enjoyed a national circulation and whose editorial stands were emulated by many Northern journalists, wrote that, "Mr. Davis is unquestionably the foremost man of the South today. Every Northern senator will admit that from the Southern side of the floor the most formidable to meet in debate is the thin, polished, intellectual-looking Mississippian with the unimpassioned demeanor, the habitual courtesy and the occasional unintentional arrogance, which reveals his consciousness of the great commanding power…He belongs to a higher grade of public men in whom formerly the slave-holding democracy was prolific."[66]

Davis's strident leadership of the Southern support for the Lecompton Constitution gained him many admirers. His forcefulness in speaking on behalf of slavery in the Senate debates brought him fame in the Southern states, but his skillful management of the Southern faction in the discussions and his behind-the-scenes politicking impressed legislators both North and South.

But the stress created by the Kansas debate nearly cost him his life.

❧

Jefferson Davis: Early Years

Jefferson Davis lived a life that a romantic novelist might have invented. The handsome, elegantly dressed senator and West Point graduate was a successful planter who had married a much younger, beautiful, and brilliant woman, Varina Howell. She would bear him two adorable children. Davis had also been a war hero in not one, but two wars—the Black Hawk War and the Mexican War—and even worked as secretary of war. He had risen rapidly up the ladder of power, serving as both a congressman and U.S. senator.

Jefferson Davis was born in 1808, one of ten children, and grew up on his father's modest plantation near the Mississippi River, where as a child he enjoyed the friendship of the family's slaves. He graduated from Transylvania College in Lexington, Kentucky, and then went to the United States Military Academy at West Point. At the same time, his brother Joseph, twenty-four years his elder, was becoming one of the wealthiest businessmen in the South.

When Davis was twenty, he graduated from West Point, twenty-third in a class of thirty-three, and went into the army. Davis the soldier looked dashing. His neatly pressed uniforms, always spotless, fit him perfectly. The young lieutenant had become one of the finest horsemen in the country too, and galloping across a field on horseback in his uniform he looked like a character from a Sir Walter Scott tale. The newly-minted lieutenant was lucky; he was assigned to Iowa under the command of Colonel Zachary Taylor, one of the army's best officers. The gruff Taylor, who later earned the nickname "Old Rough and Ready" when he became a hero in the Mexican War, saw a brilliant future for Davis and took him under his wing.

His luck improved even more when the Black Hawk War broke out on the frontier. Taylor received a tip that Chief Black Hawk himself was hiding on an island in the middle of the Mississippi River. He sent his protégé, Davis, to capture him. Black Hawk surrendered without a shot being fired and young Davis became an instant military hero in the eyes of the public.

Davis did not enjoy the army as he had hoped, because his high-strung emotional demeanor always prevented him from doing so. The suddenly famous lieutenant was constantly involved in arguments with other officers, wrote nasty letters to Washington when he was overlooked for promotions, and was even court-martialed over an argument with a superior officer. He could not get along with many people in the service. The only thing he liked about the army was Sarah Taylor, the commander's daughter. She and Davis were married on June 17, 1835.

Sarah brought joy to the entire Davis family, whose members embraced her. She was an attractive, bright, lively, and remarkably cheerful girl who, his brother Joe hoped, would help cure his younger brother of his dangerous intensity. Joe liked her so much that he gave the couple two thousand acres of land with a cabin next to his own plantation, plus ten slaves. The two plantations were on the eastern bank of the Mississippi River, some thirty miles south of Vicksburg, Mississippi.

The newlyweds moved to their new plantation—they named it Brierfield after its hundreds of brier bushes—and prepared for their first summer as man and wife. It would be their only summer. Both came down with severe cases of malaria, a common affliction in the torrid summer months in the South. Jefferson, a physically strong man, survived it—barely. Sarah did not. The twenty-one-year-old bride, sweating profusely as a high fever crippled her, passed away on September 15, her husband clinging to her hands, hardly able to move himself.[67]

Davis, devastated by the death of his wife and extremely weak, went to Cuba to recuperate. He soon had the first of numerous bouts with herpes and spent his first weeks in bed, his swollen left eye covered over with a slick film, that hideously pockmarked face with black pimples. His nervous system was also debilitated. The disease, which must have been transmitted by a sexual encounter, would be with him all of his life and would, at times, threaten to kill him.

Over the next few years, Davis turned Brierfield into a successful cotton plantation. He built a larger home for himself, cabins for his 72 slaves (the number would rise to 106 by 1860), storehouses for baled cotton, corn, and other crops, warehouses, stables, and blacksmith shops.

He developed Brierfield with the help of slaves with whom he shared a close relationship and was a benevolent master. He and his brother Joe were good to their slaves, lenient in discipline and always mindful of their welfare. Davis never whipped his slaves; he set up a slave courthouse where slaves determined punishments for infractions of work rules, such as slowdowns or stealing. Workers were not assigned nicknames as they were at most plantations, but selected their own names. They were permitted to travel through the Mississippi River basin alone, often to New Orleans and Natchez, and trusted to return. None fled. They were encouraged to read and the faster learners were given supervisory jobs that ordinarily went to white overseers. Slaves could grow their own food for consumption or sell it at local markets. Violent overseers were fired.

At first, Davis brought the best doctors to Brierfield to make house calls for his slaves when they were ill. Later he built his own slave hospital on the grounds of the plantation with a full-time nurse, thought to be the only one of her kind in the South. He hired a minister to visit the plantation each Sunday to preach to the slaves and the Davis family, and paid a dentist to call regularly to treat his laborers. He purchased new dresses for the slave women when their old ones looked worn and always bought a brand-new wedding dress for a slave girl who was about to be married. Davis paid for a lavish reception for the new couple. He played with the offspring of the slave families as if they were his own and often referred to them as his children.[68] Davis was so close to his slaves, whom he referred to as "his people,"[69] especially James Pemberton, that he frequently dined with them. Planters who knew Davis called his slaves "his devoted friends."[70]

Other planters ridiculed Davis, referring to his slaves as "Jeff Davis's free Negroes" and joking that if anyone wanted to see the latest women's fashions from New York or Paris they should not look for high society matrons in New Orleans, but rather Jeff Davis's slave girls in Brierfield. He was lampooned for bowing in greeting to any slaves or freed blacks he met on the street.[71]

In 1843, after years of a lonely existence at Brierfield as a widower, Davis emerged to begin a life in politics and to once again fall in love.

ᘄᓚ

THE ACCIDENTAL CANDIDATE

The thirty-five-year-old Davis seemed like a natural political figure for the leaders of the Democratic Party in Mississippi. He was a sophisticated, handsome, wealthy man and a staunch supporter of slavery. Best of all, he was the renowned hero of the Black Hawk War.

In the fall of 1843, he found himself the accidental candidate for Congress. The original nominee dropped out of the race just two weeks prior to the election. The Democrats begged Davis to fill in for him, assuring him that they did not expect him to do very well in such a short span of time against his Whig opponent. Davis was glad to help out the party and surprised party leaders, and himself, by winning 43 percent of the vote in the losing cause.

A year later, he ran for a full term in Congress (the state chose at-large congressmen). In his second campaign he was a better speaker and had plenty of time to plan. He delivered more than a dozen major speeches, attended barbecues, corresponded with political allies, and appeared as if he had been a politician for years. He favored fair tariffs, river improvements, the annexations of Texas, California, and Oregon, and demanded a stronger national bank and treasury system. Party officials were pleased with his conduct during the campaign and his victory. "He left behind him fame as an orator and statesman," wrote one editor.[72]

Shortly after his election, Jefferson Davis fell in love for the second time. His brother Joe had invited Varina Howell, 17, the beautiful, well-educated daughter of a prominent family in Natchez, to a Christmas party at his plantation. Davis and the Natchez beauty were smitten with each other at that first meeting.

He was an older man, eighteen years her senior, and at first the slender, brunette Varina worried that he would see her as a daughter and not a lover, but that feeling changed. "He is most agreeable and has a peculiarly sweet voice and a winning manner of asserting himself," she wrote her mother, adding that he looked thirty, not thirty-five. Varina, a very political woman who read the Washington, D.C. newspaper, the *National Intelligencer*, every day, wrote light-heartedly that Davis "was refined and cultivated…and yet he is a Democrat!"

Varina Howell was five feet ten inches tall, thin and graceful with a lovely olive complexion; her large, dark brown eyes captured the attention of everyone who ever met her. She had become a young woman by the Christmas of 1843 and began to show far more maturity than girls her age. The lovely brunette was one of the belles of Natchez, the teenage girls who had been taught all the refinements of life as they prepared for marriages to well-bred husbands. Yet Varina was a strong-willed, independent woman who had no intention of subjugating herself to a domineering husband. She did not share the commonly held view of the Southern aristocracy that in a marriage wives existed only to serve their husbands; her husband would be her partner in life, not her master.

Davis hadn't thought that he could ever love a woman again as much as he had loved Sarah, but he found himself writing Varina romantic letters and dreaming about her. He wrote that he had "longings of love" for her and that "I have to be with you every day and all day."[73] Of their future, he wrote her, "Your spirit is with me. I feel its presence. My heart is yours."[74] They shared common interests. Davis loved music; Varina played the piano. She too was an accomplished horsewoman. They both enjoyed discussing politics; both loved to read.[75]

Early on in their courtship, though, Varina detected the stubbornness and defensiveness that others found alarming in Davis. "He impresses me as a remarkable kind of man, but of uncertain temper, and has a way of taking for granted that everybody agrees with him when he expresses an opinion," she wrote. In another letter, she wrote that "it was this sincerity of opinion which sometimes gave him the manner to which his opponents objected as domineering."[76]

The arrival of Congressman Jefferson Davis and his young wife in Washington caused quite a stir. The two quickly became much sought after guests at dinners and parties and hosted some of the capital's most well attended soirées. The youthful Varina was rapidly acknowledged as one of the Hill's best dressed women, especially when she wore simple but elegant white dresses, a pin in the cleavage and either a rose or camellia in her hair.[77] She charmed everyone, North and South, and those who attended dinners at her home marveled at the way that she and her husband were able to get along with the radical Republicans in the House and Senate, such as William Seward of New York and Charles Sumner of Massachusetts. Sumner, even more radical than Seward, talked often about how much he enjoyed socializing with the Davises.[78]

One social lioness said of Varina that, "Nor must we fail to acknowledge the social influence of Mrs. Jefferson Davis, one of the most cultivated women of her time—greatly sought by cultivated men and women."[79]

She was more than a popular hostess. Varina Davis was her husband's personal goodwill ambassador, working hard to help him win friends and influence legislators. She hosted numerous dinner parties, making certain that each year every single member of Congress dined at the Davis home at least once. She helped her husband with his social and political correspondence and subscribed to several newspapers for him so he always knew what was going on in the country. She worked directly on his behalf too, spending one day each week at her home on G Street to meet anyone who wanted to talk about his bills or policies.[80]

Varina was adamant in her beliefs and would never back down in disputes. To argue with Varina was "to the annihilation of all who had the temerity to cross swords with her," said her friend Virginia Clay, the wife of Senator Clement Clay.[81]

Most freshmen congressmen said little during their first term, but Davis plunged into the business of the nation, delivering several major speeches and quickly becoming one of the Southern states' rights contingent's most successful spokesmen in the House of Representatives. Some even said that Davis might become the Speaker of the House one day. But the Mexican War intervened.

War with Mexico

To protest the American occupation of Texas, Mexican troops crossed the Rio Grande in April 1846, and attacked a U.S. Army force led by Davis's former father-in-law, Colonel Zachary Taylor. Dozens of Americans were killed and Congress declared war on Mexico. Davis, the army veteran, left Washington as soon as he heard the news and went back to Mississippi to join a volunteer force that was headed to Mexico. "I felt my services were due to the country and believed my experience might be available in promoting the comfort the safety and efficiency of the Mississippi regiment...I could not delay until the close of the congressional session," he told Mississippians in a letter published in many newspapers in that state.[82]

In Mexico, Davis captured twenty Mexican soldiers practically single-handedly in his first battle and led his men to a second straight triumph the following day. Two months later, Davis took his men into battle against the legendary Mexican general Santa Ana, the man whose army captured the Alamo in 1836, at Buena Vista. He led his 370 Mississippians in a surprise assault on the Mexicans, scattering them. During the attack, Davis was shot in the foot. Later that day, another Mexican force of two thousand cavalry attacked his volunteers and some other regiments across an open plain. Outnumbered by more than three to one, the quick-thinking Davis, bleeding through the handkerchief he had wrapped around his foot, ordered his men to form a right angle and opened up with nonstop volleys against the stunned Mexicans, who soon fled in defeat.

The soldiers who served under him were impressed by the bravery of their wounded officer. "He could lead them into hell!" said one of his men of the regiment's respect for their commander. Later, one of the Mexican generals he encountered that day at Buena Vista said his army lost because of "the flashing sword of Davis."[83] Zachary Taylor cited Davis for "highly conspicuous bravery" and President Polk offered to make the Mississippian a general, an honor Davis refused.

Davis, still hobbling from his war wounds, was seen as a national hero upon his return to the United States. Following a round of parties in Mississippi, Davis was appointed to fill one of his state's two unexpired U.S. Senate seats. He was, in the eyes of the public, a military legend and national hero.

His life changed with the introduction of the Compromise of 1850 four years later. The legislative bill was yet another measure designed to give both the North and South something each wanted in an effort to hold the Union together as the slavery issue grew in volatility. The Compromise abolished the slave trade in the District of Columbia, admitted California to the Union as a free state, set boundaries for Texas and New Mexico, admitted Utah and New Mexico as territories with the slave question unresolved there, and included a fugitive slave law that required Northerners to return runaway slaves to their owners. It was no compromise for Davis, who argued against it in the Senate. For him, it was yet another effort to end slavery and demean Southerners.

The senator, who rose to denounce the Compromise fifty-four times, speaking more than anyone else in the Senate chamber, still could not understand the uproar over slavery. What was so bad about it? He treated his slaves well and assumed that others did, too. Where was the evil?

There was nothing wrong with it; its abuses, he said, arose when slave owners treated their workers badly. "It is enough for me to know," he declared, "...that it was established by decree of Almighty God, that it is sanctioned in the Bible, in both testaments...that it has existed in all ages; has been found among the people of the highest civilization, and in nations of the highest proficiency in the arts."

And, he always told friends, blacks were better off in slavery than on their own. "In a moral and social condition they had been elevated from brutal savages into docile, intelligent, and civilized agricultural laborers, and supplied not only with bodily comforts, but with careful religious instruction, under the supervision of a superior race."[84]

He and other Southerners defended slavery for several reasons: no one should tell Southerners what to do with property—and slaves were property; the loss of slaves would cripple the agricultural economy of the South; freed slaves would take jobs away from whites, rob stores, and marry white women, tainting the race; the simple-minded slaves could not function on their own. Despite the fact that slaves learned to read and write, slaves were not intelligent, he said, and because of their diminished intellectual capacity they therefore had to be subservient to the white race. He engaged in name-calling, referring to them as "pygmies" at times.[85] He said that slavery allowed them to enjoy rewarding lives under the guidance of well-intentioned masters who had the welfare of their workers at heart. And he lectured his audiences that the freed blacks in the North had accomplished nothing with their freedom, insisting that he had thus proved his point.[86]

He explained his view clearly in Aberdeen, Mississippi, in a May 1851 speech. A reporter for the *Monroe Democrat* wrote, "Colonel Davis said that he always thought and sincerely believed that the institution of slavery, as it now exists among us, is necessary to the equality of the white race. Distinctions between classes have always existed, everywhere, and in every country...destroy them today and they will spring up tomorrow. Menial services have to be performed by someone and everywhere the world over persons [slaves] by whom menial services have been performed as a class have been looked upon as occupying, and are reduced to, a state of inferiority."

Concerning whites, Davis told the crowd, "The rich, by siding with the party in power...will always be safe. Not so with the poor. Their all is suspended upon their superiority to the blacks...the social equality of their wives, daughters, and sons are all suspended and involved in this question."[87]

He told another audience, "Can anyone believe, does anyone hope, that the southern states in this confederacy will continue...to support the Union, to bear its burdens, in peace and in war, in a degree disproportioned to their numbers, if that very government is to be arrayed in hostility against an institution so interwoven with its interests, its domestic peace, and all its social relations?"[88]

Callous Northern domination of the South was a theme that Davis would embrace all of his life, cleverly reminding people that the bedrock of the

Constitution was the protection of the rights of the minority (slaveholders) against the will of the majority (non-slaveholders). "A moral crevasse has occurred; fanaticism and ignorance—political rivalry, sectional hate, strife for sectional dominion—have accumulated into a mighty flood and pour their turgid waters through the broken Constitution," he argued.[89]

Again and again in the 1850s, he told audiences that "I see nothing short of conquest on one side or submission on the other."[90] In letters to friends, he referred to politicians from states north of the Mason-Dixon Line as "our northern aggressors."[91]

As early as 1851, he hinted at secession.[92] "The bitter waters [of North-South disagreement] have spread far and wide and as the torrent rolls on, it will acquire volume and velocity, from inexhaustible source of supply. When it becomes palpable to every man's sense, that from the free states we have nothing to expect but eternal war upon the institution of slavery, I believe the southern people will awake and unite, not to preserve the Constitution, or the union, but to organize a government for themselves."[93]

He told friends that if that day came, the South would leave the Union peacefully, but added ominously that if the Northerners tried to stop the Southern states, "I will meet force with force!"[94]

Davis was so angry at the passage of the Compromise that he left the Senate and went home to run for governor against a man who favored it to make his point. He misjudged not only the feeling of his fellow Mississippians, but the political climate. He lost.

Davis was not gone for long. His friend Franklin Pierce was elected president in 1852 and asked Davis to be his secretary of war. Who better? Davis had been a genuine hero in two wars and served on Congressional and Senate military committees. He was probably the most qualified person in the country for the position.

And he did a fine job. He authorized the issue of brand-new rifles to soldiers, obtained pay raises for officers and enlisted men, streamlined the military's cumbersome chain of command, founded the first Army Medical Corps, won approval to permit the Army Corps of Engineers to build two wings for the Capitol building, had new maps drawn of the western territories, and worked with large railroads in planning routes through the Southwest. He even pioneered the use of camels instead of horses to transport soldiers. One of the accomplishments of which he was most proud was working with the new superintendent at West Point, Robert E. Lee, the gifted colonel who had also won renown in the Mexican War, in making the military academy a more comprehensive training facility for the army.

Davis returned to politics in 1857, winning election to the Senate again, but by a narrow margin. He arrived just in time for the acrimonious debates on the Lecompton Constitution for Kansas, debates that affected him so profoundly that he once again became vulnerable to herpes, which had caused him untold pain throughout his adult life and now threatened to kill him.

ILLNESS AND POLITICS

The herpes that brought him down in 1858 was his nemesis. It flared up frequently in the form of a neuralgia that incapacitated his left eye, made his face swollen, drained his strength, and left him unable to function for weeks at a time. Sometime in the middle of that cold February, physically frail from the vigors of the lengthy and heated debates and always susceptible to illness, he caught a bad cold that quickly turned into laryngitis. Once his system was weakened by the cold and laryngitis, he was again vulnerable to neuralgia of the eye. It struck again—and hard.

Neuralgia is a condition of the eye clinically known as herpes simplex; it can be debilitating. Herpes simplex usually strikes men between the ages of sixteen and twenty-five following sexual relations with women who have it. Davis probably contracted herpes when he was in the army or just afterward. The condition causes hundreds of tiny black growths to appear around the eye, inflaming and infecting the eyelids and cornea. It then creates a liquid film that covers the eye and cornea and causes temporary blindness. The disease drains the muscular system of its victim, causing him to remain bedridden for weeks at a time. Neuralgia usually attacks for between four and six weeks and then gradually disappears. It can be activated at any time by high fever, winds that hit the cornea, prolonged exposure to sunlight, or severe emotional stress.

To alleviate the condition, doctors would scrape the cornea to bring back some eyesight until the inflammations decreased. The whole area was then constantly bathed with a solution of mercury chloride and iodine ointment. For Davis, a flare-up would occur when he worked too long in the sun on his plantation fields in Mississippi or when he was under any kind of stress, personal or public, such as political campaigns or spirited congressional debates such as the one over the Lecompton Constitution.[95]

The senator from Mississippi came down with neuralgia four or five times each year. It always wreaked havoc in his life, sending him to bed for lengthy periods of time when he was needed on his plantation or in public life. Sometimes he simply refused to follow his doctors' orders and appeared in public anyway, coping with his condition the best he could. His wife wrote her mother about it when they first arrived in Washington and he started to work hard. "He has not been well since we arrived here. He sits up until two or three at night, until his eyes lose their beauty even to me. They look so red and painful."[96]

In his 1851 Mississippi governor's race his neuralgia immediately flared up, yet he campaigned throughout the state, giving speeches on the steps of public buildings and mingling with voters at large outdoor barbecue parties. He was an odd sight to the voters. Blind in his left eye, Davis could barely see where he was going and had to wear thick goggles with tinted green glass to navigate his way through crowds and across lawns. He also covered his hideous looking eye and face with large bandages that wrapped around his head. To stay mobile and continue the campaign, he had a doctor who traveled with him treat his faulty eye with chloroform sponge baths each day and administer liberal doses of quinine and opium, plus several teaspoons of castor oil. When his neuralgia became intolerable, he asked the doctor to cut open the film that covered his eye, but that did little good. And even with all that medical attention he had to stop campaigning for weeks at a time to recover in bed.

That experience in 1851 was not uncommon for the senator. Again and again, when under stress, Davis's neuralgia returned. He contracted a bad case of the illness in the hot summer of 1852 after spending too much time in the fields. That attack forced him to sleep all day, with the curtains of his room drawn. Once awake, he was up all night, pacing back and forth through his plantation home, half blind. His condition deteriorated so badly that summer that friends who saw him make a feeble appearance at the state's Democratic Convention thought he was going to die.[97] So did Franklin Pierce. Pierce, who would be elected president two months later, wrote him a letter of relief that he had survived his latest attack.[98] In the fall of 1857, Davis embarked on a series of campaign stump speeches for fellow Democratic candidates in Mississippi, but had to stop when his neuralgia took away his sight and crippled him yet again. He admitted to friends that during many attacks over the years he had gone blind for weeks at a time.[99]

His home hospitalizations over the years not only prevented him from achieving political goals, but were genuine setbacks for the men in his party, who saw him as one of their most gifted leaders. Writing him that the Southerners saw the world through his eyes, one politician, E. M. Hitchcock, wrote to Davis, "We look to you to sustain the South and you can't see through any eyes but your own."[100]

The latest neuralgia attack, which came toward the end of the Lecompton debates in February 1858, crippled Davis. On the day of the crucial vote itself, the Mississippi senator, his eye bandaged, was too weak to walk and a friend had to carry him into the Senate chamber so he could cast his ballot. He was then carried out of the chamber to the dismay of the senators, placed gingerly in his carriage, and taken home. He nearly died.

At his Washington, DC, home, he had to remain in the darkness: all the drapes closed during the day and both eyes perpetually covered with a blindfold, because they were so overly sensitive to light. Even the dull flicker of a single lighted candle in the corner of a room caused his cornea pain. This time he not only had his usual eye troubles and weakness, but he lost all power of speech, which alarmed him. And he could barely move. Unable to speak, he had to write his words with a thick piece of white chalk on a black slate his wife purchased. A week after he was stricken by the attack, he went blind in his left eye and remained unable to see out of it for an entire month.[101] The longtime Davis family doctor, Thomas Miller, rushed to his side and visited him every day. Davis's wife Varina brought in a number of doctors from around the United States to treat him, including Dr. Robert Stone, an ophthalmologist from Washington, and Dr. Isaac Hayes, generally acknowledged as the nation's top ophthalmologist, who traveled from Philadelphia to treat him on many occasions during his near-fatal illness that winter.[102]

They all wanted him to eat more because his time in bed had caused him to lose weight. His appearance was deplorable. His wife tried to feed him, but he was often physically unable to eat. "His anguish was intense. No one but I knew how much he suffered, and I only because one day I begged him to try to take nourishment, and he gave only one smothered scream." He gasped to her, "I am in anguish. I cannot."[103]

No one could help him. Dr. Hayes said, "I do not see why his eye has not burst." The Philadelphia specialist could not believe the courage Davis showed in the face of the intense pain the neuralgia brought on. The physician, who had seen numerous cases of the disease, was dumfounded and told the senator's wife that "such patience is God-like."

He relied on his wife's care, physically and emotionally, throughout the calamity. Varina bathed him, changed his bandages, treated his eye with drops and ointments, and cooked all of his meals and brought them to his bedroom. She sat with him for hours, reading books and newspapers, plus letters from friends and political associates. Sometimes she just sat next to him and held his hand.

At the same time that she cared for her husband, she continued to raise their two children, Maggie and Jeff Jr., maintain the home, shop for food, and keep up the family correspondence.

Her husband appreciated her attention and love. At one point, when the neuralgia had made it impossible for him to talk any longer, a doctor asked him how he kept his eye functioning. With a small smile on his face, he scribbled on a piece of paper, "My wife saved it."[104]

Ironically, this horrific case of neuralgia and the brush with death in the winter of 1858 brought the Davises, who had been quarreling, together on a very deep emotional level. Often holding hands, they spent hours with each other as Davis lingered near death in his darkened bedroom. The bond between them became very strong and the love they knew in the early years of their marriage returned. Their lives as man and wife would never be fractured again. The Davises would become a strong and resourceful couple, able to withstand anything. His wife's love and support—and advice—would serve him well when the nation was plunged into Civil War, and their marriage would give him strength.

An Unlikely Friendship

Among the men who visited him regularly during his convalescence were not only senators and congressmen from the Southern states, but legislators from the Northern states, too. Lord Napier, the cheerful British minister, visited him as often as he could in an effort to pick up his spirits. Senator Clement Clay of Alabama dropped in on many evenings and read books, newspapers, and magazines to him, giving Varina some free time to simply rest. Davis was kept informed about activities in his party by his friend Alexander Stephens, the Democratic senator from Georgia, who stopped by frequently to discuss legislation and give him copies of bills.[105] Perhaps his most unlikely visitor was Senator William Seward of New York, the fire-breathing Republican. If Davis was the champion of states' rights, then the radical Seward was the standard-bearer for the antislavery forces in the North.

The New Yorker was one of the most intriguing men in the Senate. He was a slight man, just five feet six inches tall, with large ears, sandy hair, penetrating eyes, bushy eyebrows, and a sharp, hawklike nose. He was a garrulous personality, loud and bombastic at times, the center of attention wherever he went. Seward read everything he could get his hands on, whether newspapers or novels, and was one of the capital's most ardent theatergoers. He was in the middle of one of the most accomplished political careers in U.S. history. Seward, who turned fifty-seven that winter, had been the governor of New York as a Whig from 1839–1842. He was later elected to the U.S. Senate as a Whig, but changed to the Republican Party in 1856, after the Whigs collapsed over the slavery issue. Seward, the leader of the antislavery cause and one of the nation's most polished orators, was the overwhelming favorite to win the Republican presidential nomination in 1860.

On the surface, the two men had little in common. Seward never understood Davis's ownership of slaves and Davis had often publicly cast Seward as the symbol of Northern aggression, once asking an audience who had been "more industrious, patient, and skillful as a sapper and miner against the foundations of the Constitution" than the New Yorker? Yet they had become close friends.[106]

Seward was one of Davis's first visitors when he became ill and, throughout his nearly eight weeks of recuperation, saw him often, sometimes seven days a week. Seward went to his friend's home on foot and, after the visit, walked home to his house in Washington in the wintry weather, sometimes in snowfalls or rainstorms.

Davis and the charming Seward were friends, but their colleagues in both the House and Senate could not understand why; neither could any of the political writers in the capital. The two men had never met until they were introduced to each other in Congress in 1846. They did not share common friends; their wives did not socialize together. They had no mutual business interests and did not share personal interests or hobbies. Yet they were as close as two men could be. Perhaps it was politics that gave them their special bond.

During Davis's illness, Seward would stop at his home at the end of the day and recount the entire day's activities in the Senate, relating to him what bills had been introduced and approved or voted down. He discussed at length who had supported the bills and who had opposed them and why. Seward referred to a Northern Republican politician as "his man"; if they were friendly to the Mississippi senator, he called him "your man." Seward brought a smile to his sick friend's lips and a twinkle to his eye when he mimicked their colleagues in the Senate. His deft impersonations skewered not just the Democrats, but his trusted Republicans too, and on some evenings Seward would practically stage a one-man show, imitating a Republican and Democrat arguing back and forth on the floor of the Senate.[107]

They swapped stories about efforts to cajole other senators to vote for their bills and support their causes over the years and exchanged political "war stories" about their past campaigns, filled with anecdotes about colorful men and women in their states. Davis would relate his stories about campaigning with his green goggles and the raucous barbecues where so much politicking was accomplished in Mississippi. Seward would regale him with stories of his battles with the New York political machines, such as Tammany Hall, and his feuds with newspaper editors like Horace Greeley.

William Seward's affection for Davis was genuine, as was the Mississippian's admiration of the New Yorker. Varina did not understand the attraction. She always upbraided Seward for his antislavery stands, which had become more vocal over the years. Seward always explained his staunch opposition to slavery to her and her husband as cordially as any discussion of the explosive issue would allow. Senator Davis always disagreed with him, in an equally friendly manner.

The Davises disagreed with Seward's rather callous view of the political world, too. Davis loved to give lengthy speeches to large groups of people gathered in public squares or in assembly halls or to debate in the Senate, because he enjoyed questions from crowds or the back-and-forth arguments with his fellow legislators. Seward did not. He preferred to talk to newspaper reporters and editors because his remarks reached the largest number of people in the columns of the most influential journals in America. He never enjoyed arguing with senators, he said, and deflated the Davises whenever he told him that he preferred "talking to the empty Senate."

The New Yorker told the couple that he took stands that he did not like and supported bills that he did not think were useful purely for political purposes. He had supported public figures with whom he did not agree and made appearances for party nominees for whom he did not much care. Seward told the Davises on several occasions that, in fact, he had few genuine political convictions. His enemies charged that his politics were at worst duplicitous; even friends said he practiced "dexterity" in politics. The Davises were also amazed at this lack of commitment from the New Yorker. Varina Davis wrote that Seward was "a problematic character full of contradictions."[108]

During the long hours that Seward sat at Davis's bedside during his terrible illness in February and March of 1858, the subject came up once more. Seward again reiterated his stand that he did not have any real conviction about any public issue and found it impossible to genuinely care about many public policy questions. Davis, appalled as always, turned to his friend and told him with great fervor that he himself had nothing but conviction. He had been completely committed to every single bill he had offered in the Senate and every vote he had ever cast. The weakened Mississippian gasped to Seward, "Do you never speak from conviction alone?"

"Ne-ever," said Seward, stretching out the word as he leaned forward in his chair.

Davis raised his head from the pillow, looked right at his Northern friend, and said in a low voice, "As God is my judge, I never spoke from any other motive."[109]

Perhaps it was the fact that they had had this discussion on many previous occasions, or that his close friend was so ill and his face looked so disfigured from poor health, but Seward, apparently for the first time ever, was genuinely moved. He rose from his chair, went to Davis's bed, half sat in it next to him, put his arm around his ailing friend, and whispered in his ear, "I know you do."[110]

Regardless of their political differences, Varina, who attended almost all of Seward's daily visits, liked the New Yorker. "There was an earnest, tender interest in his manner which was unnaturally genuine. He was thoroughly sympathetic with human suffering and would do most unexpected kindnesses to those who would…anticipate the opposite only," she said.[111]

Seward was disturbed by Davis's condition and watched him grow weaker as the weeks passed. At one point a doctor turned to Varina and told her he was certain an operation was needed to remove Davis's bad eye and that he would spend the rest of his life with one eye and a patch. That might force the senator to leave public life. Seward, sitting there with them, nearly burst into tears. "I could not bear to see him maimed," he said to the doctor and Varina Davis. "He is the embodiment of manhood."[112] (Seward saved Varina Davis's life during a snowstorm. Varina, suffering through a very difficult pregnancy, was home alone that afternoon and suddenly became very ill. She got word to Seward, who had a nurse race to her home in his sleigh and take Varina to her doctor immediately; the doctor said Seward's quick action prevented her death.[113])

Drained of nearly all energy, Davis insisted on writing a letter to former President Pierce to let his good friend know how bad his condition had become. He wrote, "[I am] suffering under a painful illness which has closely confined me for more than seven weeks and leaves me at the time quite unable to read or write."[114]

One doctor told him bluntly that if he got out of bed to make a political speech the stress on his eyes would kill him.[115]

Davis feared that too, but was determined to deliver an important speech in the Senate in support of a coastal survey bill that would help a personal friend of his, Dallas Bache. His doctor, wife, and friends told him that it was too dangerous for his health. Davis dressed warmly, pulled his jacket tight around his chest, and walked to a carriage outside his house for the ride over the cobblestoned streets to the Capitol. "I must go if it kills me," he said. "It is good for the country and good for the friend of my youth."

It nearly did kill him. The senator delivered his speech and then sat down behind his Senate chamber desk and consumed some beef tea and wine to give him sustenance. He felt badly, though, and he nearly fainted. Men had to help his wife escort him out of the Capitol, back into the carriage, and then home, where he promptly collapsed and was put into his bed once again as his wife rushed to summon doctors.[116]

Again, in April, when a crucial vote on the Lecompton Constitution was to be taken, Davis disregarded his doctors' orders that a visit to the Senate might be his last. He had servants carry him into the Senate chamber and help him take his seat. The Lecompton vote was delayed one day and Davis returned, in much worse shape, this time physically held up by his wife on one side and his doctor on the other. Friends who saw him shuddered. One said he "was a pale, ghastly looking person, his eye bandaged with strips of white linen, his whole aspect denoting feebleness."[117]

Davis would not be muzzled, though, and worked out an agreement with his doctor that if the physician would let him spend just one hour in the Senate each day he would take care of himself at home. He resumed his Senate duties in May, an hour a day.

DUELIST AND ANTAGONIST

Weakened and irritated from the neuralgia, Davis slowly recovered his old arrogance. A senator from Louisiana, Judah Benjamin, a very successful lawyer who maintained his practice while in the Senate and one of the few Jewish public officials in America, offered some mild criticism of Davis's assessment of rifles during a June 8, 1858, discussion on the properties of a new breech-loading rifle as part of a hearing on an army appropriations bill. The Mississippian snapped angrily at Benjamin and Benjamin snapped back. Heated words followed and Davis sarcastically called Benjamin a "paid attorney," referring to his refusal to give up legal fees while in office. Benjamin was insulted.

Davis had offended someone yet again because of his truculence and anger. He knew he had a problem with his emotions. "I have an affirmity [sic] of which I am horribly ashamed. When I am aroused in a matter, I lose control of my feelings and become personal," he once said of his hair-trigger temper.[118]

All of his life, Jefferson Davis exhibited a rigid, dismissive, unforgiving personality. He always assumed he was right and could never admit that he was wrong. He firmly believed that anyone who disagreed with him had to admit he was in error. He was stubborn, as his wife often told him, and would never change his mind. Davis would never overlook a social slight, even if unintentional, and would hold a grudge against people for years. He would not compromise on issues. Davis found it difficult to deal with mild-mannered people and could not and would not work with strong-willed and personally difficult people.[119]

His belligerence was evident in public speeches as well as private conversations. Edward Pollard, the editor of the *Richmond Examiner*, who wrote about him often, put it best. "[He] was haughty and defiant, and his manners singularly imperious. He spoke as one who would not brook contradictions, who delivered his torrents of truth as if without regard to anything said to the contrary and who disdained the challenges of debate."[120]

Students at West Point respected his intellect and love of the army, but disliked him personally and wondered how anyone with such personality problems could succeed in public life. "His four years at West Point…instead of inculcating in him the pliancy and assumed cordiality of the politician, was to develop a personality of the reverse order," wrote one.[121]

And now that difficulty had surfaced again in his dispute with Senator Benjamin.

Benjamin promptly challenged Davis to a duel with pistols. The shocked Davis dismissed the confrontation. "I will make this all right at once. I have been wholly wrong," said Davis and apologized to Benjamin on the floor of the Senate the next day, ending the dispute. He may have been persuaded to do so by his wife, who did not think that Benjamin was as timid as most suggested. She saw deep rage in the Louisiana senator and wrote of his well-known public courtesy that it was "like the salute of the duelist to the antagonist," whom he hoped to kill "with the fiercest joy." She also was afraid that both men were too hot-headed and that if a duel occurred one or both might die. "They both [possess] nervously excitable temperaments," she wrote of their anger. Benjamin was satisfied with Davis, but the incident created a frosty relationship between the two. In time the rift healed, and when Davis became the president of the Confederacy he named Benjamin his Attorney General.[122]

Davis's doctor was disturbed by the incident. His patient had almost died from neuralgia and now he had just managed to avoid a deadly duel. It was not the first time Davis had nearly engaged someone in a duel or become involved in a brawl when his famous temper flared. In 1847, recovering from his wounds in the Mexican War, Davis, still walking with one crutch for assistance, became so enraged with something that his fellow Mississippi congressman, Henry Foote, said to him that he attacked him in Gadsby's Hotel, where both resided, beating him severely with his fists and the crutch. Davis screamed that he would kill Foote, but before he could lunge at him again another legislator pulled him back. Davis then beat up the second legislator. Foote demanded a duel, but mutual friends prevented it.[123] Prior to that, when he was in the army, Davis challenged another officer, W. H. Bissell, to a duel with muskets at fifteen paces. That, too, was halted by friends.[124] Davis saw nothing wrong with anger and duels; his own brother-in-law had shot a man in a duel.

The physician ordered Davis to take a lengthy vacation far from Washington to obtain needed rest, both physical and mental. Just about everyone of prominence evacuated Washington, DC, in the summers of the 1850s. The city and the surrounding Chesapeake Bay region was oppressively hot and humid in the summer. The wide streets of the city, most still dirt, became dusty in summer; the dust was so bad that people returned home from work on a breezy day covered in it. The city had still not developed a system to water down the streets in summer, as other communities had. The combination of dust and heat drove hundreds of families, including the Davises, out of town. Some, of course, remained. Robert E. Lee remained that summer at his home in Arlington House, the plantation across the Potomac River from Washington. Lee had been a friend of Davis's since the latter named him superintendent of West Point.

Senator Davis's wife and family were thrilled by the doctor's suggestion. At first, the Davises made plans to sail across the Atlantic Ocean to the south of France to join former president Pierce and his family for a vacation of several weeks, at the president's invitation. The arrangements for the trip became complicated, though, and instead Davis decided to take Varina and his children, Maggie and Jeff Jr., to Maine. The journey of the national leader of the proslavery supporters in the South to New England, the home of the country's most ardent abolitionists, would become one of the most important vacations anyone in the United States took in the summer of 1858, but for reasons that no one could possibly foresee.

〰

ABOLITIONIST COUNTRY

As soon as Jefferson Davis stepped on board the *Joseph Whitney*, moored in Baltimore harbor, he felt relieved. His doctor was right, the easy rumble of the ocean and the fresh sea air helped his neuralgia recede, and within just a few days aboard the ship he realized that the anger that had brought him close to a duel had disappeared. By the time he reached Portland, Maine, where he had been invited to use a vacation cottage owned by his friend, Montgomery Blair, he seemed better, much to the relief of Varina and their two children.

Davis was leery of traveling to anywhere in New England, the hotbed of abolitionism, home to radical antislavery newspapers such as the *Liberator*. To his surprise, a group of friendly townspeople serenaded the senator and his family when they stepped off the boat on July 9 in Portland, Maine. He and Varina felt comfortable right away. In gracious remarks, the Southern senator began by reminding the crowd gathered that Mississippi and Maine were not enemies, but "sister states" whose people had "one voice and one heart." In an unprepared but stirring speech, he applauded the rich heritage of the people of Maine and New England, especially their participation in the American Revolution. He spoke out against the practice of English ships stopping American merchant ships in search of slaves and said it was as much a nuisance to the New England merchant ships as to any slave ships. Finally, he advocated building a transcontinental railroad that would help industry in New England. He brought cheers when he said that their warm welcome made him feel "that I was still at home."

His audience was thrilled by what he said and even more by his appearance. Jefferson Davis was not a two-headed slave-owning dragon at all. He was a well dressed, well mannered, amiable man, a family man with an attractive, attentive wife and two adorable children. He didn't preach about slavery, but issues that were important to New Englanders. Perhaps he was not the devil portrayed in the abolitionist press after all.[125]

The Mississippi senator had been calling for American unity since he left his sickbed in Washington, DC. Just before he sailed for Maine, he wrote several Pennsylvanians a letter in which he declined an offer to speak in Philadelphia on Independence Day because of his health. But he told them that, "so long as their descendants may emulate their patriotism, their virtue and their wisdom, why may not the union of the Constitution stand?"[126] During the voyage north on the Fourth of July, the captain of his ship asked him for an impromptu address and he pleased the assembled crowd of passengers and crew gathered on the deck of the vessel with "a beautiful speech," that emphasized national unity, according to a reporter from the *Boston Post*, not on board, who later scribbled notes about the speech from details provided by those who were present.[127]

Davis's speech at Portland made him popular, and the Maine Democratic Convention, meeting at that time, asked him to address it. Davis strode into the convention of the northernmost wing of his party, where so much antislavery talk had been heard, and delivered another heartwarming speech calling for unity in a time of crisis. At one point, as he looked about the room he asked the assemblage, "Shall narrow interests, shall local jealousies, shall disregard of the high purposes for which our Union was ordained, continue to distract our people and impede the progress of our government towards the high consummation which prophetic statesmen have so often indicated as her destiny?"

He paused and hundreds jumped to their feet shouting "No! No! No!" and cheering.[128]

He was heralded as the hero of the Mexican War when he inspected a local militia company in Belfast, Maine. There, he reminded the men of their ancestors' victory in the Revolution and their own neighbors' victory, fighting with him, in Mexico. Again, he called for unity, telling the troops that the American flag was "the emblem and the guide of the free and the brave…"[129]

The visitor from Mississippi was asked to speak at just about any event he attended. He was drowned in sustained applause wherever he appeared, such as at the Maine State Fair, an annual event that attracted tens of thousands of people. He told that crowd that he saw himself and the people of Maine as "brothers." He said that in the South the word "Yankee" was usually a term of reproach, but now, having met so many residents of Maine, he knew that it meant "honorable." He wound up telling the huge crowd at the state fair that the disintegration of the Union was "not the sentiments of the American heart; they are the exceptions and should not disturb our confidence in the deep seated sentiment of nationality which aided our fathers when they entered into the compact of Union and which has preserved it to us."[130]

Everywhere he spoke in Maine, Jefferson Davis emphasized three things: 1. all Americans, North and South, share a single, proud heritage; 2. all local matters, like slavery, should remain just that—local; and 3. Americans, regardless of their home state, have common national interests that unite them, not divide them.[131]

The trustees of Bowdoin College, Maine, the town where Harriet Beecher Stowe wrote the antislavery best-seller *Uncle Tom's Cabin*, bestowed an honorary LLD degree on the senator from Mississippi amid thunderous applause from a large crowd that had gathered.

Davis and his family accepted just about every social invitation extended to them. It was a summer vacation like none that Davis of Mississippi, so far from home in Maine, had ever experienced. Relatives of the Blair family entertained them and took them on boat trips to the islands in Casco Bay. They were invited to a succession of large communitywide clambakes at

Cape Elizabeth and enjoyed individual picnics with families there. Someone invited them to the graduation ceremonies at Portland High School and to the reception afterward, where the Davises thoroughly enjoyed themselves, congratulating the happy graduates and mingling with those in the crowd.

Jefferson Davis carried his three-year-old daughter Maggie around the clambakes and picnics on his shoulders, to her delight. Sea captains in Portland between voyages regaled Maggie with stories about their adventures in the Pacific. Davis's daughter had become the center of attention in town. People fawned over her wherever she went and continually offered her cakes, cookies, and candies. She was such a familiar figure in Portland that when people introduced Jefferson Davis he was often not presented as the U.S. senator from Mississippi, but rather as "little Maggie's father."[132]

The family accepted an invitation from a Professor Bache to travel with him to the top of Mount Humpback to make astronomical observations. His wife remembered riding on horses through a lengthy valley filled with enormous granite outcroppings that reminded her of the pyramids of Egypt. They spent several nights camping out on a plateau at the top of the mountain. They joined Bache in an ad hoc barbecue, dining on recently caught speckled trout, and were entertained by the professor, who read to them since Davis's eyes were still weak. The professor then played a Verdi song on a music box and Davis, delighted with the song, sang it. His love of music, reported those who were there with great humor, was not equaled by his skill as a tenor.[133]

His two months in Maine had made him the toast of New England, and on his way home he was asked to speak at Boston's Fanueil Hall on October 11 and to stop off at New York on October 19 to talk at the Palace Garden. In Boston, where they stayed at the Tremont House Hotel, Jeff Jr. was stricken with the croup. The Davises were overwhelmed with advice, help, and medicine for Jeff Jr. In the middle of the night, Mrs. Harrison Gray Otis, a leading abolitionist who was from the influential Otis family, arrived with her own medicines, tonics, advice, and genuine concern for the little boy. Varina Howell was impressed with Mrs. Otis and the people of Boston. "This memory is clear and blessed to me, and her name has always been honored in our household," Varina wrote thirty years later.[134]

The senator was met with jubilant receptions in both Boston and New York. To capacity audiences, he again reiterated his admiration for Northerners, the common history of North and South, brotherhood among Americans. He also tried to dampen the fires about slavery. "There is nothing of truth or justice with which to sustain this agitation, or grounds for it… I plead with you now to arrest fanaticism which has been evil in the beginning, and must be evil in the end… The danger lies at your door, and it is time to arrest it. Too long have we allowed this influence to progress," he told cheering audiences in both cities.[135]

Throughout the North, newspaper editors praised Davis's speeches and the warm reception he received in New England. Horace Greeley of the *New York Herald Tribune* wrote that his speeches were not only imbued with patriotism, but that Davis exhibited the type of common sense that politicians North and South needed. In some quarters, his newfound Northern admirers said that the Union-loving Mississippi senator would make a fine president of the United States in 1860.[136]

The reaction in the South, however, was just the opposite. Davis was severely criticized for his olive branch approach to the people of New England and roundly castigated for trying to appease the Yankees. The strident states' rights politicians and the editors of some of the most important newspapers in the South roundly condemned him in virulent language. They damned him for his speeches and even for being so accepting of New England hospitality. One editor savagely criticized Davis just because he "had praised the Yankees" and another wrote with venom that in befriending the people of New England, Davis had become "a propagandist for disunion."[137] One of the loudest salvos fired against him in the newspapers was a scathing editorial in the *Charleston Mercury*, where editor Robert Rhett wrote that Davis was "a Union Mormon," a "pitiable spectacle of human weakness" who should have stayed in Boston. "Of all the signal examples of startling Southern defection that the venality of the times has afforded, there is none that can at all compare with this…the Jefferson Davis we knew is no more!"[138]

Davis was shaken by the tidal wave of vituperative editorials in the Southern press. He wondered if he had gone too far in trying to serve as a bridge between North and South. Perhaps the critics were right; maybe he had been too friendly. Maybe the warm reception he had received and the generosity of people in Maine to his wife and family on a personal level had blinded him to their true nature as a people politically devoted to the destruction of slavery and Southern rights. Was it in fact no longer possible, given the events of the 1850s, for harmony to be attained anywhere in the United States? Maybe the time was past when a political leader could tell people on both sides of an issue what they wanted to hear in order to bring them together.

He was reminded of that in a letter he received from a man named Campbell. He wrote, "I think the time is coming when the people will prefer to know exactly what a man's views are and then they will know exactly what to expect from him."[139]

Davis and his family returned to Brierfield, the plantation on the banks of the Mississippi River, for three weeks in September to oversee damage from a summertime flood. The trip to Maine was undertaken so he could recover physically. Now it was time for him to recover politically. At his beloved Brierfield, Davis had time to think about what he had said in New England and the animosity his words had engendered throughout the South. The senator knew the time had finally come to make up his mind about what course of action he was going to pursue, permanently, on the slavery issue. He did.

In November, he traveled to Jackson and Vicksburg to deliver two important speeches. There, in the two largest cities in his home state, he made it very clear what he felt about slavery, the abolitionists, and the Northerners, and it was not friendship.

He began his speech in a packed Representatives Hall in Jackson in which, the *Jackson Mississippian* reported, "the lobby, the aisles, and every part of the Hall were densely thronged." There was sustained applause from the crowd when he walked into the hall and even louder cheering when he rose to address it. Davis began his speech by reminding the gathering that he had almost died of "protracted, violent disease" the previous spring and that he only went to Maine to recuperate. He then carefully explained that his kind remarks in New England were spoken to thank the people there for the generosity extended to his family, not as political forgiveness, and insisted that he had been misquoted in the *Joseph Whitney*. The senator explained, too, that he was a politician and party leader and many of his remarks were meant to help Democrats in Maine and Massachusetts get elected in the fall contests. He then delivered a blistering defense of slavery and a fierce admonition to Northerners to stop their harassment of the South. He not only denounced the "black Republicans," but savaged members of his own Democratic Party, particularly Stephen Douglas, who he said had been far too conciliatory to the North on the questions of slavery and states' rights.[140]

He repeated his condemnation of Northerners who opposed slavery in a second speech in Vicksburg a few days later. Then, in a blistering finale, he told the crowd that if the Republicans gained control of the Senate, House, and the presidency in 1860 it would serve as a "revolution" that would destroy the U.S. government. That done, he told the crowd, the South would have no other choice than to secede from the Union. An antislavery president should not be allowed to take office, Davis told the crowd in a speech that became increasingly aggressive as he continued. The senator called Northerners "hostile" and "enemies," and said he would be in "favor of holding the city of Washington…and the glorious star-spangled banner, declaring the government at an end and maintaining our rights and honor, even though blood should flow in torrents throughout the land." He concluded, "As for himself…[he] would rather appeal to the God of Battles at once than to attempt to live longer in such a union."

He warned that if an abolitionist was elected president in 1860, "Let the star of Mississippi be snatched from the constellation to shine by its inherent light, if it must be so, through all the storms and clouds of war." And, he added ominously, Southerners would have to begin building armories, hoarding weapons, and expanding railroad lines in case the Northerners attacked them.[141]

The two speeches in Mississippi had not only placated his supporters and critics, but renewed the faith of Southerners in the Mississippi senator. He had not swung over to the other side after all. The editor of the *Montgomery (Ala.) Confederation* wrote that Davis had shown that he was a "distinguished and beloved son of the South." The editor of the *Oxford (Miss.) Mercury* promptly forgave all of his sins in New England, telling his readers that the speech "effectually clears away all doubts about his fidelity to the South and shows that he is still as true to her as the needle to the pole. [Critics] will now be forced to acknowledge that he is the champion of principles…inimical to the glory and honor of the South."[142]

His brush with death, his recuperation in Maine, and the stinging denunciation of Southern editors and leaders over his conciliatory remarks in the autumn of 1858 had led him down a path of physical, emotional, and mental transformation. The man who had toyed with the idea of secession for years had now made up his mind that it was necessary if the 1860 elections gave the country a radical Republican president. Jefferson Davis had become, with his two scalding speeches in Mississippi in the last days of 1858, the unquestioned leader of the secession movement.

THE WHITE HOUSE

EARLY 1858: ONE YEAR OF *DRED SCOTT*

Dred Scott was an obscure sixty-two-year-old slave who accompanied his Virginia owner, Peter Blow, from the slave state of Virginia to St. Louis, Missouri, in 1830. Blow died there two years later. Scott was then bought by an army doctor, John Emerson, who took him to Illinois, a free state, where they lived for two and a half years. Emerson then took Scott with him to a U.S. Army fort in the free territory of Wisconsin, where Scott married another slave, Harriet Robinson, whose ownership was transferred to Dr. Emerson. The army physician was transferred to St. Louis and then Louisiana. After Emerson died in 1843, his widow, who was living in St. Louis, unsuccessfully tried to hire Scott and his wife out to others for income.

In 1847, Dred Scott went to court in St. Louis and filed suit, contending that since he had lived with Emerson in a free state, and both he and his wife had lived in a free territory, they were therefore free. John Sanford, her brother, represented Mrs. Emerson in the suit. Scott lost in the initial verdict, but won on an appeal. The Missouri Supreme Court reversed that decision and that court's ruling was upheld by a federal court. Scott then took his case, and final appeal, to the U.S. Supreme Court in 1856 for a legal fight that did not end until March 1857.

In Washington, the Scotts faced an uphill legal battle. Seven of the nine Supreme Court justices were appointed by presidents from slave states and five of them were from families that had owned slaves. The two attorneys who would argue the case for Sandford against Scott before the court, Reverdy Johnson and Henry Geyer, were not only staunch antislavery advocates, but two of the best courtroom lawyers in the country.

The case was also more complicated than it appeared. The court not only had to rule on Scott's freedom, but whether, as a slave, he had the legal standing to file a suit, whether residency in a free state or territory meant that a slave was free, whether the government could prevent an owner from bringing a slave into a free state or territory if, in fact, the slave was "property."

Even more important, the ruling would determine whether slaves could be brought into the new territories, such as Kansas, where slavery had become an incendiary political issue and triggered violent wars between proslavery and antislavery factions. It could also result in a federal ruling that since all slaves were property, Congress could not ever free them as human beings.

Ironically, the case should never have involved President Buchanan. The justices were prepared to issue an opinion in February, a month prior to the inauguration, but the death of Justice Peter Daniels's wife caused a delay in all court business and the Scott case was pushed back for a month.

The five Southern justices were against Scott's plea and in favor of maintaining slavery's status quo. The two announced dissenters were Justice John McLean of Ohio and Benjamin Curtis of Massachusetts, both Republicans, who told Chief Justice Roger Taney that they would not only vote for Scott's freedom but, if he lost the case, would publish their minority opinion, denouncing slavery in the territories. The other two justices, Democrats Samuel Nelson of New York and Robert Grier of Pennsylvania, seemed noncommittal. The Southerners had the votes to turn down Scott, 5–4, and wanted Taney to write the official court opinion. The jurists, though, and many Southern congressmen—and especially President Buchanan—were emphatic that one of the two Northern Democrats had to be convinced to vote with the Southerners for a 6–3 decision to give the appearance that justices North and South were in favor of upholding the slave laws. A slender, five-vote majority ruling with all Southerners voting against Scott would appear too regional and bolster Republican charges that a slave conspiracy ruled the nation's capital.

To gain that crucial Northern vote, President Buchanan secretly wrote his fellow Pennsylvanian, Justice Grier, who was also a graduate of Dickinson College, as were Buchanan and Taney, lobbying him to vote against Dred Scott. He did so because Justice John Catron of Tennessee had discreetly written him in early February that he should pressure Grier in order to facilitate a proslavery decision. Grier had frequently defended the Fugitive

Slave Act and the president thought he could convince him to vote against Scott too. The seemingly unethical behavior by the president was successful; Grier did so. Grier admitted his role in the executive/judicial impropriety in a letter to Buchanan, in which Grier said, "We will not let any others of our brethren know anything about the cause of our anxiety to produce the result," and that what he was doing in writing Buchanan was "contrary to our usual practice."[143]

The Catron-Grier-Buchanan correspondence was fact, but there was a rumor that Buchanan's whip in the House, J. Glancy Jones, also knew that the Court was going to rule against Scott and had told Buchanan so. Another rumor was that somehow Buchanan had been shown an advance copy of Taney's decision.[144]

The final vote against Scott was 7–2 (Samuels voted with the majority; Curtis and McLean dissented).

In his majority opinion, written in scathing language, Chief Justice Taney, one of the many who believed that the Northern aggressors would not be content until they had eliminated slavery, declared that slaves were not humans and therefore had no standing to file legal suits. He went further, writing that residence in a free state or territory did not mean that Scott or any slave was free, and in twenty-one pages, ruled that the Missouri Compromise was unconstitutional. The decision angered Northerners, but what really enraged them was Chief Justice Taney's harsh language. He wrote that Negroes were "unfit to associate with the white race…and so far inferior that they had no rights which the white man was bound to respect."[145]

At his inauguration, prior to his swearing in, President Buchanan and Justice Taney met on the inauguration platform and whispered to each other. No one knows what was said, but Taney might have told the president what the *Dred Scott* ruling was going to be and that it would be made public in two days. Critics of the president were certain that happened because in his speech the president, pretending he did not know what the *Dred Scott* decision was, told the crowd that he would abide by whatever the court ruled. "To their decision, in common with all good citizens, I shall cheerfully submit, whatever this may be."[146]

Buchanan, of course, was pleased with the ruling. He had favored that view for years, writing that "all American citizens have an equal right to take into the territories whatever is held as property under the laws of any of the states…"[147]

The reaction to the landmark court ruling was predictable. Southerners and proslavery Democrats and their newspapers endorsed it and the Republicans blasted it. The editor of the official Democratic Party organ, the *Washington Union*, said that the ruling would "[restore] harmony and fraternal concord throughout the country." The *New York Journal of Commerce* said the decision was the "authoritative and final settlement of grievous sectional issues," and asserted that it was "almost the greatest political boon which has been vouchsafed to us since the foundation of the Republic." The *Richmond Enquirer* chortled that the abolitionists had now been "staggered and stunned." The *Richmond Whig* went even further, predicting that the *Dred Scott* decision had "set at rest all those vexed Constitutional questions" and decided the legality of slavery forever.[148]

The Republicans were outraged by the decision, and President Buchanan's unethical role in it, as soon as it was announced and continued to criticize the high court's ruling throughout 1857 and 1858. They were joined by numerous newspaper editors, who denounced the decision in their columns. Horace Greeley, editor of the *New York Tribune*, called it "atrocious," "wicked," and "abominable," described the judges who voted against Scott guilty of a "detestable hypocrisy," and labeled Taney the Supreme Court's "cunning chief." Other Northern editors wrote of the ruling with equal venom. The editor of the *Chicago Democratic-Press* declared that he had a "feeling of shame and loathing" for the Court, that he termed "this once illustrious tribunal, toiling meekly and patiently through this dirty job." The *Chicago Tribune* editor wrote that the decision had hurled America back into "the barbarian ages." It was, he wrote, "shocking to the sensibilities and aspirations of lovers of freedom and humanity." Dozens of public figures, some at their own expense, printed pamphlets on the court case; the Northerners attacked it and the Southerners embraced it.[149]

The two loudest opponents of the ruling were Abraham Lincoln, rumored to be the Republican U.S. Senate candidate in Illinois in the fall of 1858, and William Seward, the Republican New York senator who was the leading candidate of his party for president in 1860. Both complained that the ruling was not merely an affirmation of slavery for Dred Scott and others like him, but a signal that the Supreme Court, the White House, and the Democratic Congress were all part of a massive slave conspiracy that would turn the United States into a slave nation.

Lincoln charged that the *Dred Scott* decision was a precedent that would be used often to promote slavery. The proponents of slavery, he said, would "push it forward till it shall become lawful in all the states…North as well as South." They would accomplish that goal, he said, "Simply by the next *Dred Scott* decision." Since precedent had now been set, "it is merely for the Supreme Court to decide that no state under the Constitution can exclude it, just as they have already decided that…neither Congress nor the Territorial Legislature can do it." Lincoln added, too, that since the Supreme Court had ruled that slaves were property, no state legislature or state court could overrule it.

Lincoln predicted that soon the Supreme Court would start ruling that thousands of Southerners could move to Northern states with their slaves, and that one morning he and his neighbors "shall awake to the reality that the Supreme Court has made Illinois a slave state."[150]

Southerners dismissed Lincoln's remarks as just more Republican agitation on the slavery issue, but he was one of hundreds of Republicans, many important elected officials, who agreed. They all looked at the legal precedent: if slaves were property, then no state could ever abolish slavery because they could not abolish property holding. Even state legislatures, such as New York's, issued pronouncements in which dozens of members declared that they honestly feared the *Dred Scott* decision would soon make them slave states.[151]

Seward was even angrier, accusing Buchanan of conspiring with the justices. He said that the president had "received them as graciously as Charles I did the judges who had, at his insistence, subverted the statutes of English liberty."[152]

President Buchanan seemed pleased with the *Dred Scott* decision, often referring to it when approving of slavery in the territories or the Southerners' right to maintain the institution. As late as December of 1859, less than a year before he would leave office, Buchanan was extolling the *Dred Scott* decision in his annual message to Congress, telling members that "the right has been established of every citizen to take his property of any kind, including slaves, into the common territories belonging equally to all the states of the confederacy and to have it protected there under the Federal Constitution. Neither Congress nor a territorial legislature nor any human power has any authority to annul or impair this rested right." Following several more paragraphs of support for the *Dred Scott* decision, Buchanan happily told both houses of Congress of the case, "Fortunate has this been for the prosperity of the territories, as well as the tranquility of the states."[153]

ONE YEAR LATER

After one year of debates over the *Dred Scott* decision, Buchanan was hopeful that the anniversary, and the entire slavery issue, would pass quietly. It would not. The first anniversary of the *Dred Scott* decision, coming on March 6, 1858, fell right in the middle of the acrimonious debates in Congress over the newly passed, proslavery Kansas Constitution, defended by Buchanan and Jefferson Davis and opposed by Stephen Douglas and others. The *Dred Scott* ruling had not ended anything, as Buchanan and the Southerners had anticipated.

One year later, the *Dred Scott* decision had become a political albatross around James Buchanan's neck. It had not solved anything and had merely reminded Northerners that, despite what Buchanan frequently said about national harmony, he was in the Southern camp on slavery. On March 6, 1858, President Buchanan and everyone else in America realized that the *Dred Scott* decision was never going to go away—as the president had blithely hoped that crisp March day twelve months before when Chief Justice Taney had whispered what appeared to be such good news into the president's ear.

Chapter Four

COLONEL ROBERT E. LEE LEAVES THE MILITARY FOREVER

On February 4, 1858, the same week that his old boss, Mississippi senator Jefferson Davis, delivered his rousing speech on the Kansas issue, Colonel Robert E. Lee arrived on horseback at White House, one of his wife's Custis family plantations in central Virginia. White House, a historic 5,100-acre farm, was the home of Martha Washington during her marriage to Daniel Custis, who died when she was twenty-six. Exactly one hundred years prior to Colonel Lee's arrival at White House that day, in the winter of 1758, George Washington had proposed to Martha in that same home and she accepted, marrying him ten months later and leaving White House for Mount Vernon, her new husband's home on the southern banks of the Potomac River.

All of the grandeur of White House, the scene of so many elegant parties in the eighteenth century, was gone now. The main house was in disrepair, the lawns were unkempt, and the outbuildings nearby were in even worse shape. The slave quarters were in need of repair. Lee wrote in his diary, "Found the buildings dilapidated, no funds, no corn for sale." Nearly all the plantation homes that belonged to the Custis family, including Romancoke (4,656 acres), were in shambles in 1858, the victims of neglect by the stepgrandson of George Washington, George Washington Parke Custis, Lee's father-in-law. Lee scribbled in his diary, "Went to Romancoke—found that things there were more dilapidated than at White House—nothing looks well." On further inspection of Romancoke, he noted that the wheat for the spring was "unpromising" and that the mill dam had not been repaired in months.[154]

Everyone at the plantations—slaves, overseers, hired white workers, domestics—knew when Lee had arrived to tour their farms. He was a handsome man whom several friends later wrote was the novelist's hero come to life, the man of the marble statues. He was fifty-one years old that winter, but appeared much younger. Lee was a superb horseman, a tall, trim man, nearly six feet in height, who carried himself in a way that made him appear even taller. His eyes were dark brown, animated, and caught the attention of all who were introduced to him. Lee possessed thick, wavy black hair, a neatly trimmed moustache (his fabled gray beard would not appear until 1862). Those who knew him said he was a man of elegance and poise, the perfect soldier. "His limbs, beautiful and symmetrical, looked as though they had come from the turning lathe, his step was elastic as if he spurned the ground upon which he trod," wrote a classmate at West Point.

Walter Taylor, later a military confidant of Lee's, wrote that the colonel was "admirably proportioned, of graceful and dignified carriage, with strikingly handsome features, bright and penetrating eyes, his iron-gray hair closely cut, his face cleanly shaved except for a moustache, he appeared every inch a soldier and a man born to command."

One man who met him said that when Lee entered a crowded room he immediately looked like the most important man in it; women flirted with Lee all of his life. It was not just the middle-aged men or ladies who were impressed by his handsome demeanor, though. Even young men were struck by his elegance. "He is the handsomest man in the army," gushed one young lieutenant about Lee when the colonel was forty-eight.

Another individual who met him, Paul Hayne, wrote that he could see Lee approaching because he was much taller than any of the men around him. Lee was, Hayne wrote, "the most striking figure we had ever encountered, as erect as a poplar, yet lithe and graceful, with broad shoulders well thrown back, a fine, justly proportioned head *posed* in unconscious dignity, clear, deep, thoughtful eyes and the quiet, dauntless step of one every inch the gentleman and soldier. Had some...stone in Westminster Abbey been smitten by a magician's wand and made to yield up its legendary knightly tenant restored to his manly vigor, with a chivalric soul beaming from every feature, some grand old crusader...we thought that thus would he have appeared."[155]

Robert E. Lee was the descendant of not one, but three great American families. He was the youngest son of "Lighthorse Harry" Lee, who commanded

Lee's Legions under General Nathanael Greene in the Revolution and afterward served as governor of Virginia. Prior to the Revolution, the Lees had become wealthy planters and were influential in the government of the Virginia colony and scions of its social scene. His mother was Anne Hill Carter, the daughter of Charles Carter and the descendant of Robert "King" Carter, the largest land owner and slaveholder in the South. The Carters were the leaders of the vast and enormously prosperous tobacco industry in Virginia and had, over the years, sent several members of the family to the colony's state legislature and, prior to the Revolution, maintained cordial relations with Virginia's many Royal Governors.

Lee, who had two brothers, a half brother, and two sisters, had married into America's greatest family, the Washingtons. Mary Custis was the daughter of George Washington Parke Custis, the stepgrandson of the nation's first president. He and his sister were brought up by George and Martha Washington after their father Jackie Custis died in the Revolution. When President Washington and his wife died, Custis was left a considerable amount of land, buildings, and money. He became a moderately successful planter and amateur landscape painter, although his fortunes had declined as he aged.

Lee had previously visited some of the other Custis farms in his February 1858 inspection tour and was exasperated at the condition of what had once been one of the most impressive collection of plantations in the United States. Disheartened at what he saw on his inspections, Lee wrote his cousin, Anna Fitzhugh, "Dear Cousin Anna, what am I to do? Everything is in ruins and will have to be rebuilt."[156]

What was he to do?

On October 21, 1857, Colonel Lee had received a telegram at his barracks in Camp Cooper, in San Antonio, Texas, informing him that Custis, his father-in-law, who was seventy-seven, had died ten days before. Lee's wife Mary and several of his children were at Custis's side when he slipped away.

Colonel Lee requested a furlough and came home as soon as he heard the news of Custis's death. He arrived at Arlington House in deep mourning. Lee wrote in his diary, "Found all sad, suffering, and sick...who had always met me with fraternal kindness and affection vacant."[157]

He had learned that the old man, who always admired Lee, had designated him as the executor of his estate; he had also been informed that Custis had left an extraordinarily complicated will that would eventually require Lee to spend substantial time back home in Virginia to sort out.

The colonel, who had fought gallantly in the Mexican War in 1846 and later served as an able superintendent at the United States Military Academy at West Point under then Secretary of War Jefferson Davis, was overwhelmed by the paperwork of the will. The will required him to apportion lands and money to every single member of the family and pay off the large debt left by Custis, who died owing more than $10,000, a considerable sum at that time.

He was also overwhelmed by the chance, suddenly presented to him in the winter of 1858, to leave the U.S. Army forever and live the comfortable life of a rich Virginia planter, something he had always dreamed about. The old man's will was complex, but local attorneys and judges he talked to carefully pointed out to him that although he was technically bequeathed only a small lot in Washington, DC, there were simple steps that he could take that would make him the manager of all the Custis properties, assets, and the family's 150 slaves. Properly run by a skilled administrator like himself, these properties and businesses could make him a wealthy man and permit him to live comfortably among the gentry of his beloved Virginia. Robert E. Lee, tired of the army, could forsake the grimy military outposts and desolate plains where he had spent much of his adult life and enjoy mornings riding through the rolling countryside of Virginia and evenings sitting on the porch of Arlington House, the magnificent Custis home that overlooks the Potomac on one side and Washington, DC, on the other side, a drink in his hand and his loving family at his side.

He had been in the military for twenty-nine long years and was often bored and exhausted by his job and depressed from the long absences from his family. He was married to a woman whom he loved deeply and missed desperately when he was away in the army, whether fighting Mexicans, chasing hostile Indians, training cavalry, or administering forts thousands of miles from home. His wife was stricken with rheumatism in 1835, when she was thirty-seven, and had suffered from lengthy bouts of it, plus arthritis, throughout the rest of her life. Her health had disintegrated rapidly since 1856, when she last saw her husband following the end of his tenure at West Point and transfer to the West. With little mobility, she was unable to spend much time overseeing the housekeeping at the mansion. In her personal life she had become untidy, leaving her rooms messy and continually complaining of tiredness. She was now practically an invalid. The family wondered if she could run Arlington House without her father and her husband away in the army.[158]

Colonel Lee, always concerned about his wife, was shocked to see how much her health had deteriorated during his latest absence. The arthritis had practically immobilized her right hand and arm and caused her substantial pain. The arthritis often forced her to wake up in the middle of the night and she had difficulty falling back to sleep, spending much of the day tired from lack of rest. She had trouble holding on to banisters and plates and moved about very cautiously. She was a forty-nine-year-old woman who had the mobility of a disabled woman in her eighties. She had hid the spread of arthritis and her declining health in letters to her husband in San Antonio. "I almost dread him seeing my crippled state," she wrote a relative just before his arrival from Texas. Now that he was home again, he would know what had happened to her and how she suffered.159

The shock of her condition was one more reason Lee now thought seriously about leaving the army. Not only could she no longer live with him at army posts, but she needed him at home in order to live at all. By 1858 she had deteriorated so badly that she was no longer able to attend balls, dinner parties, and other social functions with her husband; she and he had become prisoners of their home because of her decline. A melancholy Lee wrote upon his return to Arlington House after Custis's death, upon seeing his wife for the first time in seventeen months, "I fear Mary will never be well enough to accompany me in my wandering life."160

Lee's dream of the quiet life of a planter was not new. He had expressed that yearning often to members of his family for more than twenty years. Wrote his son Rob, "He often said that he longed for the time when he could have a farm of his own, where he could end his days in peace and quiet."161

As the winter of 1858 progressed—amid the growing rancorous arguments just across the Potomac River in Washington over slavery in Kansas—and his inspections and meetings with lawyers and plantation overseers continued, Colonel Robert E. Lee had a decision to make as he attempted to fulfill his responsibility as the will's executor. Should he spend the rest of his life in a monotonous and uneventful career in the army, never promoted to general, away from his ill wife and seven children, or should he become a gentleman planter and live a life of ease?

∽

ARLINGTON HOUSE

Arlington House was one of the grand old homes of Virginia, a large, elegant mansion with a lovely two-story-high portico held up with eight thick, Doric columns on the southern shore of the Potomac River, directly across the water from the nation's capital. Its grassy lawns stretched to the edge of the Potomac in gentle slopes, many of them lined with sweet-smelling flower gardens filled with jasmine, lilacs, jonquils, hyacinths, violets, and roses, and clusters of fruit trees, such as apple and apricot. Visitors who saw it for the first time said that Arlington House and its grounds looked as magnificent as those of any European palace.

Lee felt comfortable at the mansion. He wrote that it was "where my affection and attachment are more strongly placed than at any other place in the world." Lee's wife Mary spent nearly all her life there and missed it dearly when she was away with her husband on an army assignment. "What…would I give for one stroll on the hills of Arlington this bright day," she wrote during one absence. All in the family knew of her love for the plantation. Daughter Mildred wrote that "[Mother's] heart was ever turned to Arlington and the fair scenes of her life's best happiness. Her thoughts were ever in the past at Arlington—always Arlington."[162]

Lee's daughters loved Arlington House too, as did all who visited the home of the Custis family. Daughter Mildred luxuriated in smelling the yellow jasmine flowers in the gardens and gathering up flowers that she and her siblings wove into necklaces that they laid on their bedsheets. "None [gardens] ever seemed so fair to me as this Kingdom of my childhood," Mildred recalled wistfully as an old woman. Her sister Agnes agreed. She wrote when she turned sixteen, "Arlington, with its commanding view, fine old trees, and the soft wild luxuriance of its woods, can favorably compare with any home I've seen!"[163]

Custis, Robert E. Lee's father-in-law, had lived a checkered life. An irresponsible teenager who was ejected from three different colleges, Custis moved to his father Jack's 1,100-acre plantation and its four-room brick cottage in 1802. Ownership of two other Washington family plantations, White House and Romancoke, were also passed down to him by the president.

Custis hired experienced managers to run the much larger farms at White House and Romancoke, and they were reasonably successful; he used the Arlington plantation for experimental farming and the cultivation of his beloved flower and vegetable gardens. Custis wrote several plays that were produced, many articles about his grandfather, and delivered memorial addresses about George Washington. He also memorialized his grandfather in dozens of paintings of his military exploits during the Revolution. Many of his patriotic paintings adorned the walls of the rooms in Arlington House. During the last year of his life, he helped to oversee plans for the Washington Monument, still in the planning stages in 1858 (it would only be two-thirds completed when the Civil War began).[164]

Custis also became an accomplished landscape painter and used the Potomac and the rolling lands of his plantation for backdrops for those works. His niece once encountered him standing alone on one of the hilltops of the plantation. She wrote, "I saw G.W.P. standing, wrapped in contemplation of the western sky robed in all its gorgeousness of color. I asked him if he was enjoying nature's painting, he replied, 'I am studying the effect for my picture.'"[165]

When the president died, Custis wanted to continue living at Mount Vernon, but Washington had left that home to Bushrod Washington, a cousin who himself later became an important public figure in Virginia. It was understood that Parke would move to his father's plantation. Intent on living in a mansion as grand as the manor house at Mount Vernon, Custis hired architect George Hadfield and contractors to build Arlington House, a large, eye-catching edifice modeled after old Roman and Greek temples. The rooms in it were oversized and the family made much use of them. Mary Lee, the colonel's wife, and Custis's other children joined him for breakfast each morning (Lee placed a rose on the plate of each lady at the table on those days when he was home on furlough or living there while working in Washington), and then adjourned to the family parlor, where Curtis lead morning prayers. Much of the evening was spent in that room; Parke Custis sat for hours in a large chair next to the fireplace, a succession of cats on his lap. A north wing housed the Lee family following the marriage of Robert E. Lee and Custis's daughter Mary in 1831. The Lees, like the Custises, celebrated many holidays at Arlington House. Christmas was everyone's favorite; Lee obtained furloughs from the service so he and his family could spend the holiday together. The Lees spent twenty-four of the thirty Christmases prior to the Civil War at the mansion.

Robert E. Lee missed any Christmas he was not home with his wife, children, and the extended family at Arlington House. He wrote sons Custis and Rooney at the 1846 Christmas, when he was away in the Mexican War,

"I hope good Santa Claus will fill my Rob's stocking tonight; that Mildred's, Agnes's, and Anna's may break down with good things. I do not know what he may have for you and Mary, but if he only leaves for you one half of what I wish, you will want for nothing!"[166]

And when any of his sons were away from Arlington at Christmas when he was at the mansion, he wrote lengthy letters describing the holiday festivities, sometimes in mouth-watering language. "The children were delighted at getting back [on a visit] and passed the evening in devising pleasure for the morrow. They were in upon us before day on Christmas to overhaul their stockings...I need not describe to you our amusements, you have witnessed them so often; nor the turkey, cold ham, plum pudding, mince pies, etc., at dinner," he wrote Custis, at West Point during Christmas 1851.

Besides the mansion, Custis oversaw the construction of several gardens, a dance hall, and a dining pavilion several hundred yards from the home, a grove of bushes, trees, and vegetation, a spacious horse stable that was designed as a miniature Arlington House, with a portico and four Doric columns serving as its entrance. Nearby were large wooden sheds for carriages and some cattle. An eight-hundred-square-foot ice house was located near the slave quarters, along with an outbuilding that served as a kitchen.

The highlight of the plantation was a large park called Arlington Springs that was similar to city parks. Anyone in Washington, DC, Alexandria, or other nearby communities could use "the park" without charge for picnics and parties. The park was a succession of lawns and English-style gardens off the Alexandria and Georgetown Turnpike entrance to the plantation, easily reached by carriage or horseback on the Virginia side of the Potomac or from the Washington, DC, side on the Georgetown Ferry. The park contained walking and bridle paths through its woods that were populated with oak, chestnut, and elm trees, well-manicured lawns, and several stone benches where visitors could sit and look out at the Potomac and the nation's capital. A writer for *Harper's* magazine wrote, "In front, sloping towards the Potomac, is a fine park of 200 acres, dotted with groves of oak and chestnut and clumps of evergreens and behind it the dark of forest."[167]

Visitors who walked into one of the gardens often encountered Mary Lee, along with several of her children and some slaves working feverishly on the rows of flowers. Daughter Mildred remembered, "My mother spent hours here, digging, weeding, and directing Old George, Little George, Uncle Ephraim, Billy, and the swarms of small Ethiopians. I can see her now with a white sun bonnet hanging down her back! Visitors from Washington, Alexandria, and Georgetown always ended by a stroll in the gardens."[168]

Everyone who saw them was enraptured by the Arlington gardens. Wrote Lee's niece Elizabeth Calvert of them, "Is it at the touch of memory only that flowers bloom here in such exquisite perfection, or did the yellow jasmine from its raised arbor in the center of the garden send forth a widespread fragrance and shower its countless trumpet shaped flowers down? Did the encircling bed of daily roses send their offering of perfume in the air from their brilliant blooms, did the pines in points of the garden beds shade masses and masses of lily of the valley from which we gather in lavish quantities beauty and fragrance? Did hyacinths, tulips, tall lilies all the 'beauties of sisterhood' bloom in unconstrained delight?"[169]

The residents of Alexandria and Washington, who visited the park often, remembered them, and the hospitality of G. W. P. Custis, who greeted many fondly. The editor of a Washington travel guide wrote in 1852, "Still, retired walks, inviting lawns, shaded by beautiful groves, and the finest view of the river and the city imaginable. The fine manners and instructive conversation of the venerable proprietor often add to the life and social enjoyment of those who seek [refuge] from the dust and crowds of the city a few hours' relaxation and retirement amid the charms of this cool and quiet spot."[170]

The park had numerous visitors. From April through October, several hundred area residents strolled through the park or picnicked there each weekend, and on holidays there were far more. Between five and ten thousand visitors jammed the park for the annual Fourth of July celebrations, sitting on the grassy lawns to watch the fireworks displays in Washington.[171]

The Lees enjoyed the grove, too. It was a place to play but also a place of reverence. The children buried their cats there. "The grove was a place of mystery to me," wrote Mildred Lee. "It was the part of the park enclosed in the garden and was the special resort of squirrels, blue bells of Scotland, and grape vines, where we used to swing. Here too there was an arbor covered with a grape vine, with a big mossy natural stone for a seat, a capital place to crack hickory nuts... Just on the edge of the grove, under a spreading tree, was my own little garden, a white lilac in one corner and the violets forming the borders of the beds..."[172]

No one loved Arlington more than Mary Lee, who wrote of it, "I never saw the country more beautiful, perfectly radiant. The yellow jasmine in full bloom and perfuming the air..."[173]

Her husband, the colonel, had enjoyed Arlington on visits as a teenager and never lost his appreciation for the home and the grounds around it, especially in springtime. Early one May when the cherry blossom trees and gardens were in full bloom, he wrote, "The country looks very sweet now, and the hill at Arlington covered with verdure and perfumed by the blossoms of the trees, the flowers of the garden's honey-suckles, yellow jasmine is more to my taste than at any other season of the year."[174]

A NEW ERA AT ARLINGTON HOUSE

Custis fell ill with pneumonia on the evening of Saturday, October 3, 1857, and his condition became much worse by morning. The family was summoned and told by his doctor that he was going to die and only had a few days remaining. They had to pay their final respects. Custis met with all of his family during the mornings and afternoons of the next few days and slipped away quietly on October 10. One of his last acts was to thank his daughter Mary and her husband, Colonel Lee, stationed in Texas at the time of his death, for their love and devotion throughout their lives.

Lee's daughter Agnes, who had lived most of her life at Arlington House with her mother and father (when he was back from the army), was grief stricken at the death of her grandfather. Agnes described his death in her journal on October 11, 1857, "just to try to relieve my bursting heart." She wrote, "Who will supply his place to me? O, no one. No one! We knew death had to come. I trust I am grateful that he was given to us for so long. But each year I prized him more…clung to him. What is Arlington without its master? None can ever fill *his* place. So kind he was, so indulgent, loving us so fondly."

The grief that fell like a veil over Arlington House lasted for months. On January 3, 1858, Agnes was still in deep mourning, writing in her journal that she had lived yet another year, but with her grandfather gone, lived "with a sad, sad heart."[175]

Lee's heart was sad too, as he arrived at Arlington House from Texas, but just walking on its rolling lawns and sleeping in the huge mansion conjured up wonderful memories. It was here that he visited so often as a young man and here that he met and married his wife Mary.

The colonel was born in a mansion on his family's plantation, Stratford, in Westmoreland County, Virginia, but his childhood was not a happy one. His father, despite his political influence, had gone bankrupt after a series of irresponsible financial investments and often left home to raise money or hide from his debtors. Lighthorse Harry was also a sickly man and traveled to find cures for his ailments. His wife and children rarely saw him, and Lee's mother barely paid her bills and clothed and fed her children and the slaves on the money the Carters gave her. Her husband had to sell some of their land and assets to pay off some of his debts. She left Stratford when Robert was three. Lighthorse Harry left his family to roam through the Caribbean when Robert was six. The boy never saw his father again; Harry died on Cumberland Island, Georgia, in 1818, at the age of sixty-two.

The Lees moved to Alexandria, Virginia. The Carters and Lees were friendly and young Robert was permitted to enroll in a private school the Carters ran at their plantation nearby for their children. The Lees were also friendly with the Custises because Henry Lee and his father had been friends with President Washington; the family often visited Arlington House to see Custis, the president's stepgrandson. Robert and Mary Custis played together often as children, developed longings for each other as teenagers, and finally married in 1831, when he was twenty-four and she was twenty-three. Mary bore him seven children.

Friends were eager to have him admitted to the United States Military Academy at West Point, founded in 1804, but a lengthy waiting list put that off until 1825, when Lee was eighteen years old. The Virginian was a superb student, graduating second in his class. At the military academy, he had the opportunity to meet men from all over the country, including Jefferson Davis of Mississippi, who was one class behind him. Lee chose the Corps of Engineers for his life's work in the army; it was considered a prestigious position in the military.

Upon graduation in 1829, Lee was granted a two-month leave of absence. His mother died just as he arrived home, bequeathing him some money and six slaves. Shortly afterward, he married Mary Custis at Arlington House. He explained to her very carefully that as a soldier he would often be away, serving his country at posts around the United States. Some might be as nearby as Washington, DC, and Baltimore, but others might be in the West, near the Mississippi River or the plains territories. She would be able to accompany him to some posts, but not to others. Mary was not happy about it, but agreed. Her great-grandmother Martha had been able to spend each winter of the Revolutionary War with her husband when he served in the rebellion, but that was because he was the commander-in-chief.

ᴄᴏ

LEE'S MILITARY CAREER TAKES OFF

Lee left soon afterward. He had been assigned to Savannah, Georgia, to build Fort Pulaski. That assignment kept him away for two years, but he was back home in 1831, brought back to help plan and construct Fortress Monroe in Virginia. That was followed with work on a military post in Hampton Roads, Virginia, and then an assignment at army headquarters in Washington, where he was promoted to first lieutenant in 1836. One year later, the army sent him to St. Louis, Missouri, to oversee work on the reconstruction of the Mississippi River harbor of that city. Lee spent three years there and then four years in New York City working on improvements for its harbor, one of the largest in the nation. His life was changed in 1844 when he was asked to sit on the annual examinations board at West Point. On that board, he met and became close friends with General Winfield Scott, the army's highest-ranking officer, who liked Lee immediately.

The United States became entangled in a war with Mexico in 1846 and Lee was sent there to help the engineers build roads and fortifications for the army. The U.S. Army was led by Scott, who plucked Lee out of the engineering department and gave him the authority of a battlefield leader. Lee the engineer scouted and developed attack routes at several battles—bringing victory to American troops—and at one battle personally led a group of reinforcements from Scott's army back to his division to ensure a triumph over the Mexicans the next day. He had taken it upon himself to embark on dangerous night rides across the plains of Mexico to meet with other officers and confer with General Scott, rides on which he might easily have been captured or killed. He once spent a night hiding in a gully within a few hundred yards of the enemy, while scouting terrain and trails for what turned out to be one of the most successful assaults of the conflict. General Scott called his reconnaissance work "indefatigable and daring."[176]

He was also instrumental in assisting Scott to lead American forces to victory in the battle of Chapultepec. For his valor and leadership in the Mexican conflict, Lee was first promoted to captain and then to lieutenant colonel. In the battles in Mexico, he met many men he would not have encountered had he been restricted to the Corps of Engineers. He was certainly not the dashing hero that his classmate Jefferson Davis was in the widely publicized war, but Lee was mentioned in numerous newspaper accounts and applauded for his work at army headquarters back in Washington. The war had shown his administrative skills, courage, grit, determination, and the ability to use foreign terrains to his advantage, all skills that would help him later in life.

His mental capacities were admired by all. Jefferson Davis later wrote that "his mind led him to analytical rather than perceptive methods of obtaining results."[177] All saw him as a rather complete man, with a fine military education at West Point, and a good family; a man who loved children and animals and led a good Christian life.[178]

FROM WEST POINT TO MEXICO

His family did have the chance to reunite with him when the war in Mexico was concluded. He was transferred to Baltimore, where his wife and family happily joined him. In 1852, classmate Jefferson Davis, who became the secretary of war under President Franklin Pierce, and fought with Lee in Mexico, named the Virginian the new superintendent of West Point.

Lee had his hands full at the Academy as he tried to establish tighter discipline. Jefferson Davis, who had nearly been kicked out of West Point when he was a cadet, chuckled after one visit there that the disciplinary problems of the Academy had not changed since his escapades. Lee, too, had been exasperated by the rowdy cadets. Davis wrote that he was "surprised to see so many gray hairs on his head" and that they had been caused by his sympathy for the problems of young people. Lee wrote that his troubles came from the unusual nature of West Point, that was neither completely a college nor a military school. "Cadets can neither be treated as schoolboys or soldiers," he wrote.[179]

The real pleasure of that assignment, however, was that he could once again bring his family to live with him at West Point, a school that sat on the western banks of the Hudson River, one of the prettiest locations in the country. Mary Lee and the children loved their time there.

Davis, a hard-working and effective secretary of war who saw himself as a visionary, started two new cavalry units to help the army secure the new territories in the West that the United States had won from Mexico. He pulled Lee away from West Point in 1855 to put him in the Second Cavalry, second in command to Albert Sidney Johnston, a West Point classmate and friend of Davis's and an acquaintance of Lee's. The Virginian became a lieutenant colonel in the cavalry and eventually replaced Johnston as head of the unit and remained in charge of it, assigned at first to St. Louis and then to posts in Kansas and Texas. In those positions, as in all of his posts in the army, he showed significant administrative abilities and an ability to get along with everyone—veterans in their forties as well as young lieutenants fresh out of West Point and the enlisted men. Lee worked well with peers and higher-ranking officers in the army and, happily for the army, with civilian leaders wherever he was stationed. Although he continually tried to get promoted to general, he was not a politician, as were so many officers in the army, to the delight of his superiors.

Those who knew him in those years remembered that he was a reserved man who kept his distance from the rowdier officers. His men did not see him as aloof though, and many referred to his personality as a "quiet dignity." Lee had a mercurial ability to remember people's names and faces, and later in life could recall the names of men he had met in the Mexican War in 1846. Sometimes he would forget the name of a man he saw at a church service or reception and become angry with himself because of it; sometimes, forgetting a name, he would seek out others who knew the man, obtain his name, and then find him and address him properly. He was an obsessive letter writer and answered just about every piece of correspondence sent to him in the army, regardless of the sender. Officers and men who knew him noted that one of his skills as a commander was the ability to listen to the comments of others, much like his wife's great-grandfather, George Washington. Like the leader of the Continental Army, Lee listened to all and then made up his own mind.

Colonel Lee did not smoke, drink, or curse and he attended church regularly. Although often away from home, he did not enter liaisons with other women, although he was known to flirt with some from time to time.

When engaged in disputes with his wife, he would deliberately write her to say that he had accompanied some woman to a church service or reception as part of his army duties, although apparently his relationships with other women went no further.

Throughout his career, unlike Jefferson Davis, he was never involved in a dispute with superiors or fellow officers or enlisted men. Lee was parsimonious, a holdover reaction from his youth, when his family was nearly bankrupt, and instructed his children to be careful with their money. The colonel always paid his own debts, remembering them despite the considerable stress in his life. In 1860, while a farmer at Arlington, Colonel Lee purchased a piece of equipment from a store in Washington for two dollars. During the next eighteen months the federal elections, secession, bombardment of Fort Sumter, and the outbreak of war carried him far from Arlington. The store owner had long ago forgotten the small debt. One morning a boy arrived at his store and handed him two dollars, informing him that it was the money Lee owed him, and that Lee was very sorry it had taken him so long to pay the bill.[180]

He was always immaculately turned out in his blue U.S. Army uniform, wore fashionable wide-brimmed hats in the scorching western sun, was a superb horseman, became an expert at firearms and cannon, was well read in military history and tactics, and exhibited a genuine love for the army, even though as he aged, he became restless in it.

⌁

THE FAMILY FIRESIDE

Lee's children loved him and missed him whenever he was away, stationed thousands of miles from home in New York, Mexico, Texas, or elsewhere. In the fall of 1855, after Lee had been sent west with the cavalry, his daughter Agnes wrote that "Our dear Papa is at Jefferson Barracks, far away from those he loves. It is too bad."[181]

Lee, in turn, missed his family. On Christmas 1856, he wrote several emotional letters home that described his longing to be with them and to be back at Arlington House rather than his dusty army barracks. He wrote his wife, "The time is approaching, dear Mary, when I trust that many of you will be assembled around the family hearth at dear Arlington to celebrate another Christmas. Though absent, my heart will be in the midst of you. I shall enjoy in imagination and memory all that is going on. May nothing occur to mar or cloud the family fireside and may all be able to look with pride and pleasure to their deeds of the past year. I can do nothing but love and pray for you all."

Several days later, at the holiday, he wrote a mournful letter home and told his loved ones that he hoped they had a joyous Christmas and knew that they would have many more. He reminded them that he had purchased a Dutch doll, one of the new crying babies, and little French teapots for the girls and knives and books for his sons. Their father, he wrote sadly, had Christmas dinner with a fellow officer and a clergyman. "Mine was gratefully but silently passed," he said.[182]

One flaw in Lee's make-up was his refusal, in either his professional or private life, to confront people over disagreements. The colonel avoided adversarial conversations with his wife and children as well as superiors and fellow officers in the army. His disdain for disputes often caused delays in the completion of tasks, military or personal, and when he returned to Arlington House in 1857 that unwillingness to confront people would bring him face to face with the biggest decision of his life and the life of his country.

Custis named Lee as the executor of his estate because the colonel was an accomplished administrator. If he could run the U.S. Military Academy at West Point, he could certainly run Arlington House. It is unclear, though, why he wrote a convoluted will. Custis must have realized that work on the will would be extraordinarily time-consuming for Lee and might require a lengthy furlough to come back to Virginia to fulfill its requirements. Since the will involved every member of the family, and debt that had to be paid, it might take years to straighten out.

Custis knew how debilitating that could be. His own grandmother, Martha Washington, found herself in that same predicament when her father-in-law, John Custis, died. His will, which also included the payment of numerous debts, was intricate, filled with inane dictates, such as one that required anyone who received money from the estate to carry the name Parke. Martha had to hire several lawyers to begin to administer the estate after her husband died. George Washington then took that responsibility upon himself when he married Martha and spent another decade working on it, constantly frustrated by the job. Custis had heard his grandparents complain about the Parke estate will and its troubles; why did he leave a similarly difficult will for Robert E. Lee to administer? Did he secretly hope that the estate and his daughter's illness would combine to make Lee leave the army? He had no male heirs, only his daughter Mary. Did he do it in order to force Lee to come home to Arlington House to take over the Custis heritage and the legacy of George Washington?

Under the terms of the will, Mary Lee was given Arlington House and its grounds, plus all of George Washington's furniture and relics that were housed there. It would pass to her son Custis upon her death, not her husband. The plantation at White House was not bequeathed to Lee, but to his son Rooney. Romancoke was not left to Lee either, but to his son Rob. Lee's daughters Mary Anne, Agnes, and Mildred were given the sums of $10,000 each from the sale of Smith Island, in Northampton County, and other lands in Stafford, Richmond, and Westmoreland counties, and the income from the plantations, but their father was given nothing. In fact, all Robert E. Lee was left was a small lot in Washington, DC.

Custis, like his grandfather George Washington, also freed all of his slaves in his will, directing that they be given their freedom within five years of his death, but—he added, in a line that would cause Lee innumerable troubles—they could only be emancipated within that period of time if his debts were paid.[183]

The problem with the terms of the will was that the Custis children and grandchildren were left money that he did not have and money that would not be available until the total sum of $10,000 in debts was erased. The old man seemed to owe everyone money, even the manager of his mill at Arlington, who had not been paid in six years. From time to time as he rode about Virginia, Lee was accosted by men who had been owed money by Custis, some as much as $1,300; he promised to pay them all. The sale of Smith Island would bring little. His run-down farms did not turn much of a profit. There were also no Lee men in Virginia to run those farms. Lee's son Custis was in the army and posted in California; his son Rooney had just left for an army expedition to Utah to put down what President James Buchanan termed a Mormon revolt. In fact, the only male member of the family left in Virginia to renovate and run those farms was Colonel Lee.[184]

His sons understood his predicament and wanted to help him financially. Custis sent him an official document transferring his inheritance of Arlington House to his father, insuring his financial security if his mother passed away first. Lee, as always, never wanted his sons to give up anything in order to lend him assistance, even if it was needed.

He wrote a gentle letter back to his son, telling him, "I am deeply impressed by your filial feeling of love and consideration, as well as your tender solicitude for me, of which, however, I required no proof, and am equally touched by your generosity and disinterestedness… I cannot accept your offer. It is not from an unwillingness to receive from you a gift you may think proper to bestow, or to be indebted to you for any benefit great or small. But simply because it would not be right for me to do so. Your dear grandfather distributed his property as he thought best and it is proper that it should remain as he bestowed it. It will not prevent me from improving it to the best of my ability, or of making it as comfortable a home for your mother, sisters, and yourself as I can. I only wish I could do more than I shall have it in my power to do."[185]

Complications with the Custis will began immediately and Lee had to hire lawyers to help him sort out the provisions of the document and assess the conditions of the old man's finances. Everything the colonel did with the lawyers took time, and the two-month furlough he had been given by his superiors in the army ran out in December. He was granted another furlough, this one for an entire year, and a frustrated Lee wondered, as the paperwork piled up at Arlington House, if even that would give him enough time.

Lee had moved back into Arlington House and loved the stately home, but it too had fallen into disrepair since his departure in 1855 for the frontier cavalry posts. The aging Custis had no real enthusiasm for the management of the plantation. The roof of the mansion leaked, many wooden fences on its 1,100 acres had collapsed, and the fabled lawns, neglected by Parke Custis for years, had been infested with weeds.

⌒

SOUTHERNERS AGAINST SLAVERY

Lee's return to Arlington House brought him back to slavery and once again challenged his feelings about the institution and the conflicting opinions about blacks that plagued him all of his life, views that had been evident to all at Arlington since he married Mary in 1831. The colonel always maintained that he was morally opposed to slavery, but like so many in the South, he did nothing to end it, always writing that Southerners against slavery had to leave its eventual elimination to God, Congress, or the courts.

In 1856, he wrote his wife Mary, "Slavery as an institution is a moral and political evil in any country. It is useless to expatiate on its disadvantages. I think it is, however, a greater evil to the white than to the black race, and while my feelings are strongly enlisted on behalf of the latter, my sympathies are most strong for the former. The blacks are immeasurably better off here than in Africa, morally, socially, and physically. The painful discipline they are undergoing is necessary for their instruction as a race and I hope will prepare and lead them to better things. How long their subjugation may be necessary is known and ordered by a wise Merciful Providence. While we set the course of the final abolition of human slavery and we give it all the aid of our prayers and all justifiable means in our power, we must leave the progress as well as the result in his hands who sees the end; who chooses to work by slow influences and with whom two thousand years are but a single day."[186]

After the war, publicly, Lee told anyone who would listen that he was in favor of the elimination of slavery. He expressed his disdain for slavery after the war too, telling a congressional committee that "I have always been in favor of emancipation—gradual emancipation."

John Jones, a clerk in the Confederate War Department, later backed him up, telling biographers that Lee was "a thorough emancipationist."[187] So did Herbert Saunders, a British journalist who interviewed Lee when the Civil War ended. He claimed that Lee told him he had always been in favor of freeing his slaves, and had in fact freed some during the war. Saunders said Lee assured him that many Southern planters wanted to abolish slavery because it was no longer a productive labor system. The abolitionists had created such an uproar over slavery, he told Saunders, that the same people intent on releasing their slaves kept them so that it would not appear they were backing down in the face of Northern harassment.[188]

Lee told a Presbyterian minister, the Rev. John Leyburn, a pastor in Baltimore after the war, that the purpose of the war had not been to continue slavery. In fact, he told the minister, he was glad that the result of the war was the end of the institution. "So far from engaging in a war to perpetuate slavery, I am rejoiced that slavery is abolished. I believe it [emancipation] will be greatly for the interests of the South. So fully am I satisfied of this, in regards to Virginia especially, that I would cheerfully have lost all I have lost by the war and have suffered all I have suffered, to have this object attained."[189]

Yet another journalist who talked to Lee after the war, Myrta Avery, a reporter for the *New York Herald,* said Lee claimed again that he was against slavery. He said he was one of many Southerners who felt that way. "The best men of the South had long desired to do away with this institution and were quite willing to see it abolished. But with them in relation to this subject, the question has ever been: what will you do with the freed people?"[190]

George Washington frequently questioned how pre–Revolutionary War Americans could complain that they were slaves to England and yet hold black slaves themselves. Lee felt the same quandary. He wrote, "Is it not strange that the descendants of those Pilgrim fathers who crossed the Atlantic to preserve their own freedom of opinion have always proved themselves intolerant of the spiritual liberty of others?"[191]

The family of G. W. P. Custis had been publicly opposed to slavery for decades. Custis, his wife Mary, and his daughter Mary Lee were members of the American Colonization Society, a group started in 1817 to educate blacks and to transport emancipated slaves to Liberia, on the western coast of Africa, to form a new colony there. The society's leaders reasoned that these educated and Americanized slaves would help build a democratic, Christian civilization in Liberia. The group raised money throughout the United States; the three Custises were substantial contributors. Mary Custis and her daughter had also been influenced by the Second Great Awakening, an evangelical Christian movement that swept the country in the 1840s. The movement taught that people who wanted to go to heaven had to lead moral lives—and moral lives meant fighting slavery.

The two women not only gave their own money to the group, but organized a group of slaves to pick sweet-smelling "nosegay" flowers, such as roses, lilies of the valley, and chrysanthemums, from the Arlington gardens and, with the two women and Mary Lee's daughters, bundle them into bunches. The slaves would then be sent to flower markets across the river in Georgetown to sell the flowers. The proceeds from the sales were turned over to the Colonization Society. Over the years, the Custises contributed a significant amount of money to the society and sent one of their slave families, William and Rosabella Burke and their four children, to Liberia with other Colonization families.

Agnes Lee taught the plantation slaves how to read and write at a small one-room schoolhouse her father built at Arlington. She told visitors that Robert E. Lee fondly referred to her young pupils as "the ebony mites."[192]

Custis lost interest in the Colonization Society after a decade or so, but on his own he manumitted nearly a dozen slaves over the years. They were all mulatto men and women, and neighbors gossiped that some of the females were his lovers and the others his offspring. Still, the total number of slaves freed by the Custises in their lifetimes amounted to less than twenty; they kept hundreds of others, over several generations, in bondage. In his will, the old man intended to make up for all those years by granting freedom to all of them. He left that to Robert E. Lee, who was ambivalent about the idea.

Lee had owned several slaves most of his life, as had many of the members of the Lee family. The colonel maintained a low opinion of blacks, and until 1856, in a single letter to his wife, never protested their condition. When he was thirty-two, he disdainfully told his wife that at best, they might have two good workers in an entire household of slaves and that the rest were useless. He told Mary to "do with all of them as you please if opportunity offers, but do not trouble yourself about them as they are not worth it." He cautioned his son that "you will never prosper with the blacks, and it is abhorrent of a reflecting mind to be supporting and cherishing those who are plotting and working for your injury."[193] He even adapted a policy of always having as many slaves as possible in order to make up for the lazy workers. "What they want in quality we must make up in quantity," he said. Exasperated by the behavior of slaves all of his life, he sometimes told his wife to simply ignore them and hire free whites to get things done.[194]

Lee made no effort to disguise his low opinion of blacks, and all of the slaves at Arlington knew that he felt they were worthless. Lee wrote in 1839 that Arlington's proximity to the Alexandria canal and capital city, and its public park, distracted the slaves. He wrote, "The whole place will be exposed to the depredations of the public; his [Custis's] own people [slaves] will have more opportunity for gossip and idleness and greater temptations and inducement to appropriate the small proceeds of their labor to themselves."[195]

Over the years, those opinions never changed. He once wrote fellow planter Thomas Carter about blacks that "I have always observed that wherever you find the Negro, everything is going down around him, and whenever you find the white man, you see everything around him improving." He wrote Virginia senator Andrew Hunter that "the relationship between master and slave, controlled by humane laws and influenced by Christianity and enlightened public sentiment, is the best that can exist between the white and black races...”[196]

At the end of the Civil War, he very reluctantly agreed with a plan to grant freedom to Southern slaves who fought in the Confederate Army. He only did so because he needed troops desperately, reminding the Confederate Congress of his dim view of slaves as he went along with the proposal. He wrote, “Considering the relation of master and slave, controlled by humane laws and influenced by Christianity and an enlightened public sentiment, as the best that can exist between the white and black races while intermingled as at present in this country, I would deprecate any sudden disturbance of that relation unless it be necessary to avert a greater calamity to both. I should therefore prefer to rely upon our white population to preserve the ratio between our force and those of the enemy, which experience has shown to be safe...”[197]

So when Robert E. Lee took over the stewardship of Arlington House and its farms in 1858, the slaves there were not happy about it. They knew that he did not like blacks and had little interest in their welfare. He exhibited that feeling when he announced that he was going to make money by hiring out dozens of his slaves to work for other farmers in the Virginia and Maryland area. He engaged a hiring agent who specialized in that work, a Mr. Winston who lived in Richmond, and sent him three male slaves and three females who had experience in domestic work.

He wrote Winston, “I wish you to hire them [women] out, in the same manner as the men, for one or more years, to responsible persons, for what they will bring—should you not be able to hire any or all of these people, you may dispose of them to the end of the year to the best advantage, on some farm, or set them to work at the White House, as you may judge best....”

A rather cold-hearted Lee also told Winston that if he could not find work for the slaves, he should turn them over to any other agent he knew for the same purpose. He told Winston that if the man bringing the slaves did not reach his office during working hours, he would not rent rooms for them in the city overnight, but told the man to put them in the local jail. He advised Winston of his blacks, too, that “I cannot recommend them for honesty.”[198]

His hiring schemes often backfired. Workers whom he had sent to some other owner quickly realized that if they performed poorly they would be sent right back to Lee. This happened often. In one scheme, three of his hired-out men were returned after only one day. They claimed the work was too hard and would not do it. A disenchanted Lee wrote of the men, "Among them is Reuben, a great rogue and rascal whom I must get rid of some way."[199]

Lee wrote his son Rooney that his workers rebelled, that some had fled and had to be forcefully apprehended. "I have had some trouble with some of the people, Reuben, Parks, Edward…rebelled against my authority—refused to obey my orders and said they were as free as I was, etc. I succeeded in capturing them, however, tied them and lodged them in jail. They resisted till overpowered and called upon the other people to rescue them."[200]

The new master of Arlington House was attacked by some critics, who wrote to newspapers accusing him of flogging his slaves and inventing the codicil in Custis's will that the slaves could not be freed until the old man's debts had been paid. The published letters also charged that Custis fathered fifteen children with slave women. Lee refused to answer the charges, but someone else did, calling them malicious. Few paid any attention to the newspaper letters, Lee included.

What did concern Lee was the news that unhappy slaves had set fire to the barn of a Virginia neighbor. It struck home at Arlington House. In 1801, Lee's wife's great-grandmother, Martha Washington, announced that she was going to free her slaves upon her death. The slaves of Mount Vernon insisted that she free them immediately and when she refused they apparently set fire to a barn there. Martha's friends feared that they would torch the manor house itself or even harm the former First Lady, and they convinced her to emancipate her slaves right away. Lee did not want history to repeat itself at Arlington House and attempted to calm down the slave fervor there with more lenient work practices. He later wrote his son Rooney of any dealings with slaves when he came back from the army, "I trust you will so gain the affection of your people, that they will not wish to do you any harm."[201]

Mary Lee was even angrier than her husband. After all, she had educated many slaves, raised money for the Colonization Society, and sent an entire slave family to Liberia. What kind of thanks was this? She called her slaves "a host of idle and thankless dependents" and sarcastically wrote that "we should be most deeply indebted to their *kind friends* the abolitionists if they would come forward and purchase their time and let them enjoy the comforts of freedom at once."[202]

The slaves at Arlington quickly discovered that Custis had granted them freedom in his will and were angry that they had to wait until the old man's debts had been paid. Abolitionists, who visited Arlington's park as members of the public and talked to numerous slaves on the plantation, reminded them of the will whenever they could. It seemed unfair, they told the slaves. Why couldn't the Lees free them right away? The slaves' response was to complain loudly about it to the Lees, to exhibit disagreeable behavior, and to engage in work slow-downs.

Lee may have understood their feelings; he scowled to his son Custis in a letter that "He [G.W.P. Custis] has left me an unpleasant legacy."[203] However, he did not appreciate their constant complaining and continually criticized them. Lee and his wife reminded the slaves that the hiring program he had initiated, that they may not have approved, was to raise money to pay Custis's debts so that he could free the very slaves who complained about him. His workers scoffed at the idea.

Lee could not ignore the slavery issue, though, because in 1858 it seemed to be the only topic of conversation in Washington, DC, and at Arlington House. Lee's inspection tours of his plantations and meetings with his lawyers took place during the same weeks that the debate in the Senate over the proposed slavery constitution for Kansas raged. He read the newspaper accounts like everyone else of all the Senate speeches—such as those by his friend Jefferson Davis—and the opinions of newspaper editors.

Lee loved his country, but he did not fear that the storms raging in those years would tear it apart. He wrote, "I wish for no other flag than the star-spangled banner and no other air than 'Hail Columbia.' I still hope that the wisdom and patriotism of the nation will yet save it...the North would cheerfully redress the grievances complained of. I see no cause of disunion, strife, and civil war and pray it may be averted."[204]

He added also that he was against any division of North and South. "Secession is nothing but revolution," he wrote. "I can anticipate no greater calamity for the country than a dissolution of the Union. It would be an accumulation of all the evils we complain of, and I am willing to sacrifice everything but honor for its preservation."[205]

However, Lee, like so many Virginians, saw the attacks on slavery by Northerners not as mere criticism of the institution, but as a serious assault on the Southern way of life.

"The South, in my opinion, has been aggrieved by the acts of the North… I feel the aggression and am willing to take every proper step for redress… A Union that can only be maintained by swords and bayonets, and in which strife and civil war are to take the place of brotherly love and kindness, has no charm for me," he wrote, but told radical Southerners that he did not support any of the public figures loudly advocating secession. He recognized, though, that the country was approaching a crisis. He wrote later, "As far as I can judge by the papers, we are between a state of anarchy and civil war. May God avert both of these evils from us."[206]

Like many Southerners, Lee placed the blame for the North-South bitterness squarely on the shoulders of the abolitionists, charging that they were deliberately provoking the South. He wrote, "The abolitionist must know this and must see that he has neither the right or power of operating except by moral means and [per]suasion and if he means well to the slave, he must not create angry feelings in the Master; that although he may not approve the mode by which it pleases Providence to accomplish its purposes, the result will nevertheless be the same…"[207]

Yet at the same time that he was spouting these antislavery and pro-Union sentiments, he vilified his slaves on a daily basis.

⟶

The Army or the Plantation?

In the autumn of 1858, in the middle of his fourteen-month leave from the military, Lee gave himself a deadline to decide what kind of life he wanted—to return to the army or remain a planter. Colonel Lee had often toyed with the idea of resigning from the army. He had gone to West Point and forsaken the life of a Southern gentlemen to devote his days to the military, but from time to time he tired of it, complaining that there had been few rewards and little satisfaction. He had only been in one real military action, the Mexican War, where he had distinguished himself. Prior to that conflict, and for years after it, he had lived the mundane life of an underpaid and unappreciated officer. He was fifty-one years old and had never been promoted to general, a position he felt he deserved. It rankled him. Others with lesser skills had become generals, yet he had not. Complaining of "a system of favoritism," he often daydreamed about resigning.

While he was home at Arlington House in 1858, Lee would again be denied that promotion. He felt that Congress had never allocated the funds required for him to do his job as a soldier, whether as an engineer, superintendent at West Point, or cavalry leader and post administrator. The army was rife with petty politics that appalled him. Lee feared living out his army life as a mere colonel while others his age in the private sector were spending their golden years in the ease and comfort of their homes. In fact, most of the men he had served with in Mexico, such as U. S. Grant and Jefferson Davis, had left the service.[208]

He missed Virginia, too, where he could enjoy a wonderful life in retirement. Lee was not just a man who was born in Virginia, but a man who loved his home state and, as the offspring of a Revolutionary War hero, was one of its favorite sons. His wife was the great-granddaughter of George Washington. And of course he never really enjoyed leaving his beloved wife and children behind and riding off to some desolate army base far away, as he had been forced to do quite often. Now, too, with rheumatism and advanced and crippling arthritis, plus the responsibility of running Arlington following the death of her father, his wife could no longer accompany him to far-off posts.

The idea of quitting the army had intrigued him for nearly twenty years. As early as 1838, when he was just thirty-one years old, Lee considered leaving the military. He wrote a friend, "I wish all were done and I was back again in Virginia. I volunteered my services last year to get rid of the office in Washington and the [army] at last agreed to my going. I was cognizant of so much inequity in more ways than one, that I feared for my morality, at no time strong, and had been trying for two years to quit. I spent last winter partly on duty and partly not. Had a pleasant time with some friends in Virginia and now here working for my country."[209]

That conflict about the service remained with him all of his adult life and from time to time, when friends and relatives asked whether Lee thought the military was a good career for their sons, he told them no.

Lee was very conflicted about his future. A few months later, he wrote a friend that the camaraderie he had always enjoyed in the army was a major reason that he wanted to stay. He would have his family back in Virginia, but he would be leaving his longtime confidants in the service.

His love of the army was so great that at one point in 1858 he wrote that he felt guilty being away from it, even though he was with his wife and family. "I feel that I ought to be with my regiment and this feeling deprives me of half the pleasure I derive from being here."[210]

Lee's deadline of autumn 1858 to make up his mind on whether to resign from the army and end his long military career came and went. He could not make up his mind because there was still much physical work to be done to refurbish Custis's homes and lands and too much legal work in the courts over the will. He had not resolved the old man's debts, either. Lee gave himself another deadline to make a decision: December 1, 1858, the end of his army furlough. He was frustrated, writing of the interminable legal delays, "I have never proceeded so slowly before in anything I have undertaken."[211]

That December deadline came and went too because Robert E. Lee had still not turned the Custis farms into profit-making enterprises, no matter how hard he tried. He wrote his son around that time that, "It does not aggrieve me to tell you that it will take a stronger man than I am to supply funds for...Arlington [and] the White House if this state of things is to continue. When will it end?"[212]

By then, Colonel Lee realized too that running a plantation was very hard work, full of frustration, and not at all the charming, casual life of moonlight, magnolias, and late-afternoon mint juleps served on the veranda depicted in the romantic novels about the Old South that enjoyed popularity at the time.

Lee's estate transactions, due to their complexity, then became hopelessly bogged down in the courts. Probate judges told Lee that he had to turn to the Circuit Court of Virginia to make a determination about the terms of the will. The reason, as Lee feared, was that Custis had directly linked the distribution of $10,000 to the sale of the lands and the emancipation of his slaves within five years, but *only* when that had been accomplished. Could the court free the slaves while land sales were still pending? Would the land sales revenue cover the $10,000 debt? Would the debts have to be paid before the slaves could be freed? The issue was as complicated for the court as it had been for Custis. At the end of November, when his old boss Jefferson Davis was making his secessionist speeches in Mississippi and laying claim to being the leading secessionist in the nation, a disheartened Lee was told that the court could not hear his case until May of 1859.

He put off his decision about returning to the service once again, writing General Winfield Scott, head of the army, that "I have been occupied ever since my arrival from Texas in settling the estate of the late G.W.P. Custis and have earnestly endeavored so to arrange it, so as to enable me to return to my regiment this fall. I find it, however, impossible to do so and without going into a narration of matters still unfinished and requiring my personal attention, I will only state that the terms of Mr. Custis's will are found to be so indefinite and admit of so many different versions, that I have been compelled to apply to the Circuit Court."

And then, at the end of the letter, after building such a strong case to remain a planter at Arlington House until the Circuit Court heard his case, Lee told General Scott that he would, however, if the army deemed his presence "necessary," rejoin his regiment.

General Scott responded that his presence was not important since the country was not at war and there were no prospects for a war. Scott told Lee to remain home on an extended leave of absence until he had straightened out all of his family's estate businesses. Lee did not appeal that decision and by the end of 1858 still wrestled with the great question of his life: the army or the plantation?[213]

Chapter Five

THE WHITE HOUSE

FEBRUARY 1858: SHOWDOWN WITH STEPHEN DOUGLAS

President James Buchanan was angry with anyone who opposed the proslavery Lecompton Constitution for Kansas, which he strongly endorsed, but none of its opponents drew his wrath as much as Stephen Douglas, the short, portly, brilliant Democratic senator from Illinois. It was Douglas, after all, who introduced the Kansas-Nebraska Act that gave residents of the Kansas Territory the right to authorize slavery if they so desired. It was Douglas who had heralded "popular sovereignty," or the people's right to decide issues, for years. Now Douglas, a former state court judge, opposed the Lecompton Constitution, which authorized slavery in Kansas, in a rebuff of Kansans, his own party, and the president. Douglas's opposition, the president felt, was not based on his convictions about the people's right to choose, but on his hatred of Buchanan. It was yet another chapter in their feud, now a year old, that had threatened to split the Democratic Party in two.

The enmity between Douglas and Buchanan began just before Buchanan was inaugurated as president in March 1857, but the roots of it went back to the 1856 Democratic Convention in Cincinnati that nominated Buchanan for president. Buchanan, incumbent president Franklin Pierce, and Douglas were the three front-runners for the nomination, but none had a majority of votes during the first fourteen ballots. Douglas then conspired with Pierce to have him drop out of the race and throw his votes to Douglas. Even with Pierce's delegates, though, and strong support from the South, Douglas did not have enough strength to capture the party's nomination. Buchanan, sixty-five, a party veteran and moderate, was seen by most as the candidate who could mollify both North and South over slavery and get the country through four more years. Douglas graciously dropped out of the race and urged all to support Buchanan. He told those who pleaded with him to remain in the balloting that his public policy goals of national unity and political goals of a united party were far more important than his career. Besides, Stephen Douglas was just forty-three years old. He had time to satisfy his enormous ambitions; many at the convention assured him that the presidential nomination would be handed to him in 1860.

Douglas naturally assumed that Buchanan would be grateful that he stepped aside, permitting the Pennsylvanian to win the nomination and move on to defeat John C. Fremont in the general election, with Douglas campaigning hard for him (Douglas had contributed $42,000 of his own money to the Buchanan campaign).

The president-elect was not.

Buchanan arrived in Washington one month prior to his inauguration, and in a succession of busy days and nights met with outgoing President Pierce at the White House and then, separately, with leaders of the Democratic Party, including Douglas. The Little Giant felt that he was entitled to personally name several members of the cabinet and contribute to the shaping of national policy. He assumed that Buchanan would listen carefully to everything he had to say. He owed his nomination to Douglas. The Illinois senator was a powerful force in politics, the darling of the South since he introduced the Kansas-Nebraska Act, the champion of the emerging northwestern states, and a favorite with the party in general. He was also the best debater and public speaker in the country, along with Republican William Seward. Washington was also a very socially conscious town and Douglas's recent marriage to a much younger and extremely attractive woman, Adele Cutts, who possessed a penchant for parties, would ensure his place as a social lion in the political community.[214]

Buchanan did not feel he owed Douglas anything, was annoyed by his blustering about cabinet choices and let him know that he would not play any role in the administration. Buchanan was the president, after all, and did not need the impertinent Douglas to succeed. Douglas was furious that he had been frozen out. Another senator told a Buchanan friend that Douglas would "run amok" against the president and his policies in the Senate.[215]

Douglas knew that most farmers in Kansas were free-state men, opposed to slavery, and that most of the proslavery faction in Kansas were recent arrivals from Missouri. Under his popular sovereignty theory then, the free-state men should be able to abolish slavery in the territory when the day came for its residents to become a state, and that day had now arrived. His two-year-old Kansas-Nebraska bill was also unpopular back home in Illinois, where he was up for reelection in eleven months. Fifty-five of the state's fifty-six newspapers were against the proslavery Lecompton Constitution. He had gained enormous popularity with Southerners when he introduced the Kansas-Nebraska bill, opening the door to slavery in the territories if residents desired to live in slave states, even though Northerners, and his neighbors in Illinois, were furious with him over his stand. Illinois crowds continually booed him and often shouted him down when he tried to discuss slavery, forcing him to leave in disgrace. Dozens of ministers signed petitions denouncing him. Some had accused the ambitious Douglas of supporting slavery in Kansas for personal political profit, that the people of Kansas "were mere hazards of [his] Presidential game." Now, could he change his mind to please his constituents in Illinois but anger the same people that so heartily approved his original stand, the Southerners?[216] They were already calling the free-state Kansans the "Topeka Traitors" and would lump Douglas with them. Could one important Democrat turn his back on the most important Democrat, President Buchanan?

SMALL BUT MIGHTY

A correspondent for the *Chicago Tribune* wrote, "I can hardly conceive it possible that [Douglas] will break with the South and the administration."[217]

The iron-willed Douglas had no qualms about a rift with the administration. In one angry conversation about Buchanan, the Illinois senator blurted out, "By God, sir, I made Mr. James Buchanan, and by God, sir, I will unmake him."

By late November, Buchanan had made it obvious to insiders that he was going to support the Lecompton Constitution, approving slavery in Kansas if the residents of the territory voted for it, and expected everyone in the party to fall in line with his policy. Douglas was the chair of the Senate Committee on Territories, and the bill would go to his committee first. Buchanan should have consulted Douglas but, as usual, he ignored him.

An irate Douglas confronted Buchanan about Lecompton in December 1857, at the White House. He told the president that he expected much of the year 1858 would be filled with legislative and public arguments over Lecompton and slavery in the territories and that the president should work with him on the issue. Buchanan heatedly reminded Douglas that he would suffer harsh consequences if he broke with the administration on Kansas. He reportedly told him of two Democratic senators who had opposed Andrew Jackson twenty years earlier. "Mr. Douglas, I desire you to remember that no Democrat ever yet differed from the administration of his own choice without being crushed. Beware of the fate of Tallmadge and Rives."

Douglas looked back at him and said chillingly, "I wish you to remember that General Jackson is dead, sir."[218]

Buchanan was not afraid of Douglas. He was the president and his will, and his Lecompton bill, would prevail. If he had been an astute politician, Buchanan would have worked with Douglas and tried to earn some compromise victory over Kansas. An alliance with Douglas would not only strengthen the party in the South, but in the North, where it had been roughed up in the last elections by upstart Republicans. The president refused to even acknowledge Douglas's influence, despite the Little Giant's political capital in the Senate, his fame across the country, and the political clout he maintained in the Democratic Party—even more than that of Mississippi senator Jefferson Davis. Douglas was such an important political figure at the beginning of 1858 that a correspondent for the *New York Times* wrote that his skills and power "combine to make him an influence which will be decisive in the settlement of this controversy," and several other papers wrote that he was the key to the administration's success.[219]

Buchanan had ignored Douglas yet again, following the cabinet appointees snub just prior to the inauguration, and turned a simmering feud into a political conflagration between the two men. It was personal, too, because the president continually refused to permit Douglas to visit the White House, refused to meet with him, and on occasion, just for spite, called him "Samuel Douglas" in letters he mailed to him.[220]

Douglas plunged into the work of defeating the Lecompton bill with a fury, writing public officials and friends days before the matter was introduced in Congress that this was a political Armageddon. He wrote one man, "The battle will soon begin. We will nail our colors to the mast and defend the right of the people to govern themselves against all assaults from all quarters. We are sure to triumph. Keep the ball rolling and the party united."[221]

He was not only determined to lead that crusade in the Senate, but called for people throughout the United States to debate Lecompton and Kansas. "The time has now arrived when the democracy of the whole country should hold meetings in the cities, towns, and counties, and proclaim in tones that will command respect their devotion to and determination to sustain and carry out in good faith the great principles of self government," he wrote, adding that Lecompton was "a scheme so monstrous as to force a constitution at the point of the bayonet down the throats of an unwilling people."[222]

He took the floor of the Senate seconds after the president's annual message, including his proslavery stand on Kansas, was read. The dynamic Douglas cut quite a figure, as always. He was a very short man, about five feet two inches tall, dark complexioned, with an unusually large head. Much of his brown hair had turned thin and gray by 1858. The senator also had gray eyes with thick eyebrows, connected by a deep wrinkle between them, and a large and firm mouth in the middle of an oval-shaped face. The Judge had, one man wrote, "small white ears, small white hands, small feet, a full chest, and broad shoulders." Reporters always noted his oversized face that, one said, "seems too large for shoulders as support it."[223]

He was nearly always described as "thick set" or "burly" and possessed, many said, a "fierce, bull dog bark." But Douglas was an electric figure to behold. "Small as he was, you would choose him out of a crowd," one reporter who covered his campaigns wrote. Carl Schurz said he was "the very embodiment of force, combativeness, and staying power." Egomaniacal and defiant, he was sometimes portrayed as a cocky rooster and a few newspapers even ran drawings of a rooster in stories about him.[224]

Douglas's great strength was public speaking. One reporter wrote of him, "He is haughty and imperative, his voice somewhat shrill and his manner positive, now flattering, now wild with excess of madness. That trembling forefinger, like a lash, was his whip to drive the doubting into the ranks. He is a very tyrant..." Anther man added, "No one among the gray beards in the United States Senate commands such instant attention when he rises to speak." He delivered "brilliant, sledge hammer speeches," wrote one reporter. A woman who listened to him often from the Senate gallery wrote that Douglas had "the power of thrilling his hearers through and through…his language is always sharp, clear, and strong."[225]

"I totally dissent from all that portion of [President Buchanan's annual] message which may fairly be construed as approving of the proceedings of the Lecompton Convention," Douglas roared that day.

The next day, following administration efforts to muzzle him, Douglas exploded again. He angrily told the Senate that his Kansas-Nebraska bill had been twisted by the administration to mean something it did not. He said that if slavery had to be approved by the residents of a state or territory, then so did every single article of the Constitution, adding that the Lecompton Convention was not legal. He said that his hopes for the territories to adopt popular sovereignty were being "frittered away" by the administration, that the plan was "a system of trickery and jugglery to defeat the fair expression of the will of the people." He told the Senate that since the proslavery faction had hammered together the Lecompton Constitution and that antislavery residents stayed away from the polls when it was proposed in referendum it could not possibly reflect the will of the people—the cornerstone of both popular sovereignty and the Kansas-Nebraska Act. He asked the Senate if the plan of Buchanan and others was "to force a constitution on the people against their will?"

Finally, Douglas said, "If this constitution is to be forced down our throats, in violation of the fundamental principle of free government, under a mode of submission that is a mockery and insult, I will resist it to the last!"

As he finished speaking, the packed gallery of the Senate, equally divided with proslavery and antislavery forces, broke into jeering and applause at the same time, causing general havoc.[226]

Reaction to Douglas's defection from the administration was explosive. Southerners were genuinely shocked, not just by Douglas's stand against the proslavery constitution, but by his 180-degree change of heart on the subject. They not only felt abandoned by the Illinois senator, but betrayed.

Buchanan reveled in that, writing close friend J. B. Baker that "Douglas has alienated the South on the Kansas question." The Southerners were afraid, though, that Douglas's stand against Lecompton, and what appeared to be the irreparable rift with Buchanan, who never made an effort in all of those months to meet with Douglas, would cause the Democratic Party to split in half, just as the Whigs had only six years earlier. Clearly Buchanan, a slavery defender, would lead the Southern half of the party along with Jefferson Davis. Douglas would lead the Northern half.

Douglas had support all over America. He had letters from residents of many Northern states urging him to hold his ground on the Lecompton issue. Typical was the plea of Daniel Morton, of Cleveland, Ohio. He wrote Douglas, "Yield not one inch. Consent to no compromise. Stand firm by the right and God and country will stand by you."[227]

Buchanan not only refused to negotiate policy or discuss politics with Douglas, but would not listen to rumors, many true, that the Republicans in Illinois and nationally were courting Douglas, trying to convince him that his feelings on Lecompton, and on slavery in general, were far more within the Republican camp than the Democratic. Several Republican leaders met with Douglas and hinted that he should become a Republican.[228]

OPTIMISM IN POLITICS

The president became paranoid about Douglas as the Kansas debate droned on through February and March of 1858 and his obsession with the Illinois senator caused just about all business at the White House to grind to a halt. Buchanan came to the conclusion that thousands of Democrats had drifted into the Douglas camp and that they were all secretly working to undermine the party and the White House. He wrote later of the Kansas debacle and the Civil War in general, "It is clear that the original cause of the disaster was the persistent refusal of the friends of Mr. Douglas to recognize the constitutional rights of the slaveholding states in the territories, established by the Supreme Court."[229]

And by 1858, Buchanan was starting to blame all of his woes on Kansas and Douglas. He wrote that the Supreme Court decision on *Dred Scott* should have ended the slavery debate, but "the Douglas Democrats disregarded this decision altogether. They treated it as though it had never been made and still continued to agitate without intermission."

The besieged president said too that it was Douglas who led the South to believe that everyone in the North was against them. Again and again, he told Democrats that the South had "utterly repudiated" the idea of popular sovereignty in the territories, and yet Douglas continued to insist upon it. In doing so, the president said, the Illinois senator had turned Democrats and non-Democrats alike against the South.[230]

The spat with Douglas once again underlined Buchanan's shortsighted view of the toll that slavery was taking on the country. In private correspondence with friends, the president said that he honestly believed that if Kansas was admitted to the Union as a slave state it would end the national debate on slavery and demolish the Republicans. He wrote one friend, "The admission of the state will annihilate the Black Republican Party to end the question of slavery…[it] will equally end the strife on that subject," and blithely added that "I am an optimist on my politics and have ever looked upon the bright side of things."[231]

The efforts of Douglas and others failed to defeat the proslavery Lecompton Constitution in the Senate because there were few Democratic defectors to the banners of Douglas and the Republicans. The bill had to be passed in the House of Representatives also, though, and the fight in the Senate ignited an equally heated battle in the House that included a fist fight between two congressmen. In the House, the Republicans wooed twenty-two Democrats to their side and Lecompton was defeated, 120 to 112. To save face, the administration managed to get through both houses a bizarre bill that permitted Kansas to enter the Union if residents approved of new federal land grants; rejection would defer any chance for statehood for two long years. The carrot of immediate entry failed and Kansans rejected the offer. Kansans elected a new free-state legislature a year later, in 1859, that called for a new constitutional convention and the territory entered the Union as a free state in 1861.

The defeat of the proslavery Lecompton Constitution ended the most controversial intra-organizational fight over a piece of legislation in the history of political parties up to that time. Buchanan, in his rosy world, hoped that the dispute over Kansas had ended the national debate on slavery. Kansas "is now a very peaceful and quiet community," he wrote. The country was back to normal, he thought, ignoring all evidence to the contrary. "All is peace and all express devotion to the Union," he trumpeted to his close friends.

Even so, he told them that Douglas was the devil who wrecked everything on Kansas and that Douglas and his supporters were out to ruin him. He said to one friend, "My great object in public life is to leave a fair name behind me, by honorable means," but that Douglas was making that difficult. Buchanan told an Illinois man, "The…[Douglas] men of your state are not even content to acquiesce in a measure which has been stamped by the national democracy of both houses of Congress." In the final line of that savage letter, the president wrote that he was having trouble preserving the Union against "its opponents in Illinois."[232]

Publicly, the president said nothing about the Douglas crusade to undermine him and his administration, but privately he began to take jobs away from Douglas Democrats, hurting the Little Giant's state party machine, an organization that he would need desperately if he was going to be reelected to the Senate in 1858 and set himself up to fulfill what he believed—and many others believed—was his destiny: to become president in 1860. "Old Buck," as the Douglas Democrats sneered at Buchanan, had no interest in using the president's considerable power over job patronage during his first days in office. Now, his hatred for Douglas growing daily, he turned to those powers and began an effort to dismantle Douglas's political empire in Illinois.[233]

Those who spent time with the president in private said that his hatred of Douglas was almost uncontrollable, that the mere mention of the senator's name brought on long and loud outbursts from Buchanan. Some of his friends thought that his ire for Douglas would cause him to have a nervous breakdown or even a stroke.[234]

And Douglas? The Little Giant was as defiant of the White House as ever. He wrote one newspaper editor, "We will fight the battle boldly and triumph in the end. Let the enemy threaten, proscribe, and do their best or worst; it will not cause any honest man to falter or change his course." And he told another senator, "The administration are determined to crush every public man who dissents from their policy…you may rest assured that I will take no step backwards and abate not one iota of the position I have taken, let the consequences be what they may to me personally."[235]

The Kansas debate was only round one in the political boxing match between the two powerful and stubborn men, though. There would be more throughout 1858, and in the end one would triumph and one would be ruined.

❧

BUCHANAN FIGHTS BACK

President Buchanan's anger with Senator Stephen Douglas did not die down after the contentious winter debates in the Senate over the Lecompton Constitution for Kansas. As the summer approached, Douglas returned home to Illinois to begin his senatorial reelection campaign against up-and-coming Republican state legislator and Douglas's personal friend, Abraham Lincoln. The president believed this might be the right time to turn up the pressure on Douglas to conform to Buchanan's vision of America and to support his administration on every issue.

Even though it appeared Douglas would have an easy race against Lincoln, one of many former Whigs trying to revive his stalled career as a Republican, the Little Giant would be seeking all the assistance he could receive in order to win in convincing fashion, thus setting himself up for a White House run in 1860. He would need all of the resources of the national Democratic Party, which was controlled by Buchanan. He would receive none.

The elections reminded the president once again of the many reasons he disliked Douglas. Paramount was his rudeness to the president two years earlier when Buchanan and Douglas were trying to line up votes to win the Democratic nomination in 1856. The men met by chance that May in the National Hotel in Washington. Buchanan, who saw himself as a political veteran, offered Douglas some convention strategy advice. The offended Little Giant shot back, "I expect to choose my Constitutional advisers soon, and am most happy thus to receive your acceptance in advance."[236]

Most of all, he always blamed Douglas for the collapse of the Lecompton Constitution. In the spring of 1858, Douglas suddenly found that friends of Buchanan in the Senate were publicly aligning themselves against him in the discussions over Kansas and other topics. He saw it as a conspiracy orchestrated by the president. Douglas accused them of trying to ruin him, writing one man, "There are men under [the president] busy at work to convince everyone that I have betrayed my party and my principles, in order to see if they cannot crush me among my Democratic friends." At another point, angry at Senator William Bigler from Pennsylvania, a friend of

Buchanan's, Douglas shouted, "I do not recognize the right of anybody to expel me from the Democratic Party!...I shall maintain my views of right whether there be harmony or not... If, in so doing so, I shall happen to come in collision with any of my friends I shall deeply regret it...[but I] must maintain my independent course of action inside the Democratic party."[237]

To another he wrote, "If the party is divided by this course it will not be my fault... The contest is a painful one to me, but I have no alternative but to accept the issue and stand by what I deem to be my duty."[238]

Douglas seemed to do everything he could to encourage the animosity of the White House. He even met secretly with William Seward and Thurlow Weed in what many saw as a conspiracy by the Republicans to persuade the influential Illinois senator to switch parties. Another persistent rumor flew through Illinois that Douglas, Seward, and Kentucky Democrat John Crittenden were going to form a third "radical" party to serve as a home for all antislavery voters. Another rumor was that a deal had been agreed upon in which new Republican Douglas would support Seward for president in 1860 and then Seward would support him for president in 1864.[239]

Buchanan believed that the ouster of Douglas's friends in Illinois would not only weaken the strength of his wing of the party, but set the removed politicians against him and make all of Douglas's other patronage appointees fear for their employment. He was right.

The president then appointed Dr. Charles Leib as a federal mail agent. Leib grilled federal workers on whether they supported the president in his feud with Douglas. Leib reported back to the White House that most Democrats in the state wanted the Douglas men removed right away, to the delight of Buchanan.

The president then turned his attention on the Illinois newspapers. The party had been awarding lucrative government printing contracts to the *Chicago Tribune* and the *Illinois State Register*; Buchanan canceled them. The president then threatened to cancel government printing jobs that had been given other newspapers unless they supported the administration.

The feud became ugly. Buchanan supporters skewered Douglas and one even seethed that "fealty to Senator Douglas is treason to Democracy."[240]

His friends encouraged Douglas to remain firm in his resolve and to steer clear of any rapprochement with the president because a truce would show Douglas as the loser in the dispute, a cowardly figure who had crawled to the

White House, hat in hand, to ask forgiveness. Usher Linder wrote him that "any reconciliation between you and the Administration party *soils* you."[241]

There would be no truce.

The National Democrats of Illinois, Buchanan's national party organization, announced that it would field candidates against Douglas in each county. One speaker, John Dougherty, warned the crowd that Douglas would be "crushed and ground to powder." Members, who called themselves the "Buchaneers," urged the president to boot the senator out of the Democratic Party.

Leading Democrats understood that Buchanan and his Illinois operatives, called the "Danites" by the Douglas people, were behind everything done to undermine Douglas in Illinois. They defended the chief executive. Cabinet member Howell Cobb wrote, "If Judge Douglas had done as he promised…all of us ought to have sustained him. Such has not been his course. Publicly he attacks the Administration; privately he indulges in the coarsest abuse of the president. Under these circumstances, to ask our support is in my opinion asking too much... [Douglas is] determined to break up the Democratic Party…to unite with anybody and everybody to defeat us."[242]

The president believed in his policy of destroying Douglas, but other leading Democrats did not. They thought that it was the type of misguided politics for which Buchanan had become famous. Senator Henry Wise of Virginia, whom Buchanan had offended as soon as he became the president-elect, was one of them. Douglas's triumph "without the aid of the administration will be its rebuke; his defeat with its opposition will be the death of the administration…"[243]

Animosity by supporters of Douglas soon spilled over the borders of Illinois into other states, where newspapers from the Midwest to the Northeast not only blamed Buchanan for the attacks on Douglas, but charged that he was trying to destroy an entire wing of the party. Newspapers charged that even Buchanan's supporters on Kansas were appalled by his efforts to unseat Douglas. The editor of the *Dubuque (Iowa) Express* wrote, "Even a majority of men who agree with the Kansas policy of the Administration dissent from the course of the president in Illinois and Mr. Buchanan would find himself in a hopeless minority among Democrats was the propriety of his policy towards Douglas submitted to a popular vote of the party."[244]

Even the staunchly pro-Buchanan *Cleveland Plain Dealer*, which routinely criticized all of his opponents and constantly demeaned the antislavery leaders of Ohio, backed Douglas in the dispute. Its editor wrote, "He was hunted and hounded...denounced, vilified, and menaced with political extermination. All of the engines of power were turned against him, every accessible avenue of influence was closed to his appeals, every office holder who would not join the [White House] crusade was expelled from office. He had dared to doubt the essential divinity of the Great Mogul of his party and the decree forthwith went out that he was to be hamstrung, beheaded, tied in a sack, and thrown into the sea."[245]

Support for Douglas, and denunciation of the president, across the country was so great that even Buchanan's own vice president, John Breckinridge, announced on October 22, 1858, that he not only supported Douglas but, if called upon, would travel to Illinois and campaign for the Little Giant.[246]

Douglas denounced his detractors in Illinois and even the opposition of Buchanan cronies in the Senate itself, calling on true Democrats to rally around him. Shrewdly, he told the Senate that he did not think the president was behind this effort to deny him reelection, but just White House renegades, surmising that the tact might lead Buchanan to call off his political assassins.

The White House naturally assumed that Douglas wanted a reconciliation and feared that the party split in Illinois would be followed with intra-party battles elsewhere. A quiet campaign was started to achieve peace with Douglas. Friends of both Douglas and Buchanan continually told Douglas how important he was to the party. Advisers to the president and cabinet members went to Douglas and his friends to bring about reconciliation. The Democratic newspapers that the White House controlled urged Douglas to make peace with the president.[247] Douglas's own father-in-law was recruited by the administration to help persuade Douglas to return to the fold. But the one man who might have convinced Douglas to return to the national party, President Buchanan, showing his political ineptitude once more, never asked Douglas to the White House to discuss their mutual problem; it was something he refused to do.

A stubborn Douglas would not surrender. If he had to run against Lincoln without any help from the national party, so be it. As the summer of 1858 began, Douglas came to several conclusions. There was growing public and press support for him in his war with Buchanan. Congressmen and senators from around the country had rallied around him, as had numerous Democratic newspapers, even the hometown paper of Buchanan's attorney general, Jeremiah Black. Minnesota governor William Gorman said that "999 out of every 1,000 in our party, except for the office holders under the present administration, are with you."

A Democrat in Vermont said his fight would not only defeat slavery in Kansas, but win him the White House in 1860. Southerners even supported him. He must have smiled when he received a congratulatory letter from Virginia governor Henry Wise, whom Buchanan had now lost as an ally. Douglas was a popular man in Illinois and believed that he did not really need the Buchaneers to win the Senate election and, if he could defeat Lincoln *and* the Buchaneers, the dual victory would make him invincible in the 1860 presidential election.[248]

DOUGLAS LAUNCHES HIS CAMPAIGN

If there were any doubts in his mind about his decision to forge on in the Illinois Senate race against Abraham Lincoln without White House support, they disappeared on July 9. On that day, Douglas returned to Chicago from Washington for the beginning of what would be the historic campaign against Lincoln. He boarded a special four-car train in Michigan City, Indiana, and proceeded slowly to Chicago, passing through dozens of communities where thousands of residents lined the train tracks to see his cars pass, cheering loudly for the Little Giant. His well-orchestrated arrival in Chicago might have rivaled that of Alexander the Great when his army entered Babylon. Douglas's train was met with a thunderous cannon salute from 150 pieces of artillery.

He rode through the city streets in an open carriage pulled by six horses and waved to thousands of supporters who lined every avenue. Small Douglas banners hung from the windows of buildings and huge banners were strung over the wide thoroughfares of the bustling Midwestern metropolis. Douglas revelers crowded the rooftops of buildings, alleyways, porches, and windows and roared for the senator as loudly as they could as his carriage passed and a smiling Douglas waved to all, nodding his head in thanks.

The huge throngs followed the parade through early evening as it slowly made its way to the Tremont House where Douglas stayed, their numbers filling several city streets. He spoke to the crowd, estimated at close to thirty thousand, for a few moments; his combative, booming voice carrying over the multitude with their signs and banners. When he finished, a bit hoarse and very tired, rockets were fired up into the sky and a huge fireworks display began. The celebration ended with another burst of rockets soaring high into the night, framing a carefully lettered fireworks explosion of his theme, "Popular Sovereignty." Below it, on the streets of Chicago, thousands cheered as bands played "Yankee Doodle."

Could he defeat the Buchanan wing of the party *and* its candidates *and* Lincoln at the same time? As he waved back to the thirty thousand cheering supporters in the crowd gathered in front of the hotel and watched the rockets burst high over Lake Michigan, he had to ask himself, how could he not?[249]

Chapter Six

HONEST ABE AND THE LITTLE GIANT

THE LINCOLN-DOUGLAS DEBATES, PART ONE

"I wish to preserve a set of the late debates…between Douglas and myself. To enable me to do so, please get two copies of each number of your paper containing the whole, and send them to me by express; and I will pay you for the papers and for your trouble. I wish the two sets, in order to lay one away in the drawer, and to put the other in a scrapbook."

—*Abraham Lincoln to Charles Ray, editor of the*
Chicago Press and Tribune, *November 20, 1858*

Abraham Lincoln wanted to remember his debates with Stephen Douglas in their race for the United States Senate seat from Illinois in the fall of 1858; so did the rest of the nation.[250]

The race was the most closely watched contest of the year; it attracted national attention from numerous large eastern newspapers. The contest was widely covered for several reasons: 1. the Democratic candidate was incumbent Stephen Douglas, one of the most famous men in the country, who had to win the election to become the next president; 2. Douglas was being undermined by President Buchanan, the head of his own party; 3. the Republican candidate, Abraham Lincoln, while unknown outside of Illinois, represented the fiery new Republican Party; 4. it was a showdown over the Kansas constitution and slavery in general; 5. Illinois had become the fourth most populous state in the country and was evenly divided into proslavery and antislavery regions with key central counties where feelings on the issue were mixed; and 6. it featured seven debates that gave those in the audiences, and national correspondents, a complete and vivid picture of the two candidates.

Both men were veteran politicians and skilled public speakers. Both had strong opinions about slavery. Both were also overly ambitious. Everyone knew that Douglas wanted to be president. Of Lincoln, a friend wrote that "his ambition was a little engine that knew no rest."[251]

⌒

A HOUSE DIVIDED

The campaign began in a firestorm on June 16, when Lincoln stunned the Republican convention, and all of Illinois, with his "house divided" speech, which he delivered when accepting the party's nomination for the Senate. Lincoln told the convention that the United States could not go on with half of the country condoning slavery and the other half abhorring it. "A house divided against itself cannot stand. I believe this government cannot endure permanently half slave and half free. I do not expect the Union to be dissolved—I do not expect the house to fall—but I do expect it will cease to be divided. It will become all one thing, or all the other," he said, referring to the familiar biblical line.

The crowd jamming the convention leapt to its feet at the conclusion of the speech, the hall echoed with thunderous applause. Party leaders grimaced as they heard the riveting speech. They wanted Lincoln to maintain his moderate policy of accepting slavery where it existed and opposing it only in the territories. Now, in this unexpected radical turn, he had just about predicted a Civil War.[252]

The major issue in the Illinois Senate race was slavery, as it was in every contest that autumn. The men disagreed sharply over it. Douglas believed that the United States was always going to have free and slave states and that the residents of new territories should be able to decide whether they wanted the institution. Lincoln grudgingly accepted slavery where it was already in place, but believed that the founding fathers wanted it to be abolished eventually. Universal emancipation could not occur if the residents of new territories could choose slavery. Lincoln argued that was evident in the language of the Northwest Ordinance of 1787, which forbade slavery in the land above and west of the Ohio River that the United States also acquired from England—including his own Illinois.[253]

Lincoln traced his hatred of slavery back to an early 1830s boat trip on which he saw several slaves chained to one another. He wrote, "That sight was a continual torment to me and I see something like it every time I touch the Ohio, or any other slave border. It is...a thing which has, and continually exercises, the power of making me miserable."[254]

In 1855, after he joined the Republican Party, he wrote a friend of slavery, "Our progress in degeneracy appears to me to be pretty rapid. As a nation, we began by declaring that 'all men are created equal.' We now practically read it all men are created equal, except Negroes, and foreigners, and Catholics. When it comes to this, I should prefer emigrating to some country where they make no pretense of loving liberty—to Russia, for instance, where despotism can be taken pure, without the base alloy of hypocrisy."[255]

Although he was willing to let slavery exist in the South, he had repeatedly denounced it throughout his life, always reminding his audiences that slaves were human beings, and not property, as slaveholders insisted. In Peoria, Illinois, in 1854, he turned the issue upside down and asked the crowd why hundreds of people, many from the South, had found "something" to liberate their slaves. "What is that something?" Lincoln said. "Is there any mistaking to it? In all these cases it is your sense of justice, and human sympathy, continually telling you that the poor Negro has some natural rights to himself—that those who deny it and make mere merchandise of him deserve kickings, contempt, and death. Why ask us to deny the humanity of the slave?"[256]

He was always angry about slavery, telling one crowd that "as sure as God reigns and school children read, that black, foul lie can never be consecrated with God's hallowed truth." It was, to him, "a moral, social and political evil" that was wrong and had to be ended. Of those who put up with slavery, he said, "Do they really think the right ought to yield to the wrong? Are they afraid to stand by the right? Do they really think that by right surrendering to wrong, the hopes of our Constitution, our Union, and our liberties can possibly be bettered?" He scoffed at Southerners such as Jefferson Davis and Robert Rhett who argued that slavery was a good thing because Negroes could not care for themselves. "We never hear of the man who wishes to take the good of it, *by being a slave himself*," he said.[257]

Lincoln never framed his opposition to slavery more eloquently than he did in 1854, when he attacked Douglas and his Kansas-Nebraska Act, a bill that permitted residents of the territories to decide whether or not they wanted slavery within their borders. He said of slavery, "I hate it because of the monstrous injustice of slavery itself. I hate it because it deprives our republican example of its just influence in the world—enables the enemies of free institutions, with plausibility, to taunt us as hypocrites—causes the real friends of freedom to doubt our sincerity, and especially because it forces so many really good men amongst ourselves into an open war with the very fundamental principles of civil liberty—criticizing the Declaration of Independence, and insisting that there is no right principle of action but self interest."[258]

❧

THE TEN-THOUSAND-MILE CAMPAIGN

It was an exhausting campaign. The two candidates, traveling mostly by train, had maintained a hectic schedule all summer. Douglas tried to speak in a different town every single day of the summer, reaching small hamlets by carriage, stagecoach, or river packet if they were not located near a train stop. He would not cancel speeches because of train delays or unruly weather. Once his 10:40 p.m. train did not arrive at its destination until 3:30 a.m., but he waited for it, boarded it, and, with little sleep, hit the campaign trail again at 6:00 a.m. when it reached its next stop. "Senator Douglas is taxing his strength severely, but it does not seem to impair his health," wrote a reporter for the *Chicago Times*.[259]

Lincoln was just as busy. By November, each candidate had delivered one hundred speeches. Between them, by carriage, steamboat, and train, they had traveled more than ten thousand miles. The Senate race, and its debates, became historic. It was the first Senate race in U.S. history in which both sides hired stenographers (Robert Hitt, James Sheridan, and Henry Binmore), skilled at shorthand, to record the debates, word for word, for publication in the state's newspapers (although both parties later complained that the stenographers missed words or entire phrases and took what the candidates said out of context).[260]

It was a colorful campaign full of heated debates, rousing speeches, huge and colorful banners that hung across city streets, thousands of broadsides, tens of thousands of pamphlets, raucous torchlight rallies, songs and poems written especially for the contest, and seemingly never-ending parades that snaked their way through large cities and small villages with equal enthusiasm. It was a campaign that was dominated by the great issue of the day: slavery. It also involved one of the most important political leaders in the country, Douglas, whose re-election would, all assumed, guarantee him the Democratic nomination for president in 1860 (some newspapers were already calling it "the great battle of the next presidential election"). And it was a campaign, Illinois residents insisted to eastern reporters who did not know much about him, that would introduce the little-known Abe Lincoln to the country.[261]

ᕲᕲ

DEMOGRAPHICS IN ILLINOIS

Politics had always been tricky in Illinois. The state's residents would vote for one party's presidential candidate and then the other's for the Senate and House. One party would win national races and the other state contests. There was a heavy Chicago vote that was very different in its composition than the vote in the rest of the state. The southern section of Illinois that bordered on slave states was like a different country than the northern part; the Free-Soil candidates did poorly there in both 1852 and 1856. As an example of the southern leanings of the geographical sections of Illinois, a proposal to hold a convention to permit slavery in the state received the approval of just 23 percent of the voters in northern Illinois, 41 percent in central Illinois, and 62 percent in southern Illinois. Parts of the state were industrial and others were agricultural. Illinois had a large German population, which often voted for its own immigrant interests, as well as a substantial Irish and Swedish population. It was a great railroad and transportation center, whose workers sided with politicians who favored bills to help their industry.[262]

Both Lincoln and Douglas fretted about Illinois, especially Lincoln. He was one of the founders of the Republican Party in the state. He understood first-hand the intricacies of campaigning on national issues there. In 1856, the Republicans did well in congressional elections, capturing several seats, and in the statewide races they won over 40 percent of the legislative districts. Yet the 1856 presidential candidate, John C. Fremont, who should have run as well as the others on the ticket, lost the state. His pattern of votes was unbalanced too, and this alarmed Lincoln as he prepared for his Senate race. Fremont did well in the northern part of the state, but won a meager 23 percent of the votes in the south and just 37 percent in the central section. Lincoln would lose the election if he captured a similar vote in the central and southern sections of the state.[263]

Always a man who learned from the mistakes of others, he targeted the critical central counties; half the debates were scheduled there—Quincy, Alton, Charleston. That's where he had to stop the Democrats. Wrote a reporter for the *Chicago Daily Democrat*, "The Republicans will sweep the North. The Democrats will sweep the South. Douglas hopes to get his balance of power in the center of the state…his only chance is to hold the balance of power [there]…"

The eleven counties in the central section of the state were evenly split between the Democrats and Republicans and a swing of just a few hundred votes there could determine the entire race. The vote was so close that in the 1856 state races in those eleven counties, the Republicans won 19,344 votes and the Democrats won 19,122. Lincoln had a plan to succeed in the central counties. He insisted that the party support Owen Lovejoy, an abolitionist and the brother of Elijah Lovejoy, a murdered newspaper editor, to win antislavery votes. He put together a strong German-based campaign organization.

It was there, beginning in 1856, that the Illinois Central Railroad expanded its lines deep into the heart of Illinois. To attract residents who would use the line, the railroad sold one million acres of land near the tracks in the central part of the state to settlers they attracted through newspaper ads. About half were transplanted New Englanders, who tended to be liberals, and the other half were newly arrived German immigrants. The Germans numbered over 300,000 by 1858, one-fifth of the state's population; no one was certain how they would vote.[264]

Lincoln started a large voter registration drive. The Republicans learned that new voters tend to join new parties and vote for new candidates. The Republicans had been successful in amassing large numbers of registered voters who supported them in Illinois. The party registered 133,000 voters in 1854, its first official year, and then increased that to 238,000 in 1856. They sought even more members in 1858. He strengthened his relationships with all of the Republican newspaper editors in the state.[265]

But Lincoln had problems, too. Several national Republicans, led by *New York Tribune* editor Horace Greeley, actually wanted to have Douglas elected on a fusion ticket because they now saw him as an antislavery champion. Lincoln, if elected, would have no influence in Washington, but the famous Douglas would. A Douglas landslide would also ruin Buchanan and pave the way for the Republicans to capture the presidency in 1860.

Lincoln complained bitterly about their efforts to support the Democrat. He wrote of the powerbrokers in his party who talked about Douglas, "Have they concluded that the Republican cause, generally, can be best promoted by sacrificing us here in Illinois?" He wrote later that those who thought so highly of Douglas would have been disappointed in him and if they were stuck with him in office, they would "cut their own throats." He argued that Douglas did not care whether anyone had slavery, and that supporting Douglas or Buchanan would be "to reach the same goal by different roads." He wrote that if the Republicans had turned to Douglas, "The Republican cause would have been annihilated in Illinois and…everywhere for years, if not forever."

And then there were the leftover antislavery American Party voters, the former Know-Nothings, and disgruntled Whigs, who had made such an impact in the 1856 elections. In 1858, the Douglas Democrats worked hard to win their support. Lincoln wrote a party operative, "We must not lose the district. Lay hold of the proper agencies and secure all the Americans you can at once."[266]

All seemed aware of the importance of the state's 1858 race. "The present political canvass in Illinois is a singular one and, I think, without a parallel in the history of electioneering campaigns in the history of this country," wrote a reporter for the *New York Evening Post* who followed it.[267]

Lincoln was the underdog. Douglas had enjoyed a long career in politics, was a famous U.S. senator, had nearly won the Democratic presidential nomination two years earlier and seemed the certain nominee in 1860. He had a large and formidable political organization in Illinois and a well-financed campaign to which he himself had heavily contributed. A reporter for the *New York Herald* wrote of the race, as did others, that of "the re-election of Douglas there appears to be at present very little doubt." Besides, few in the national press, or anywhere outside of Illinois, knew much about Lincoln.[268]

Even in Illinois, though, where many were familiar with Lincoln and where his stature as a political strategist and public speaker was well known, the Republican candidate was seen as the underdog. Douglas had, after all, changed his mind about Lecompton, and now argued against it, as everyone in the state had hoped. Thousands of local workers owed their jobs to Douglas. His party owned or controlled several of the state's largest newspapers. His triumphant return to Chicago to start the campaign was proof that he was a very popular man.[269]

Lincoln was saddled with defending a questionable conspiracy theory that he had harbored for months, in which he charged that Douglas had been part of a massive national plot to destroy the Missouri Compromise, attain slavery in Kansas, and promote the *Dred Scott* decision for, he said, "the sole purpose of nationalizing slavery." He also had to defend his "house divided" speech, a speech that would bring him much acclaim throughout history, but one that brought him nothing but problems in his 1858 Senate race. The speech, his advisors told him, might lead voters to think that Lincoln might indeed want to eliminate slavery someday. He easily tired of the constant references by Douglas and other Democrats to his "abolitionist platform." The constant need to defend himself curbed his chances to attack Douglas.[270]

He insisted too that the election was not only about slavery and spoke up frequently for the transcontinental railroad project, workers' rights, the power of labor unions, land grants for agricultural colleges, a homestead act to permit newly arrived German immigrants to buy up farmlands cheaply, and federal money for the improvement of harbors and riverfronts. He did gain support from these arguments; many newspapers agreed with him that permitting slavery in the territories would ruin the chances of white workers gaining employment there. He also reminded voters again and again that he championed the rights of the white race as well as the black. "It is well known that I deplore the oppressed condition of the blacks; and it would, therefore, be very inconsistent for me to look with approval upon any measures that infringe upon the inalienable rights of white men," he said.[271]

THE PRINCE AND THE PAUPER

Lincoln ran as a pauper to Douglas's prince. Douglas wore elegant suits; Lincoln's were inexpensive and fit badly. Douglas dined at the best hotel restaurants; Lincoln preferred local taverns. Douglas hired his own richly appointed train car, decked with bunting and flags, for campaign travel; attached to the private car was a flatcar that carried a cannon that two men fired whenever Douglas arrived at or departed from a town. Lincoln rode in the coach cars with everyone else. Douglas traveled with his exquisitely dressed wife, whose appearance connoted her wealth; Mary Todd Lincoln stayed home until the final weeks of the campaign.

Lincoln was confident that Douglas could be beaten, even if others were not. The popular senator had stepped into a political briar patch over slavery in Kansas. In the years since Douglas's last election, Illinois residents had increasingly rejected slavery. The growth of Chicago had made the state the key to the middle of the country's trade with the east and west, and Lincoln wanted to do all he could to promote that advantage. Douglas, so embroiled in the intemperate debates over Kansas in Washington, had not traveled back to Illinois as often as he should have to shore up his political strength. Lincoln told friends that the Little Giant could be defeated. He wrote one man that the crowd at his speech just one day after Douglas's talk in the same city was just as large—even though his supporters had only twelve hours to organize— and he had as many supporters as Douglas in his Democratic crowd. "Douglas took nothing by his motion there," Lincoln wrote. "In fact, by his rampant endorsement of the *Dred Scott* decision he drove back a few Republicans who were favorably inclined towards him."[272]

Lincoln dismissed Douglas's enormous crowds, well-attended parades, and frenzied, well-received speeches. He wrote a friend, "It is all as bombastic and hollow as Napoleon's bulletins sent back from his campaign in Russia."[273]

Douglas was vulnerable.

Lincoln believed that events had given him an opportunity to defeat Douglas. At the same time that Douglas and the Democrats seemed to weaken, Lincoln and the Republicans were gaining strength. The new party was just as strong as the Democrats by 1858 and on the verge, its national leaders believed, of taking control of both the House and Senate. Locally, Republican Lyman Trumbull had won election to the U.S. Senate in 1855 and Republican Richard Bissell had been elected governor. The Republicans now controlled nearly 45 percent of the state legislature. The Republicans had much momentum. Lincoln, who had spent one uneventful term as a congressman, had roared back into politics with the Republicans, who had given him new life as one of their party leaders. He had always been a fine public speaker, but now he was even better, impressing people and drawing large and enthusiastic audiences wherever he went. He scribbled in a notebook that "speeches at once attracted a more marked attention than they had ever before done."[274]

He had mastered the art of polling as a Whig, and now as a Republican he used polls to enable him to campaign shrewdly, concentrating on the districts he needed to win and ignoring the areas in which he was either far ahead or far behind. Lincoln talked to just about anyone he encountered—neighbors, courthouse personnel, strangers he met at hotels when he traveled—about politics, always eager to know what the people were thinking. He and his associates had run colorful and successful campaigns. One reporter wrote of the work of the new party in Illinois, "The drive and energy of the Republicans astounded their opponents."

Now, in 1858, he was serving as his own campaign manager, plotting strategy, raising money, booking speaking dates, working with newspaper editors, planning rallies, renting hotel rooms, mapping travel itineraries, and hiring campaign workers.[275]

Most of all, though, he lived in a turbulent decade and was running for the U.S. Senate in 1858, a chaotic year. The swirl of events and feverish climate might just bring him victory. He had almost won a Senate seat three years earlier. Lincoln was the front-runner in the legislative race for the post but, realizing he could not win, stepped aside in order to permit another antislavery candidate, Trumbull, to defeat a Douglas supporter. Now he had a second chance and he was not going to let it pass him by.[276]

He had once said, "I claim not to have controlled events, but confess plainly that events have controlled me," and in his race against Stephen Douglas his belief would be severely tested.[277]

ᜒ᠍

LINCOLN'S LESSONS IN ELOCUTION

Lincoln did not fear Douglas, but shrewdly insisted in public, as he always had, that he was no match for his opponent. He had been doing so since 1848. Again and again, he had warned legislatures, newspapers, and crowds at rallies that he was always at a disadvantage in any disputes with the great Douglas. In 1854 he invited a Springfield crowd to return after supper to hear him refute Douglas, who spoke in the afternoon, reminding them that Douglas's "high reputation and ability" gave him a distinct advantage over Lincoln. He joked to the crowd that they should "stay for the fun of hearing him skin me."[278]

Privately, he knew that he was as good at speaking and debating as Douglas, and he eagerly looked forward to proving it. Lincoln had always been jealous of Douglas, for whom everything in life had seemed to come so easy. Douglas was one of the most famous people in the country and Lincoln was barely known outside of his home state. Lincoln wrote in 1856, "With me, the race of ambition has been a failure—a flat failure; with him it has been one of splendid success. His name fills the nation; and is not unknown, even, in foreign lands. I affect no contempt for the high eminence he has reached. I would rather stand on that eminence than wear the richest crown that ever pressed a monarch's brow."[279]

And too, Lincoln lamented that Douglas had such a national presence that anything he said molded public opinion.[280] There was some anger, too, that the famous Douglas paid little attention to Lincoln, his friend of twenty years. "He indulged himself in a contemptuous expression of pity for me," Lincoln once wrote of a Douglas speech delivered back in 1839.[281]

Douglas was wary of Lincoln. His aides assured the Little Giant that following his years of besting the titans of American politics in Washington again and again he had no need to worry about the local Republican challenger. Douglas knew better. He told one man, "I shall have my hands full. He is the strong man of his party—full of wit, facts, dates—and the best stump speaker, with his droll ways and dry jokes, in the West. He is as honest as he is shrewd and if I beat him the victory will be hardly won."[282]

Douglas knew what a moving speaker his friend Lincoln could be. He had sat in numerous audiences that burst into unrestrained cheering following Lincoln's speeches. The Republican was not only full of humor and a great storyteller, but an emotional speaker who spoke directly to the hearts of those in the audience—and with great effect. One reporter who covered a speech that Lincoln delivered at the State Fair in Springfield in 1856 wrote, "For an hour he held the assemblage spellbound by the power of his argument, the intense eloquence. When he concluded, the audience sprang to their feet and cheer after cheer told how deeply their hearts had been touched, and their souls warmed up to a generous enthusiasm."

Another reporter wrote that in his life he had never heard anyone like Lincoln. "All the strings that play upon the human heart and understanding were touched with masterly skill and force, while beyond and above all skill was the overwhelming conviction pressed upon the audience that the speaker himself was charged with an irresistible and inspirational duty to his fellow man..."[283]

This praise for Lincoln as a speaker was not new. As early as 1839, the *Sangamon Journal* wrote of his oratorical prowess in a speech that was "characterized by that great force and point for which he is so justly admired." A Boston reporter wrote in 1848, "He spoke in a clear and cool and very eloquent manner for an hour and a half, carrying the audience with him in his able arguments and brilliant illustrations." Lincoln remembered those speeches now, in 1858; so did Douglas.[284]

While Douglas had been hailed in Illinois and Washington as the nation's greatest debater, Lincoln had quietly become a vaunted debater himself. He began his career as an oral gladiator while still a boy, friends remembered, standing on top of boxes and tree stumps to talk to a group of children. As a young man in New Salem, he joined the New Salem Debating Society and studied books about debating, such as Kirkham's *Grammar* and William Scott's *Lessons in Elocution*. He studied the Bible for stories and memorized quotes from famous men. He filled his early talks and arguments with analogies and metaphors, created a universe of bears, dogs, bees, and birds that he substituted for political opponents. One American Party leader who switched to the Republicans because of Lincoln said he "was one of the most remarkable speakers of English living. In all that constitutes logical eloquence, straightforwardness, clearness of statement, sincerity that commands your admiration...strength of argument...he is infinitely superior to Douglas."[285]

He developed a genuine wit, too, regaling crowds with his humorous stories. All of the reporters covering the campaign and debates noticed that. "A shrug of the shoulder, an elevation of his eyebrows, a depression of his mouth, and a general malformation of countenance so comically awkward that it never fails to bring down the house," wrote one reporter. Another observed that when his wit surfaced, "his body straightened up, his countenance brightened, his language became free and animated." And yet another told readers that "the tones, the gestures, the kindling eye, and the mirth-provoking look defy the reporter's skill."[286]

No one appreciated Lincoln's debating prowess more than Douglas. The men had tangled in politics, directly and indirectly, for more than twenty years. They first faced off in the Illinois state legislature over a slavery bill in 1836–1837. The pair met again as they campaigned for party candidates in the 1838 congressional elections. In 1839–1840, the two directly debated each other as local representatives for the party presidential candidates. The two opposed each other in several court cases in Illinois and even in a murder trial, with Douglas serving as county prosecutor, when Lincoln managed to win a surprise acquittal for a man who killed another in a hotel room. In various elections in the 1840s and 1850s, the two men campaigned for candidates throughout Illinois, speaking separately to the same crowds on the same day or on the next day. Each would often remain to listen to the other's speech.

❧

SETTING THE STAGE FOR THE HISTORIC ILLINOIS DEBATES

Lincoln was not physically attractive. His law partner, Billy Herndon, said of him, "He was not a pretty man by any means…he was a homely man, careless of his looks, plain looking." He seemed awkward with his extraordinarily long arms and legs, lanky frame, huge head, large ears, distinctive Adam's apple, facial wrinkles, thick eyebrows, and always unkempt hair. Everything about him seemed the wrong size. One man remarked that "his body seemed a huge skeleton in clothes."[287]

His face was clearly defined by sharp features, his eyes dark under heavy brows; his forehead high and his hair seemingly uncombable, leading one reporter to write that "[His] appearance is not comely."[288]

His presidential secretary, John Nicolay, who knew him well, always insisted that photographers and artists never captured his real essence. He wrote that he had a face "that moved through a thousand delicate gradations of line and contour, light and shade, sparkle of the eye and curve of the lip, in the long gamut of expression from grave to gay and back again, from the rollicking jollity of laughter to that serious, far away look." And a journalist added that when telling stories his famous melancholy look disappeared. "The eyes began to sparkle, the mouth to smile, and the whole countenance was wreathed with animation."[289]

All were struck by his gargantuan size, six feet four inches, and enormous physical strength. He had worked with his hands as a farmer and rail-splitter as a young man and retained his strength over the years; men swore they had seen him lift six hundred pounds. In one of the debates, he insisted that a Douglas supporter on the platform explain something and when the man refused Lincoln playfully grabbed his jacket collar with one of his huge hands and, rather easily, picked the man up and carried him several feet—to the laughter of the crowd.[290]

Lincoln made up his mind to force Douglas into a series of debates during the middle of the summer in order to win the race. The way to do that, he decided, was to attend Douglas's speeches and then, when the Judge finished, invite the crowd to return after an hour or so to listen to him refute the Judge's charges, or to return the next day. It was a very effective ploy because it not only gave him a chance to answer Douglas right away, but to add the sizable Douglas throngs to his own. Lincoln thought it was an almost perfect plan. He wrote later, "Speaking at the same place the next day after Douglas is the very thing— it is, in fact, a concluding speech on him." To let Douglas know what he planned to do, Lincoln released a schedule of his speeches and locations so the Democrats could see that he was following their candidate, intent on stealing his audiences. It was a subtle way to get Douglas to debate him.[291]

Douglas followers, not realizing the ploy, were appalled at Lincoln. They accused him of trying to kidnap the senator's crowd. Douglas joked to audiences, and to Lincoln himself, that he was welcome to follow him around the state because that is the only way he would attract large crowds. One Douglas supporter, a newspaper editor, noted that Lincoln had scheduled one speech in a circus tent. That was proper, he wrote, because Lincoln followed everyone and now he was following circus clowns, too.[292]

The press poked fun at Lincoln's tactics. A reporter for the Lowell, Massachusetts, *Journal and Courier* wrote, "Douglas and Lincoln are stumping the state and a right merry time they are having of it; wherever the Little Giant happens to be, Abe is sure to turn up and be a thorn in his side."[293]

Lincoln could accomplish several goals if he could talk Douglas into a series of debates: 1. standing on the same platform, he would give himself equal stature as Douglas and eradicate his status as an underdog running against a famous U.S. senator, 2. the debates would garner extensive press coverage in Illinois and, perhaps, the nation, giving Lincoln national visibility, and 3. they would give him the chance to attempt to force the easily irritated Douglas into statements he would regret.

Some Democrats warned Douglas not to debate Lincoln and to dismiss Republican charges that the Little Giant was afraid of an oratorical donnybrook with him. The editor of the *Illinois State Register* wrote that Douglas did not have to debate Lincoln at all, and that in so doing he would only help Lincoln's campaign. "Mr. Lincoln's political necessities may have needed this boosting of him into prominence..."[294]

Douglas had not only been goaded into the debates by Lincoln, but by the vitriolic Republican newspapers, too. A writer on the *State Journal* accused the Little Giant of "...sneaking about the country by himself, assailing, misrepresenting, and vilifying the man whom he has so ignominiously refused to meet in open, manly debate, before the whole people." A writer for the *State Register* challenged his oratorical manhood by charging, "The idea of a man who has crossed blades in the Senate with the strongest intellects of the country...dreads encounter with Mr. A. Lincoln is an absurdity that can be uttered by his organs only with a ghastly phhiz."[295]

Douglas knew that Lincoln would not quit shadowing him until he agreed to debate. He suggested debates in several towns and cities in Illinois and Lincoln agreed. The men would meet first at Ottawa on August 21, and then meet again at Freeport on August 27, Jonesboro on September 15, Charleston on September 18, Galesburg on October 7, Quincy on October 13, and Alton on October 15.[296]

Both men had developed a stand on the issues by the time the first debate took place in Ottawa. Lincoln was confident that everyone in the state knew his positions and that they were the opposite of Douglas's. Their differences were, Douglas said, "direct, unequivocable, and irreconcilable." A reporter for the *New York Evening Post* who had covered the race agreed, writing that "two men presenting wider contrasts could hardly be found."[297]

What Lincoln needed to do, and believed he could do, was take advantage of Douglas's bluster on many issues and his simplistic analogies, such as comparing the right of a people to have slavery in a territory to their right to have liquor stores.[298] And whenever pushed on his positions, Douglas would proudly reply that "I go for...the right of the people to decide for themselves."

Douglas was always careful, making certain he appealed to those in favor of slavery, those opposed to it, and those opposed to it who wanted freedom for blacks, but not too much of it. "I am opposed to Negro equality," he thundered throughout the campaign, reminding crowds how equality had ruined countries in Central and South America. He told listeners, "This government is founded on the white basis... It was made by the white man, for the white man, to be administered by white men." Then, the traditional white vote in his grasp, he assured all that within that white government blacks could have rights assigned to them by their states and territories. Lincoln believed that he could trip him up on that stand.[299]

The two men had distinctly different assessments of the debates. Lincoln saw them as his best chance to defeat Douglas by showcasing his considerable oratorical and argumentative skills. He believed that the debates would not only show him as the equal of Douglas in Illinois, but also give him much-needed national visibility. Douglas's view was different. To him, the debates were but a small part of the larger campaign and certainly would not be the deciding factor.[300]

Besides, Douglas believed that verbally he could out-duel anybody in the country. He had been doing so for years, impressing audiences with his deep, rich voice, animated descriptions, and uncanny ability to win over farmers in villages on the Illinois western frontier just as he could woo well-educated merchants in Chicago. On any speakers' platform he appeared as a man of great intensity, constantly waving his arms, jabbing his fingers into the air, and heaving his short body back and forth for effect. Even Lincoln's friends conceded that the Judge was the nation's top debater. Lincoln's law partner Billy Herndon wrote, "He had extensive experience in debate...had been trained for years with the great minds and orators in Congress. He was full of political history, well informed on general topics, eloquent almost to the point of brilliancy, self-confident to the point of arrogance, and a dangerous competitor in every respect."

Journalist Horace White added that Douglas's experience gave him other strengths in debate. "He could make more out of a bad case, I think, than any other man this country had every produced," and added that he had "unsurpassed powers of debate and strong personal magnetism."[301]

The public was delighted that Lincoln and Douglas would engage in seven head-to-head debates. Political campaigns had, by 1858, become high entertainment, especially in the Midwest, where politicians had to travel great distances throughout states to reach all of the voters. The two- and three-hour-long "stump speeches," with their before and after receptions, boisterous parades, and roaring bonfires, had become staples of politicking, and debates between candidates were always the highlight. Debates not only enabled both candidates to reach thousands of people at a single location, but permitted them to exhibit the full range of their oratorical skills, personalities, wit, and understanding of the issues. The stump speaker merely delivered a speech and left town, with someone from the other party coming through a day later to refute his charges. In a debate, both combatants, like Roman gladiators, directly rebutted each other.

The people could cheer for their man, jeer his opponent, and argue politics with their neighbors in the crowd at the same time. Most important, though, the debates were a wonderful opportunity to size up candidates for office based on their views and personalities—on display right in front of them.[302]

Even with all their preparation for the debates, and their hopes and dreams, neither Senator Stephen A. Douglas or Abraham Lincoln could foresee the dramatic consequences that the seven debates in Illinois would have on the Senate election, the presidential election of 1860, and the history of their country.

THE WHITE HOUSE

JULY 1858

Senator Stephen Douglas's triumphant parade through the streets of Chicago on July 9, packed with thousands of cheering supporters, had energized him. That night, as the parade ended, he stepped onto the balcony of the Tremont Hotel to address the crowd in the street below him, kicking off his reelection campaign against Abraham Lincoln. He explained the differences between his policies and Lincoln's, but could not stop himself from taking yet another swipe at President Buchanan and his lieutenants, whose campaign against him had gained steam over the last few weeks.

Yet again Douglas denounced the Lecompton Constitution and told the crowd that popular sovereignty meant that the people, and not Congress, had the power to decide whether they wanted slavery in their state, that it was "as a permanent rule of public policy in the organization of territories and the admission of new states."

And then he blasted the Buchanan Democrats, warning his supporters that they were determined to see him defeated, that they were "as much the agents, the tools, the supporters of Mr. Lincoln as if they were avowed Republicans."[303]

The president, no longer content to stay in the shadows, fired back. Buchanan was friendly with the editors of the *Washington Union*; they had been dinner guests at the president's summer quarters where, the editors of the *New York Times* charged, he gave them instructions for their virulent campaign against the Illinois senator. The *Union* turned up the vehemence of its attacks on Douglas, accusing him of "treachery" and of being a closet

Republican—a "traitor" to his party. The *Union*'s editors charged that he was not only "a knave," but the nation's leading abolitionist.

The White House seemed to orchestrate the press campaign against Douglas because the Illinois Democratic newspapers loyal to Buchanan reprinted the vituperative attacks in the *Washington Union* within days of their publication. The editor of the *Quincy (Illinois) Whig*, as an example, quoted another paper's assertion on July 21, 1858, that Douglas could not be considered a presidential candidate in 1860 given his dispute with the president and because he was a Northerner. His nomination was "entirely out of the question." They all hammered away at the same theme—Douglas was finished.[304]

❧

PERSONAL OR POLITICS?

By the time the Lincoln-Douglas debates began in August, many political observers felt that the White House witch hunt of Douglas was no longer just about political disagreements. "It is wholly a personal matter," wrote the editor of the *Illinois State Journal.*

A Douglas friend, editor John Heiss of the *Washington States*, wrote him that President Buchanan "hates you in the most bitter and unrelenting manner." When he was in a good mood, the president informed party members in letters and conversations that his bitterness toward Douglas was not personal. He despised him, the president told them, because Douglas had led the fight against the Lecompton Constitution. It was just politics, and it was Buchanan's job to "preserve, protect, and defend the Constitution."

But in private, he said that he would destroy the Little Giant. Thomas Harris told Charles Lamphier, a Douglas-supporting newspaper editor, that the president was telling people in Washington that he would fire every single federal office holder who opposed him in the feud with Douglas.[305] One of the leaders of that campaign was Buchanan's long-time friend, Congressman J. Glancy Jones of Pennsylvania, the Democratic whip in the House and the most important leader of the Democratic Party besides the president. Letters from him had a chilling effect on their recipients.[306]

The theme that Douglas was an abolitionist was reflected in the columns of the Buchanan Democratic newspapers in Illinois. The *Jonesboro Gazette* said Douglas "was slowly sinking into the unfathomable depths of the filthy sea of abolitionism."[307]

The National Democrats nominated candidates for each of Illinois's congressional seats and stumped the state campaigning for their men, derisively labeled "the Danites" by the Douglas Democrats, after Leib's Danites in Kansas. The stump speakers ripped Douglas apart wherever they went.

Several newspapers reported that, in addition to Lincoln, Douglas was running against "the entire administration…with its vast patronage of hundreds of millions of dollars, with its army of mercenaries and expectants, organized and rallied against [him]." One reporter wrote that Douglas was fighting "the whole Republican Party" by himself.[308]

The president also gave a warm nod of approval to Illinois National Democrats' efforts to link up with the Republicans to undermine Douglas; rumors flew that the Lincoln campaign was subsidizing the new Danite newspapers. It was not Lincoln, though, but the White House that was doing so. It was no secret that the leading Republican newspapers were cooperating with the Buchanan supporters to undermine Douglas. By the summer, President Buchanan was determined to see Douglas go down in defeat. "Judge Douglas ought to be stripped of his pretension to be the champion of Popular Sovereignty," the president wrote Jeremiah Black, who fronted for him in public attacks on the Illinois senator.[309]

The Republicans were naturally pleased with the feud. "We are glad the fight goes on so bravely and shall herald its progress with much satisfaction," wrote one editor, certain that the split could only help Lincoln. They were pleased too, as the summer went on, that many newspapers—Republican and Democratic, in-state and across the country—reminded the public that Buchanan was at war with a man who had been responsible for his election as president. An editor for the *Philadelphia Evening Bulletin* wrote, "The State (Illinois) was carried for Mr. Buchanan more through Mr. Douglas's efforts than through the united efforts of any other half dozen men."[310]

Douglas said publicly that these orchestrated and vicious assaults did not bother him, but privately he admitted that they did—and that the heat had been turned up. He wrote one friend, "The hell hounds are on my track."[311]

None of the "hell hounds" would stop him, Douglas bellowed to one crowd at the start of the campaign. He told his cheering audience that the

White House and the Republicans had entered into "an unholy alliance" and that "I intend to fight that allied army wherever I meet them. I shall deal with these forces just as the Russians dealt with the allies at Sebastopol. The Russians when they fired a broadside at the common enemy did not stop to inquire whether it hit a Frenchman, an Englishman, or a Turk, nor will I stop to inquire, nor shall I hesitate, whether my blows hit the Republican leaders or their [White House] allies."[312]

Douglas had the editorial support of the overwhelming majority of the Illinois Democratic newspapers (sixty-five out of seventy) and of dozens of newspapers throughout the nation, North and South. Numerous important public figures, Northern and Southern congressional leaders included, endorsed him.[313]

Oddly, nowhere was his national support stronger than in the Deep South. The *New Orleans Crescent*'s editor, while acknowledging "the influence of the Administration bitterly arrayed against him," not only supported his candidacy, but noted that 75 percent of all the Southern newspapers were for him, as were "hundreds of Democratic statesmen of the South." The reason: Lincoln. The *Crescent* editor wrote, "Lincoln is as dirty, cowardly, and malignant an abolitionist as can be found out of Massachusetts."[314]

The support of one eastern newspaper, the *Philadelphia Press*, delighted him. That was John Forney's paper. The president's former friend had not only become one of Douglas's chief press supporters, but an admirer who had urged him to fight the White House all year. "You must not be cast down by these difficulties; upon you the whole heart of our nation reposes; a million men look to you as their leader..."[315]

And there were powerful Democrats who backed him in the battle with the White House, too. One of the most prominent was Senator John McClernand, who had been cheering Douglas on since February, when, discussing Buchanan, he told him to "Agitate! Rouse the people!...Never before did any political struggle so thoroughly possess and sway the hearts of the masses."[316]

Douglas knew, too, that the president was not campaigning just against him, but the entire Illinois Democratic machine. The Illinois state legislature elected its U.S. senator, regardless of the public vote. Douglas could actually lose the election to Lincoln and still be sent back to the Senate by the legislature. There, his polls showed, the Douglas Democrats maintained a slight lead in all the statewide House and Senate races (one newspaper survey put Douglas's lead in the Illinois Senate at 14–11 and in the House at 40–35). If his fellow Democrats could hold those leads, and his newspapers were certain they could, he could be reelected regardless of what Buchanan accomplished.[317]

Many in Illinois could not wait until the election, so that Douglas could defeat Lincoln and show up the president at the same time. Wrote one supporter, "Carry the state and by Christmas the hoary-headed old sinner at Washington will be at your feet, a supplicant for mercy."[318]

The president's campaign to denigrate Douglas baffled many Democrats as much as it amazed the Republicans. Douglas was already the front-runner for the Democratic presidential nomination in 1860. If he lost the election to Lincoln because of the Danites, he would be out of the race for president and there was no one else as popular as the Little Giant to lead the Democratic Party. In fact, if he lost the Senate election in Illinois, no one doubted that Seward, the obvious Republican nominee, would be elected president, much to the consternation of Democratic Southerners—and Buchanan. Why then was the president conducting this campaign against Douglas? The president had nothing to gain beyond personal satisfaction and was risking the unity of the party, the 1860 elections, and all of the federal patronage that came with victory. He was also spending so much time on his feud with Douglas, and similar feuds with others, that he was accomplishing very little as president. The nation was splitting apart even further in 1858 than it had in 1857 over the *Dred Scott* decision, and the president, so tied up in his personal disputes, did little to heal the wounds.

What was wrong with President James Buchanan?

Chapter Eight

HONEST ABE AND THE LITTLE GIANT
THE LINCOLN-DOUGLAS DEBATES, PART TWO

"There will be some rare speaking done or we are much mistaken."
—Central Illinois Gazette, *August 4, 1858*

No one in Illinois politics could recall a scene like the one that greeted Abraham Lincoln and Stephen Douglas as they arrived in Ottawa for the first of their seven debates in the late morning of August 25, 1858. At eight in the morning, four hours prior to the debate, the streets of the town were congested with men, women, and children in wagons, elegant carriages, two-person buggies, and riders on horseback. Trains arrived regularly, the smoke from their engine stacks visible for miles, and their passengers formed lengthy processions as they emerged from the cars, many unfurling DOUGLAS and LINCOLN banners as they left the train depot. Amateur militia regiments marched alongside civilian bands playing festive tunes that had been brought in for the occasion. Cannon salutes were fired throughout the morning, their boom reverberating throughout the town. Peddlers jammed the streets trying to sell their wares. "Vanity Fair never boiled with madder enthusiasm," wrote one reporter there. "Excited groups of politicians were canvassing and quarreling everywhere…" wrote another.[319]

Throughout the morning, thousands of people arrived in Ottawa (population 7,000) by train, canal boat, wagon, carriage, buggy, and on horseback. Many had come a day or two earlier. All of the town's hotels were full and several reporters from eastern newspapers had to sleep on hotel lobby floors, their coats rolled up and used as pillows. The press had never seen anything like it. "The prairies are on fire," wrote one journalist.[320]

Douglas disembarked from his private train car in Peru, Illinois, sixteen miles from Ottawa, in early morning on August 25 and stepped into an elegant carriage drawn by four horses. Several miles outside of town he was met by a throng of hundreds of supporters carrying large banners and signs. Douglas appeared as he did for each of the August debate sites, looking as much a theatrical figure as a political candidate. He wore a handsomely cut blue broadcloth suit and, to shade his eyes from the sun, a white, wide-brimmed hat. The Douglas supporters, with their bands, led the Little Giant into the town, where more than ten thousand people jammed the streets and alleyways. The carriage slowed to a crawl as the multitude of people surrounded Douglas, shouting his name.

Lincoln arrived just before noon on a train from Rock Island carrying seventeen cars full of people bound for the historic debate; the railroads had sold debate-excursion tickets at half the normal fare and would for all of the debates. Lincoln was escorted in his own large carriage decked out in freshly cut flowers. In front of him hundreds of well wishers, led by several loud bands, formed a parade that transported him the half mile to the home of the mayor, where he had lunch.[321]

The public square was so crowded with people that they pushed up against the hastily constructed platform where the debate would take place and reporters covering the event had to shove through the mob to reach it. Thousands filled the streets and many people sat on the roofs of nearby buildings.

∽

THE OPPONENTS

The fierce opponents had been personal friends throughout their adult lives; they had dined together often, visited each others' homes, traveled alongside each other, spoke at rallies together. Prior to her marriage to Lincoln, Mary Todd had been courted by Douglas. Lincoln told one rally, "He and I are about the best friends in the world." Years later, after Douglas died, Lincoln placed a photo of him in his family album. Douglas added that he had known Lincoln as a friend for twenty-five years and that "I regard him as kind, amiable, and intelligent gentleman."[322]

The residents of Illinois knew that in the Lincoln and Douglas debates they were getting three hours of discussion from two of the most fiery speakers in the country. Everyone in America was familiar with Douglas's well-known oratorical bombast; only those in Illinois were familiar with Lincoln's skills.

Lincoln always began his speeches and arguments slowly, a little uncertain, his timing off a bit, his voice shrill and unpleasant. Physically, there was always visible awkwardness in Lincoln as he pulled his lanky body up from a chair, unbending his long, thin legs and standing erect. His unkempt hair was never combed properly; his suits never fit right. After eight or nine minutes, though, he usually found his rhythm and then completely engaged his audience for an hour or more.

Law partner Billy Herndon wrote that as Lincoln continued to speak, his voice lost its shrillness and "mellowed into a more harmonious and pleasant sound."[323] A New Yorker found his style "weird, rough, and uncultivated," but ten minutes into his speech, that changed. "The voice gained a natural and impressive modulation, the gestures were dignified and appropriate, and the hearers came under the influence of the earnest look from the deeply set eyes."[324]

He rose with his hands clenched together behind his back, walking forward with a bit of an odd gait caused by the combination of his size and his long legs. One writer compared his odd walk to a cross between a derrick and a windmill. He grasped his jacket lapel with his left hand and gestured with his right. He shook his head back and forth to make many points, used his hands and arms for emphasis, and punctuated the air with the forefinger of his right hand. "There was a world of emphasis in the long, bony finger as he dotted the ideas on the minds of his hearers," wrote Herndon.

And there was an emotional appeal to his speeches. He was, a New York writer said, "a thoroughly earnest and truthful man, inspired by sound convictions in consonance with the true spirit of American institutions... Lincoln always touched sympathetic chords."[325]

One of the best speakers in the country had not started out that way. In his first years in the state legislature, his speaking ability was without polish and raw. His Kentucky accent caused him to mispronounce words, intoning "Mr. Cheerman" for *chairman* and "sich" for *such*. An observer wrote of him in 1832 that he "was a very gawky and rough looking fellow." In 1839, reporters criticized his speaking as clumsy and warned that he had to change his style. "His entire game of buffoonery convinces the mind of no man and is utterly lost on the majority of his audience," wrote a reporter for the *Illinois State Register*. "We seriously advise Mr. Lincoln to correct this clownish fault before it grows upon him."[326]

He did.

Douglas was different. He was a master of historical facts, public policy initiatives, and could remember just about any position an adversary had taken on an issue. Harriet Beecher Stowe wrote that "he has two requisite qualities of a debater—a melodious voice and a clear, sharply defined enunciation." Others noted his resonant voice. "There was a certain quality of broad, deep, vibrant energy in the tone that was strangely enthralling alike to one or two, or to a throng of many thousands. His voice rose and fell, round, deep, sonorous with the effortless volume of a great organ tone," wrote one man.

Many newspapers predicted that Douglas would humiliate Lincoln in their seven joint encounters. "Douglas is matchless in debate," wrote one editor emphatically.[327]

Douglas had his detractors, though, who claimed that he often muted his successful speeches with physical tantrums. John Quincy Adams said of Douglas, "His face was convulsed, his gesticulations frantic, and he lashed himself into such a heat that if his body had been made of combustible matter it would have burnt out." Labor leader Carl Schurz added, "He was from the start angry, dictatorial, and insolent in the extreme…and he went on in that style with a wrathful frown upon his brow, defiantly shaking his head, clenching his fists, and stamping his feet."[328]

Douglas had convinced himself that President Buchanan's henchmen would insist that a third candidate—a Danite—share the platform with the pair. If so, Douglas told Lincoln, he would not participate. No third candidate ever asked to join them, though.[329]

THE PRESS

The state press reporting of the campaign and the debates, beginning in Ottawa, was highly biased. The Republican-controlled newspapers applauded Lincoln and the Democratic journals hailed Douglas. Lincoln's key papers were the *Illinois State Journal* and the *Chicago Press and Tribune*; Douglas's primary journals were the *Illinois State Register* and the *Chicago Times*. Each candidate was supported by dozens of other newspapers throughout the state.

The election generated surprisingly comprehensive coverage throughout the Midwest and the nation. Several key newspapers in neighboring Missouri and Indiana covered the race extensively, as did some papers in Ohio. The race and debates captured the attention of newspapers in the east too, and they sent reporters from eastern cities such as New York and Boston. Newspapers in many other cities did not send reporters but reprinted stories about the debates published in other newspapers, a common practice at the time.

The debates, and the race, were seen as special by everyone and the press often presented the candidates' appearances as boxing matches or brawls. One Indiana reporter wrote, "Perhaps of many the pitched battle between Douglas and Lincoln of Illinois is on the whole as interesting, as severe, and reviewed by as many anxious spectators… Douglas is a perfect specimen of the adroit politician, whom the American system seems calculated to engender…" He added, however, that "Lincoln gives him blow for blow."[330]

⟋⟍

THE SEVEN DEBATES

The crowds at all of the debates responded warmly to both men. There was prolonged cheering for each when they were introduced, when they sat down, or when either spoke with some great passion or skewered the other. People took it upon themselves to shout out their feelings. "Stick it to him!" a man would shout to Douglas or Lincoln when a rejoinder seemed necessary. Others called out, "That's right! You told him!" "Give him an answer!" "Bravo!" "Three cheers for (Lincoln or Douglas)!" "You've got him now!" "I'll never vote for him!"[331] The crowd would roar with laughter when either man told a humorous story or poked fun at his adversary.

The debates were not similar to contemporary debates in which the candidates actually discuss the previous statements of the other. In the Lincoln-Douglas encounters, the first speaker (they alternated) spoke for an hour, the second for ninety minutes, and then the first had thirty minutes for rebuttal. It was standard procedure for the era.

Ottawa: The First Debate

That first debate set the tone for all seven. Lincoln attacked Douglas over his different positions on the Kansas sovereignty question, accused him of being part of a national slavery conspiracy, and harangued him for refuting the Missouri Compromise with his Compromise of 1850. Douglas defended himself. He accused Lincoln of wanting to repeal the Fugitive Slave Act and other antislavery measures that had been passed by Congress, of belittling the white race in his constant defense of blacks, and of being the blackest of the "Black Republicans."

The Little Giant surprised Lincoln in that first match with his aggressiveness. In that debate and in later encounters he derided Lincoln's constant references to slavery's "ultimate extinction" while at the same time insisting that he did not mind its existence as it was. He hit Lincoln with a long list of accusations, shrewdly connecting them to show, he said, that Lincoln was opposed to the people making any decisions at all unless they supported his Black Republican "abolition party." He insisted that at the Republican state convention in Illinois in 1854 Lincoln had approved of the party platform that called for the overturning of the Fugitive Slave Act, opposed the admission of any more slave states even if the people wanted them, favored abolition of slavery in Washington, DC, was against slave trade between states, and would be opposed to any territory's admission to the Union if its residents had approved slavery there. The charges refuted Lincoln's moderate stand on slavery. To back up his claims, Douglas even described the hall where Lincoln had spoken in 1854. He named the other Republicans around him at the time. It was a bombshell from which the Democrats did not think Lincoln could recover.

Lincoln was flustered. He could not remember what he said about his 1854 party convention plank and tried to remember his stand on issues by reading a copy of a published speech he made in Peoria, Illinois, that year. He had trouble seeing it and had to fumble for his glasses. He then spent long moments trying to find passages in the news clipping to read as Douglas looked at him smugly.

He had not abandoned the white race for the black, Lincoln assured the crowd. "There is a physical difference between the two, which in my judgment will probably forever forbid their living together upon the footing of perfect equality… I…am in favor of the race to which I belong having the superior position." He said he believed in obeying the Fugitive Slave Act because the Supreme Court had upheld it. He did not want Southern states to do away with slavery. He then lamely tried to frame what he called the "national conspiracy"—engineered by Douglas—to legalize slavery everywhere and insisted that it be kept out of the territories. He ripped the Kansas-Nebraska Act and the Lecompton Constitution.[332]

Each side in the partisan press proclaimed their man the winner at Ottawa. The reporter from the Democratic *Freeport Weekly Bulletin* wrote that "the triumph of Senator Douglas was complete" and that Lincoln was "exceedingly lame throughout." One man wrote, "The Illinois Giant at the first onset pushed his adversary to the wall, and never ceased for a moment his blows, until Abraham was taken by his friends, dispirited and overcome."

A reporter for the Republican *Chicago Press and Tribune*, however, wrote that Lincoln "chewed him up." He then blithely wrote that "Douglas is doomed," the Democrats would not be able to recover, and that the "contest is already practically ended." A reporter from the Republican *Daily Pantagraph* agreed, telling his readers that "the speech was one of the most powerful and eloquent ever made by Lincoln."[333]

Many of the eastern reporters who covered the debates expected oratorical acrobatics from Douglas, but all saw something special in Lincoln, despite his faltering. A reporter for the *New York Evening Post* wrote about Lincoln, "Stir him up and the fire of his genius plays on every feature. His eye glows and sparkles, every lineament, now so ill-formed, grows brilliant and expressive and you have before you a man of rare power and of strong magnetic influence. He is clear, concise, and logical; his language is eloquent and perfect." And a reporter for the *New York Tribune*, at another debate, echoed those feelings, reporting that Lincoln stated his principles "with more propriety and with an infinitely better temper."[334]

The Ottawa crowd loved both candidates. The audience of twelve thousand erupted in sustained cheers for both men when the first debate ended. Men grabbed the astonished lanky Lincoln, put him on their shoulders, and carried him through the multitude of people as a band played "Hail Columbia!" over the din.[335]

Lincoln had not fared well in the first encounter and he knew it. Party leaders were disappointed. "I thought Douglas had the best of it," said Theodore Parker. "He questioned Mr. Lincoln on the great matters of slavery and put the most radical questions, which go to the heart of the question, before the people. Mr. Lincoln did not meet the issue. He made a technical evasion. They were the vital questions, pertinent to the issue, and Lincoln dodged them. That is not the way to fight the battle of freedom."[336]

Party leaders and Republican newspaper editors urged him to stop being defensive and attack Douglas, as he had throughout the summer on the campaign trail.

That first debate and the enormous press coverage it attracted changed the nature of the campaign, too. The crowds of both men increased in size, especially Lincoln's. Douglas introduced a question-and-answer format to his campaign, tackling any and all questions from the audience after he finished speaking. The senator also began to shake hands with hundreds of cheering people in the crowds at his campaign stops, adding an appreciated personal touch to his appearance.

Douglas was also determined to let every audience know that his remarks on slavery and popular sovereignty in the debates reflected his convictions, so he repeated them again and again. He told one crowd, "I stand by my principles and follow them to their logical conclusion, and I will not depart from them either to the right or to the left to flatter one section or the other… I have acted honestly and faithfully in my political course."[337]

Showdown at Freeport

The reception for the two candidates at their second debate—in Freeport, a tiny town of five thousand in northern Illinois—six days later dwarfed the outpouring at Ottawa. It seemed as if all the people that lived in Illinois had caught "debate fever." Long trains filled with thousands of supporters for both men began arriving at nine in the morning and the streets of the town were overflowing with people. The train from Amboy, Dixon, and Polo, with Lincoln on board, carried twelve cars and two thousand people. The train from Galena carried eight cars, the train from Marengo and Rockford had eighteen cars, all of them overcrowded with loud supporters of the two candidates. The Carrol County Lincoln Club held one parade and the Galena Lincoln Club held another. Local Republicans fired off several cannon when

Lincoln emerged from the train. He was greeted with huge banners such as "Lincoln the Giant Killer" and "All Men Are Created Equal."

The Douglas supporters arrived by every mode of transportation possible and held similarly loud parades throughout the morning. Douglas himself had arrived the night before and was met by hundreds of well-wishers who staged a torchlight parade for him. Organizers and press estimated the size of the debate crowd at between fifteen and twenty thousand—quadruple the size of the entire community. A reporter wrote, "All the main streets, backroads, lanes, and byways of Freeport appeared to be literally alive with men, and the suburbs for a long distance around were filled with vehicles of all descriptions."

The weather was not good. It had been cloudy all morning, chilly and damp, with intermittent rain, and the sun rarely broke through. Organizers breathed a sigh of relief when, just before the debates began at two o'clock, the rain stopped.

Both men were greeted with sustained roars from the crowd. Lincoln received an especially tumultuous ovation from the overly Republican audience when he arrived seated on a Conestoga wagon pulled by six large white horses at the head of a parade full of ardent supporters.[338]

Lincoln needed to win the second debate and was certain that he would. Freeport was a stronghold for the antislavery movement, the Republicans, and Lincoln. The crowd would be on his side. He also had opportunity, because Douglas had asked him several questions at Ottawa that he now had to answer. That opened the door for him to query Douglas and gave him the chance to pin the Judge down on his view of the territories and slavery. If it was acceptable for the residents of Kansas or any territory to reject slavery when they adapted a constitution and became a state, was it also acceptable for them to approve of it?

Lincoln knew how Douglas would answer the question; he would defend the right of territories to either approve or disapprove of slavery—his familiar popular sovereignty argument. The Judge had been answering the question the same way since 1856 and never wavered in his defense of that belief. He had said in a hundred places but in the same way: "Every people ought to possess the right of forming and regulating their own internal concerns and domestic institutions in their own way." Several months before, on July 18 in a speech at Springfield, Douglas had stated his position yet again.[339]

Lincoln also knew that by forcing him to answer, Douglas would become defensive, bristling at yet another attack on his stand, and respond with confidence, as he had done for years. "I never dodge a question. I never shrink from any responsibility. I never hesitate to give an unpopular vote or to meet an indignant community, when I know that I am right," he was quoted as stating in the *National Intelligencer*.[340]

Lincoln's advisers were against raising the question at Freeport because Douglas's expected answer—that territorial voters could bar slavery—might win him the Illinois Senate race. True, Lincoln answered, but "I am killing larger game; if Douglas answers, he can never be president, and the battle of 1860 is worth a hundred of this."[341]

He could never be president, Lincoln told them, because if Douglas answered yes in such a public forum, and in front of so many reporters from around the United States, the Southerners would turn on him and he could lose half the country's electoral votes in a presidential election; the reaction might be so great that he might even lose the 1860 Democratic nomination.

At Freeport, Lincoln began by answering Douglas's queries, telling the crowd that he did not favor the repeal of the Fugitive Slave Act. He was against slavery in the territories, and he made it clear that under no circumstances could any territory in any way be allowed to permit it. The answer, on top of his well-known reluctant acceptance of slavery in the Southern states, made his position clear.

Lincoln then astonished the gathering by providing incontrovertible proof that Douglas's charges made in the first debate at Ottawa were not true. Douglas had contended that the Republican Party of Illinois had passed abolitionist resolutions in their state convention in 1854 at Springfield, supported by Lincoln. The resolutions had been passed, but by other parties and in Kane County, not at any Republican convention—and Lincoln had not been at the Kane County meeting and had nothing to do with those in attendance. Douglas was shaken; he had been given bad information.

Lincoln berated Douglas for the false accusations. He reminded the crowd what an esteemed position the Judge held as a U.S. senator, a man "of worldwide renown," and then skewered him, charging that it "is most extraordinary that he should so far forget all the suggestions of justice to an adversary or of prudence to himself, as to venture on the assertion of that which the slightest investigation would have shown him to be wholly false…"[342]

Lincoln then asked Douglas, "Can the people of the United States Territory in any legal way, against the will of one citizen, exclude slavery from their limits, previous to the formation of the state constitution?"

Douglas answered, as Lincoln knew he would, by defending the will of the people to do what they wanted about slavery in the territories. Douglas stated yet again that residents of a territory could approve slavery. However, if they so chose, those territorial residents could also prohibit slavery. He reminded all gathered there that this view was based on the Kansas-Nebraska Act, his own bill, cheered at the time by proslavery forces. Now he told the crowd that voters in a territory could approve slavery or ban it; it made no difference to him.[343] His answer was branded "the Freeport Doctrine" and was promulgated by the Republicans to show that Douglas believed the same way Lincoln did about slavery in the territories and to hurt his credibility with Southerners and Southern-leaning residents in the lower part of Illinois. In fact, though, the historical "Freeport Doctrine" was no different from anything else Douglas had said over the previous two years. Lincoln's skill was in baiting him into stating it at an important public forum. Many have claimed that Lincoln somehow tricked Douglas into his answer. He had not; he forced him into stating it clearly in front of an enormous crowd, and journalists reported the answer throughout the nation.

The applause for Lincoln at the end of the Freeport debate was deafening. He had forced Douglas to endorse popular sovereignty everywhere and firmly positioned himself as a public figure who grudgingly approved of slavery where it was in the United States, but was determined to halt its advance in the territories. He was at times serious and at times witty. His performance was far superior to that at Ottawa. Lincoln's supporters were thrilled. Wrote a Republican journalist, "[Douglas] was completely wiped out and annihilated."[344]

The Final Five Debates

The remaining five debates did little to illuminate issues for the public; the two candidates did not say anything more than they had at the first two debates and in their many speeches throughout the summer and fall. The third was in the far southern part of Illinois, actually below the Mason-Dixon Line, at tiny Jonesboro, held at the Union County fairgrounds. This was Douglas's country and Lincoln side-stepped just about all of the Judge's attempts to get him on record about his antislavery views. It mattered little; less than two thousand people turned out.

In the fourth debate, at Charleston, again shoring up his position as a moderate on slavery who was not interested in forcing anyone to fraternize with blacks, Lincoln told the crowd, "I am not, or have ever been, in favor of bringing about in any way the social and political equality of the white and black races...of making voters or jurors of Negroes, not of qualifying them to hold office, not to intermarry with white people. There is a physical difference between the white and black races which I believe will forever forbid the two races living together on terms of social and political equality." He added that the white race was superior to the black race and that he did not foresee himself or his friends ever marrying any blacks.[345]

The debates had been planned to run from the middle of August through late October in order to keep up public interest. In between each debate, the two candidates traveled extensively. The debates and the travel took their toll on Douglas, as could be expected of any candidate who was completing a grueling campaign, and rumors that he had returned to drink during the autumn surfaced often. He was clearly exhausted by the time the Senate race entered its last weeks and it showed in the final debates. One man in Jonesboro said that he had trouble hearing Douglas. A reporter wrote at Jonesboro that Douglas had a "desolate look" and that he "looked very much worse for wear." The reporter added that "bad whisky and wear and tear of conscience have had their effect. He speaks very slowly, making a distinct pause at the end of each word." In the last debate, at Alton, Douglas was so hoarse that he had trouble speaking and those beyond the front rows of the crowd complained that they could not hear him.

Lincoln, though, seemed to gain a second wind during the last weeks. He had far more energy than Douglas and even more than he had exhibited throughout the summer. His jokes were funnier, his speeches crisper and better organized, and he seemed full of passion. One man wrote that in the last few debates Douglas had rambled and lost his concentration, but Lincoln had not. "[He] kept strictly to the question at issue, and no one could doubt that the cause for which he was speaking was the only thing he had at heart."[346]

In fact, Lincoln was not only winning the battle against campaign fatigue, but becoming a demonstrably stronger speaker, debater, and public presence at the same time the Judge was fading. In their last three encounters, Lincoln, looking ebullient and full of fire, continually blasted

Douglas as part of the national slavery conspiracy and for his mistaken charges that Lincoln was at the Kane County convention. He charged that the Judge had misquoted him in the debates and on the campaign trail, that he had failed to put forward intelligent policies on slavery, and that he had, in fact, abandoned the principles of the Declaration of Independence. At Galesburg, using one of Henry Clay's favorite lines, he said that Douglas "is blowing out the moral lights around us" and cared more for jingoistic foreign adventures in Mexico and South America than he did problems in the United States. Finally, in the last of the debates, at Alton, Lincoln ended with a glorious flourish, telling the overflowing audience—which swarmed the intersection of Broadway and Market Streets where the debate platform had been erected—that the campaign was about slavery and whether it was right or wrong.

Lincoln said, "That is the issue that will continue in this country when these poor tongues of Judge Douglas and myself shall be silent. It is the eternal struggle between these two principles—right and wrong—throughout the world. They are the two principles that have stood face to face from the beginning of time; and will ever continue to struggle. The one is the common right of humanity and the other the divine right of kings."

Lincoln paused, and then went on. "It is the same spirit that says, 'You work and toil and earn bread, and I'll eat it.' No matter in what shape it comes, whether from the mouth of a king, who seeks to bestride the people of his own nation and live by the fruit of their labor, or from one race of men as an apology for enslaving another race, it is the same tyrannical principle."[347]

Crowds who saw him in his appearances throughout the state in the last days of September and during October marveled at his energy and determination. His enthusiasm even rivaled that of the enormously popular William Seward, not running but campaigning for the Republican ticket in New York.

In the final debates, Lincoln made frequent use of his famous humor. At Charleston on September 18, he told the crowd that controversial issues such as black equality and racial intermarriage were local and would be decided by the state legislature. Then, eyes twinkling, he quickly added that, "And as Judge Douglas seems to be in constant horror that some such danger is rapidly approaching, I propose as the best means to prevent it that the Judge be kept at home and placed in the state legislature where he can fight the measures."

Of his very last speech in Springfield, a reporter for the *Illinois State Journal* wrote that it "was one of his very best efforts, distinguished for its clearness and force...one of the most eloquent appeals ever addressed to the American people" and that it "was received with spontaneous bursts of enthusiasm unequalled by anything ever before enacted in this city."[348]

Even though polling suggested that the Democrats were running slightly ahead in many key counties in the state, Lincoln, his spirits aroused by the reception in the last days of the campaign, was very hopeful that he would win. He wrote Republican state chairman Norman Judd, "I now have a high degree of confidence that we shall succeed." Douglas also sensed victory, and victory over both Lincoln and Buchanan. Each had their supporters in the press. In the South, though, newspaper editors denounced both men. The editor of the *Mississippian* called them "a pair of depraved, blustering, mischievous, lowdown demagogues."[349]

Who won the Lincoln–Douglas debates? It is impossible to tell. The newspapers provided no intelligent assessment of who triumphed because they were all partisan. There were no exit polls on election day that could be used to evaluate the vote between those who attended the debates and those who did not. The huge crowds that they attracted—some seventy thousand people—were not a barometer either because not everyone who attended the encounters voted and many were children.

Many in the press pronounced the American political system the winner because the campaign and debates gave the entire nation electrifying dialogue on slavery from two well-prepared debaters. "Douglas and Lincoln are both giants, and the way they discuss political questions before immense crowds of people is an admirable illustration of the workings of our institutions," wrote one eastern reporter.[350]

Douglas and Lincoln each believed that they had presented themselves well. Douglas had reminded the liberal voters of Illinois again and again that he was in favor of territorial residents prohibiting slavery if they so chose and had again, in his oratorical wizardry and grasp of issues, shown all why he had been such an effective U.S. senator.

All Honest Abe and the Little Giant could do after the final debate and last stump speech was wait for the verdict of their neighbors in Illinois on election day, an election that would conclude a furious campaign that the Republicans hoped would install them as the dominant party in the United States and somehow bring the end of slavery one step closer.

THE WHITE HOUSE

AUTUMN 1858: THE FORNEY FEUD

No one in America had supported the political ambitions of President James Buchanan more strongly, or for a longer period of time, and served as a closer and more loyal friend than John Forney. The president's fellow Pennsylvanian had, over twenty years, worked tirelessly as Buchanan's aide, ran his campaigns, gave him advice, raised money, and twisted the arms of politicians to curry favor for his friend. Forney had also been the editor of the *Washington Union*, the Washington, DC, newspaper controlled by the Democratic Party that served as the official organ of the White House when the Democrats occupied it. Forney loved the newspaper job because it enabled him to work as a journalist and, at the same time, as a political operative for the party. As editor, he used his powerful post to promote the career of his friend, James Buchanan.

Forney had joined Buchanan in the late 1830s when Forney was in his early twenties and had been with him ever since. Forney worked hard for Buchanan and was always faithful, but Forney could be a difficult man. He had a reputation as a drinker. He was an energetic, impetuous, excitable, and sometimes very angry person who, even his best friends admitted, could talk a man to death. He had no regard for money; he was often broke and borrowed funds from friends, sometimes forgetting to repay them. He had a violent temper, took umbrage at the innocent remarks of others, misread people's intentions, and exhibited a great deal of paranoia. These negative traits, always apparent in his defense of his friend Buchanan, annoyed people. Yet no one could question his devotion to the politician. Forney, who was forty years old, had enjoyed his finest hour during the months of September and October of 1856. Buchanan's presidential campaign sputtered in those months, especially in his native Pennsylvania, which he had to win to capture the White House.

The devoted Forney, the head of the state Democratic Party in Pennsylvania, became a dynamo in those two critical months. He personally took charge of the Pennsylvania state campaign, changing its tactics to combat the surging third-party threat, the American Party, dispensing funds, dispatching speakers, arguing with newspaper editors, and, with a small army of volunteers, helping to get out one of the largest voter turnouts in state history, especially newly registered Irish voters. In those last few tumultuous weeks, amid evening torch-lit parades, afternoon rallies, and endless receptions, Forney, operating on little sleep, did much to win Pennsylvania for his friend, Buchanan, by just a thousand votes, and with it, the presidency.

He greatly admired Buchanan and had urged him to run for president for years. He had argued with him that Buchanan could have won the 1844 Democratic nomination if he had campaigned through the Northeast and let the party leaders know he wanted the job. Buchanan ignored his advice, did nothing, and was never a contender for the nomination. Forney said his friend could have captured the 1852 Democratic nomination over Franklin Pierce with even more ease if he had only tried. He did not. Buchanan always thanked Forney for his work, noting in 1852, as always, "the warmth of your friendship."[351]

In the weeks and months following the successful 1856 presidential election, the normally grating Forney was simply overbearing in his relationship to the president-elect's other political aides, many of them newcomers. He was intent on drawing attention to himself in newspaper stories. Others in the Buchanan inner circle were mad at him for trying to make the public believe that he carried far more influence with the president than anyone else. The president's other advisers, U.S. Senator William Bigelow, John Appleton, who had worked with him in England, and Congressman J. Glancy Jones, of Pennsylvania, were among them. Jones, a minister-turned-politician from a safe Democratic district, admired in the halls of Congress by Southerners as well as Northerners, quickly became the new president's right-hand man and was made the "whip," or presidential legislative captain, in the House of Representatives.[352]

A rift between the president and Forney started in those frantic post-election days. Forney pressed Buchanan to make him the editor of the

Washington Union again, but the two men who owned the paper disliked the argumentative Forney and refused to go along with his stewardship of the influential journal. The editor of the *New York Herald*, James Gordon Bennett, whom Buchanan had just brought back into the Democratic fold after Bennett supported Fremont in the last election, despised Forney and complained to the president that he was the wrong man for the job. Several powerful Southern senators who did not care for Forney also argued against him.

Instead of ordering them to take Forney for the *Union,* which he could have done, the president caved in and told Forney that his other aide, John Appleton, would get the post. Forney was furious, but soon had another idea. Why not make him the other U.S. senator from Pennsylvania, filling a recently vacated seat? The state legislature was scheduled to vote on a successor in January 1857. Why not pressure them to pick Forney? Would not his substantial foreign experience as Buchanan's long-time aide enable him to serve as a good senator?

The president agreed to do so but never fully used his political muscle to win the post for Forney. Buchanan wrote a few letters and talked to several state legislators on his behalf, but did little more. Because the president's endorsement of him was so weak, Forney lost the seat to Simon Cameron in the legislature's vote. Forney placed all the blame on Buchanan, whom he said had deliberately bungled the job. Forney, disenchantment with his friend growing daily, then tried to win himself an appointment to the cabinet, but Buchanan turned him down.

Forney not only felt abandoned but betrayed, and by an old friend for whom he had worked tirelessly all of his life. He wrote a passionate letter to Jeremiah Black, the new attorney general, in the spring of 1857: "Read this letter to Mr. B. Ask him if he is dead to the past in which I have served him almost like a slave. Ask him if he forgets the dark hours when his friends fled from him and I stood alone, a monument to fidelity."

Buchanan, as usual, did not understand, or care to understand, Forney's deep-seated unhappiness. Telling Forney that he was "grateful for the services which you have rendered to the Democratic Party," he offered his old friend two posts that he thought would satisfy him, head of the Naval Office in Philadelphia and consul at Liverpool, England. The president told him that he had "the earnest hope that you will accept one or the other," and wrote that "I…gratify my own warm feelings of friendship for yourself."

Forney not only turned down the posts, but dispatched a savage letter to Buchanan, telling him that the president knew very well why Forney would not work in his administration. He then reminded him how hard he had labored for the Democrats over the years and told Buchanan that he was "a man to whose cause I have given the best years of my life, and upon whose election to the Presidency I have expended every effort I could command, and nearly every dollar I had in the world."

He angrily told his former mentor that he would find his own job and never rely on party patronage or Buchanan's charity again. "I am about to embark once more upon the ocean of the future. I have suffered deep and bitter humiliation since you have been elected, the gibes of false friends and the open exultation of open foes."[353]

Finally, with no decent job or prospects of a job as a reward for his work on the campaign and twenty years of friendship, and with mounting debts for his family of five children, a distraught Forney asked his wife to write a letter to the president in which she pleaded for work for her husband and suggested the job of postmaster in Philadelphia. Mrs. Forney's request was set aside too.[354]

Buchanan felt badly for the irate Forney and offered him several poorly paying government jobs—an insult, really—and Forney, scorned, turned them all down. He did some freelance writing to pay his bills, but little else.[355]

No one in the national Democratic Party helped Forney either, since no one was in a hurry to back the wrong side in the quarrel, and so Buchanan's former close friend floundered. He had become a political pariah. His crime? He told everyone, with great bitterness, that it was spending his life helping his close friend become president.

Buchanan was unable to patch up his differences with Forney. Someone in the state party made arrangements for him to return to his old job as the editor of the *Pennsylvanian*, one of the party's newspapers, and he soon founded the *Philadelphia Press*, a paper that he turned into a very powerful journal in just a year, even introducing a national edition. The new job not only gave Forney a forum for his opinions of the party, public policy, and Buchanan, all of them unfavorable, but once again significant influence as a party leader in Pennsylvania. He now had a chance, too, to use the newspapers to help win election of, or defeat, state and national candidates.

The president, of course, never considered for a moment that the falling-out with John Forney was his fault and told everyone that Forney had caused the deep wound between them and had made no effort to heal it. He wrote friend and party political operative Joseph Baker at the beginning of January 1858, that he was sorry that Forney had abandoned him. "I mourn over Forney. I fear he can never return to us and yet he must feel awkward in his new associations. They will, I trust, at least make the fortune of his paper."[356]

FORNEY FIGHTS BACK

Forney never forgave the president for casting him aside and spent the rest of his life castigating Buchanan in the columns of his newspapers, speeches, and later in his memoirs. His criticism was relentless. The loquacious Forney, with an acidic sense of humor, became a popular speaker at dinner parties, outdoor festivals, and barbecues and regaled crowds by telling them, "We were all working to make J.B. president for twenty-five years before we got him in [long pause] and a pretty mess we made of it!"[357]

Worst of all, from the White House point of view, Forney spent much of 1858 blasting the administration over its Kansas policy. Buchanan denounced Forney and took away some government advertising from his journals. Forney used the White House assaults to present himself to the public as a maligned victim of a savage witch hunt. "It was a dark hour…instantly, the whole government power was organized against us. Everybody who sympathized with us in office was removed. The press…was the target of merciless abuse. Our subscribers dropped off like leaves in October. My heart sank under the pressure, but we were right and that carried us through."[358]

Forney told his followers that he had met the same fate as Stephen Douglas and others who disagreed with Buchanan; he was ostracized. Forney warned Democrats throughout 1858 that Buchanan's petty party politics would only result in Republican victories at the polls in the autumn.

Forney called Buchanan and his men "traitors" to the Democratic Party. In blistering editorials and speeches throughout the fall of 1858, he accused Buchanan of "petty proscriptions which village politicians would despise and which honorable men would laugh at." He added of the president's campaign against him that "this transaction proved not so much the prejudice of my old friend, Buchanan, as it did his littleness."[359]

Following his letter to Baker early in the year, Buchanan appeared to have forgotten John Forney and their dispute. But Forney did not forget. Now, as the political campaigns began in the fall of 1858, two years after their acrimonious parting, Forney, through his newspaper, speeches, and friends, had become a major player in the Democratic Party and a national figure in his own right. Newspapers began referring to the Northern wing of the organization as the "party of Douglas and Forney." And now, as election day approached, Forney had a plan to exact terrible revenge against his former friend in the White House.[360]

OBERLIN, OHIO: THE RESCUERS

On a chilly winter evening in January 1856, slave John Price fled his Kentucky farm on horseback with two other slaves. They reached Brown County, Ohio, after a dangerous crossing of the swirling Ohio River near the town of Ripley. Price—a stout, five-feet-eight-inch tall man in his twenties with a deformed left foot—and his companions met a Quaker on the Ohio side of the river that night. The Quaker turned out to be a member of the Underground Railroad, which consisted of intricately connected routes in Ohio and other Northern states followed by slaves who had fled their plantations. There were hundreds of them that took runaways to cities in the Northern states, where they moved in with members of the black community or to Canada, where slavery had been outlawed earlier in the century. The slaves' rescuer moved Price and his friends to Oberlin, a small, quiet town of tree-lined streets that surrounded a village green in the northern part of the state that was home to Oberlin College. Many of its professors were staunch abolitionists. Two of them, James Monroe and Henry Peck, were also among the most active Underground Railroad leaders in Ohio; Monroe was a state legislator.[361]

There, the trembling runaways found an integrated, liberal-thinking village of 2,250 residents that had prided itself for years on protecting fugitive slaves. Oberlin was one of several dozen "utopian" communities founded in the early 1830s where devoted religious people could live and work in harmony free from racism and economic strife. These towns reflected the new religious ideal of Protestant sects, particularly the Presbyterians, that men and women had to lead moral lives in addition to worshipping God in order to be saved. That meant integrated residential villages and schools, such as Oberlin College, with its eight hundred students, the centerpiece of the town. It was one of the few integrated colleges—men and women, blacks and whites—in the country.[362]

Blacks had lived in Oberlin since 1835, when the community formed one of the first antislavery societies in Ohio; 230 residents were members.[363] In 1853, the community even assumed the responsibility for the medical care of Lee Dobbins, a frail four-year-old slave child who was too ill to travel by the time he and his mother reached the community during their escape from a Southern plantation. The town's doctors and nurses did all they could, but the child died a month later. His funeral was attended by over two thousand residents in a very public display of the area's hatred of slavery. More than a dozen runaway slaves lived in town by 1858. For these reasons, and because his health was poor when he arrived, John Price decided to reside in Oberlin and not to travel on to Canada.

Price, however, with few skills beyond those of a farmer, had floundered. He had been unable to make enough money to pay rent, so the local townspeople cared for him as a pauper. He had roomed in different houses, rent free, for a year. Price worked for a dollar a day harvesting crops in nearby farms in good weather; he performed odd jobs around town in the winter. He felt bad that he was depending on the charity of others and let everyone in Oberlin know that they should contact him if there was any work to be done so he could earn money for his own rent.

He was working at the farm of Lewis Boynton just north of Oberlin on September 13, 1858, a crisp autumn day. The farmer had hired him to pick potatoes. Boynton's teenage son Shakespeare picked Price up in a buggy at the home of his black freedman farmer landlord late in the morning. The two drove away, intent on reaching the Boynton farm by lunchtime. Shortly after noon, just as they had driven across the Oberlin town line, Shakespeare Boynton started to slow down as he spotted another buggy following them on the roadway, its horse trotting at a rapid clip after them, kicking up clouds of dust on the highway. John Price, cleaning his teeth with a pocket knife and casually looking out at the woods and farmland they passed, paid no attention to what was going on.

A moment later, the second buggy, carrying two slave hunters from Kentucky, Samuel Davis and Richard Mitchell, and Jacob Lowe, a deputy marshal in Oberlin whom they brought along for protection, caught up to the slowly moving carriage. Lowe had the writs and papers of Davis and Mitchell that gave them permission to bring Price back to his plantation south of the Ohio River.[364] The teenager, who turned out to be an accessory to the plot, brought his vehicle to a halt. Two of the three men in the other buggy jumped out, shouting, grabbed a startled Price and pulled him into their carriage.[365]

The men held on to Price and told him they would return him to his owner. They were headed for Wellington, a nearby town with a train station. They planned to wait at a hotel and then board the 5:13 p.m. train south to Columbus, Ohio, and from there take Price back to Kentucky. A short time later their buggy passed two Oberlin College students, Ansel Lyman and Seth Bartholomew, on their way back to the campus. Price cried out for help but the two young men did not seem to hear him.

Hoping that the two men they passed on the road did not understand that Price had been kidnapped, the three slave hunters drove to Wellington at a leisurely pace and took a room at the Wadsworth Hotel. A handsomely designed three-story building with wide, columned porches on the first and second floors that faced the town's sizable public square, the hotel was located just three doors down from one of the community's churches. A bar and restaurant on the first floor were favorite dining and drinking spots for the town's residents; the porch and half dozen trees in front provided shade in the summertime. The slave hunters had a fourth accomplice, Anderson Jennings, who was on his way from Oberlin. Jennings, a neighbor of the farmer who had owned John Price, was in the area to capture a runaway of his own and decided to go after Price, too.

❧

RESCUING JOHN PRICE

At the same time that the three kidnappers and Price were eating lunch at the Wadsworth Hotel, telling their waitress that jittery Price was a business colleague, the two young college students they passed on the highway arrived back in Oberlin. Ansel Lyman began to walk briskly through town, looking for leaders of the antislavery movement, of which there were many. In hurried conversations, Lyman told men he knew that John Price had been abducted and was probably headed toward Wellington. Word spread quickly. The men whom Lyman told about the abduction ran to stores and homes to tell others. Those men fanned out through the community to alert anyone they could find. One man, Simeon Bushnell, a thirty-two-year-old, short, bearded, talkative printer, burst into the local bookstore owned by James Fitch and yelled at the customers there, including Fitch and Oberlin professor Henry Peck, "They have carried off one of our men in broad daylight and are an hour on their way already."

Someone else in the stored yelled, "They can't have him!"

The people in the store rushed into the street, where other angry townspeople were gathering and shouting that John Price had to be rescued.

Resident Artemas Halbert said that many men began looking for guns. "Simeon Bushnell...was talking to Oliver Wall. One of them said they ought not to go without a gun and the other said he knew where he could get a gun," Halbert said, adding that when he reached Wellington he saw numerous men armed with revolvers.[366]

Within minutes, word of the kidnapping spread throughout the town and to the campus of the college. Dozens of men arrived in the town center, running and walking, in front of John Scott's store on South Main Street. There were no speeches, just the repetition of the story. Men then ran to procure weapons. Some jumped on their horses and others into their buggies and wagons. Many commandeered wagons from townspeople or farmers in the village after explaining the urgency of the moment. Bushnell carried a gun and told others thinking of going to Wellington that they had no business there without a gun.[367]

Ironically, one of the men was Richard Winsor, a twenty-three-year-old college teacher, who had witnessed the deportation of another kidnapped black man, Anthony Burns from Boston, four years earlier. As the instant army of abolitionists raced out of Oberlin toward Wellington in a caravan of vehicles, a passerby in the growing crowd asked Winsor, riding in a buggy with John Scott and Jackson Chestnut, where he was going.

Waving three rifles in one hand and his floppy hat in the other, Winsor yelled out as loudly as he could, "I am going to Wellington to rescue John Price!"[368]

Everyone roared as the armada of abolitionists sped northward. Oddly, one of those cheering on the crowd as it left for Wellington was Henry Peck, who decided not to go. It was Peck, however, who would become a central character in what would soon unfold as one of the most important dramas of the Civil War era.

Peck, the thirty-seven-year-old married father of four, was a graduate of both Oberlin College and its Theological Seminary. The well-dressed teacher, who fancied bright white shirts and dark ties, was of medium height and sported a moderately sized beard, no moustache. Peck had a high forehead, large ears, and a noticeable wart on his upper lip. He was one of the state's most distinguished Underground Railroad leaders, and in early September had sent five fugitive slaves from Oberlin to Canada. He made no secret that he had raised money to purchase guns for John Brown's 1856 attacks against slaveholders in Kansas and Missouri. Peck had campaigned actively for the Republicans in the 1856 presidential election, earning the enmity of area Democrats and the *Cleveland Plain Dealer*, the state's leading Democratic newspaper.

The army of horses, buggies, and wagons moved as fast as it could, so fast, in fact, that several wagons suffered broken wheels when they hit ruts in the road. The men leading the caravan hailed everyone they passed and urged them to join them in their assault on the slave hunters in Wellington. Hundreds did so. When the men from Oberlin arrived in Wellington, they discovered a huge crowd gathered in the public square that had been there since morning, when its members watched the fire department put out a blaze that ruined three wood buildings in town. Those people joined the abolitionists as they arrived. The crowd swelled over the next few minutes as more and more wagons and riders arrived as the alarm over John Price's kidnapping spread. "The leaves of the forest seemed to carry the news," said an eyewitness.[369]

The members of the crowd, many brandishing rifles and revolvers, surged through the square and its adjacent streets. The spacious square was so crowded that there was no room left to stand, so many people slipped into public buildings to peer out from their windows. Dozens made it to the rooftops of buildings to watch the commotion below. Teenagers climbed trees and perched themselves on sturdy limbs to witness what transpired next. One observer put the size of the crowd at five hundred people, another counted one thousand. It was not a typical abolitionist crowd, made up of wealthy members of the community and ministers. The gathering did contain the usual abolitionists: wealthy landowners, merchants, and ministers from both Oberlin and Wellington. But there were also poor farmers, cobblers, carpenters, an undertaker, a grocer, harness master, shoemaker, brickmaker, and dozens of students and professors from Oberlin College—people from every walk of American life. Many of them were black freedmen. One bystander described the scene, "It was a very noisy time; a great deal of excitement and confusion."[370]

The smell of charred timber from the morning fire was still in the air and those who watched the enormous armed crowd gather were transfixed by the sight. "A fire in the morning and war at night!" exclaimed one woman.[371]

As the tension built among members of the angry crowd, ready for action, John Watson, one of the leaders of the rescue, obtained a warrant for the arrest of the slave hunters from a judge in Wellington. He returned to find the mob on the edge of revolution because someone had started a rumor that either Deputy Marshal Lowe or the Wellington mayor had wired for a large contingent of federal troops that would arrive on the 5:13 p.m. train to restore order. The crowd now began to scream for Price's release in order to free him before the army appeared.

A frantic Oliver Wadsworth, fearful that the mob would attack his hotel and destroy it, posted employees at all of its doors to keep people out. Despite his employees' presence, several of the abolitionists from Oberlin, and newly arrived recruits from Wellington, walked inside the hotel and up to a third floor attic room where Price was being held. They were joined by the local constable, Barnabas Meacham, who told everyone that he wanted to avoid violence. The slave catchers insisted that they had met every legal provision of the Fugitive Slave Act of 1850. They had a federal warrant for the return of Price, had signed certificates authorizing their apprehension of the runaway, and had gone directly to a local U.S. marshal, Lowe, who was bound by law to aid them in their search for Price. That seemed obvious under the Fugitive Slave Act of 1850 and even more appropriate under the 1857 U.S. Supreme Court's *Dred Scott* decision that a slave living in a free state was still a slave and belonged to someone. But the Oberlin men believed that their arrest warrant for the Kentuckians superseded the slave hunters' federal writs. Inexplicably, Constable Meacham then left to seek legal advice from a local judge.[372]

Wadsworth and the slave hunters agreed that something dramatic was needed to avoid an attack by the furious mass of people in the village square. There was talk of violence throughout the crowd and one man, pointing to the store that had burned in the morning, said that the crowd had to do the same thing to Wadsworth's Hotel. Another said, "They would have [Price] if they had to tear the house down."[373] Jennings asked Price if he would talk to the crowd and explain that he was amenable to going back to Kentucky because he was legally obligated to do so. Price agreed. Jennings walked on to the porch on the second floor and told the suddenly hushed crowd that he had legal papers to take Price away. "This boy is mine by the laws of Kentucky and of the United States," he bellowed.

"You dry up!" shouted someone in the crowd. "There are no slaves in Ohio and never will be north of the Ohio River."

"This boy is willing to go to Kentucky," Jennings said.

The people did not believe him. There were more loud jeers. One man yelled that the only way to prove that contention was to have Price address them.[374]

Price, afraid of being harmed by his captors, walked slowly out on to the balcony and looked down at the crowd. All eyes were upon him. Uncertain what to say, he told them, "I suppose I've got to go back to Kentucky."

Walter Soules from Oberlin was suddenly on the second-story wooden balcony near him. He yelled, "Had you not rather go to Canada?"

The runaway did not have time to answer. John Copeland, a twenty-four-year-old black freedman carpenter from Oberlin appeared, pointed a gun at Jennings, and told Price to jump off the balcony while he "shot the damned old rascal."

People in the crowd started shouting "Jump! Jump!" The Kentuckians and Deputy Marshal Lowe, afraid that either Copeland or someone else would start shooting at them, fled the balcony. They grabbed Price by his arms and hustled him inside and again took him up one flight of stairs to the small attic room.

There, the kidnappers were constantly visited by unarmed members of the crowd who attempted to talk them into releasing Price. "They would come in about two or three at a time," Jennings said later. Some left and some remained.[375]

Two men, Charles Marks and Norris Woods, Democratic Party leaders in Oberlin, then climbed up the ladder as others held it on the ground. As they did, Judge Isaac Bennett emerged on the balcony and tried to quiet the noisy crowd. He attempted to shove the ladder from the building but could not; he then pulled out his revolver and aimed it at Marks and Woods, who had been drinking earlier, and forced the pair to scramble back down the ladder to the ground.

Judge Bennett then left the hotel to study the papers that Lowe had handed him and the writ to arrest the kidnappers. Men from Wellington and Oberlin, including some college students, moved through the crowd, trying to pacify the angry, gun-toting abolitionists in order to prevent the incident from evolving into a full-scale riot in which dozens of people might be killed. Constable Meacham still could not figure out what to do and dispatched a man to a nearby town to procure a writ of habeas corpus in case he decided to arrest the slave hunters. Deputy Marshal Lowe kept insisting he had the legal right to put Price on the train to Columbus and reminded anyone he could find that the rumor about the soldiers on their way via railroad was true. But while Lowe had wired for help, he did not know if men would be forthcoming.

A COMEDY OF ERRORS

What followed was a comedy of errors, misunderstandings, miscommunications, and a total breakdown of law enforcement and jurisprudence. Judge Bennett went back to the hotel, met with the slave hunters, and then left. The local justice of the peace, William Houk, was summoned to verify Lowe's writs, but the justice forgot his glasses and had to go back to his office to retrieve them. On the way, he bumped into Judge Bennett, who assured him the writs were in order and he did not have to double-check them. But the justice forgot what Bennett said and went on his way, meandering through the crowd toward his office, not to be seen again.

Each time Lowe looked out the window at the mob below, he saw more men with guns. "The colored people seemed the most warlike," said Jacob Wheeler, a local farmer who was an eyewitness. "[I] think some of the younger lads among the white folks had some guns, too."[376]

Throughout the crowd, the marshal heard loud shouts of encouragement to free Price no matter what the cost. Most men were yelling that people should rush into the hotel and grab the runaway, but a few urged genuine destruction of property. "Some said they'd tear the [hotel] down," said one bystander, Chauncey Wack. Norris Woods said, "I expected there'd be shooting up there and I wanted to see it."[377]

Deputy Marshal Lowe, certain that people were going to be hurt if the standoff continued much longer, then asked a group of men to accompany

fighting, dozens of other men, several brandishing weapons, had charged into the hotel and began to climb the stairs. Winsor and another man placed Price on the shoulders of the first men on the staircase; they passed him downward on their shoulders, flight by flight, and eventually to the lobby. Winsor and the men there brought Price out of the building as the melee in the room continued; no one engaged in the fist fight was even aware that Price was gone.[380]

Those in the room were scared. "Good many got through the window. Don't know how many. Ten or fifteen at least. Others come in at the door. They crowded all around John and moved towards the door. I made no demonstration to fight at all," said the clearly rattled slave catcher Anderson Jennings.[381]

Outside, shouts of jubilation went up as Winsor suddenly emerged from the hotel with the runaway. The buggy that John Scott had driven to Wellington from Oberlin was waiting in the square, close to the porch of the hotel. Simeon Bushnell was driving it. Winsor pushed Price into the buggy and climbed in next to him. The crowd parted as the trio sped out of Wellington and headed north for Oberlin, Price smiling but still worried, Bushnell urging his horse to trot faster, and Winsor, a wide smile on his face, lifting both arms into the air in triumph.[382]

Throughout the evening all of the rescuers returned on horseback or in buggies and wagons, proud that they had worked together to prevent a man's return to slavery. They celebrated in the homes of neighbors, in dorms at the college, on streets, and on the village green.

Winsor celebrated, too, but first he brought John Price to the home of Calvin Fairchild in Oberlin. Fairchild was against slavery but was not a member of the Underground Railroad and not one of the fiery public advocates for the antislavery cause in town. If federal marshals came searching for John Price, the home of Fairchild would be the last place they would look.

There was joy and relief in Oberlin. The members of the Underground Railroad had done their job again, this time very publicly, and the whole community was proud of them. For Price's rescuers, the incident was over. For the federal government, it was not. The abolitionists wanted to make a public example of John Price? Then the federal government was going to make an example out of them.

Price's rescue was not new. The first successful recorded escape was by a slave from Albany, New York, who left his farm in 1705 and fled to Canada, where he was given refuge. By the 1760s, on the eve of the American Revolution, thousands of slaves were escaping from their owners each year; in 1760 alone there were more than nine hundred ads for runaways in Southern newspapers. Despite severe punishment for the runaways who were caught, tens of thousands of slaves continued to flee over the years.

Slaves made it to the homes or businesses of men and women, black and white, who hid them during the day and transported them by carriage, wagon, and horse by night to the next community on the trek to safe cities in the North or to Canada. Those who aided the runaways were sometimes beaten and sometimes shot. Some were killed. Others were given stiff prison terms lasting up to four years. The Underground Railroad workers had established well-run networks by the 1820s. A slave could be moved from Virginia to Canada, by land or sea, in just a few weeks. One of the most efficient railroads was in Ohio, with twenty routes and over two hundred safe houses.

Despite these efforts, slave catchers apprehended many fugitives and returned them to their plantations. Sometimes groups of Northerners prevented them by staging public rescues. These had taken place since 1851, and by 1858 there had been at least one each year.

All of the rescues of captured slaves by mobs in Northern states received substantial coverage in both the mainstream newspapers and abolitionist journals, but no rescue in American history would receive the media coverage that the freeing of John Price did in the autumn of 1858. No rescue would have as much impact on the nation, either. It was a rescue that would grow from a single, widely publicized incident into a much larger one and, by the time the story was over, would push millions of fence-sitters on the slavery question into the radical camp, reenergize the abolitionist movement that had been weakened by the *Dred Scott* decision of 1857, and dramatically affect American politics.

THE FEDERAL FALLOUT

On the day following the rescue of John Price, as the slave hid in the home of Fairchild, deputy marshal Jacob Lowe was back in town, walking through the public square, stopping in stores and visiting the college campus, questioning everyone he could find. So was federal marshal Matthew Johnson, who had arrived from Cleveland. He sought out the town's proslavery residents, among them merchant Chauncey Wack and postmaster Edward F. Munson, and peppered them with questions about townspeople who might have been involved in the rescue.

Within weeks, Cleveland's Democratic-leaning *Plain Dealer* reported that a federal investigation of the Oberlin rescue was underway, targeting the men who freed Price, and that they were going to be "immediately prosecuted."[383] Shortly afterward, federal district judge Hiram V. Willson impaneled a grand jury to consider evidence in the Oberlin case. Every single member of the grand jury was a Democrat, and it even included Lewis Boynton, the father of the teenager who lured Price to his kidnappers.

Judge Willson was biased against the Oberlin and Wellington men from the start. He told the grand jury that their job was to simply decide if the men who freed Price had violated the fugitive slave law. It was not to decide whether their views on slavery were right or wrong. They were now referred to in the press as the "Rescuers," with a capital *R* to honor their national notoriety as a group. Willson added that while the Rescuers were obsessed with fighting for the rights of their own property and beliefs, they had no regard for the property and beliefs of others. Their antislavery feelings were religious but wrong, he said. He told the jurors that it was "a sentiment semi-religious in its development, and is almost invariably characterized by intolerance and bigotry. The leaders of those who acknowledge its obligations and advocate its sanctity are like the subtle prelates of the dark ages. They are versed in all they consider useful and sanctified learning— trained in certain schools in New England to manage words, they are equally successful in the social circle to manage hearts."[384]

Willson and many others believed all abolitionists such as the Rescuers were simply too strident. Most Americans opposed to slavery were willing to work with Southerners so that over the years slavery might be eliminated. The abolitionists, though, wanted that elimination right now. Many Northerners saw that all-or-nothing approach as unreasonable and often obnoxious. Perhaps some time behind bars would chasten the whole bunch of them.[385]

The grand jury, reportedly made up of men who loathed abolitionists, heard witnesses over a period of two months and on December 6, 1858, handed down indictments against thirty-seven Rescuers, twenty-five from

Oberlin and twelve from Wellington. There would have been even more indictments, but witnesses could not identify many of those in Wellington that day.

Those indicted represented a broad spectrum of American life. They included a bookseller/printer, a clerk, a carpenter, two cabinetmakers, two lawyers, a harness maker, a book and shoe merchant, two cobblers, six farmers, and a doctor. They included Ansel Lyman, who alerted the town to the abduction, William Lincoln, who led the assault on the front door of the hotel, John Scott, who led the charge on the rear entrance, and Richard Winsor, who spirited Price out of the room. Many of the indicted men were black.[386]

Among the several professors named was Henry Peck, who had not even been there. It was Peck, though, who became the focus of the media stories because of his previous political activities, in which he campaigned for Republicans on platforms filled with men armed with muskets to strike a radical note. "Wonder if the Professor will be found on said platform now, with his musketeers about him ready for the fray?" the reporter for the *Cleveland Plain Dealer* mocked, adding that "he may shut up his college for a few days and not only come into court himself, but bring his students and his *shades* with him."[387]

Controversy arose immediately. All of the men indicted were Republicans and many were leaders of the area's Underground Railroad. Why wasn't Norris Woods, a Democrat, indicted, questioned the local newspapers. It was Woods, after all, who tried to climb up the ladder that day. Why were James Fitch and Ralph Plumb indicted? Like Peck, they did not even go to Wellington that day.

The next afternoon, half the Oberlin Rescuers arrived by train in Cleveland for their arraignment. The rest of the men from Oberlin and those who lived in Wellington—except for eight—were arraigned separately over that week.[388] Seven of those indicted were runaway slaves themselves; they fled. Four others, including black freedman John Copeland, disappeared. William Lincoln, who led the assault on the hotel, was on spring break from college and agreed to turn himself in later. That morning, the Rescuers procured the services of two of the best lawyers in Ohio, Rufus Spalding, the former speaker of the Ohio state legislature, and Albert Gallatin Riddle, former county prosecutor and state legislator. They added a third attorney, Seneca Griswold, a thirty-five-year-old Oberlin graduate. The trio, all fierce antislavery advocates, worked for free.[389]

The Rescuers were released on their own recognizance and told to return for a trial in March. The Rescuers and dozens of other townspeople in Oberlin held a victory dinner on January 11, 1859, at the Palmer House, whose roof was still covered with snow from an earlier storm. The event was jokingly nicknamed the "Felons' Feast."[390]

At the Palmer House, following some levity, several men who gave speeches or read letters mailed to them from others warned that the federal government's prosecution of the Oberlin Rescuers might lead to serious national events. It was the first time that civil war had been discussed in Ohio. In a letter, local attorney Stevenson Burke said he could not tell the purpose of the prosecution by the "ruling madmen" and said with great passion, "Nor can I tell what further sacrifices it may yet become necessary for the lovers of freedom to make, to render our own beloved and beautiful Ohio—indeed, and in truth the land of the free and the home of the brave—to deliver our people from the demoralizing spectacle of slave catching and slave hunting in our midst—to render it safe for the humanely disposed among us to feed the hungry, clothe the naked, or relieve the distressed, without fear of government spies or running the risk of fines, forfeitures, and prison bars and bolts."

John Mercer Langston, a black freedman whose brother Charles was indicted, rose and told the crowd that the government had struck down both the Declaration of Independence and the Constitution with the Fugitive Slave Act and this prosecution. "How shall we meet our duty? To do it, we must make sacrifices—go to prison, or, if necessary, go out on the battlefield to meet the slave oligarchy." And, in a menacing letter, John Brown Jr., the son of the fire-breathing abolitionist leader, wrote the Rescuers that by the actions of the government, "We are forced into the attitude of resistance to the government. I am glad the work of judicial 'cursing out' is progressing not only out of Kansas, but in Ohio."[391]

The federal government was not amused by the "Felons' Feast." Just three days later, federal marshals burst into a small, local schoolhouse where rescuer William Lincoln was teaching to arrest him. They not only physically restrained the young educator and forcibly removed him from the class but manacled him in front of his students. An angry Lincoln begged to have the tight handcuffs removed, but the marshals ignored him. Lincoln was then taken on a long carriage ride to Columbus and tossed into a tiny jail cell without food or water. When the other inmates were told who he was and why he was there, they cheered him. Lincoln could not sleep and the next day was taken by train to Cleveland, where he was arraigned and finally released, his reddened wrists cut and badly bruised from the tight handcuffs.

The prosecutors smirked over their tough treatment of Lincoln, but it unnerved the nation when it was made public in an article from the *Columbus State Journal* that was reprinted in *The Liberator,* the country's leading abolitionist newspaper, and other publications. The Oberlin rescue, and the prosecution, was no longer just another slave-rescue account but a national story.

❦

Trial by Jury

The trials were held in a relatively new, three-story-high stone county court-house, with handsome arched windows that fronted Cleveland's busy public square. Reporters from newspapers in several Midwestern states, plus the *New York Herald Tribune,* were in the building to cover it as well as reporters from all of the leading newspapers in Ohio. The media view of the trial was mixed. The *New York Times* correspondent in town, twenty-three-year-old John Kagi, easy to spot anywhere with his lengthy beard, provided sporadic stories. The controversial Kagi had previously worked as a soldier for John Brown in the Kansas wars and was clearly on the side of the defendants. Several other papers provided a pro-defendant view, too. The *Free South,* an abolitionist paper, favored the defendants and its editor even asked William Lincoln to serve as its reporter for the judicial proceeding. The editor of the *Cleveland Herald* wrote at the start of the hearings that "no criminal court ever had a more respectable class of prisoners in the criminal docks," and added that the trial was "disgraceful to our country."392

But there were other journals represented in the courtroom whose editors saw the Rescuers as genuine evildoers. The *Cleveland Plain Dealer,* Ohio's paper with the largest circulation and the most influence, as an example, alternately referred to Oberlin as "that Babylon of abolitionism" and "headquarters and hotbed of Negro fanaticism in the North." Any rallies or protests of abolitionists were referred to as "carnivals." Not content to write that the Oberliners were charged with breaking the fugitive slave law, the *Plain Dealer* insisted that they were all guilty of treason (their new editor was humorist Charles Browne, who wrote as Artemas Ward).[393]

The public was divided, too. Most residents of Ohio sided with the Rescuers, while others sided with the prosecutors. A few who considered themselves liberals drew the line at violent interference by U.S. marshals. They shared the opinion of Seth Gates, a liberal on most issues, who criticized his friend, radical congressman Joshua Giddings, for his "audacious letters in justification of the Oberlin law breakers."[394]

The federal government did not want to try all of the men together and decided to put Simeon Bushnell, the local printer, on trial first. Then they would proceed with individual trials for the others in a predetermined order agreed upon by both teams of attorneys. The government was confident that it had a solid case against Bushnell. George Belden, the overeager prosecutor, who had bragged, "We will drive those Oberlin fellows *to the wall*,"[395] proved without doubt that John Price was a runaway slave and that the slave hunters had legal writs to capture him and return him to his owner. Kentuckian John Bacon, a well-dressed man, appeared in court to tell the story of his ownership of Price.

Numerous witnesses identified Bushnell as one of the men who had spread the word of the kidnapping in Oberlin; others identified him as one of the Rescuers in the crowd at Wellington. Judge Willson admonished the members of the jury that their only job was to determine whether or not Bushnell assisted in rescuing Price. If so, they had to find him guilty under the federal Fugitive Slave Act. Some said the judge was hopelessly biased and called his instructions to the grand jury "an intemperate assault upon the character and motives of conscientious objectors to that law."[396]

Bushnell was certain he would be acquitted. So were all the other defendants, who traveled to Cleveland and sat in the courtroom in a show of support. Dozens of family members and friends went to Oberlin so that they could cheer the not guilty verdict and escort Bushenell back to town for a victory celebration. Their confidence was bolstered following a strong case made by the defense team. They offered standard arguments that the slave catchers each told a different story and therefore all of their testimony was unreliable. They turned the indictment upside down and said that since what the Rescuers had done was a morally good thing, they could not have committed a crime. "There is not one among you," one attorney told the jury, "that would look upon [them] as a thief or one convicted of a moral wrong."[397]

The defense attorney reminded the jurors that in Ohio everyone was free and therefore the defendants not only had the right to rescue Price but were obligated to do so. He told them that, in fact, those slave catchers had kidnapped an Ohio citizen. The Rescuers would have saved that citizen if he were white—skin color did not matter. He reminded them that while slavery was legal under Kentucky's laws, it was not in Ohio. "How then can the court assume that the law of Kentucky is applicable to this case?" asked Albert Riddle.[398]

The convincing Riddle made a passionate plea for Bushnell's release, and his graphic denunciation of slave hunters and those who assisted them mesmerized those in the courtroom.

He told the jury, "To one of us, every breath, every mouthful of food, or shred of clothing thus enjoyed, is a larceny from the sinews, hearts, and souls of a whole race. I can also understand why, in the half-barbaric profusion and license of southern slavery, these coarse, bloated, bullying, cowardly swaggers—great, hairy maggots warmed into life in the hot, seething carcass of rotten slavery—can exist, and the needs for such existences, for I have seen them among us. But, I repeat it, I cannot comprehend how a mass of feculence can exist at the North, in which God can tolerate life, that outrages human nature by crawling into the human form so abject and vile that it can prey upon and trade in the misfortune of these wretched fugitives from slavery."[399]

The loquacious Riddle appealed to them "as men and as Ohioans" to free Bushnell and the others. He told them that these were "issues involving the common rights, franchises, and liberties of us all as citizens of a great free state."[400]

In his charge to the jury, the judge offered the jurors no leeway in their verdict, telling them that if they believed Bushnell had aided in the rescue of John Price in any way they had to find him guilty; no exceptions could be made and the law could not be interpreted by them. Even so, all in the courtroom were startled when the foreman rose from his seat in the jury box and barked out "guilty" when asked for the jury's verdict. Before any of the defendants in the courthouse or in the audience had a chance to react, the prosecutor further astonished the court by demanding that the next defendant be put on trial right away—Professor Henry Peck. But Henry Peck was not the second scheduled trial. That "honor" belonged to black freedman Charles Langston. The defense lawyers had not even prepared a defense for Henry Peck yet. Judge Willson agreed that Henry Peck should be put on trial—immediately.

At that point, chaos reigned in Willson's courtroom. There was cheering by those in the chamber who believed the Rescuers were guilty and jeers from the residents of Oberlin and Wellington who thought they should all be freed. Others howled that it was unfair to put Peck on trial next, out of order; no jury should hear a case of a man whose lawyers had not put together a defense. Prosecutor Belden told the judge he was ready to proceed against Henry Peck. Defense counsel Rufus Spalding said that the government appeared ready to try the men out of order, one after the other, in an illegal manner. He would have nothing to do with it; the legal team would offer no defense if Belden went that far.

Belden smirked that he could do what he wanted, and to make certain that the Rescuers remained in Cleveland so he could put them on trial, he wanted them all arrested and thrown in jail. Judge Willson agreed. Another defense attorney, Franklin Backus, was livid. He called the decisions of Belden and the judge "a most villainous outrage on the sense of justice of the civilized world, and no one of the defendants would so stultify himself as to attempt a defense before such a jury…a monstrous proceeding."[401]

Belden, fearful of a riot, suggested to the judge that he might let the men go home if they posted $1,000 bail each, an amount they could easily obtain.

The Rescuers gathered in a large huddle in the middle of the high-ceilinged courtroom and engaged in a heated discussion. Marshal Johnson stood by, waiting for them to agree to bail so he could let them leave the building and walk to the train station with their families. The Rescuers had decided to take a bold step, though, one that surprised Johnson and, as soon as it was reported, the entire nation. The Rescuers would not post bail. The men would remain in jail for as long as it took for each trial to be heard, even if that took months. In a "manifesto" they published, the Rescuers said that they were confident the judge and prosecutor were acting out of "personal malice and a determination to humble them." They were going to "enter a most emphatic protest against the insult and legal injustice which they had suffered," said rescuer Jacob Shipherd.[402]

〰

Wightman's Castle

That afternoon, in a light drizzle, the men marched together out of the courthouse and across the public square to the Cuyahoga County Jail. The sheriff in charge of the facility, David Wightman, who privately sympathized with them, was so startled to see the group walking toward his front door, their luggage in their hands, friends at their side, that he did not believe it. He insisted on papers authorizing him to take them as prisoners; the men stood in the rain until the documents arrived some time later.

The Cuyahoga County Jail was a foreboding structure that looked more like the medieval dungeon of a deranged warlord than a nineteenth-century correctional facility. It consisted of two connected, three-story stone buildings, one higher than the other. The roof contained battlements and watchtowers, hence its long-time nickname, "Wightman's Castle."[403]

Wightman told his new prisoners that he welcomed them as guests, not criminals, because, the antislavery sheriff said, "I cannot regard you as criminals for doing only what I should do myself under similar circumstances."[404]

Wightman and the jailer, John Smith, told the Rescuers that they would be made as comfortable as possible. Wightman let some of them live in his own apartment at the prison. They were allowed the use of all the administrative rooms and permitted to roam throughout the building at will; the cells where they slept were cleaned regularly.

Wightman and Smith suspended all the rules for visitation and told the Rescuers' families that they could arrive whenever they desired; he let it be known that anyone could join them. They did. Throughout their incarceration, thousands of people came to visit and encourage the Rescuers. At first they came from blocks away in Cleveland, then by stagecoach from Lorain and by train from Oberlin and Wellington. Soon afterward, supporters began to arrive on horseback and in carriages from all over Ohio and later, by train from all over the United States. The first visitors were wives, children, and friends, but soon huge organizations arrived to lend their support.

The first large group to turn up consisted of dozens of women from the Cleveland Plymouth Church, a Congregational sect. Wightman let them stay for hours and the reception rooms at the jail became festive, as they would for the dozens of large groups of visitors who would follow. The atmosphere was so party-like that the *Cleveland Morning Leader* wrote that "President

Buchanan hardly holds greater levees." The *Herald* reporter noted that the jail "appeared more like a fashionable place of resort than a prison."[405]

The size of the crowds of visitors grew quickly into the hundreds and then into the thousands. On the first Sunday of their imprisonment, more than seven hundred visitors jammed the prison yard and the perimeter of the jail, and hundreds more crammed into windows of the courthouse and other nearby buildings, to hear Professor Henry Peck read from scriptures and lead a choir in singing hymns. Peck told the crowd with great firmness that, as William Seward had often said, there was a higher law than the Constitution: the law of God. "Divine will is to be paramount law with us," Peck told the assembly. "We must obey God always, and the human law, social and civil, *when we can.*"[406] Later, a group of more than four hundred Sunday school students from Oberlin took a train to visit the Rescuers. More large groups followed, week by week, in a long procession.

The most intriguing visitor of all was John Brown, the abolitionist leader of the murderous wars in Kansas who was wanted by the federal government for his illegal raids in that state and neighboring Missouri. Brown arrived in Cleveland unseen. He not only managed to slip unnoticed into Cleveland but delivered a virulent antislavery lecture to a large crowd that was advertised in dozens of broadsides nailed to trees and buildings in downtown Cleveland. At a well-attended and publicized auction, Brown sold off horses and mules he had stolen. The audacious Brown even managed to walk past courthouse guards and for one day sat in the courtroom observing Simeon Bushnell's trial. To elude detection, Brown simply tucked his famous long white beard into the top of his shirt and pulled a hat down over his forehead.

Encouraged by his courtroom deception, he then sneaked into the Cuyahoga County Jail and visited the Rescuers, even trying to recruit some of them for the raid he planned somewhere in Virginia (it would be the notorious Harper's Ferry attack). One of them was William Lincoln. Brown told Lincoln that not only did he want him with his band of raiders, but would make him one of the leaders. Lincoln asked him how many men had been recruited and when Brown answered that he had twenty-two, Lincoln scoffed.

"Brother Brown, twenty-two are enough for death; I shall reserve myself for better and wiser plans," Lincoln said.

Brown understood and departed. "God bless you, young man," Brown said. "God bless you and good-bye."[407]

The huge crowds soon became routine as the abolitionist press and many mainstream newspapers not only embraced the cause of the Rescuers, but saw them as the descendants of the Christian martyrs of old, remaining in prison to defy the Romans and anyone else who opposed Christianity.[408] Congressman Joshua Giddings spoke for many when he said, "They are no longer for themselves in this business, but for justice, for liberty, for the cause of freedom. The eyes of the nation are upon them… Cleveland is the Boston of 1775."[409]

The Rescuers understood their newfound acclaim and realized they could use it to promote their cause. Republican Party officials did also, rallying to the Rescuers' defense.[410] "May the God of the poor use us, and these stirring events, to awaken a sleeping Church and a sleeping state to acknowledge the fact that the bolts of heaven are hanging over us, and the wrath of heaven is out against us because of our indifference to these miseries of his suffering poor," said bookseller Jacob Fitch from jail.[411]

Charles Langston was tried next, but with a new jury. Langston, too, was found guilty, but the black defendant electrified the courtroom when he spoke before sentencing was imposed.

"I shall never be taken into slavery. And in that trying hour I would have others do to me, as I would call upon my friends to help me, as I could call upon you, your honor, to help me, as I would call upon you, Belden, to help me…and upon you [his lawyer] *so help me God*! I stand here to say that I will do all I can, for any man thus seized and held, though the inevitable penalty of six months' imprisonment and one thousand dollars fine for each offense hangs over me! We have common humanity. You would do so; your manhood would require it; and no matter what the laws might be, you would honor yourself for doing it; your friends would honor you for doing it; your children to all generations would honor you for doing it; and every good and honest man would say, you had done *right*!"[412]

As he finished, the spectators in the jammed courtroom erupted in cheers that continued for several minutes despite the judge's efforts to calm them down.[413]

The Rescuers' lawyers decided to try to persuade the Ohio Supreme Court to free their clients from Belden's detainment. Needing some legal leverage, they pressured Sheriff Herman Burr, of Lorain County, to arrest the slave hunters who abducted John Price on kidnapping charges. The Rescuers' lawyers demanded, and received, a guarantee that each case would be heard by a separate jury. To add yet more pressure on the government, the attorneys told the press that by the time all of the trials were over, the proceeding would be the costliest in the history of the Ohio courts, more than $5 million.

~⌒

RESCUERS IN PRISON

Each side threatened the other. The Rescuers' attorneys warned that they were seeking lengthy prison terms for the Kentuckians; prosecutor Belden replied that he had decided not to keep any convicted Rescuers in the Cleveland jail, but to transport them to the notorious state prison in Columbus, where the worst murderers in the Midwest were incarcerated. In one effort to pressure all of the Rescuers to make bail and go home, charges were dropped against two defendants who had nothing to do with the actual freeing of Price. Prosecutor Belden then convinced three of the Wellington Rescuers that he would drop the charges against them if they would leave the jail and return to their community. They did. That left fourteen defendants, all from Oberlin. Belden said later that they were the real culprits, telling a reporter, "The Oberlinites are the ones the government wants to punish."[414]

The defense team made a lengthy plea before the Ohio Supreme Court, arguing that the federal government could not make a state government enforce the Fugitive Slave Act and that made it null and void and their clients innocent. The Rescuers' attorneys also argued that the right against detainment was not only protected by the U.S. Constitution, but by English law back to the Magna Carta of the thirteenth century.[415]

Their gallant appeals did no good; the Ohio Supreme Court refused to aid the Rescuers. The judges ruled that a state court could not intervene in federal judicial proceedings; it crushed the hopes of the Oberlin prisoners.

Throughout this time, the Rescuers in prison made the best of their circumstances. There were problems, such as the common criminals and lunatics incarcerated with them who sometimes assaulted them. The food was not good or plentiful and there was little sunlight. Their jailers permitted them extraordinary freedom within the walls of the prison, however. John Scott was allowed to manufacture saddles in a shed. The students from Oberlin were permitted to bring their books, study, and set up an ad hoc library. Henry Peck, who had become the leader of the group, preached at two prayer meetings a day and held two Sabbath services every Sunday. The men organized a letter-writing drive to keep friends, family, and local newspapers informed of their welfare. They wrote over two thousand letters and many were copied and sent to newspapers around the country. The men even produced their own newspaper, called *The Rescuer*. The pages of the newspaper, which was published every other week, were filled with sermons and antislavery columns, all written by the Rescuers.[416]

The defendants kept as busy as they could because the trials had been suspended while the Ohio Supreme Court heard a second, and more important, plea from the defense team to have the Fugitive Slave Act overturned in Ohio, making the Rescuers innocent. All sides waited for the Ohio Supreme Court to hand down its decision. The court may have refused to step into a federal judicial proceeding, but it could certainly authorize a way to free the men while they awaited their trials.

All dreaded the consequences. The apprehensive U.S. attorney general, Jeremiah Black, stated in Washington, DC, that no state court could overrule the federal government on any matter concerning the trial and that any such decision violated the U.S. Constitution. Black ordered Marshal Johnson to defy the court and to do whatever was necessary to keep the Rescuers in prison if the Ohio court ruled in their favor. "You will respectfully decline to produce the bodies of the prisoners before the state court or to let them be taken of your own custody," Black declared.[417]

Throughout the country, rumors flew. One oft-repeated story was that Governor Salmon Chase had already called up the state militia and that if the court ruled in favor of the prisoners, the militia would assault the Cuyahoga County Jail and free the Rescuers. Another was that in order to prevent any state officials from releasing the men, President Buchanan had ordered federal troops stationed in Kentucky to attack the city of Cleveland by land while the USS *Michigan* shelled it from the waters of Lake Erie. One rumor not on the streets at the time, but confirmed later, was that John Brown's raiders planned to lead a small group of armed men to storm the county jail and free the Rescuers.[418]

On May 24, 1859, on the same day that the State Supreme Court was expected to rule on the writ of habeas corpus that would free the Rescuers, a massive rally was held in the public square in front of the county jail. The rally, sponsored by the Ohio Antislavery Society, attracted several thousand angry Ohioans (two thousand was a figure offered by the Democratic *Plain Dealer* and ten thousand by the Republican *Leader*). They arrived individually and in groups. Entire trains were rented to bring them in. A thirteen-car train was needed to transport more than two thousand residents of Oberlin alone. A fifteen-car train from Columbus arrived filled to capacity, as well as jammed twelve-car trains from Cleveland and Toledo. There was even a car filled with Rescuer supporters from Pittsburgh. Some of the railroads, eager to support the cause, sold half-price tickets. Three groups arrived with brass bands and large banners with slogans such as: "Sons of Liberty, 1765," and "Down with the Fugitive Slave Act." The men and women from Oberlin marched from the train station to the county jail two abreast, their brass band playing the French national anthem, "Marseilles." Dozens of large American flags were carried by other groups.[419]

At the rally, speaker after speaker denounced the county prosecutor, the judge, and the federal government. Finally, Joshua Giddings just about urged the crowd to take the matter into their owns hands and storm the jail. "Let all those who are ready and resolved to resist when all other means fail—when the yoke is fixed upon your necks—and when the heel of oppression crushes our very life out—all those who are thus ready to resist the enforcement of this infamous Fugitive Slave Act...speak out!"

Giddings's oration was met with a thunderous roar from the crowd. Then suddenly, unannounced, the governor of Ohio, Salmon Chase, who had earlier sent word he would not attend the rally, appeared at the podium.[420]

All hoped the state's slave-hating governor would be there to lead the attack. Over the last few years, Chase, a tall man whose regal carriage made him look even larger, who was interested in seeking the presidency in 1860, had become one of the loudest critics of slavery. Chase had denounced the caning of Senator Charles Sumner of Massachusetts by Senator Preston Brooks in the Senate in 1856, telling Sumner then, "All acts against antislavery showed the true character of the men that slavery makes more than 10,000 speeches."[421] He loathed the Fugitive Slave Act, having often called it with great sarcasm, "a symbol of the supremacy of the slave states."[422] The governor had written the country's new political star, Illinois's Abraham Lincoln, that "it is unnecessarily harsh and severe and marked by many repulsive features."[423]

Surely, their governor would ask the people to rise up and free the prisoners. He had been urged to do so not only by Ohioans, but by politicians outside the state and by influential national newspaper editors. Joseph Medill, editor of the *Chicago Tribune,* wrote that the Fugitive Slave Act was "the worst blow freedom has yet received" and urged Chase to "let the great, broad seal of the great state of Ohio be put upon the illegality of that accursed act and it will be the heaviest blow yet that has been struck at the aggression of the slave power."[424]

Chase did not. In fact, the governor had no desire to attend the rally. He was talked into an appearance and did his best to quiet the crowd after the speakers had driven it into a frenzy. The governor may have agreed with the Rescuers' actions, but he would not advocate violence. Chase, who always kept one eye on politics, also did not want to wreck his presidential dreams by being responsible for a riot.

"Citizens of Cleveland! Law abiding citizens of Cleveland!" he said, opening his speech, and went on to urge the crowd to be calm and to let the courts decide what would happen to the Rescuers. He "had not come to counsel any violence," he said, and told the thousands in front of the prison that the only way to truly defeat any government, state or federal, was at the ballot box.

The organizers of the rally were disappointed. They blamed Chase for holding back a crowd that seemed ready to attack the county jail, free the Rescuers, and carry them throughout Cleveland on their shoulders.[425]

Chase knew that he had disappointed the people. "I was most coldly received," he wrote later.[426] But there were others at the rally that day who believed he had acted properly. A *New York Times* editorial writer said that the governor's speech was "sensible."[427]

The governor was not the highlight of the rally; the Rescuers were. The crowd turned from the square and marched a block to the county jail, where the Rescuers were all in the yard, near a fence, listening to the speeches. Several Rescuers climbed on boxes on their side of the fence to address the crowd, whose members roared when each began to speak. Charles Langston told them that America was the "home of the brave, but not the land of the free." James Fitch asked the crowd if they were ready to submit to the Fugitive Slave Act. "No!" they shouted in unison. He told

JEFFERSON DAVIS AND MRS. DAVIS, 1849.

This portrait of Jefferson Davis was taken sometime in 1854, while he was secretary of war, when he first met Robert E. Lee.

Courtesy of the Museum of the Confederacy

Jefferson Davis married Varina Howell in 1845. It was his second marriage and her first. Varina cared for him throughout his near-fatal illness in the winter of 1858.

Courtesy of the Museum of the Confederacy

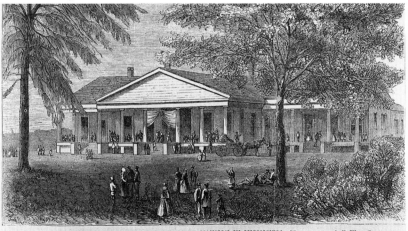

PICTURES OF THE SOUTH—JEFFERSON DAVIS'S MANSION IN MISSISSIPPI.—[Sketched by A. R. Waud.]

Brierfield, the Davises' Mississippi plantation on the banks of the Mississippi River, was one of the state's largest.

Courtesy of the Museum of the Confederacy

These two photos show how rapidly Robert E. Lee aged as the nation plunged into the Civil War. The photo at the left was taken in the early 1850s, when Lee and his family resided at Arlington House between army assignments. The one at the right was taken in the spring of 1862.

Courtesy of Arlington House, the Robert E. Lee Memorial

Robert E. Lee and his son Rooney

Courtesy of Arlington House, the Robert E. Lee Memorial

Mary Lee aged rapidly during the 1850s and by 1858 was infirm and confined to the grounds of Arlington House. Her poor health was the primary reason Lee considered retiring from the army that spring.

Courtesy of Arlington House, the Robert E. Lee Memorial

This Benson Lossing painting of Arlington House captured the serene beauty of the mansion and estate overlooking the Potomac River that was home to the Lees for thirty years.

Union troops seized Arlington House in 1861 and used it as a camp throughout the Civil War. The Lees never returned.

Courtesy of Arlington House, the Robert E. Lee Memorial

In 1858, Abraham Lincoln was a relatively unknown Illinois politician, but he had developed into a powerful public speaker and skilled debater.

Courtesy of the Lincoln Museum, Fort Wayne, IN (Ref. # O-17)

Stephen Douglas, the Little Giant, was considered the finest debater in the United States and his followers had no fear that he would easily best Lincoln in their seven historic encounters in 1858.

Courtesy of the Lincoln Museum, Fort Wayne, IN (Ref. # 65)

The enormous height difference between the six-foot-four Lincoln and five-foot-two Douglas is evident in this sketch of the pair during one of the debates.

Courtesy of the Lincoln Museum, Fort Wayne, IN (Ref. # 173)

President James Buchanan's refusal to deal with the slavery issue throughout 1858 was one of the primary causes that North and South split apart so badly that year and why the Civil War followed in 1861.

Courtesy of Dickinson College

When Seward first came to Washington his family remained at their Auburn, New York, home. In the lower photo, Seward sits with his family in the gardens of the Auburn house.

By 1858, the Sewards spent most of their time at their Washington, DC, house. Above, Seward talks to family members on the veranda porch at the rear of their home.

Courtesy of the Seward House Museum

Seward became Abraham Lincoln's secretary of state. Here, he sits in front of the table in a painting of Lincoln's cabinet.

Courtesy of the Lincoln Museum, Fort Wayne, IN (Ref. # 2825)

Seward often traveled as secretary of state. This photo was taken of the secretary and the captain of the USS Waywayanda as it sailed the Atlantic.

Courtesy of the Seward House Museum

Seward sometimes traveled to army camps with members of his staff and/or family during the Civil War in visits similar to this trip to the headquarters of General Joseph Hooker.

Courtesy of the Seward House Museum

Former slave John Price was taken to the Wadsworth Hotel in Wellington, Ohio, where he was rescued by hundreds of local abolitionists. The much-publicized rescue and the trial of the men involved helped revive the anti-slavery movement the year after the Dred Scott decision was issued by the U.S. Supreme Court.

Courtesy of Oberlin College

Professor Henry Peck, although not one of the Rescuers, went to jail with them and became their spokesman.

Courtesy of Oberlin College

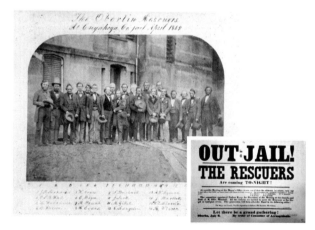

This photo of the Rescuers in the yard of the county jail was published in numerous newspapers throughout the country and rallied millions of northerners to their cause.

Hastily printed broadsides such as this were posted throughout Oberlin and Wellington on the day the Rescuers were released from prison and scheduled to return home.

Courtesy of Oberlin College

In this composite photo/illustration of the Union high command, President Lincoln is surrounded by his top generals and admirals. Sherman is to Lincoln's right and Grant is to his left.

Courtesy of the University of Notre Dame

This popular photo of General William Tecumseh Sherman shows him as the much-heralded Union General just three years after what appeared to be the end of his career selling corn at a road stand in 1858.

Courtesy of the University of Notre Dame

Sherman rapidly became one of the Union's most successful generals. He is seen here on horseback during the campaign to capture Atlanta, Georgia, in 1864. That victory was followed by his infamous "march to the sea."

Courtesy of the University of Notre Dame

Sherman's image as the tough, despotic general seems betrayed by his gentle artwork, such as these drawings of a bird and a tent. Sherman enjoyed sketching and was an accomplished artist.

Courtesy of the University of Notre Dame

This is one of the last photos of a clean-shaven abolitionist John Brown. It was taken before the Missouri raid in which he and his men freed numerous slaves and took them to Canada.

Courtesy of the Kansas State Historical Society

Brown grew a beard just before the Missouri raid; those who saw him said the long, flowing white beard gave him the look of a Biblical prophet.

Courtesy of the Kansas State Historical Society

Mary Brown with two of Brown's twenty children.

Courtesy of the Kansas State Historical Society

One of John Brown's final acts on his way to be hanged for his raid on Harper's Ferry was to kiss a black child. The image helped to make Brown a martyr throughout the North.

Courtesy of the Kansas State Historical Society

them that Jesus Christ was with them, and that he was a higher law than the District Court of Northern Ohio, and that prompted lengthy cheering from the crowd. Ralph Plumb climbed onto the box and said the people of the United States would never submit to the Fugitive Slave Act and the crowd roared again.

By then, a number of people in the crowd had become agitated. "Let's tear the old jail down!" several shouted. The police feared a riot and so did many in the crowd. Suddenly, an unknown man whose coat was decorated with numerous pink ribbons climbed on to a box on the outside of the fence and very calmly announced that the marshal requested everyone to turn around, form an orderly procession, and leave. Remarkably, they did, preventing what might have been the largest riot in the history of the United States.[428]

On May 30, to the disappointment of the jailed Rescuers, the Ohio State Supreme Court again ruled in favor of the prosecution. By 3–2, the court upheld the Fugitive Slave Act. Chief Justice Swan, aware of the overheated political climate, wrote, "I must refuse the experiment of initiating disorder and governmental collision, to establish order and evenhanded justice."[429]

The news depressed antislavery proponents throughout the state. When they heard of the decision, several ministers in Painesville, Ohio, ordered their church bells tolled slowly all afternoon to mourn the decree.[430]

The imprisoned Rescuers received word of the defeat that evening. "I suffered more on that dreadful night than I did when my dear firstborn died in my arms," said Henry Peck.[431]

Let down by Governor Chase, the prisoners realized that they had no backing from any political leaders in the Midwest, Democrat or Republican. The country's leading Democratic senator, Stephen Douglas of nearby Illinois, urged everyone to obey the fugitive slave statute because it was the law. He wrote to a newspaper editor, "It is the duty of Congress to pass all laws necessary to carry that provision [Fugitive Slave Act] into effect; no act calculated to render that provision inoperative can ever receive my approval." Douglas had no love for the supporters of the Rescuers either. He called Rep. Giddings "the high priest of abolitionism."[432]

The Rescuers expected that admonishment from a Democrat, but not from Abraham Lincoln, the leader of the new Republican Party in Illinois. Lincoln, who had thrilled abolitionists in Ohio with his scalding "house divided" speech in June at the start of his 1858 Senate campaign against

Douglas, wrote Chase that he disagreed with Ohio Republican pledges to overturn the Fugitive Slave Act. In the letter Lincoln said, "I have no doubt that if [it] be even introduced into the next Republican National Convention, it will explode it," and added that "the cause of Republicanism is hopeless in Illinois if it be in any way made responsible for that plank."[433] Lincoln also coldly disavowed the crusade to help runaways, telling Columbus lawyer Samuel Galloway that it was illegal. "They [the Rescuers] are viewed by many good men, sincerely opposed to slavery, as a struggle against and in disregard of, the Constitution itself," Lincoln said.[434]

The court ruling meant that Bushnell would have to spend sixty days in jail. Langston would have to serve twenty days. It brought the fourteen Oberlin Rescuers to a crossroads. Should they remain in prison in their show of defiance, and then risk prison terms when convicted, as they surely would be, or give up the fight and go home? The judge announced that the court calendar had ended for the spring and that the Rescuer trials would not resume until July, two months away, or even later in the summer. Each man would be tried individually and the proceedings could drone on into the following winter or even the spring of 1860. Following much debate, the men decided to remain in jail, certain that they could do more for the cause in prison than out of it.

The lawyers for the Rescuers continued their campaign to have charges against them dropped by pressing their own accusations against the abductors of John Price under Ohio's kidnapping law. In early May, they managed to have the Kentuckians arrested and held in jail for several days. In June, they forced the state to bring the kidnappers to trial, where they, too, would face prison terms.

The legal crusade against the kidnappers was just one of the troubles the government faced. The trial, the rallies, and the continued defiance of the Rescuers had attracted enormous national newspaper coverage, most of it attacking the government. Assistance for the Rescuers was no longer local. They were being sent money from all over the country, ministers were leading congregations in prayer for them throughout the Northern states, and tiny weekly newspapers were reprinting the Rescuer stories from the large city dailies; almost all were supportive. A group photo of the Rescuers in the prison yard, defiant as always, was published in numerous newspapers and further strengthened their support around the country. Groups of small children visited them with parents and schoolteachers. It was clear to everyone that all of the men were going to be found guilty and given jail terms, and with each verdict there would be more bad publicity. The federal government began to look for a face-saving way out of the uproar it had created. The Oberliners had become far more trouble to the continually embattled government of James Buchanan than they were ever worth.

ᐧᑌᐧ

VICTORY

The way out came during the first week of July. The kidnappers realized that they might go to prison for substantial periods of time if their trial was heard in front of a jury full of antislavery fanatics determined to seek revenge for the Rescuers' trials—as the defense team assured them they would. The Kentuckians announced that they would not appear as witnesses in any more of the Rescuers' trials in exchange for a deal. They received it. The federal government agreed to drop all charges against the remaining fourteen Rescuers and the state government agreed to dismiss the charges against the kidnappers. The Rescuers could go home.

After thanking their jailers for their goodwill and saying good-bye to fellow prisoners, the tired Rescuers took two somber final steps before leaving the Cuyahoga County Jail after their eighty-five-day stay, happy in the knowledge that the man they saved the previous autumn, John Price, had now established a new life for himself—free—in Canada. They held a prayer service, led as always by Henry Peck, and then issued a statement to let the federal government know of their view toward fugitive slaves in the future, now that they knew how harsh the government could be. Defiant to the end, they wrote that "hereafter, as heretofore, [we will] help the panting fugitive to escape from those who would enslave him."[435]

The Rescuers were released at five o'clock in the afternoon on July 6, 1859, to the cheers of hundreds of supporters gathered outside the walls of the prison; one hundred cannons on the shores of Lake Erie fired a thunderous salute to them. The editors of the *Cleveland Plain Dealer* prepared to admit in their columns the next day that the Rescuers had won. The now ex-prisoners, incarcerated for nearly three months, walked to the train station behind a large and boisterous band that played "Yankee Doodle."

By the time their train arrived home in Oberlin, town officials had organized a historic welcome. More than six thousand people, the entire population of the town, turned out at the train station to greet them. The crowd was so large that it extended up the tracks. "Joy beamed in every eye," noted James Fitch as the train slowed to a halt. As it approached Oberlin, the engineer was careful not to hit the hundreds of people swarming around and across the tracks. When the train came to a stop, Professor James Monroe gave a short speech from a platform between cars and told them, "We have never, for a moment, ceased longing for the sight of your faces among us."[436]

A large band played for the Rescuers as they were led down the streets of Oberlin toward the Quaker meeting house for a formal ceremony. Uniformed firemen lined the parade route and small chidden threw flowers at the feet of the Rescuers as they walked, waving their arms in triumph, cheered on by multitudes at every block.

The jubilee continued at the large white clapboard meeting house at the village green where a choir of 125 singers had been assembled in just a few hours for the event. The celebration in the meeting house was long and rousing, lasting until midnight. Public officials and leaders of the antislavery movement spoke, as did some of the Rescuers and members of their families. Father John Keep, speaking for many, told them that what they had done was legendary and that they were "the friends of human freedom."

The assemblage passed a hastily written resolution to remind the nation of their resolve. It underscored the residents' "determination that no fugitive slave shall ever be taken from Oberlin either with or without a warrant, if we have power to prevent it." And then, near midnight, the residents of Oberlin, who filled every square inch of the meeting house, accompanied by every available instrument in the building and the energetic choir, sang the "Marseilles" with all of the passion and strength their lungs could muster.

"No mortal would ever hear it again as it was heard that night," wrote a young girl who had been there that evening.[437]

The rescue of John Price, and the well-publicized prison ordeal of the men involved in it, had an enormous impact in Ohio and across the country. Their actions showed Congress and the nation that the Underground Railroad was stronger than ever, that the *Dred Scott* decision was not going to be effective, and, concerning the thousands of people who visited the Rescuers and attended rallies for them, that there was a pent-up public fury against slavery that was far deeper than anyone had believed.[438] The rescue, reported in mainstream newspapers all over the country, gave new life to the antislavery movement, whose opponents had hoped would be crushed by the combination of the 1856 election of James Buchanan, the *Dred Scott* decision, and the proposed proslavery Lecompton Constitution for Kansas. William Lloyd Garrison, the editor of *The Liberator*, wrote Oberlin's James Monroe that the incident "gave fresh impetus to our noble cause."[439]

THE WHITE HOUSE

OCTOBER 1858

During October, the last month of the 1858 political campaigns, the White House threw caution to the wind in its efforts to sink Stephen Douglas in Illinois, and decided to do it by any means possible. President Buchanan had used the phrase "honor" throughout the campaign, continually reminding leaders of both the Democratic and Republican parties that he would not engage in underhanded tactics in any race. Yet, as the historic debates in the Illinois Senate race between Democrat Stephen Douglas and Republican Abraham Lincoln ended in the middle of October it became obvious to all that the White House was willing to do anything to defeat Douglas.

The president never said a word about the unscrupulous campaign against the Little Giant, but everyone seemed to know that he was the one directing the attacks. The White House increased the tempo of its "dump Douglas" campaign because Lincoln had performed well in the debates. Lincoln had pinned Douglas down, forcing him to admit that he was just as much in favor of prohibiting slaves in the new territories, if the residents so chose, as he was in favor of slavery, if the residents so chose. Lincoln had also proved to the tens of thousands of Illinois voters who went to the debates, and to millions around the country who read about them in the newspapers, that he was the Judge's equal as a debater, politician, and prospective U.S. senator. Lincoln, an underdog at first, had made up significant ground and in the campaign's fading days had pulled even with Douglas in the race. Now was the chance, the White House decided, to aid Lincoln's surge with a growing shadow campaign of duplicity and skullduggery.

The president, who felt the Oberlin abolitionists should be dealt with quickly and severely, threatened any Democrats who supported Douglas, reminding them that the president's powers in patronage, federal funds, and political support could wreck their careers if they did not follow strict instructions from the White House. Buchanan was blunt, telling operatives around the country about the Douglas defectors, "I shall deal with them after the election as they deserve."[440]

Men who supported the president in his battle with Douglas were given railroad agent jobs so they could travel from town to town in Illinois to denounce the Little Giant. Friends sent him names regularly and reminded him that the prospective agents were authentic Douglas haters. The rail agents were even quoted in recommendation letters to the president. Buchanan's friend, Isaac Sturgeon from St. Louis, in recommending a man name George Coles, told the president that Coles had publicly called Douglas "the basest traitor of our party."[441]

The administration located men from ethnic backgrounds to speak out against Douglas in Illinois's many immigrant conclaves. Sturgeon advised Buchanan to fire Douglas's officeholders throughout Illinois and replace them with administration men, but Sturgeon insisted that the new appointees' ethnic background should match the largest ethnic groups in the area. In one area, he recommend Henry Oaverstabz, a German; he wrote the president, "We have the Irish vote. We must court the German vote." Roman Catholics were recruited to criticize Judge Douglas in Illinois communities with heavy Catholic populations.[442]

During the final month of the campaign, local operatives told the president which postmasters in Illinois sided with Douglas in the feud with the president and urged their removal, often suggesting strong administration supporters to replace them. One operative wrote, "The P.M. at Belleville, Ill., is a decided enemy if not really abusing his position. Trust no time will be lost in giving [a job] to Mr. Casper Thiell."[443]

Sturgeon urged the president to publicly attack any Democrats who wavered in their support of the attack upon Douglas. "We can not—dare not—sustain Douglas in his charges against the Administration," he insisted.[444]

It also appears that the administration coerced newspaper editors in Illinois and elsewhere by buying additional political ads if the paper came out for Lincoln against Douglas or urged its Democratic voters to stay home on election day.[445]

Democratic newspapers around the country that supported the president were urged to run stories that were critical of Douglas, branding him a closet Black Republican or worse, a closet abolitionist. It was rumored in these stories that Judge Douglas was constantly meeting with Republican Party leaders and that he might abandon the Democrats to join the Republicans as soon as the elections were over. Democratic papers in Illinois then reprinted these stories to hurt Douglas's chances.[446]

And so, by October, as the voters of Illinois were deciding whether to return Judge Douglas to Washington or replace him with Abraham Lincoln, the White House crusade to undermine the Douglas campaign was at full throttle. The underhanded program was doing so well, in fact, that with just weeks to go before election day James Hughes, another of the president's operatives in Illinois, wrote Sturgeon of the "dump Douglas" effort with great satisfaction that "we are getting along very well, and that we have most cheering news from all parts of the state. You will have seen that the president has gone to work in earnest, 'chopping off' heads in this state."[447]

President Buchanan was confident that his lieutenants in Illinois could defeat Douglas, and in so doing deny him the 1860 presidential nomination. All that remained now was to somehow derail the presidential ambitions of New York Senator William Seward, the certain Republican presidential candidate in 1860, so the Democrats could retain the White House.

Chapter Twelve

WILLIAM SEWARD: THE "IRREPRESSIBLE CONFLICT"

William Seward, smiling and nodding to people in the crowd, sat comfortably on his chair on the stage of Corinthian Hall in Rochester, New York, on a Monday evening, October 25, 1858. It had been windy and raining all afternoon. A drizzle still fell on the city as several thousand people shuffled into the building to hear the famous New York senator, whom everyone expected to be president in 1860. Seward was about to give one of his traditional fire-and-brimstone stump speeches for the Republican candidate for governor of New York, Edwin Morgan. The speech was one of many planned for dozens of Republican rallies held that week as the gubernatorial campaign headed into its final phase.[448]

Certain that Morgan would win handily, Seward, who was not up for reelection in 1858, had at first declined any interest in the campaign and went to Niagara Falls in September for an extended vacation with his family. Party leaders begged him to stump for Morgan, though, as the race tightened and a third, and then fourth, party nominated other candidates, creating a wide-open, four-way contest. He decided that it would be wise to leap into the race to clinch the governor's mansion for Morgan and perhaps claim credit for a Republican sweep.

Seward had been introduced to the local political leaders on the platform earlier that night and waited his turn to address the crowd. It was one of hundreds of platforms he had shared with other Republicans. One of the most recent had been Abraham Lincoln of Illinois, who he joined at a rally in Boston a few weeks before.[449] The rain and wind caused problems with the lighting system and at first it was difficult for those in the crowd to see Seward because the lamps in the auditorium flickered from time to time.[450]

Seward, who had arrived in town earlier that day by train, had no doubts about the speech he was about to deliver. It would be the New York senator's traditional antislavery storm, full of thunder and bravado, denouncing the slavers and their supporters in Congress, embracing the support of God and the people in his cause to free the slaves, and ending with a call for the people to rise up, vote Republican, and send the hated Democrats home where they belonged. An advertisement the local Republicans ran in the Rochester newspapers that day to draw a crowd heralded the presence of one of the most famous men in America and promised a speech "which will be read throughout the country and exert a great influence in the present crisis of our affairs."[451]

It was yet another speech he hoped would convince everyone in the United States that he was a staunch leader of the antislavery movement with no qualms about his radical position. There had always been doubts. The friends of the antislavery movement and all the other liberal groups that Seward had championed over the years appreciated his support, but always wondered if he defended them out of pure belief in their cause or as yet another means to further his own gargantuan political ambitions.

Those ambitions had worried many in the antislavery movement and the new Republican Party. Some had accused him of being a puppet of New York's conniving political boss, Thurlow Weed. Massachusetts's Daniel Webster had called Seward "subtle and unscrupulous." South Carolina author William Grayson called him "a sly schemer." Mississippi senator Henry Foote thought him ruthless and labeled him "cold and unexcitable." Many called the senator a cynic.[452] Senators said that he was "bedeviled" about party loyalty and could never be trusted to vote with the organization. In the winter, when his friend Jefferson Davis had come so close to death, Seward acknowledged to him and his wife that he never really had convictions about what he said in public. Just four months earlier, in July, he wrote abolitionist Theodore Parker that the fierce commitment of the abolitionists to their cause always surprised him. "It is strangely true that they believe what they write themselves," he wrote him, almost in amusement.[453]

Tonight was also another chance to sting his critics, and there were many. He wrote a friend about those who savaged him of "the malice of a thousand political assassins who undertake that job."[454]

SILVER-TONGUED SEWARD

William Henry Seward had become, by the autumn of 1858, one of the country's most spellbinding orators, a man who could hold the attention of any crowd for hours—uneducated country farmers or college graduates. In public appearances he carefully described the "slave power" domination of American politics, noting that from the White House on down to clerical jobs, politicians who sympathized with the slaveholding Southerners dominated the government, even though the number of states with slaves, and their populations, constituted a minority of the American nation and people. He loved to read off a lengthy statistical analysis that showed that one-half of the men appointed to federal jobs were from the South, even though that region made up only 33 percent of the population.

Seward's speeches were not only well written but organized, permitting him to begin his remarks slowly and lead his audience to a crescendo at the conclusion. They were all laced with the history of his topic, whether loud indictments of slavery or pleas for a national railroad or better pay for the working man. He was a master of language, able to craft his phrases carefully, and used colorful words to drive home his point. Whether speaking to a group of legislators in the well of the U.S. Senate or in front of a crowd of twenty thousand farmers at an outdoor gathering, William Seward was the country's most gifted speaker, so mesmerizing that people rode on trains and wagons for miles to hear him. Tonight in Rochester he would work his oratorical magic once again to get Edwin Morgan elected governor.

Ironically, when Seward was younger he dreaded speaking in front of people. He could not put words together and suffered from intense stage fright. He was a brilliant student at Union College in Schenectady, New York, but his one weakness, a professor there wrote of him, was "his inability to speak in public."[455]

In the Senate, he was ineffective at first, his public responses spoken, one man wrote, "like clanging oracles into the night." He was such a disappointing speaker that for several years he preferred to hand out copies of his speeches to reporters rather than deliver them. Years of speeches in the

Senate and stumping for Whig—and later Republican—candidates on the campaign trail gradually turned him into a fine orator, even though at times his style was peculiar.

One observer wrote of his speaking ability, "His voice was harsh and unpleasant, and his manner extremely angular and awkward…[yet] I at once observed that he commanded the attention of the Senate." Diplomat Charles Francis Adams wrote of Seward's oratorical style that at first it did not seem impressive, yet "he had in a remarkable degree the faculty of fixing the hearer's attention—the surest test of oratorical superiority."[456]

Like all politicians, Seward developed standard speeches on certain topics and improved his arguments over the years. Tonight in Rochester he would deliver the same basic antislavery talk he had given many times before, as early as 1848 in Cleveland and later in the Senate in 1850, Buffalo in 1855, Auburn in 1856, and in the Lecompton debates just a few months earlier, in only slightly different language. [457] In Buffalo, as an example, he framed the contest as the "tyranny of slaveholders over the non-slaveholders."[458] In Albany in 1855, he told a crowd that slavery "will be overthrown either peacefully and lawfully under the Constitution or it will work the subversion of the Constitution, together with its own overthrow."[459]

Everyone expected oratorical melodrama from Seward as well. Senator Henry Wilson of Massachusetts wrote later, "There is scarcely a prominent orator or writer in the Republican ranks who does not go as far, or further, than Mr. Seward."[460] Tonight he would add a phrase and an argument, though, that would make the speech not only a national sensation, but one of the most important speeches in the history of the United States.

A handsome man, Seward was a portrait of fashion as he sat on the stage of the hall waiting to be introduced. The New York senator was thin, slight, about five feet eight inches tall, with sloping shoulders, sandy hair that had been red when he was younger, large ears, a slightly recessed chin, bushy eyebrows over blue gray eyes, and a hawklike nose. His small frame enabled tailors to dress him well. He favored the most expensive suits from the best stores in New York, white shirts and large, dark cravat ties. The senator insisted on buying suits and appropriate clothes when he started college, beginning a feud with his father over clothing that lasted all of his college years. [461] He never understood why his father, Sam, a successful merchant, landowner, and real estate speculator, preferred simple clothing. With

Seward, as always, was his treasured silver snuff box that he used frequently, a yellow handkerchief, and his signature unlit cigar, that he held nimbly in his fingers as he spoke. [462]

Corinthian Hall was jammed for the speech. A correspondent for the *New York Times* wrote that the hall was "crowded to excess" and a reporter for Thurlow Weed's *Albany Evening Journal* said it was "an immense meeting."[463]

ᗧ

SEWARD AND WEED: POLITICAL TWINS

Seward had come a long way since the day he first met Thurlow Weed. Seward was elected to the New York state senate in 1830; at twenty-nine, he was one of the youngest members in its history, and there became an ally of Weed, already one of New York's most powerful political bosses. Weed, a tall, brazen man with a natural inclination for writing and politics, had become the editor of the *Albany Evening Journal,* one of the state's most influential newspapers. Weed used the pages of his newspaper, located in the state capital, to become a political powerbroker and, within a few years, the indisputable boss of the Whig Party.

Weed first met Seward in 1838. He liked Seward right away because he held the same political views as the party boss. He said of the young state senator that he was "strong and earnest in exposing and denouncing misrule… in sympathy with the masses."[464]

Horace Greeley, editor of the *New York Tribune,* a friend and later foe of the party boss, saw Weed as a man who accomplished his goals but was certainly not a deep thinker. He said the boss was "coarser mold and fiber, tall, robust, dark featured, shrewd, resolute, and not overscrupulous. [He is] keen sighted, though not far-seeing."[465]

A Weed-Seward-Greeley triumvirate began in 1838, when Weed and Seward convinced Greeley to spend the campaign publishing a propaganda Whig newspaper, the *Jeffersonian,* to get Seward elected governor. The three were kindred spirits, devoted to liberal causes, hard workers, and men determined to remake the United States and to eliminate slavery.

Weed always said that he and Seward were political twins. Weed wrote that Seward possessed "unmistakable evidences of stern integrity, earnest patriotism, and unswerving fidelity. I saw also in him a rare capacity for intellectual labor, with an industry which never tired and required no relaxation, to which was added a purity and delicacy of habit."[466]

The two men seemed like brothers to those who knew them. Each savored a good joke, enjoyed life to the fullest, loved children, studied history, admired businessmen, appreciated literature, especially the works of Charles Dickens, and enjoyed talking politics endlessly. They relied on each other, as Seward acknowledged in a note to his mentor in 1850, "I need your advice every day and your help in many things." They were so alike that someone who knew both men remarked, "Seward is Weed and Weed is Seward."[467]

The Seward-Weed alliance to advance Seward's career began badly when Seward lost the gubernatorial race in 1834 and considered not only quitting state politics, but moving to faraway Michigan for a new start in life. [468]

Weed talked him out of leaving. Four years later, in 1838, Seward became governor. By that time he had more experience, a track record in the state senate, and the backing of Weed's ever-growing political machine. For Seward, it was the start of a long career of public service and national politics as a Whig and then a Republican. Right away, Weed saw the clever and intelligent Seward not only as the perfect political figure for his well-oiled political machine, but also as a man who might be elected president of the United States.[469]

SEWARD IN THE SENATE

The 1848 campaign was fruitful for Seward. He stumped for Whig candidates throughout the country, telling the boisterous crowds he addressed that slavery "can and must be abolished, and you and I can and must do it."[470]

In March 1849 the U.S. Senate seat became available, and with the help of Weed, Seward scrambled to win it. Seward had enemies within the Whig Party and they tried to derail his crusade for the seat. Offering several other candidates, they charged that Seward was too radical on slavery and questioned his devotion to the national ticket. Weed, jockeying feverishly behind the scenes, made deals, twisted arms, and lined up votes for his friend and disparaged the skills and experience of Seward's opponents. Seward wrote several letters reiterating his desire to maintain harmony between

North and South. He wrote James Watson Webb, a friend of the president, that he was not a radical on slavery who would hurt the moderate position the party had taken on the issue.

"I shall labor by free, and kind, and peaceful discussion to form public opinion and direct it to a constitutional, lawful, and peaceful removal of it," he said of slavery, but added quickly that he viewed a Southern state's decision to continue slavery, if it so desired, as "sacred."[471] On February 6, the New York state legislature put Seward in the Senate by a lopsided 121–32 vote.[472]

Right after he was elected, he received advice from one of his former professors at Union College, Elihu Nott, whom he relied upon all of his life. Nott reminded him that he had been elected as the champion of the "poor man's rights" and should always hold that position. "The die is cast," Nott said prophetically of his election and political views. "You have crossed the Rubicon and there is no re-crossing it."

His college mentor warned him too, as did Weed throughout his life, that his stand on slavery and assistance for the downtrodden would always engender animosity from Southern slavers; they would not change their view of him no matter what he did or said. So, Nott and others told him, he had to simply ignore them. [473]

Few people arrived in the U.S. Senate so well known, or with as many supporters and detractors, as William Henry Seward in the winter of 1849. The former governor of New York was welcomed enthusiastically by the antislavery forces in Congress, who immediately saw the much-publicized politician as a leader for their cause. He was also embraced as the champion of the underdog, the immigrant, and the blue-collar worker. "Probably no man ever yet appeared for the first time in Congress so widely known and so widely appreciated as William H. Seward," wrote Horace Greeley. [474]

His enemies could not stand the sight of him in the Senate chamber. The Democrats, Whig conservatives, and Southerners of both parties were alarmed by his radical views on the slavery issue and feared that his political skills might turn many others in Congress against the institution, too. They resented his constant remarks that the slaveholders permitted no one to disagree with them. "There is nowhere in any slaveholding state personal safety for a citizen, even of that state itself, who questions the rightful national domination for the slaveholding class," Seward said. Even more, they resented what they saw as his insulting descriptions of their home states. He wrote of Virginia, as an example, "…an exhausted soil, old and decaying towns, wretchedly neglected roads, and in every respect an absence of enterprise and improvement…"[475]

The new senator not only had to balance his life between New York and Washington, but his personal life as well. His wife Frances had always complained that his busy law practice, political campaigns, and incessant scheming with Thurlow Weed had too often taken him away from her and their family. She complained again when he was elected to the Senate in 1849. Frances Seward, a decidedly non-political woman and mother of three, wanted to remain home in Auburn and was unhappy that she had to accompany her husband to Washington, a town where the political crowd would not only be larger and more contentious than in Albany, but right at her doorstep.

There were problems at home, too. Seward had three sons and a daughter, ranging in age from five to twenty-three. None of them were as intellectual or as emotionally focused as their father or maintained any interest in a life of public service. Augustus, the eldest at twenty-three, had begun an undistinguished career in the army. Recent college graduate Frederick seemed rudderless and had no interest in law. Willie, who was ten, had bad eyes, read little, and had no interest in school. Daughter Fanny's health was always tentative. And then, just after his election, Seward's cantankerous father died. Seward was named executor of Samuel Seward's extremely complicated estate, so complex that it was not completely settled until 1871, twenty-two years after Sam's death. His father had put all of the inheritance money for Seward's brothers, nephews, and nieces in trust; they became his wards and their care took up much of his time.

When he started his career in Washington in 1849, Seward, who was forty-eight years old but looked much younger, plunged into two interests that would consume his life—establishing himself as a noble-minded and hard-working public servant and promoting himself shamelessly. Publicity was natural for Seward, who had courted attention all of his life and, through his friendships with Weed and Greeley, always had plenty of it. Now on a national stage, he expanded his self-promotion, always trying to keep his name in front of the public in a favorable light and continually meeting new people from around the country who would help him do it.

He proposed bills, making certain that stories were written about them, socialized with editors of Washington newspapers and began lengthy correspondence with newspaper editors from different states, such as Schuyler Colfax of Indiana. Seward asked a friend to publish the transcript of a well-publicized recent murder trial in which he won acquittal for his client. He clipped out any newspaper articles that suggested he run for president in 1852 and forwarded them to Weed for publication in his papers. He even authorized the use of his name for publicity purposes on other men's business cards. All publicity was good publicity to Seward.[476]

The new senator realized quickly that he had stepped into a maelstrom of anger over slavery when he took his seat in the Senate in 1849. He wrote friend Hamilton Fish back in New York that the proslavery forces were bold and the moderation that their foes always exhibited was doomed to failure—aggressive opposition was needed.[477]

There was no doubt where the New Yorker stood on slavery in his first winter in the nation's capital. He had argued against it all of his life and constantly urged people to do the same. Just a year before his election to the Senate, he told a Whig county conclave in New York, "Real friends of emancipation must not be content with protests. They must act—act wisely and efficiently."[478]

He was tired of slaveholders and their supporters telling him that slavery would cease "in time." In one stirring moment in the Senate, he stood to say, "Slavery has existed here under the sanction of Congress for fifty years, undisturbed…the right time, then, has not passed…it must therefore be a future time. Will gentlemen oblige me, and the country, by telling us how far down in the future the right time lies?"[479] In one of the most dramatic moments in the history of the Senate, he rose and defiantly faced the Southerners in the chamber. At the end of a powerful speech, he said, "I simply ask whether the safety and interests of the twenty-five million free, non-slaveholding white men ought to be sacrificed or put in jeopardy for the convenience or safety of 350,000 slaveholders?"

Seward paused, looked left, then right, up at the crowd in the gallery, and then, a smug smile on his face, said, "I have no answer," and sat down.[480]

At the same time that he was becoming the leader of the antislavery cause in Washington, he had introduced and lobbied into law substantial antislavery legislation back in New York. He personally shepherded so many strong slavery bills through the New York legislature—via colleagues—that his own Whig friends there said he was turning it into an "abolition party." He was one of the financial contributors to Frederick Douglas's abolitionist newspaper, the *North Star.* Seward signed the bail bonds to free the rescuers in the well-publicized case of the runaway slave "Jerry" in Syracuse. He permitted the Underground Railroad in New York to use his Auburn home as a safe house and personally hid and fed dozens of runaway slaves there. Later, he would give famed slave rescuer Harriet Tubman a home on his property where she would live out the rest of her life.

What most Americans did not understand about Seward was that he not only saw slavery as morally wrong, but as a weakness of character that intellectually and emotionally crippled the entire nation. How could any country claim to be a great republic if it permitted slavery or kept out immigrants? This view had been argued by a few men since the 1760s, but never truly understood. Seward did not merely want to end slavery, but to elevate the American people in doing so.[481]

Seward was always able to separate his political and personal life. His most dogged enemies on the floor of the Senate, such as Henry Foote and Jefferson Davis of Mississippi, became close friends from it, as did Democratic vice president John Breckinridge.[482]

The New Yorker and his wife hosted numerous dinner parties to which they invited not only Northern congressional allies, but Southern firebrands whose view of the world was the direct opposite of Seward's. No expense was spared at these dinners; they were talked about for weeks afterward. Seward was a treasured guest at receptions and dinner parties hosted by the Southerners and never failed to win their personal friendship while at the same time being the target of their political animosity.

He managed to befriend those he opposed by dividing his life into personal and professional relationships and convincing others in the federal government to do the same. A toast he offered at one party was typical. Seward raised his glass to all and said, "May many such pleasant banquets as this hereafter occur among us, and may none of them be interrupted or rendered less agreeable by the introduction of sectional talk." When he finished, others at the party, Southerners as well as Northerners, applauded him. The Southerners easily separated their friendship with the affable Seward and their politics; in contrast, Seward always had difficulty doing that, certain that if a man liked him he would put up with his politics.[483]

THE COMPROMISE OF 1850 AND SEWARD'S "HIGHER LAW" SPEECH

All of Seward's feelings about slavery and fears that the antislavery forces were not strong enough tumbled forth in the debates over the Compromise of 1850, introduced by Henry Clay to restore harmony to the country. Under its terms, the slave trade was abolished in the District of Columbia, California came into the Union as a free state, new boundaries were set between Texas and New Mexico, and New Mexico and Utah were admitted to the Union as territories, with slavery unresolved. It also included a new fugitive slave law to permit owners to retrieve runaways. It was an opening salvo in a war that he would continue this night in Rochester in 1858. [484]

The Compromise produced soaring oratory. Everybody seemed to think that the Compromise called for their best verbal work. One of the finest speeches was delivered by Massachusetts's Daniel Webster, who uttered one of the most memorable lines in U.S. history when he rose and said, "I wish to speak today not as a Massachusetts man, nor as a Northern man, but as an American...I speak today for the preservation of the Union. Hear me for my cause!"[485]

Seward wanted to defeat the Compromise, telling other senators, "I think all legislative compromises [are] radically wrong and essentially vicious." But he wanted to bring California in as a free state too, which the Compromise would sanction. He wrote, "The storm is blowing, but when it has spent, we shall admit California just as if it had not rained at all."[486]

On March 11, Seward, his eyeglasses in one hand, began what would become a legendary address on slavery by ripping into the venerable seventy-year-old Henry Clay, whose desk was right next to his. "Now if Henry Clay has lived to be seventy years old and still thinks slavery is opposed only from such motives [sectionalism], I can only say he knows much less of human nature than I supposed," he said. The New Yorker then began a lengthy speech admiring parts of the Compromise, such as the end of the slave trade in the capital and the admission of California as a free state, but denouncing it as a whole because it continued to advocate slavery and included the fugitive slave law. He said of the fugitive law that it was "unjust, unconstitutional, and immoral."[487]

Seward began in a dry monotone that morning, as he always did, hoping for some self-inspiration. He still did not consider himself a very good public speaker in 1850 and neither did anyone else. The years in the Senate, and the political climate in the country, would change that perception. [488]

Moving forward slowly, Senator Seward said that the extension of slavery into new territories was abominable because it would subvert democracy. Turning up the rhetoric, his voice rising, he told his audience that they could not just listen to the voices of the people living in the territories now, but had to listen for the voices of those who would live there hundreds of years in the future. He said they were crying out, "The soil you hold in trust for us, give it to us free—free from the calamities and sorrows of human bondage."

The heart of his argument was a brilliant intellectual parry that he was certain would win the debate over slavery once and for all. For years, slave owners had argued that since slavery was lawful and protected by the Constitution it had to be respected. No one could break the law in order to eliminate or curb slavery. Even the staunchest abolitionists had agreed that slavery was legal and attempts to overthrow it were against the law. [489]

Seward's new argument changed the debate forever. The Constitution, he said, was pledged "…to union, to justice, to defense, to welfare, and to liberty. But there is a higher law than the Constitution, which regulates our authority over the domain, and devotes it to the same noble purposes. The territory is a part—no inconsiderable part—of the common heritage of mankind, bestowed upon them by the Creator of the universe. We are his stewards, and must so discharge our trust as to secure, in the highest attainable degree, their happiness…"[490]

Seward's "higher law" speech stunned the country. Abolitionists heralded it and saw it as a justification for attacks on every aspect of slavery, from aiding runaways to harassing slave owners and publishing virulent antislavery books, pamphlets, and speeches. Senator John Hale of New Hampshire, elected as an antislavery Free-Soil Party candidate, thundered in the Senate, "Shall the united and universal shout of a regenerated people go up in one strong, swelling chorus to the throne of the Most High, unmingled with the groans or prayers of the victims of oppression…?"[491] Tens of thousands of abolitionists even began to refer to themselves, as did the newspapers, as "the higher-law people." Seward's office was asked to mail out more than fifty thousand copies of the speech; friends sent out fifty thousand more. The American Antislavery Society printed up ten thousand copies. Greeley's *Tribune* published the entire speech as a special edition, distributing hundreds of thousands of copies. All of the Northern newspapers carried the speech and stories about it, plus letters about it for weeks. The speech was even printed in German for German Americans.

Approval in the North was loud. Catholic bishop John Hughes of New York said the force of its appeal would end slavery. Wrote one college professor, "You have revived the age of Burke. All his comprehension, his eternal truth is yours."[492] Greeley wrote in the *Tribune* that "Seward's speech will live longer, be read with a more hearty admiration, and exert a more potential and pervading influence on the national mind and character than any other speech of the session."[493]

Denunciation of the speech from the South was even louder. Clay and other Southern lawmakers criticized him, dozens of Southern clergymen wrote him insulting letters and governors and state legislators throughout the Southern states lambasted him in public and private. Wrote Clay, "Mr. Seward's latest abolitionist speech...has eradicated the respect of almost all men for him." Mississippi's Foote became so angry at Seward in the Senate, calling him the "counselor to bloodshed and violence," that his own party leaders had to tell him to tone down his language. [494]

The *Washington Republic* blistered Seward in its editorial columns, as did all of the Southern editors. The *New Orleans Picayune* called him "an unscrupulous Demagogue." The *Charleston Courier* said that Seward had "sunk...to his proper level."[495] None was harsher than Edwin Pollard, of the *Richmond Enquirer*, who wrote that the New Yorker was "a wretch whom it would be a degradation to name."[496]

Seward read all the criticism, but never waffled in his belief that he had delivered an important speech. He wrote Weed, "I know that I have spoken words that will tell when I am dead, and even while I am living, for the benefit and blessing of mankind, and for myself this is consolation enough."[497]

❧

CHAMPION OF THE ANTISLAVERY CAUSE

Ironically, the "higher law" speech would ultimately pale in comparison to the address he would deliver in Rochester this night. He must have remembered the clashes across the nation over the 1850 speech that night in Corinthian Hall as he got ready for yet another loud and public joust with the slaveholders.

The "higher law" speech, eight long years ago, had made it clear to everyone where Senator William Seward stood on the slavery question. He was not only against slavery, but had become the leader of the antislavery cause throughout the country. All of the other firebrands in the abolitionist movement were local ministers, newspaper editors, or state officials. Seward was a famous and highly influential United States senator, two-term governor, an increasingly proficient public orator, and a man from the largest state in the Union. He had influential friends and allies and spread his message through his newspaper contacts. His reference to God in his "higher law" speech had not only galvanized those who hated slavery, but made them realize that it was no longer just a political or moral issue, but a religious one. The combination of those three elements gave new life and strength to the antislavery movement, all exemplified by Senator William Seward.

All of a sudden, in the summer of 1850, the New Yorker had become the champion of all the different abolitionist movements and religious sects. Several abolitionist parties tried to convince him to leave the Whigs because their stand on slavery was far more in line with his. After all, they told him repeatedly, half the Whigs are proslavery. Seward refused all offers, reminding the leaders of these small splinter groups that the Whigs were one of the major parties in the country. He could accomplish his goals as a Whig; he could not accomplish them as part of a tiny ad hoc abolitionist group. He would not even attend abolitionist party conventions as a guest speaker or observer for fear that the public would paint him as one of them. [498] Turning down one invitation to speak to an abolitionist assemblage, he wrote New York abolitionist leader Gerrit Smith that he would continue to be a Whig whether or not the party triumphed in elections. "[Whigs] are firm, fearless, resolved in the hour of defeat…willing and yet capable to take the cause of freedom into its keeping." Yet Seward always acknowledged that the abolitionists made it possible for the radical Whigs, and later Republicans, to be as liberal as they were on slavery. He wrote a friend of the abolitionists that they "played a vital role in awakening the public conscience…opening the way where the masses can follow." [499]

The Kansas-Nebraska Act of 1854 changed Seward's life, and more than any single event it drove him toward his fierce antislavery politics. Slavery in the Southern states was distasteful enough, Seward believed, but a decision to expand it to the territories, which encompassed half the United States, was unthinkable. He warned, "We will engage in competition for the virgin soil of Kansas, and God give the victory to the side which is stronger in numbers as it is in right."[500]

⤳

THE REPUBLICAN PARTY IS BORN

The Whig Party collapsed the following year, 1855, because the proslavery half of its membership found that it could no longer work with the antislavery half on any issue, not just slavery. Its fall did not hurt Seward; in fact, the dissolution might have helped him. A brand-new national party, the Republicans, had formed to replace the Whigs; it also consolidated more than a dozen growing antislavery parties, such as the Free-Soilers. To the new party, Seward was an invaluable asset because, in addition to his antislavery views, he was well known for supporting public education, public funds for parochial schools, rights for immigrants, and federal assistance for the working man; he advocated economic development and social mobility, and yet, on the conservative side, preached government assistance for business. He appeared to have something for everyone in any party. And, unlike most of the other Republicans, he was famous.

By the time Seward joined the Republicans, he had honed his hot phrases against slavery into short bursts of invective that the antislavery Republicans cherished. As an example, while many radical Republicans would require thirty minutes to explain their view, Seward would simply wail that slavery was "morally unjust, politically unwise, and socially pernicious, in some degree, in every community where it exists."

He did it time after time, in rallies inside churches and halls in the winter and in front of large crowds at outdoor addresses in spring and summer. And each time he brought the throngs of merchants, farmers, craftsmen, and people of all walks of life to their feet, cheering every barb he tossed at the Democrats, every accusation against slavers, and any and all references to the Declaration of Independence or the Constitution. He had seized upon an issue, slavery, that seemed to galvanize an entire party and half of a nation. Others had spoken out against slavery, many as brazenly as he had, but somehow Seward had made it his issue and that issue had made him the very visible and very loud champion of the new political party.

Seward was, labor leader Carl Schurz wrote, "the intellectual leader of the antislavery movement."[501]

Some of the Republican bosses courted Seward, telling him that he would not only become the leader of the party but would surely be its presidential candidate in 1856. The New Yorker, who had been promoting himself tirelessly since his arrival in the Senate in 1849, believed he now had the White House within his grasp. He would be just as well known in the new party as he had been in the old, perhaps more so because he was now one of its highest-ranking members. The Republicans spoke with one voice against slavery, too. Until 1855, the men that the antislavery parties (the Liberty Party and the Free-Soil Party) did get elected to the Senate and Congress were against the institution but disagreed on an approach to eliminate it. The few Democrats and the ex-Whigs opposed to slavery faced the same quandary. Consequently, they could not agree on how to end it. The Republicans were all united on their plans to halt the spread of the institution and were far better organized. So in 1855, Seward joined the Republicans, who warmly welcomed the veteran campaigner, political strategist, and antislavery champion.[502]

How to leave one drowning party and jump to another without looking like a political traitor? Easily, decided Thurlow Weed, who cleverly managed to merge the New York wings of both parties into one, the Republicans, preserving the dignity of all the state's Whigs while at the same time anchoring them in the vibrant, liberal new organization.[503]

The New Yorker was very happy that he did so. The Republicans may have approved of slavery where it existed, for the moment, but they were defiant about allowing it to be extended to the territories. This viewpoint had become a staple of Seward's speeches and beliefs, along with his fear that slaveholders would soon completely dominate the federal government. Furthermore, he found far more support among the Republicans than he had among the old Whigs. Upon joining in October 1855, he told a Republican conclave in Albany that the party had a "new, sound, liberal platform...equal and exact justice." He saw the Republicans as salvation for a country under the heel of the slave empire. "It will rescue and save the country," he said. "So long as the Republican Party shall be firm and faithful to the Constitution, Union, and the rights of man, I shall serve it with...zeal and devotion."[504]

Seward had made the transition to successful Republican with so much ease that he paid little attention to a terrible feud involving himself, Weed, and *Tribune* editor Horace Greeley. The editor, who had political ambitions of his own, wanted to be the governor of New York and worked hard to win the Whig nomination in 1854. Weed did not see Greeley as a successful politician and crudely blocked his efforts, getting Henry Raymond, the editor of Greeley's rival, the *New York Times*, the nomination. Greeley, accusing both Weed and Seward of betraying him, split with the pair, never to be reunited.

The angry Greeley not only left the triumvirate, but did so in spectacular fashion, denouncing the pair in a scathing letter that was printed in the *Tribune* and reprinted in dozens of leading newspapers across the country. He charged that not only had he been betrayed by Seward and Greeley, but that during all the years he worked for them he was paid low wages, just $10 a week. He railed that he was constantly overlooked as Seward and Weed gave cushy, well-paying state and federal jobs to others and that he had lost all of his money backing corporate schemes they advised him to invest in that failed. Then, at the end of his rant, he charged them with guaranteeing him the party nomination for governor and instead handing it to "that little villain [Henry] Raymond, who is of no advantage to our party, and a man whom to know is to detest."[505]

In the spring of 1855, Greeley's abandonment seemed to matter little to Seward, but it would matter greatly in just a few years.[506]

Seward could have won the Republican nomination for president in 1856, but Weed cautioned against trying to capture it. The Republicans were too new, not very well organized and gave too much influence to the members who were nativists, men opposed to immigration, a cause that Seward had long championed. The Republicans had merged with the Know-Nothings, Free-Soilers, and other traditional antislavery organizations disdained in the South. The new party was hammering together a platform with many good policies: against slavery in the territories, for the transcontinental railroad and more money for river and harbor improvements. But the new platform also contained radical language accusing the Pierce administration of numerous crimes against humanity, such as murder, that seemed questionable to radical Republicans and ridiculous to moderates.[507]

Seward could win the nomination at the convention, where he had been warmly received, but Weed insisted he would lose the election to James Buchanan, the old political war horse the Democrats had nominated. Buchanan, who vowed to leave slavery alone, had traditional Democratic support in the North and, importantly, throughout the conservative South. The Republican nominee, especially if it was Seward, would run strong in the North, but not in the South. Weed and Seward agreed that he should wait four more years, when the Republicans would be far stronger and Seward an even more famous and powerful leader of the party.[508] Weed and Seward agreed the passive Buchanan would be an ineffective one-term president who would do little good or harm to the nation. For his own political future, Weed told the senator privately, Seward had to turn back any efforts to hand him the nomination; Seward wrote his wife that he agreed with Weed. Seward's other advisers felt Weed was correct, too. George Baker, the editor of his first book and now an adviser, was against it and so was John Schoolcraft, a New York congressman and counsel, who warned him that the Republican presidential race would be "unwise and unsafe, on the grounds that the election would be impossible."[509]

Seward, always under attack for his egocentric political behavior, did not want to say that publicly, so whenever asked about the nomination, he cleverly pleaded that he could not bend his beliefs, particularly those on immigrants, to win an office. "I would not modify them [his beliefs] to secure the Presidency," he told all with an air of admirable nobility.[510]

Weed had been right; the Republican nominee, explorer John C. Fremont, lost. Reporters wrote much about the charismatic John C. Fremont's dashing adventures and romantic good looks, but little about his stand on the issues. The Democrats howled that nominating someone who was not a public figure was absurd. One Democrat called Fremont a "poor ignoramus" and another charged that his only skills were that on his expeditions he had "subsisted on frogs, lizards, snakes, and grasshoppers and captured a wooly horse."[511]

Despite the ineffectiveness of their standard-bearer, the Republicans did come close to winning. They ran a campaign filled with huge outdoor rallies, torchlight parades, and soaring speeches by supporters of "the pathfinder." Illinois legislator Abraham Lincoln, as an example, tirelessly stumped across the Midwest for Fremont, delivering ninety speeches. Veteran politicians and journalists were astounded at the fervor of the Republican campaign and the ability of its organizers to get out the vote; 83 percent of eligible voters cast their ballots in the Northern states. The Republicans had turned traditional politics upside down and seemed on the rise everywhere.[512]

Their efforts were not enough, though, as Weed had predicted. As a new party, and with the loss of prospective radical voters to the third party, they could not marshal enough support to win. The American Party members, plus many Southern politicians such as Robert Toombs of Georgia, threatened to lead a secession movement if Fremont brought home the Southern states for Buchanan (Virginia governor Henry Wise said that if Fremont won he would raise an army of twenty thousand men, march on Washington, and seize the capital).[513] In fact, many Southerners feared the very radical American Party, the successor to the Know-Nothings, more than the Republicans and campaigned actively against them.[514] Fremont soon disappeared from the national stage, leaving Seward, without question, the front-runner for the 1860 race.[515]

SEWARD AND THE 1858 DEBATE ON SLAVERY

The road to Rochester this night in October 1858, a week before the elections, began in fine fashion ten months earlier on New Year's Day for William Seward. He sat in the kitchen of his home in Washington writing letters to family and friends while scribbling notes in a daily journal that he kept from time to time. He was buoyant because he felt his Republican Party was on the march and would capture both the House and Senate in the 1858 elections. He had written in his journal just a few weeks previously that "the Administration and slave power are broken; the triumph of freedom is not only assured, but near." Now, on the first day of 1858, a sunny one, Seward wrote, "It is a bright and genial day and I trust it may be auspicious of a happy new year."[516]

Outlined in the notes he went over on the platform at Rochester that night, Seward's ire over slavery probably began during the debates over Kansas's proposed Lecompton Constitution at the end of the recent winter. That constitution favored slavery in the territory. The Kansas debate was yet another example of the way in which Seward was seen as the leading public figure in the antislavery movement. Senator William Lowndes Yancey, one of the South's most respected political leaders, was by 1858 routinely referring to the Republicans as "Seward and his...party." Seward's office was deluged with letters from disturbed residents of Kansas and political leaders in the Midwestern territory who kept in touch with him as the violence there spun out of control and when the two constitutions were forwarded to Congress.[517]

All were convinced that the Lecompton debates would be important for the future of the institution of slavery because its passage as a proslavery document would set precedent for similar constitutions in all the other prospective states that would eventually be carved out of the western territories. All of the nation's leading newspapers published stories about the upcoming Senate deliberations weeks prior to opening of the Senate session. It was a critical moment in the year, and in history. The Democrats and Republicans both understood that. President Buchanan, in presenting the Lecompton Constitution, warned Congress that "dark and ominous clouds" were passing over the Union because of the strife in Kansas. Seward's aide George Baker wrote him that "slavery will be turned inside out this session as never before."[518]

To many, Lecompton would make all of 1858 a year of debate on slavery, from the halls of Congress to taverns in New England to general stores in Kansas. Buchanan knew that slavery would dominate his term when he took office, no matter how much he tried to downplay the issue. In his annual message, he said, "The great object of my administration will be to arrest, if possible, the agitation of the slavery question at the North, and to destroy sectional parties. Should a kind Providence enable me to succeed in my efforts to restore harmony to the Union, I shall feel that I have not lived in vain."[519]

On the Senate floor on March 3, Seward blasted President Buchanan for supporting the *Dred Scott* decision, once again flayed Southern slaveholders, and said he was fed up with the illogical Southern claim that cold-weather states like Kansas would become cotton empires. He lashed out that the move to make Kansas and other territories slave states "will only fail to be a great crime because it is impracticable and, therefore, will turn out to be a stupendous imbecility."[520]

Predictably, the speech was applauded by the Republicans and abolitionists and denounced by the Southerners. Senator James Hammond of South Carolina was irate that Seward, like all Northerners, treated the South as a defeated duchy. He railed that the South was home to millions of Americans and that its production of cotton made it a worldwide force. "No, sir, you dare not make war on cotton," said Hammond in one of the most quoted lines in history. "No power on earth dares make war upon it. Cotton is king!"[521]

President Buchanan was so piqued by the attack that he barred Seward from the White House. Chief Justice Taney was even angrier and boldly vowed that if Seward was elected president in 1860, as was anticipated, he would refuse to administer the oath of office to him.[522]

LIBERTY AND THE "IRREPRESSIBLE CONFLICT"

The four-way governor's race in New York, with added candidates from the People's Party and the American Party, infuriated Seward and Weed, who knew that they now faced more hard work than in any campaign of their lives to hold the state for the Republicans. The American Party was formidable in New York. Their gubernatorial candidate in the last New York election, Erastus Brooks, won 130,870 votes, 22 percent of the total votes cast. If their candidate this year, Lorenzo Burrows, did as well, draining votes from the Republicans, Democrat Amasa Parker could back his way into office.[523] Weed and his lieutenants spent the fall in an unprecedented drive to get out the vote. The pages of Weed's *Evening Journal* and other Republican papers in New York were filled with columns urging voters to go to the polls and publishing the locations of each polling place in each town in the state. Rallies were held in large cities and small villages, concluding with a mass rally in Albany just before the election. Efforts were made to win the ethnic vote, especially the German American vote.

The Republicans fought two campaigns that autumn, one traditional campaign against the Democrats and a second unconventional campaign against the American Party and Smith's People's Ticket. They rallied the people against the Democrats with the standard denunciation, but focused more on national issues than local ones, continually castigating the administration over its policies on slavery. The Republican leadership even cleverly put President Buchanan "on trial" in their newspapers and in campaign speeches, always finding him guilty.[524]

The battle to win the votes of the antislavery American Party and Smith's supporters might have been even more critical. The Republicans bluntly told those committed to both fringe parties that their votes would be wasted. "Every vote cast for the American ticket may render the Republican triumph the more difficult, but not less certain. The Republicans, unaided, can beat the Democrats; but with the votes of Americans who are in sympathy with the cardinal principles of the Republican party, the Democrats would be hopelessly overwhelmed."[525]

Weed lobbied the editors of the pro–American Party newspapers and convinced several to leave the Americans and embrace the Republican banner. A typical example was the small *Hornellsville National American* paper. The editor, announcing the switch in loyalty, asked his readers, "Shall he cast his vote where it can do no possible good, or will he give it where it will tell most in favor of freedom and of a pure franchise?" He wrote that the American Party advocates should think of the slavery issue, and not just the party that opposes it.[526]

The Republicans had much less success in trying to bring abolitionists from the new People's Ticket into their party. They had "made war upon the Republican Party," charged Weed.[527]

Finally, two weeks prior to the election, Weed and his lieutenants tried to arrange a convention at which the People's Ticket, the American Party, and the Republicans would all merge into one party that would serve as an umbrella organization for all the antislavery, anti-Democrat groups, to be called the Union Party. The small groups refused to attend and the effort failed (during the Civil War, Abraham Lincoln did the same thing, with great success).[528]

Weed's political machine supported Morgan, as did his newspapers. Horace Greeley, who had split with Weed and Seward in 1854, backed Morgan in his *New York Tribune*. Seward decided to end his vacation and stump up and down the state for Morgan because Morgan had to win, and by a big plurality, in order for Seward to become president in 1860. The senator realized that his support and personal campaigning would help Morgan. He had enormous political influence and he knew it, as did everyone else. Abolitionist leader Wendell Phillips wrote of him, "Seward is a power in the state…his position decides that of millions." Getting Morgan elected would prove that and establish Seward as an unbeatable candidate for the Republican presidential nomination.[529]

Seward had more support from the people in New York and other Northern states than ever for his antislavery policies in 1858. Throughout the year, he had received letters from many Americans around the country applauding his stand on slavery and denouncing the administration's. Wrote Cornelius Baker in a typical note, "If there were the least spark of humanity left in the powers that be, the African slave trade would be abolished."[530] In another, F. F. Brown wrote that when the senators are called upon to show their hand for or against freedom, "you will then be heard before the nation."[531]

So, on the evening of October 25 at Rochester's Corinthian Hall, with every seat filled and many more people standing in the side aisles and at the rear of the hall, a drizzle still falling outside, William Henry Seward rose from his seat and walked the few steps across the stage to the podium to a crescendo of applause. He had an unlit cigar in his hand so he could jab the air with it to make his point, as he always did.

This time he did not slowly build toward his theme, as was his usual custom. He began with a vituperative attack on the Democrats and slavery, like an angry gladiator, telling the cheering crowd that Southerners would not only continue the slavery of the black man, but would enslave the white man, too—if they could. He looked out at a crowd of mostly white men and women, sprinkled with some black freedmen, and quickly moved to one of his lifelong beliefs, that the slave system demeans the white worker as well as the slave and is destructive to mankind. He jabbed the air with his cigar and told the crowd, "The slave system is not only intolerable, unjust, and inhuman towards the laborer, whom, only because he is a laborer, it loads down with chains and converts into merchandise, but is scarcely less severe upon the freedman, to whom, only because he is a laborer from necessity, it denies facilities for employment, and whom it expels from the community because it cannot enslave and convert him into merchandise also."

He told the crowd that the slave system would wreck America. "It is necessarily improvident and ruinous because, as a general truth, communities prosper and flourish or droop and decline in just the degree that they practice or neglect to practice the primary duties of justice and humanity," he said, adding that they were "incompatible" and that "they never have permanently existed together in one country, and they never can."

Seward explained that most of the countries in the world had outlawed slavery by 1858 because not only was it immoral, but they found that the paid labor and slave labor systems could not function together in a society. Americans, he said, would soon discover the same thing; the nation was on a collision course.

And then, about one-third of the way into his speech, he tried out his new two-word phrase, "irrepressible conflict," to define his theme, that he assumed would merely highlight his remarks, nothing more.

It is, he said of slavery in America, "an *irrepressible conflict* between opposing and enduring forces, and it means that the United States must and will, sooner or later, become either entirely a slaveholding nation or entirely a free labor nation. Either the cotton and rice fields of South Carolina and the sugar plantations of Louisiana will ultimately be tilled by free labor, and Charleston and New Orleans become marts for legitimate merchandise alone, or else the rye fields and wheat fields of Massachusetts and New York must again be surrendered by their farmers to slave culture and to the production of slaves and Boston and New York become once more markets for trade in the bodies and souls of men. It is the failure to apprehend this great truth that induces so many unsuccessful attempts at final compromise between the slave and free states and it is the existence of this great fact that renders all such pretended compromises, when made, vain and ephemeral." The crowd roared at his new phrase.

The Democrats had become the nation's controlling party and had established a detestable record on slavery that would continue if they were not turned out of office. Seward charged that: 1. they would defeat any efforts to outlaw slavery in any of the new territories and permit them to come into the Union as slave states; 2. a Democratic president, with consent of the Democratic Senate, would annex numerous slaveholding foreign countries in Central and South America to increase the empire; 3. the Supreme Court, appointed by the Democrats, would nullify any antislavery laws passed by the states; and 4. eventually the Democrats would force now free states to accept slavery within their boundaries.

If that happens, Seward vowed, voice rising, he would leave the country. "I shall never be a denizen of a state where men and women are reared as cattle, and bought and sold as merchandise. When that evil day shall come, and all further effort at resistance shall be impossible, then, if there shall be no better hope for redemption than I can now foresee, I shall say with [Benjamin] Franklin, while looking abroad over the whole earth for a new and more congenial home, 'Where liberty dwells, there is my country.'"

He did not think that he exaggerated in outlining his fears, Seward told the crowd, because "the Democratic Party is inextricably committed to the designs of the slaveholders."

Seward then launched into a history of the opposition to show, he said, that "the history of the Democratic Party commits it to the policy of slavery." Two-thirds of the party consisted of Democrats from the Southern states, he noted, giving the slaveholders a constant majority within party ranks and the power to make the Democrats from the Northern states do their bidding. As an example, he cited President Martin Van Buren, of New York, the first Democratic president from a non-slave state. He said that the Southern Democrats forced the president to accept the existence of slavery in the District of Columbia in 1836. The Democrats insisted upon the admission of Texas into the Union as a slave state in 1845, Seward contended, and forced the nation to accept slavery in the territories of Utah and New Mexico, won in the Mexican War of 1846, as part of the Compromise of 1850. The Democrats deliberately ordered the Fugitive Slave Act as part of the Compromise. Finally, in 1856, when Seward claimed that the residents of Kansas wanted to bring their territory into the Union as a free state, President Buchanan and the Democrats backed efforts by a slaveholding group to ram a slave constitution down the throats of its citizens.

Charging that the Democrats had a "dark record," Seward then set off one more verbal explosion—his belief that the Democrats would soon bring back the African slave trade, overrunning the United States with Africans in chains. How to stop all of this? Defeat the Democrats and turn them out of power. He roared, "It is high time for the friends of freedom to rush to the rescue of the Constitution."

The senator spoke for nearly ninety minutes that evening to the captivated and increasingly angry crowd in Corinthian Hall. As he moved toward his conclusion, he added yet another bombshell to his "irrepressible conflict" scenario. Seward looked out at the crowd and said defiantly, "I know, and you know, that a revolution has begun. I know, and all the world knows, that revolutions never go backwards."

And then he predicted that the only solution to the slavery problem was "to confound and overthrow, by one decisive blow, the betrayers of the Constitution and Freedom forever."[532]

The crowd erupted in wild applause and foot stomping that lasted many minutes. People in attendance banged their chairs on the floor, slammed their hands against the backs of those next to them in triumph and shouted for the downfall of the hated Democrats.

The "irrepressible conflict" speech, plus a similar speech he delivered in Rome, New York, four days later, in which, a reporter said, he "was greeted by enthusiastic cheers, long continued and often repeated," caused a national uproar.[533] What Seward had done, the highly agitated Republicans said, was to finally define the feelings of everyone in the country who was opposed to slavery and could foresee, like Seward, how the evils of the slave trade would destroy the United States. The outraged Democrats charged that what Seward had really done was, in no uncertain terms, call for a Civil War that would divide and destroy the nation.

The Republicans said that Seward had predicted an unmistakable future if slavery was not halted and the Democrats howled that he had predicted an unmistakable calamity if Southerners did not do what the Northerners (and Seward) ordered. If the United States had been two camps prior to the Rochester speech, for and against slavery, they were now ready to take up arms and attack each other over the issue of slavery.

Those in Corinthian Hall were inspired by the speech. One man in the audience that night gushed in a letter to a Rochester newspaper a week later that Seward was the "champion of freedom" and described him as a knight of the Round Table. "There he stood, [patriotism's] calm and eloquent advocate, true to his mission—undaunted by the wrath of tyrants. I have long been acquainted with Mr. Seward, and have always found every emotion of his heart to be generous and noble. He will always be found on the side of the oppressed; a despiser of aristocracy and a hater of tyrants."[534]

Just as with his "higher law" speech, many Americans wanted copies of the Rochester oration. Hundreds wrote to him personally, and thousands more wrote the Republican Party, telling him they would be honored just to read it.[535]

One of Seward's advisers, George Baker, was thrilled by the Rochester oration. He sent copies of it to dozens of newspapers and told Seward that he should reproduce the speech in a pamphlet and publish thousands of copies, reminding him that it was "the keynote for the future contest [the presidency]."[536] The speech, Baker added, was "destined to save the Republican Party from self destruction and the country from the [evils] of slavery." He said of Southerners that "it was going to make the heathens rage more than any speech you ever made." Even former friend Greeley admired it, writing that "the speech will be pondered by every thoughtful man in the land."[537]

Seward's oratory was roundly lambasted in the South. Seward was called "wicked," "malicious," "the chief black Republican," and even "treasonous." His critics all said the same thing: the bombastic Seward was trying to create an irrepressible conflict where, they said, no conflict of any kind existed.[538] The *Little Rock (Ark.) State Gazette* called Seward "an unscrupulous politician." Vice President Breckinridge, who was from Kentucky, accused Seward of "trying to turf over a volcano."[539]

No one expressed the Democratic and Southern bitterness better, and with more anger, than President James Buchanan. He cried that the Republicans lacked convictions and that he was a "politician and not a statesman," and said that he used the speech to set a policy for the Republicans that none of them wanted except him. "He thus aroused passions, probably without so intending, which it was beyond his power afterwards to control. He raised a storm which, like others of whom we read in history, he wanted both the courage and the power to quell."[540]

Buchanan added that because Seward was certain to be the Republican nominee in 1860, all of his speeches carried great weight. His views were "reckless fancies," said the president. "[Southerners] believed or affected to believe that the people of the North, in order to avoid the dreaded alternative of having slavery restored among themselves, and have their rye fields and wheat fields cultivated by slave labor, would put forth all their efforts to cut up slavery by the roots in the southern states."[541]

The Republicans scoffed at Buchanan's complaints, but some, such as *New York Times* editor Henry Raymond, understood why Seward's "irrepressible conflict" idea stirred such feelings among slaveholders and "made his name an object of so much terror to the South."[542]

Regardless of the region, party affiliation, or stand on the slavery issue— or any issue—just about every newspaper in the country commented on the speech. Most reprinted the "irrepressible conflict" paragraph and many reprinted the entire speech. Some large papers printed the speech on one day and comments on it the next. Letters about it were published long after the election, some in 1859. Wherever people gathered to talk politics, the speech and the concept were argued for hours. For many Northerners and just about all Republicans, the speech and the phrase came to symbolize the North/South split. The national reaction to Seward's speech far outdistanced the public reaction to a similar stand taken by Illinois's Abraham Lincoln in his often-quoted "house divided" speech delivered earlier in the spring.[543]

Seward was shocked by the reaction to the speech, by both its admirers and detractors. It was the same speech he had given often—all of his adult life—and his description of the "irrepressible conflict," although a new and catchy phrase, was not that different in meaning from dozens of other speeches. "[No one] dreamed more than I did that this was a new, or bolder, piece of composition," he wrote abolitionist leader Theodore Parker of his surprise.[544]

Why was the electric speech so important then, if, except for a phrase or two, there was nothing radically different in it from the same speech he had delivered, in much the same form, for two decades?

First, by 1858 Seward had become the leading Republican in the country, just as he had been the leading Whig. The Republicans' ascension to the second most powerful party in the country in just three short years had startled the political establishment. Whatever Senator Seward said as the nominal head of this new party was important to all, Republican and Democrat, Northerner and Southerner.

[handwritten margin note: REPUBLICAN PARTY ESTABLISHED IN 1854]

Second, participants and observers of that autumn's political campaigns saw the elections of 1858 as critical to halt the Democratic Party, which many viewed as the slaveholders' party, and the time to give the Republicans a majority in both houses of Congress, plus more governors. The New York gubernatorial election of Morgan was central to those goals.

Third, control of both houses of Congress might lead to victory in the race for the White House in 1860 and Seward was the indisputable favorite to be the Republican candidate for president in that race, surely running against Stephen Douglas. Most Americans discounted the constant bellowing of slaveholders and their friends in Congress that the election of Seward would bring about secession; the Southerners had been braying about secession for twenty years and were still there.

Fourth, the antislavery movement was catching fire across the nation, from the arrests of the Rescuers in Oberlin, Ohio, to other public rescues over the last few years. Hinton Helper's controversial anti-South book, *The Impending Crisis,* was being read by thousands, the abolitionist newspapers were everywhere. Harriet Beecher Stowe's novel *Uncle Tom's Cabin* continued to sell well throughout the country and in Europe.

The election of 1858, then, was the natural stage for some politician from a major party to deliver a scalding speech that would inflame the masses against slavery, convince hundreds of thousands to join the crusade, and then carry that speaker to the White House. All the elements of politics aligned themselves that rainy night in Rochester, and were symbolized in William Henry Seward and his "irrepressible conflict."

∾

"SEWARD FOR PRESIDENT"

Morgan was elected governor by 17,440 votes over Democrat Amasa Parker, a far cry from the 65,000 plurality of Republican John King in the previous election. The narrower-than-desired margin did not surprise New York Republicans or party members across the country. There were several reasons why Morgan fell far short of King's plurality.

Most blamed the four-way race, claiming that without the American Party's Burrows and abolitionist Smith in the contest the radical Republican ticket would have fared much better, and it surely would have. Burrows won 61,157 votes and Smith had 5,446. The overwhelming majority of the antislavery American Party and People's Ticket votes would have gone to Morgan, giving him an impressive plurality of some 80,000 votes.[545] Some blamed a savage Democratic campaign designed to undermine Seward's national popularity. Others said the Republicans were still a new party and not as organized as they might be, especially in New York. Some argued that while Morgan had been a successful organizer as national chairman for the Republican Party, he was not a particularly marketable candidate. Some said that the Democrats were far richer than the Republicans in New York, funded by fat cats such as August Belmont of New York City.

Some blamed Horace Greeley, the influential editor of the *Tribune,* for abandoning Seward four years earlier. Greeley scoffed at that and blamed the "irrepressible conflict" speech for the slight margin of victory, arguing that the excessively liberal Seward had gone too far in the Rochester oration. Greeley said the sword-rattling speech was too much too soon and scared the moderate center of the electorate. He wrote that the Republican victory "is one of which we cannot feel proud; we should have won by 50,000."[546]

Weed did not see it that way. Victory was victory. Morgan had won, the Republicans wound up with twenty-eight of the state's thirty-three congressional seats, an increase from twenty-one in the last election, and gained control of the state assembly. What more could anyone ask? "The revolution is perfect—the triumph is complete," Weed declared in the *Evening Journal.* "It is, in all aspects, priceless and precious."[547]

Seward did not see it that way either. In the desk drawers of his homes in Auburn and Washington, and in his desk drawers at the Senate, he had letters from people all over the country applauding the "irrepressible conflict" speech at Rochester. Newspaper reporters and editors throughout the Northern states wrote that it was not only his best speech, and one of the best of the 1858 campaign, but one of the most brilliant speeches in American history.

The New Yorker knew, too, that the speech had won him the support of some of the most prominent Republican political leaders and operatives in the country, whose assistance would be invaluable at the 1860 presidential convention and subsequent national election.[548]

Governor Nathaniel Banks of Massachusetts called the New Yorker "a renowned statesman." Michigan governor John W. Longyear, whose support in the Midwest would be critical to Easterner Seward in the 1860 race, told him, "[You have devoted] your life, fortunes, and your sacred honor to the support of the contest of freedom against slavery." The governor of Wisconsin sang the New Yorker's praises to all, rhapsodically telling them that Seward was the equal of James Madison and Thomas Jefferson.

Politically connected judges who were also party leaders gushed in their enthusiasm for Seward after the speech. Judge John North of Wisconsin hailed Seward's "political integrity and profound statesmanship." Judge Aaron Goodrich of Minnesota applauded Seward for his "undying devotion to a righteous cause, transcendent genius…high moral daring."[549]

Newspapers, too, jumped on the bandwagon of the ever-growing "Seward for president" boom. Dozens declared him the front-runner and the editor of the *New York Times* wrote just prior to the 1858 elections that it was time to prepare for 1860 and Seward's nomination. The editor of the *Rochester Union and Advertiser* even wrote that Seward was *already* the Republican candidate for president.[550] The Democratic press coined a new term to meld radical Republicans and antislavery advocates together— "Sewardism."[551]

There was one more factor that convinced Seward he had made the speech of his life at Rochester and that his oration would propel him into the White House in 1860—he was now convinced that the people of the United States had finally caught up with him. For two decades, he had felt very much alone in public life as the enemy of slavery, a radical perched on a lonely limb. He never had enough congressmen and senators on his side to make him look like anything more than a maverick. Those who did side with him often would not say so publicly for fear of defeat by moderately minded electorates in most Northern states.

The speech reinvigorated many who had tired of the losing fight against slavery. T. C. Leland was one. He wrote the New Yorker of the Rochester speech that he was "fired by it with renewed indignation against our democratic aristocracy, with renewed admiration of your faculty for historical portraiture and graphic words" and said, like so many others, that Seward ought to be president in 1860.[552]

Old Whigs were behind him, too. One man scribbled "Whig Press Office" on his stationery and wrote Seward of the upcoming 1860 presidential election, "I hope the great party of freedom [Republicans] will then have a candidate whom they can work for, and that his name will be Seward."[553]

William Seward was no longer a solitary figure standing against slavery. Winning candidates from many states had now joined him in the cause, publicly as well as privately. The New Yorker's years as a maverick had ended; he had, in fact, become mainstream. He was not only his party's best public speaker, shrewdest political operative, and best-known public figure, but now he had an enormous following in his crusade against slavery. He was confident that the antislavery following would grow over the next two years and make him the president of the United States.[554]

He was so certain he would win the presidential nomination, then easily defeat Douglas in the run for the White House, that he left the operations of the party to underlings and embarked on a triumphal eight-month tour of Europe.[555] As his ship crossed the Atlantic and fellow travelers greeted the famous senator, William Seward was convinced that his historical "irrepressible conflict" speech that rainy night in Rochester, New York, would make him the next president of the United States.

He was wrong.

Chapter Thirteen

THE WHITE HOUSE

ELECTION DAY

E lection day 1858 was one of the darkest days in the history of the Democratic Party. The Democrats did retain their control of the Senate, by the narrowest of margins, but the Republicans swept the congressional elections, picking up a surprising twenty-one additional seats in the House, and reducing the Democrats' House seats in the Northern states by a sizable 40 percent (in that era, only half of the House stood for election each year). The Republicans won control of numerous state legislatures for the first time, including New York, Pennsylvania, New Jersey, Indiana, and Minnesota. They retained their existing majorities in Ohio, Michigan, Iowa, and Wisconsin.[556] In Minnesota, the Republicans gained control of both houses in the state legislature for the first time.[557] The Democrats won the majority of the state's eleven congressional districts in Indiana in 1856, but in 1858 the Republicans captured eight of the eleven (one of the Republican victors had switched from the Democratic Party).

In Ohio, the Republicans won fifteen of the state's twenty-one congressional seats, an increase of three, captured both houses of the legislature and the governor's mansion. Hamilton County, Ohio (Cincinnati), was an example of the Republican surge there and in the nation. The Republicans lost that county by 3,300 votes in 1857, but won it by 1,500 votes in 1858.

Overall, the Republicans won nearly two-thirds of the vote in the northwestern states; it was only in Illinois that their total was as low as 49 percent. The Republicans won two-thirds of the vote in the New England and northeast states, 61 percent in the east, west, and north-central states.

They worked to get out a record 81.6 percent vote in Massachusetts and not only won the state's senate and assembly, but took the governor's mansion as well. As expected, they lost in all of the Southern slave states. The vote was spread out over all of the congressional districts in which the Republicans won, enabling them to win some seats by large pluralities, but most by small ones, meaning victories in far more districts. This pattern of triumphs without rolling up landslide numbers permitted the Republicans to maintain control of these districts for the next fourteen years. [558]

∾

THE PENNSYLVANIA CAMPAIGN

There was no mere good fortune involved in the Republican sweep, just solid strategy and hard work. The brand-new Republican Party had stunned the Democrats in the 1854 and 1856 congressional elections, capturing nearly half the seats in the House of Representatives. The leaders of the new party determined that in order to gain control of the Senate and the House and win the presidency in the 1860 elections they had to capture the electoral votes of Ohio, New York, and especially Pennsylvania.

Pennsylvania was not only a Democratic state, but it shared a border with two slave states and was home to President Buchanan. Victory there was seen as the biggest challenge because nine of its southern counties—Adams, Cambria, Clarion, Cumberland, Fayette, Westmoreland, Wyoming, Northampton, and Northumberland—bordered Maryland and Virginia, both slave states, and thousands of Pennsylvanians in those counties did business in Maryland and Virginia and had relatives living there. Those counties had been solidly Democratic for years, and any Republican incursion there would be difficult. In fact, despite Buchanan's narrow victory in the state in 1856, the Democrats did maintain their majority in the state legislature, winning fifty-three of one hundred seats, and held on to fifteen of the state's twenty-five congressional seats. Wrote one Pennsylvanian later to Abraham Lincoln of the Democratic strength there, "I lived in Pennsylvania several years and without Pennsylvania's vote you cannot be elected president."[559]

The Republicans were not daunted and went to work on Pennsylvania immediately following the '56 election. They convinced several key Democrats to leave their party and join the Republicans; some brought hundreds of followers with them and, even more important, dozens of veteran campaign organizers who could help the Republicans in the 1858 elections. Fortunately for the Republicans, the popularity of the antislavery American Party in Pennsylvania slipped precipitously as the overwhelming majority of its members became Republicans; William Hazelhurst, the American Party's gubernatorial candidate in Pennsylvania in the previous year, 1857, polled only 28,000 votes, or one-third the number cast for the American Party's presidential candidate in that state in 1856.[560]

Beginning in the 1856 elections, the Republicans cleverly played up to the American Party by joining their campaign for tougher immigration laws to keep foreign criminals from arriving in America, but did not agree with their anti-Catholic stand in order to attract the thousands of Catholics in states such as Massachusetts, New York, and Pennsylvania.[561]

The Republicans' major issue was slavery, but the party's leaders knew that they could not succeed on a single campaign plank; they needed to become a full-service party that took a stand on dozens of issues besides slavery. They found a very appealing issue in 1856 that they pushed harder in the 1857 and 1858 elections—a protective tariff. American manufacturers and their millions of workers, the people who created the industrial revolution, could not maximize their profits because products imported from Europe, particularly England and specifically iron and coal, were selling for the same prices, sometimes less. Nowhere was this a bigger problem than in Pennsylvania, whose one million iron and coal workers supplied nearly half the nation's iron. The Republicans argued long and hard for a sweeping tariff to protect Pennsylvania's iron workers and it had helped.[562]

The Republicans were not alone as they worked hard to increase their popularity in Pennsylvania; the Democrats toiled at growing their numbers, too. They had held the state in the 1854 election and won the presidency for Buchanan by carrying it in 1856, although by less than five thousand votes. Those Democrats, though, had been led by state party chairman John Forney, who had defected following his acrimonious dispute with the president. The president had done little for the party in his home state, preferring to fill his time with foreign-policy adventures. The Democrats, without presidential assistance and without Forney—and in fact with Forney working against them—floundered.

The Republicans' hard work paid off and they captured the Keystone State by 31,000 votes and, in a special non-binding question in several counties' polling booths there, voters turned down the Lecompton Constitution, 51,208 to zero.[563] An election eve analysis showed that Pennsylvania Republican congressmen running in the districts where Lecompton was on the ballot as a special question won by the widest pluralities.[564] In a real surprise, the Republicans took eleven of the state's fourteen congressional seats that were contested that year.

The biggest blow there, to the party and President Buchanan, was the stunning defeat of the powerful J. Glancy Jones, the Democratic House whip. His district was considered the safest in the country for the Democrats, earning the nickname "the Gibraltor of Democracy." Jones lost because of a well-organized Republican campaign, Buchanan's sinking popularity, and, most of all, because John Forney and his *Philadelphia Press*, and his political associates, targeted the powerful Jones as part of Forney's retribution campaign against Buchanan. Buchanan had blithely cast his old friend aside when he became president, and now John Forney had blithely cast aside James Buchanan's old friend J. Glancy Jones, crippling the Democratic congressional leadership. Buchanan knew it too, and after the elections, raged that "the conspirators against poor Jones have at length succeeded…"

And who were those wretched conspirators? "The Forney mob," answered the president.

The defeat of Jones was just one of many Republican triumphs on election day. They also won control of the state senate and equaled the Democrats' seats in the assembly. And, as the Republicans seemed to do in every state, they rolled up impressive margins in every congressional and state legislative district, except for Philadelphia and the nine southern counties, just as they did in 1856, laying the foundation for an even more impressive victory in 1860.[565]

The Democratic debacle in New York was almost as great. There, the Democrats, who had minimized Seward's effect on the race with his "irrepressible conflict" speech, lost seven congressional seats, giving the Republicans twenty-nine of the state's thirty-three seats. The Republican sweep was so complete that the new party even defeated the candidates of the seemingly invincible Tammany Hall political machine in New York City.

The Republicans swept Democratic congressmen out of office everywhere. In Vermont the Republicans captured all three congressional seats, and two of three in Wisconsin, six out of six in Maine, four of five in New Jersey, all twelve seats in Massachusetts, three of four in Michigan. The Democrats took six of the seven congressional districts in Missouri (a slave state) and five of the nine in Illinois, thanks to Douglas and not Buchanan.[566]

Altogether, the Democrats lost twenty-one seats in Congress and, with the loss of those districts, control of the House of Representatives. The Democrats clung to a slender majority of seats in the Senate and held their majority in states whose congressional seats were not up for election that fall, especially the Southern states, preventing a complete Republican takeover of the Congress.[567]

〜

DOUGLAS DEFEATS THE REPUBLICANS IN ILLINOIS

Perhaps the most significant Republican victory came in its greatest loss—the senatorial campaign in Illinois. There, the Democratic Party won or held fifty-four of the state's ninety-five state legislative seats (eighteen were not up for election), guaranteeing the reelection of Stephen Douglas, but in a surprise Republican Abraham Lincoln actually won the popular vote, 125,430 to Douglas's 121,609, with Buchanan's Danite candidate drawing a mere 5,000.

Douglas was exhilarated. To him, all that counted was the state legislative vote, not the popular vote. He had defeated both Lincoln and the political assassins of President Buchanan and was certain he would be elected president as the Democratic nominee in two years. Ironically, many newspapers heralded his victory over Buchanan and downplayed Lincoln entirely. Less than a week after the election, the *Buffalo Register and Times* ran a huge headline: "For President in 1860: Stephen A. Douglas of Illinois" (the *National Slavery Standard* proclaimed both Douglas and Seward the 1860 nominees, as did the *New York Herald*). One week after that, thousands attended a raucous torchlight parade to honor Douglas in Chicago. In Philadelphia, organizers fired off a two-hundred-gun salute to celebrate Douglas's victory.

No one was happier about the Douglas win than John Forney, Buchanan's old friend and now avowed enemy. He bragged after the election results came in that Douglas had won despite "the entire administration of the federal government with its vast patronage of a hundred millions of dollars, with its army of mercenaries and expectants, organized and rallied against [Douglas]." Douglas wired the *Illinois State Register* on election night of his victory, "Let the voice of the people rule!"[568]

The Little Giant immediately went on a tour of several Southern states to reassure voters and political powerbrokers there that he was on their side on the territorial slavery question and rashly advocated that the United States annex Cuba, Mexico, and all of Central America, permitting slavery there, too. He even traveled to Havana, Cuba, in an effort to broker an annexation of Cuba with the United States. He was confident that he could regain his popularity in the South, but just a week after the elections, while he was traveling from state to state, the South's leading politicians had already started to turn against him, angered by his repeated affirmations that he did not object to free territories in his debates with Lincoln.[569]

◌

A SLIP AND NOT A FALL

Lincoln was at first disappointed in his loss of the election in the legislature, despite his popular-vote victory. "It hurts too much to laugh and I am too old to cry," he told one journalist. He was proud, though, that he had done much for the antislavery cause, even in defeat. He wrote Henry Asbury two weeks later, "The fight must go on. The cause of civil liberty must not be surrendered at the end of one or even one hundred defeats." He told him too, that the 1858 election did not decide the slavery question for him or anyone else. "Another explosion will soon come."

As for himself, he knew that the elections had made him a national figure. He said later that after he lost on election night, he nearly stumbled while walking home on a dirt path. "I recovered and said to myself that it is a slip and not a fall," just as his loss had been a slip and not a fall. He brushed off efforts of friends to console him. He told all, "I am neither dead nor dying."[570]

Why did the Republicans, so hopeful on the eve of the legislature's balloting, lose in Illinois? Party leaders had numerous excuses: Lincoln's liberalism, poor planning, disproportioned districts, voter fraud, and a rainy election day.[571] What effect did the debates have? Some historians have claimed that the debates were a small part of the larger contest in Illinois, that they were merely seven speeches Lincoln and Douglas made out of a total of some sixty throughout the campaign. Others argued that his strong finish in the debates enabled Lincoln to defeat Douglas in the popular vote. Some said the result of the debates was pretty much a draw and others claimed that they had helped Douglas more than Lincoln.

One analyst noted that Douglas won because he carried seven of the nine Senate districts and sixteen of the twenty-one House districts in the central part of Illinois, even though the vote was close in each. Victories in those counties gave him enough Democratic legislators to bring him victory. Lincoln only carried one of the seventeen House districts in the southern third of the state and in none of its Senate districts. Lincoln did carry four of the seven counties where the debates were held, two in the northern part of the state and two in the central. Ironically, each man lost his home county; Sangamon went for Douglas and Cook for Lincoln. So, in a sense, the slavery issue central to the debates that enabled Lincoln to become a national figure may have brought about his defeat in the Senate race.[572]

However, another, stronger argument could be made. Just over five thousand Democrats shunned Douglas and voted for Buchanan's Danite candidate. Surely, some other Democrats voted for Lincoln or simply stayed home. If Buchanan had not intervened in the race, Douglas might well have won the popular vote too, and that would have made an enormous difference two years later at the presidential nominating conventions, where Lincoln's forces would not be able to proclaim him the actual "winner" in the Senate race.

❧

THE REPUBLICANS: A RADICAL NEW PARTY

The residents of Ohio, galvanized against slavery by the Oberlin rescue and the sham trials defended by Buchanan, voted Republican in large numbers in 1858, giving the new party complete control of both houses of the state legislature. A year later, in 1859, radical Republican governor Salmon Chase was elected to the U.S. Senate from Ohio. His successor as governor, the equally radical Roelliff Brinkerhoff, was elected by a wide margin of votes to replace him.

The Republicans had achieved a remarkable victory in the 1858 elections. They had managed to herald one main issue, a grudging acceptance of slavery where it had flourished for years in Southern states but opposition to the spread of slavery into the territories and new states. But they won over many converts by brilliantly tying their campaign to important economic issues. The Republican congressional and state tickets favored a protective tariff to help local manufacturing and commercial businesses thrive, freer banking practices, the building of a transcontinental railroad, cheap land sales to homesteaders to promote the development of the western territories, and substantial federal funds for the improvements of harbors and waterways to make the commercial shipping trade, domestic and foreign, more prosperous.[573] Yet the Republicans managed to connect these issues to the moral issue of slavery. In state after state in the 1858 elections, the Republicans constantly charged that it was the monolithic, evil "slave power" (the Southern slave states) that prevented Northerners from achieving any commercial or economic gains. The Republicans conducted a moral crusade but carefully framed it as also an economic one.[574]

The Republicans won because they understood that while their brand-new party contained many abolitionists, it also had as members tens of thousands of former Whigs and antislavery Democrats. It was led by some of the new radicals, but most of the leadership came from the Whig and Democratic parties; they had significant fund-raising and campaign experience. These leaders also realized that the 1850s were a time of rapid change in politics and they were able to capitalize on the people's continual desire for new leadership. For example, nearly 90 percent of the men in Congress following the 1858 elections were not there prior to 1852.[575]

The new Congress meant, too, that the Republicans now had far more seats on important policy-making committees than they did before, and more than the old Whigs previously had. As an example, following the 1858 elections, two-thirds of the members of the powerful Ways and Means Committee were brand-new members to Congress; most were Republicans.[576]

And politically the Republicans were not the old Whigs, a party that
died because it was torn apart by the slavery issue. The main reason the
Republican Party came into existence was the opposition to slavery by all of
its members. The new party was held together by that overriding policy, and
while the members may have differed on some other policies, they never
differed on slavery. That foundation held them all together. The
Republicans, on issues and on the campaign trail, were much stronger than
the old, splintered Whigs, something the Democrats did not realize.[577] The
Republicans had been born as a radical party, but by 1858 they were no
longer just a rump political congregation, but a well-organized political
organization that had replaced the Whigs as the second major party and
would be a powerful force in American politics for years to come.[578]

The Democrats were grim. In a published letter, President Buchanan
said that the numerous defeats of his party spelled doom for the nation. If
the Republicans continued to win elections, he said, "The fountain of free
government will then be poisoned at its source, and we must end, as history
proves, in a military despotism. A Democratic Republic, all agree, cannot
long survive unless sustained by public virtue. When this is corrupted...[it
will] wither and die."

Whose fault was it? The president did not blame the lingering animosity
of many people toward the Supreme Court over the 1857 *Dred Scott*
decision, the Kansas debates, or the ineptitude of his administration. He
told the party they had lost simply because the Republicans had managed to
raise more campaign funds than the Democrats, and that it was a sad day
when the richest party won the election.

Others, of course, blamed the president for not supporting many
candidates and for spending much of his time in what turned out to be a
disastrous campaign to stop Douglas in Illinois. None analyzed Buchanan's
failures more succinctly than John Forney, the man he had scorned and the
man who worked so hard to defeat J. Glancy Jones. Forney had warned that
Buchanan's betrayal of fellow Democrats would come back to haunt the
party. "Such has been the result," Forney told a dinner crowd in Camden,
New Jersey, after the fall elections. "Many and many a glorious Democrat
placed upon the Democratic ticket has been sent to obscurity because the
opposition party has risen against the mistakes of the federal administration
and because the Democratic party, through the conventions of its office

Chapter Fourteen

WILLIAM TECUMSEH SHERMAN: DEAD-ENDED

After the 1858 fall elections were held, William Tecumseh Sherman, a former U.S. Army lieutenant living in Kansas following the collapse of his latest professional venture, developed yet another scheme to make money that would fail, as all of his myriad business schemes failed. This one involved a plan to sell corn from a road stand at the side of a highway to hungry prospectors from the East and Midwest. These adventurers were on their way to Pike's Peak, Colorado, to join the thousands already there following the discovery of large deposits of gold in the foothills of the Rockies.

The redheaded Sherman was a wiry, thin man with a long, gaunt face, receding hairline, short beard, and moustache. In the middle of a bitter '58 winter, he had begun construction of roadside warehouses for his spring corn operation. Sherman had to put up with stiff prairie winds and low temperatures. It was so cold, he wrote, "I could hardly hold my pen." Sherman, his hands covered with calluses and full of splinters from the construction, was more despondent than he had been in his entire life. It had been eighteen years since he graduated from the U.S. Military Academy at West Point and went into the army, hopeful of a successful life there. Now, shivering and depressed in the winter of 1858 as he drew crude plans for the corn warehouses, the chilly, biting Kansas air harsh against his face, Sherman wrote of his sad, unfilled life in which one disappointment followed another, "I am doomed to be a vagabond. I look upon myself as a dead cock in the pit, not worthy of future notice."[580]

⌒

Sherman and Ulysses S. Grant

The year 1858 began badly for William Tecumseh Sherman. The former soldier had given up the army for a career as a banker, trading in his blue army uniform for the finely tailored suits and splendid cravats of a financial man. He had been hired by the national banking firm of Lucas and Turner, based in St. Louis, and sent to California to run their bank in San Francisco in 1853.

The banking business did not go well and by 1858 he was sick of it. Earlier that year, prior to his roadside-stand business, he left his home in St. Louis and made one final visit to San Francisco. Just before he left, Sherman bumped into another former army officer who was just as insolvent as he— Ulysses S. Grant. "Sam" Grant had served with numerous other West Pointers, such as Robert E. Lee and Jeff Davis, in the Mexican War. Sherman and Grant barely knew each other at West Point, but their chance encounter on the streets of St. Louis gave the men a chance to commiserate with each other about life after the army for men whose only skills seemed to be of a military nature.

Grant had left the army to become a farmer in Missouri. He had failed miserably in the several years he had spent trying to till the plains, struggling with the region's freezing cold temperatures in winter and its oppressive heat and dangerous dust storms in summer. Grant knew by 1858 that he was not a farmer, and by then he had lost just about everything he had trying to make his tiny set of acres prosperous. Grant's finances hit rock bottom in January of 1858. First, he had to sell several of his treasured possessions, including a gold chain with sentimental value, to a pawn shop in order to pay his bills. The money he made on the chain, a paltry $22, did not help much. [581] To make ends meet, he then traveled back and forth to St. Louis, where, appearing just like any unkempt drifter down on his luck, he stood on street corners and sold small bundles of firewood he had cut at his farm for a few dollars. That didn't bring in much money either, and Grant wrote his sister in the winter of 1858 that he was broke and could not pay a bank note on the farm due in April. "I don't see now that I shall have the money," he told her. [582] Grant had poured out his tale of woe to Sherman, who told his West Point classmate his own sad story of failure out of uniform. He was despondent in his talk with Sherman and everyone else and saw no future for himself, a washed-up former soldier with no other skills. Grant wrote his sister that he planned to travel to see his family in Ohio that spring, "One more visit home before I get old."[583] Sherman, saddened by the meeting with his old classmate, wrote later, "[I] concluded that West Point and the regular army were not good schools for farmers [and] bankers."[584]

William Tecumseh Sherman and Ulysses Grant would meet again.

Sherman departed for California right after he bumped into Grant, at the end of January 1858, to wrap up business matters at his former company's bank there, uncertain how the year would turn out, but confident that it would end better than 1857 had. He was wrong.

He found chaos everywhere he looked in the Lucas and Turner bank in San Francisco. The bank reported $200,000 in bonds, mortgages, and notes in its financial inventory, but the economic slump that swept across the country meant that their assets and paper were actually worth far less. They owned land and buildings worth over $100,000 on paper, but those had also been dramatically devalued by the panic. Sherman's job was to collect whatever monies he could, offering substantially reduced terms, so that Lucas and Turner could settle all of their accounts in California, leave the state, and try to regroup in their national offices in St. Louis.[585]

William Sherman's heart went out to the Californians who owed his bank money. They had lost much in the economic collapse; some lost everything. How could he in good conscience force them to immediately pay back all they owed? He could not. Sherman systemically went about trying to collect just small percentages of what was owed the bank, writing debtors and simply asking them to pay what they could, sometimes asking for just ten cents on the dollar. Some of the Californians could not even pay that much and the bank recovered only a small percentage of what was owed.

That 1858 trip was the final chapter of William Sherman's life in California. He had last headed for the West Coast in February of 1853, just a few years after the gold rush there, when the state boomed and tens of thousands of prospectors arrived by wagon train, horseback, and ship to make their fortune in hills that all believed were laden with gold. Their presence had turned San Francisco from a sleepy port city into a sprawling, raucous community of fifty thousand people, sixty times its size five years before—Chinese immigrants, prospectors, prostitutes, and merchants eager to make money off the men and women who made their money off the gold rush. The city that Sherman sailed to was fast becoming one of America's most important ports and metropolitan centers, Sherman described it then as "the most extraordinary place on earth."[586]

By 1858, the boom had turned to bust. "When we began [early 1850s], we were on the top of a high wave rolling towards a dangerous but hidden reef," he wrote his foster father, Thomas Ewing. "Lands and houses here were yielding fabulous rents, and gold was a drug. People paid their three and five percent a month without a blush. Houses were building in every direction and the cities were pushing their streets over hills and out upon the bay, where but a year before ships were riding at anchor...we all supposed these magical changes were the result of gold from our mountains. This was but partially the case, for our gold was going East about as fast as it came down from the mountains."[587]

He told Ewing that the financial storms had battered the city's best people. "Almost every bank has failed. A large proportion of the wealthy have become embarrassed and bankrupt. Real estate has fallen from an exaggerated rate to almost nothing."[588]

Sherman was in the army, where he had been sent to clean up and take charge of the corrupt commissary office in New Orleans, when Henry Turner, a wealthy St. Louis banker, asked him to leave the military and go to California. Turner was the partner in the successful Lucas and Turner bank there. He told Sherman that the years he had spent as a quartermaster and commissary officer in the military had made him a capable financial administrator. And Sherman knew California. That combination made him perfect to be the president of the brand-new Lucas and Turner bank in California. Sherman would not only be paid more money than he had ever earned in the army, but would be given stock in the company as well.

He did not want to leave the army, but felt enormous pressure from his wife Ellen, Thomas Ewing's daughter, who had long disdained the low pay of the military and the transitory life of army families. She wanted some financial stability and a better life. New Orleans was very expensive and the Shermans could barely get by on his army pay. Ellen had given birth to their second child in the winter of 1852, more children would be on the way, and she insisted that he leave the army and accept the lucrative banking offer.

So the sunny shores of California were appealing to Sherman for many reasons. The move there was a chance to make more money, please his increasingly unhappy wife, and put distance between himself and his foster father, whom he did not like but upon whom had always been dependent. And it was a chance to return to San Francisco, where he had been stationed with the army and had many friends.

SHERMAN'S EARLY LIFE

Tecumseh Sherman was the offspring of one of the most patriotic families in America. He was a descendant of Roger Sherman of Rhode Island, a signer of the Declaration of Independence. Another ancestor had served thirty years in the Connecticut General Assembly. Sherman's grandfather was a judge and his father led an Ohio militia company in the War of 1812. The Shermans moved to Ohio to farmlands provided by the State of Connecticut to its Revolutionary War veterans. They settled in the village of Lancaster, in the southeastern part of the state, where Sherman, nicknamed "Cump," was born in 1820; he was named Tecumseh after the Shawnee Indian warrior. His father Charles became a lawyer and later sat on the Ohio State Supreme Court. His untimely death on June 24, 1829, when William was nine, followed financial woes that left him practically penniless.

With her husband Charles's passing, Sherman's mother was left nearly bankrupt, with nothing but their small home and two hundred dollars—and a mountain of debt. She had eleven children and no resources to care for them, so in a common practice of the day she asked relatives and friends to take in her children. Her next-door neighbor, Thomas Ewing Jr., a forty-year-old businessman and political leader in Ohio, became William's protector, or foster father. He would go on to become President John Tyler's secretary of the interior and a U.S. senator. Another man in the village did the same for her son John, then six, who would grow up to become a United States senator.

"Cump" became the eighth child in the Ewing household, joining his four natural siblings and two nieces and a nephew. Ewing's wife Maria insisted that Cump be baptized and the nine-year-old redhead agreed, but a minister could find no Saint Tecumseh and the boy needed a Christian name. The day he was baptized happened to be Saint William's Day, so the boy was officially named William Tecumseh.

William was always grateful for the good life provided by the Ewings, but he never truly accepted them as his parents, always referring to them as "Mr." and "Mrs." and never "father" and "mother." He got along well with their children, did his chores, and took full advantage of his years of intense education at the Lancaster School, founded by the Ewings, where the school afforded William the opportunity to study Greek and Latin as well as literature, mathematics, and other subjects. He developed an interest in the military in the middle 1830s when he watched local militia companies march out of town to fight area Indian tribes. In 1836, thanks to Ewing's influence, he won an appointment to the United States Military Academy at West Point.

Sherman adapted easily to the strict disciplinary codes of West Point. He rose at 5:30 a.m. for breakfast and went to class or studied all day before retiring for the evening at 9:30 p.m. He was a fine student and graduated sixth in his class of forty-two cadets in 1840. Among the cadets with him at West Point were several he would fight with or against in the Civil War twenty years later: Braxton Bragg, Jubal Early, Joseph Hooker, John C. Pemberton, P. G. T. Beauregard, Irvin McDowell, William Hardee, Edward Halleck, George Thomas, Don Carlos Buell, and James Longstreet. They were all well dressed and looked like professional soldiers, all except a freshman he knew casually, the disheveled and disorganized Ulysses Grant, whom everybody called "Sam."[589]

Sherman was not only one of the best-read cadets at West Point, but the best informed. His foster father sent him numerous newspapers from Ohio and Sherman subscribed to a national newspaper, the *National Gazette*. Each fall anyone, cadets or instructors, who wanted to learn more about the political campaigns sought Sherman out. By the time he graduated, Sherman had become a Whig, like his foster father. He had little interest in pursuing politics, but was quite knowledgeable for a young man.

Sherman did well in his studies, but did not impress the men who ran the academy. He piled up ninety demerits for various infractions (two hundred brought expulsion), was sometimes belligerent to his teachers, and hated the required Sunday morning church services. He was certainly not one of the memorable graduates, such as Robert E. Lee a few years later. Sherman was not a hard-nosed military man, either. He surprised cadets with his love of the theater and surprising skills as an artist. A contemporary journalist wrote that most at West Point would have "admitted that there was nothing manifested in…[his] character…that marked him as one destined to play a great part in the greatest war of modern times."[590]

His superiors at West Point may not have loved Sherman, but he loved the army. One of the most important aspects of his years at West Point was his deep-seated passion for the military that he developed there.

He loved everything, from the army's strict discipline to the variety of people from all over the country. Most of all, he firmly believed that the military was obligated to hold the nation together in time of any foreign attack or constitutional crisis.

Sherman had always been emotionally torn in his personal life. He felt that he had been abandoned by his mother, even though he understood the necessity for the departure of the children from her home. He was grateful to the Ewings for raising him, but never believed that he completely fit in with their family or that they were his true parents.

Sherman wrote his wife about the Ewings, "I am fully aware how slight are my claims to her [Mrs. Ewing's] regard… Very often I feel my insignificance and inability to repay the many kindnesses and favors received at her hands and those of her family. Time and absence serve to strengthen the claims and to increase the affection and love and gratitude to those who took me early under their care and conferred the same advantages as they did upon their own children. Indeed I often feel that your father and mother have usurped the place which nature has allotted to parents alone," hinting that he somehow saw the Ewings as illegitimate parents.[591]

His first army assignment gave him an artillery command in Florida, where he participated briefly in the continuing wars against the Seminole Indians. He quickly decided that the war was a waste of time. He also came to understand that in war armies had to adapt to their situation—the army could not fight the Indians in the jungles of the southeast like it could a European force on an open field. It was lesson that would be invaluable later in the Civil War.

During the following years, he served in Florida, Georgia, Alabama, and South Carolina, where he saw firsthand how committed Southerners were to the institution of slavery. He disagreed with them, but he also disagreed with the growing chorus of abolitionists that wanted slavery to be eliminated everywhere, and immediately.

Along with army life, Sherman grew to love his foster sister, Ellen, now sixteen and grown up. He wrote her frequently, soliciting her advice, and the pair became close, eventually falling in love. He asked her to marry him and she consented, but with two demands—he had to resign from the army and they had to live in Lancaster, Ohio, close to her parents. Sherman balked at both requests. He did not want to live with the Ewings again as their ward, and he certainly did not want to leave the army.

His dreary days in South Carolina ended quickly when the Mexican War began. It seemed like everyone he knew was sent there for what Sherman saw as the road to military glory. Jefferson Davis, ahead of him at West Point, was there, as were Robert E. Lee, whom he had heard so much about at the Point, and many other officers who were his classmates. They even sent Sam Grant, whom many said was the sorriest-looking cadet they had ever seen. Sherman was not going to Mexico, but he would travel to California to serve in an army unit whose job was to protect the republic *in case* the Mexican War spread to the Pacific Coast.

It did not. Sherman, who had risen to the rank of captain, spent several years in the Monterey and San Francisco areas with little to do except spend time drawing, turning out dozens of remarkably good sketches of wildlife. He became a clerk to a colonel and the heavy workload made him ill. That, combined with boredom, resulted in a dreary letter to his beloved Ellen, "I am so completely banished that I feel I am losing all hope all elasticity of spirits. I feel ten years older than I did when I sailed and, though my health is good, I do not feel that desire for the exercise that I formerly did."

And he missed the action in Mexico. He wrote Ellen, whom he married in 1850, "To hear of the war in Mexico and the brilliant deeds of the army, of my own regiment and my own old associates, everyone of whom has honors gained and I out in California—banished from fame, from everything that is dear and no more prospect of ever getting back than one of the old adobe houses that mark a California ranch...there is nothing new here, no strange events, no hair-breadth escapes, no battles, no stirring parties, no nothing and this war will pass and I will have to blush and say I have not heard a hostile shot."[592]

He complained, too, that if the Mexican War ended suddenly, officers who served with distinction there would get all the promotions, not people like him who sat out the conflict in California. He told her that those men would also win the best jobs in the private sector if they left the army, not people like him.[593]

SHERMAN'S BANKING CAREER

Sherman was happy to be back in California to represent Turner and his banking companies. The return for the newly minted banker and former army officer was a disaster. His arrival was highlighted first by the wreck of his vessel, which ran aground on rocks several miles from San Francisco. After helping the captain to evacuate all of the passengers, Sherman made it to land and then booked passage on a small boat headed for the city; the boat capsized and Sherman had to be fished out of the water by the crew of a passing vessel.[594] It was an inauspicious start.

But, he added, the people who lived there seemed to be making a lot of money, and he wanted, through his bank, to make a lot of money off them. If he could succeed financially, something that was impossible in the army, then perhaps his wife would have a better view of him and their growing family could prosper. The banking business, in booming San Francisco, seemed like a good path to that goal.

There were obstacles. The Lucas and Turner bank, a new venture, had been capitalized at just $100,000, a small sum. There were only a handful of employees. Loans were given out at low 3 percent rates. The bank itself was in rented quarters in a downtown building and not impressive. Sherman argued with Turner and Lucas to capitalize the bank at triple the amount, $300,000, hire more employees, build its own structure, and open up smaller branches in other California cities. They refused.

The new bank president did not think the company could succeed under the present circumstances and threatened to quit. He traveled back to St. Louis and confronted both bosses. After much haggling, they gave in to most of Sherman's demands. The bank was capitalized at $200,000, Sherman was given money to build a bank office, and more employees were hired. He did not get the branches, but he did get more money in salary and benefits.[595]

He was pleased and asked his wife to join him in San Francisco with their daughters, Lizzie and Minnie. The Ewings balked. Thomas Ewing insisted that his daughter remain in Lancaster, Ohio. Ellen insisted that she had to be with her husband. Ewing then talked her into leaving baby Minnie with him and his wife, convincing his daughter that the trip to California would be too much for an infant. It was a way that they could protect Minnie, they said. They wanted Ellen to stay home—for good. They also pressured her into trying to talk her husband into leaving California and banking and returning home to Ohio, where his foster parents could take care of their foster son, Cump Sherman, in whom they had little faith.[596]

Ellen wrote a dismal letter to Sherman in which she told him that she did not want to go to California for any reason, and that he should come home immediately. She wrote, "My hope…is now that you will leave that country entirely never again to be lured thither by promises of wealth or even by a certain prospect of gaining it. You do me justice in believing that I will cheerfully submit to any course you may determine upon, provided we are not to be separated for years, yet you will not forget to take into account the trial it would be for me to leave my parents, now growing old, with a certainty for not seeing them again for years and a probability of never meeting them again in this world. So if there is anything to incline the balance to either side let this bring you home."[597]

Ellen Sherman's trip to California was as problem-plagued as her husband's had been the previous year. In that day, sixty years before the opening of the Panama Canal, travelers either spent long and difficult months sailing around the southern tip of South America and then northward to reach California or crossed Central America on badly hewn roads in either Panama or Nicaragua. Ellen spent most of the voyage to Central America from the United States in bed, ill, and the overland trip across Nicaragua was hazardous.

Ellen began to complain about San Francisco as soon as she arrived: his army buddies from the old days visited too often, the house they leased was too expensive, the house they then bought cost too much, there was nothing for her to do, the streets were too dusty when the weather was dry, they were too muddy when it rained. She did not like her neighbors. The residents of San Francisco were crude. The hot days and cold nights, and the fabled sharp winds, made her ill and she spent more and more days in bed. She woke up at night terrified that her baby Minnie had died back in Ohio. Ellen, a very religious woman, then tried to make her husband more religious, constantly inviting clergy to their home; this annoyed him.[598]

"This is El Dorado, the promised land?" she mocked him. "I would rather live in Granny Walters's cabin [in Ohio] than live here in any kind of style."[599]

The Ewings began yet another campaign to talk Sherman into quitting his job and coming home to Ohio. Ewing told him that he could guarantee him a respectable job in one of his businesses with a more than adequate salary. It would enable him to enjoy professional success and come back to Ohio, where his wife so desperately wanted to return.

Sherman would have none of it. "I would rather be at the head of the bank in San Francisco, a position I obtained by my own efforts, than to occupy any place open to me in Ohio," he abruptly wrote his foster father.[600]

Making the bank a success was difficult. Sherman had to oversee the construction of the new bank at the same time he ran the old one in its small rented quarters. Numerous bankers had arrived in California following the gold rush, resulting in considerable competition. None of the financial institutions were making much money loaning money at 3 percent though, and the small interest income and the cost of the new building kept the Lucas and Turner profits low. There were other troubles for banks in the city. The bank business had flourished right after the gold rush of 1849, but then leveled off. The gold rush brought corruption to the city; a scandal ensued when a city official disappeared with government money and bank notes. Needed investors had become wary of putting their money in banks.

Sherman worried that he would not be as successful as Lucas and Turner wanted him to be in this new venture. He had a personal worry, too. The new bank president had dozens of army friends still stationed in San Francisco. Many of them turned over all the money they had to Sherman for investments. Sherman feared that if the bank's business continued to go badly, he ran the risk of losing their life savings.

The stress at home and the work at the bank brought back the severe asthma attacks that had bothered Sherman all of his life. He spent many sleepless nights wheezing and then was exhausted the next day. This went on for months. His wife, too, was sickly in San Francisco, suffering from terrible colds and boils. She told her husband that her ailments, too numerous for doctors to diagnose, had made her miserable. She had become an invalid, rarely leaving their home. Sherman told her that she was a hypochondriac and that her ailments were not in her body, but in her head. They argued often about the reality of her ailments. Still, he tried everything possible to placate his wife, even buying a piano that she could play to amuse herself.[601]

Then along came another baby, a boy, William, in the summer of 1854, and he brought nothing but worry to the Shermans. The bank president who could barely pay his bills now had a wife and three children to support. His wife spent far too much money on clothes and furnishings, too. He wrote Turner, "I have a family growing at an awful rate, that I know will need a great deal to maintain and provide for."[602]

On February 20, 1855, calamity struck the banking business in San Francisco. The city's biggest bank was the local branch of Page and Bacon, the large national bank with headquarters in St. Louis. Their San Francisco branch went out of business that day.

Frantic, the bankers turned to a man whom they trusted—rival banker William Tecumseh Sherman. He rushed to the Page and Bacon bank, realized that there was a run on it as hundreds of people waited in line outside to withdraw their funds, and sought out the bank's executives. The bankers told Sherman they were going to publish an ad in the next day's newspapers assuring the public that they had funds to cover all withdrawals, even though they did not. Sherman advised them not to mislead the public and left. He had his own bank run to worry about, and that started the very next day.

The San Francisco run was a good example of Sherman's administrative skills, his way in dealing with people, and, most important, his ability to operate in a crisis and under severe pressure from all sides. His military experience turned out to be just as valuable as his banking skills. First, he made certain that, as he had always insisted, his bank had nearly enough funds to cover withdrawals if, in fact, every single depositor demanded their money. The bank did, thanks to Sherman's planning. Next, he obtained assurances from several wealthy men in town that they would lend him up to $140,000 to cover sudden withdrawals.

He then explained when other friends arrived mid-morning, loudly enough for all in the crowd to hear, that he had more than enough money to cover all withdrawals. That seemed to quiet the swelling crowd, which surged out of the bank lobby and into the middle of Montgomery Street. Next, he asked the army friends whose money he held—trusted colleagues such as Don Carlos Buell, Joseph Hooker, John Bell Hood, Braxton Bragg, Henry Halleck, and George Thomas—to keep their money, over $130,000, in the vault. They agreed. He then borrowed $40,000 to serve as a reserve. Finally, late in the afternoon, he asked friends to actually deposit money in the bank the next morning to show confidence in the bank. They agreed.

When the Lucas and Turner bank closed its doors at the end of business hours at four in the afternoon that day, there was still money in the vault, money in the drawers of the tellers, and a smile on the face of its president.

He had survived the run and in the morning, as promised, people who had faith in him deposited nearly $120,000. The bank remained solvent. [603]

A very relieved Sherman wrote Turner, "So the battle is over and we are not dead by a d—d sight." He depicted his success in the terms that a military commander would describe a successful battle, "We weathered it [the run] by excessive caution, by scattering risks, and by not having too many sinking friends to bolster up."[604]

Sherman's actions in the banking crisis were singular. Page and Bacon floundered and closed its doors. So did several of the other large and influential financial institutions in the city, including some of the oldest. Of the city's nineteen banks, seven went out of business that week, decimated by runs by their depositors.

Instead of applauding the dramatic, steely action of her husband, Ellen Sherman sighed that she had actually hoped that Lucas and Turner had gone bankrupt so that she and the family would be forced to move back to Ohio. She unnerved Sherman, who wrote that "I'd blow this house [bank] into atoms and squeeze dollars out of brickbats rather than let our affairs pass into the hands of a rascally receiver or more rascally sheriff."[605]

One month later, Sherman suffered the worst asthma attack of his life. Ellen tried to convince him to return to Ohio for his health, but he refused. She left anyway, leaving the two children with him for childrearing, for an extended visit with no set date for her return to California. She wrote Sherman letters pledging her eternal love for him, but making it clear that she much preferred life at home with her parents than the life she had complained about so bitterly and so often in San Francisco.

Ellen did come back to San Francisco in December, nine months later. During that time, left to his own resources as a father and bank president, Sherman had thrived. He devoted every spare minute to his children and, perhaps for the first time in his life, genuinely enjoyed parenthood. He took firm steps to shore up his bank, increasing deposits, maintaining a high reserve of cash, and forbidding merchants from writing overdrafts on their accounts, a practice that had helped to bring on the February run across the city.

Sherman never looked well. He was thin, pale, and his body was continually wracked by asthma attacks. One of his clerks wrote, "You would have thought he was an invalid to look at his build and peculiarly pinched look about his mouth."[606] Yet these same clerks, and anyone who met him, marveled at the high energy he maintained and his ability to complete dozens of tasks each day, at the same time caring for his two children as a single parent.

His wife seemed happier upon her return, even though she left Minnie back in Ohio with the Ewings. Sherman hired extra help to assist her in running the house, which she appreciated. And she had her pictures. Ellen had brought photos of the Ewings and daughter Minnie to California with her, framed them and hung them throughout the house. Each day, Ellen and the two children looked at the photos and held lengthy conversations with them, a practice that annoyed Sherman.

What angered Sherman more was the lawlessness that plagued San Francisco. The dramatic population boom of the gold rush had brought thousands of unsavory characters to the city and it was quickly nicknamed "the Barbary Coast." The gunplay, fights, and ever-increasing criminal activity were far too overwhelming for the civil authorities. By 1851, vigilante groups were formed to mete out justice. Sherman, as an army man, was opposed to vigilantes, but he also sided with them on occasion following revelations of pervasive corruption in the city's government. In 1856, Sherman was pulled into a vigilante dispute that might have cost him his life and brought him face to face with deciding whether rebels who believed that their way of life was being threatened had the right to take up arms and declare war against the established government.

A newspaper editor, James King of William (his actual name), was shot dead by another editor, James Casey, whom Sherman detested because of his negative stories about the banking industry during the financial collapse of the previous winter. Casey was held in jail, but the ever-growing vigilante groups in San Francisco wanted him hanged immediately, without benefit of trial.

Sherman had been made the head of the San Francisco militia a few months earlier, a job that he did not think would cause him much trouble. Suddenly, he found himself defending the city jail with several hundred militia against an armed vigilante mob whose size reporters estimated at close to seven thousand men. Sherman, the mayor, and the governor watched from a rooftop as the vigilantes descended on the city prison. He wrote of the raucous scene he observed from the rooftop of the hotel, "Parties of armed men, in good order, were marching by platoons in the same direction and formed in line along Broadway, facing the jail door." [607]

The feeble militia could do nothing to halt the vigilante mob, and they surrendered Casey. The vigilantes hung him following a sham trial several days later.

Worse, the vigilantes, emboldened by their success at seizing the prisoner and the size of their army, decided to completely ignore civilian authority and run the city of San Francisco themselves. "It soon became manifest that the vigilante committee had no intention to surrender the power thus usurped. They took a building on City Street, near Front Street, fortified it, employed guards and armed sentinels sat in midnight council, issued writs of arrest and banishment, and utterly ignored all authority but their own. A good many men were banished and force to leave the country...Yankee Sullivan, a prisoner in their custody, committed suicide, and a feeling of general insecurity pervaded the city."[608]

An alarmed Sherman attempted to crush the vigilantes. The state had promised him cannon and guns and more men for his militia. In a bold and dangerous maneuver, Sherman planned to take control of an artillery battery that overlooked the place where the vigilantes had set up headquarters and shell it as his troops assaulted the neighborhood. He then asked David Farragut, the California area's U.S. Navy commander, to give him command of a warship in the harbor to fire at the vigilante's headquarters at the same time his cannon opened up on them from the hilltop. Farragut reminded Sherman that the U.S. Navy could not do that. State officials then informed him that the promised weapons and ammunition would not be forthcoming. Unable to fight, a frustrated Sherman resigned from his position as head of the militia. He used his influence as a banker to work behind the scenes with others to restore peace to San Francisco, which came about within six weeks when the vigilantes, under growing pressure from the governor, state assembly, and the press, finally gave up control of the city. [609]

Sherman had resigned primarily because his role as head of the militia might hurt his bank business, which was true, and because he found himself in an unwinnable situation. His wife had also pressured him to resign after his life—and those of his wife and children—were threatened several times by the vigilantes.

It was a sign to Sherman, the military man, that large groups of Americans were becoming increasingly unhappy with national, state, and local governments, and were starting to rise up in violent episodes to impose their will on them.

Sherman had little time to ruminate over the future of the vigilantes in California, though, because his bank decided to close its San Francisco office in 1857 and transfer him to New York. After four years on the West Coast, Sherman had been sent to New York to open up Lucas and Turner's new branch there, but the panic of 1857 struck the nation in August, crippling the new bank, along with hundreds of other financial institutions in New York and across the country. [610] No one blamed Sherman for the collapse of the New York or California bank, but Sherman did. It seemed that everything that had gone wrong in his life had been his fault, so why not the bank failures? Sherman cursed his lack of good fortune in the banking business and, as always, lamented his decision to leave the army, the only place he ever felt comfortable. He wrote of finance and his poor luck in 1858 that "banking and gambling are synonymous terms."[611]

Sherman moved back to St. Louis, with his wife Ellen and their children, to sort out of his future following the panic and bank closures. He conferred with his foster father, the influential Ohio businessman and politician Thomas Ewing Jr., who had raised him since he was young, and then started to think about what he would do with his life.

Sherman, like all bankers, knew that the panic was one of the worst financial setbacks in the nation's history. He wrote, "The panic grew worse and worse and about the end of September there was a general suspension of the banks of New York, and a money crisis extended all over the country." Sherman was pleased, though, that his bank had survived it. He wrote with pride, "No man lost a cent by either of the banking firms of Lucas Turner & Co. of San Francisco or New York."[612]

Sherman had failed to collect significant loans or foreclose on property in California and he left for the return trip to St. Louis deflated about his business skills. "I am utterly disqualified for business," he wrote Turner. "My experience here has completely destroyed all confidence in myself and everybody else."

He had never enjoyed banking. He wrote when the panic began, "Of all lives on earth, a banker's is the worst, and no wonder they are disbarred from heaven. Bound at any and every moment to produce the very dollar deposited, compelled to keep up an expensive outshow, and yet compelled to lend the money on chance, and depending on that chance for profit!" And he hated losing people's funds. "I can lose my own money and property without feeling much, but to lose what is confided to me by others I can't stand…"[613]

He was even blunter in a letter to his wife. "You can easily imagine me here, far away from you, far away from the children, with hope almost gone of ever again being able to regain what little self-respect or composure I ever possessed. I wish I could, like most men, harden my conscience and say I could not help the downfall of this country [California] or avoid the consequences thereof, than to have dodged a cannon ball, or escape an earthquake. You know I worked as hard as anybody could, that my whole thoughts, too much so, were engrossed in this business, which kept getting worse and worse from the time Page and Bacon broke, till we got away. What I did and what dangers I avoided are of the past and must be forgotten. What I failed to do, and the bad debts that now stare me in the face, must stand forever as a monument of my want to sense and sagacity. I envy…the non-chalance of business men generally, who wipe out these old sums, like the marks on a slate, and begin anew with no feeling or regrets for the past…"[614]

That view was reflected in all of his letters and memoirs, and in all of them he always concluded about his days as a businessman, "I regret I ever left the army."[615]

Turner told him he had done his best and urged him to return to St. Louis to accept some kind of reassignment from the bank. At the same time, Thomas Ewing, who had bailed him out all of his life, wrote Sherman and offered him a job managing his salt wells and coal mines near Lancaster, a job that he knew was charity so he could collect paychecks, pay his bills, and attempt to care for his family.

Sherman did not want to go back to Lancaster to manage the salt or coal companies and he certainly did not want to work for his foster father again. He shrugged his shoulders and went, though, because he had nowhere else to go—and no confidence in himself. He wrote Turner dejectedly that, "When I leave here I shall accept some post at the salt wells or coal mines of Mr. Ewing, where at least I can do no harm if I can't do good."[616]

Just before he went, though, he demanded that Lucas and Turner send him back to San Francisco to make certain that their depositors, especially his army friends, either had their money returned or reinvested with other reputable banks. His army friends kept their savings during the crisis, and were always thankful to Sherman for his diligence.[617]

Ellen was against even that short trip and stayed home in Lancaster. She told him she was "heart sick and distressed," and that "I am entirely unwilling for you to go out there at all. I don't care what Mr. Lucas has at stake, your life is worth more and you are not to risk it. But I suppose no opposition of mine can keep you now."

And then, knowing what was on his mind, what was always on his mind, she finished the letter curtly, telling her husband, "Please do not mention the army to me again unless you have made up your mind that we are not worth working for."[618]

His wife's admonishments not to mention the army fell on deaf ears. As he prepared to go back to Lancaster, his banking days over, Sherman again wrote his wife forlornly, "I regret I ever left the army."[619] In another letter home, he wrote Ellen, "I ought to have had sense enough to know that I was fit for the army but nothing else."

He was just as apologetic to his boss, Mr. Turner. He told him that he was "disqualified" for banking and that "I seem to bring bad luck. I ought to have known California better than to risk my own and other persons' wealth in such a cursed land."[620]

His brother John had become one of the most influential men in America by the time Sherman had reached what appeared to be the end of his rope as the proprietor of a roadside stand in the winter of 1858. No one who knew them would have predicted the two brothers would turn out that way. William had been a fine student and college graduate, but John was not. His younger brother stopped formal schooling at age fourteen and went to work as a laborer. He soon became interested in politics and embarked on one of the most impressive political careers in United States history. The Ohioan served several terms in the U.S. House of Representatives, nearly becoming the Speaker in the winter of 1858–1859, was elected to the U.S. Senate and later served as the secretary of the interior and secretary of state under different presidents, holding down important jobs in public life until 1898. John Sherman gained fame early as an opponent of slavery and throughout the 1850s was seen as one of the nation's leading abolitionists. [621]

His brother William Tecumseh Sherman did not share his politician sibling's virulent hatred of slavery. William had no strong feelings about the slavery controversies in Kansas that had caused such an uproar throughout the nation. In fact, he had no feelings about slavery at all. He wrote little about it, except to tell his brother that the current status of blacks was acceptable to him. It was his view that blacks should remain in bondage in the Southern states. "The Negroes of our country should remain slaves," he wrote his brother. He did not speculate about the spread of slavery to the territories, especially Kansas, in letters to him. Ironically, Sherman was farming in Kansas at the same time that abolitionist John Brown, who had caused so much trouble there in 1856, had returned to the territory to live with his sons and plan subsequent antislavery activities. [622]

He did make a prediction to his congressman brother about politics and slavery. He told him that every issue in the country was being determined on the slavery question and not on its merits. He told the congressman that if that continued the country would be dragged into a civil war.

BACK TO THE MILITARY: THE LOUISIANA MILITARY SEMINARY

Sherman ended the winter of 1858 trying to sort out his life. He no longer wanted to be a farmer—anything would be preferable to that. He wrote, "I feel in danger, ready to run to any quarter of the world where I can do anything."[623] He was in no hurry to return to Ohio and his foster father, either.

Friends of the former soldier had numerous suggestions: superintendent of an iron company, manager of a hotel building project, participating in a cattle drive from Utah to California, or assistant manager of a bank in London. One even suggested running a grocery store.

None made any sense to him, and he traveled back to Ohio to take Ewing up on his offer of a job in his nearby salt factory. He had given in to his wife, his foster father, and what he believed to be his fate. He wrote Ewing, "If Ellen & the children are willing to live down in Hocking and you think it proper that I should leave my family there, and can satisfy yourself that I can serve you and them, too, I'll hold to my promise to come to Lancaster this fall, and go to work at Surveying Engineering or whatever you are willing to entrust to my care."[624]

He worked in Lancaster for a short time and then moved to Leavenworth, Kansas, at Ewing's insistence, to work with Ewing's sons there in a law firm they had set up. They strong-armed local legal officials to permit Sherman to become a lawyer by merely taking a general knowledge test and skipping law school. He passed and became a very unhappy lawyer, writing his wife that his legal work would be "bungle, bungle, bungle from Monday to Sunday."[625]

In the fall of 1858, after eight years of marriage, numerous separations, and fights too numerous to count, Ellen Sherman finally decided between her parents and her husband. She wrote William Tecumseh Sherman a heartfelt letter. "One thing I cannot consent to, and that is to live separate from you any longer. I will wear cheap clothes, put them on the children— eschew society *in toto*, live far from the church or near it, as I can, do as much of my own work as possible and be more amiable than you have ever known me, if you will only be cheerful and happy. I cannot lead this unnatural life any longer, suffering anxiety on your account as I do. If your means will permit no better rent [than] a log cabin or its equivalent with two or three beds and a rag carpet and a stove and if we can have fueled bread, meat, and coffee and sugar I shall not despair. I am in bad health and I am unhappy and I beg you to take me with you somewhere."[626]

He appreciated her letter but, as always in the back of the mind, there was the army. He always regretted leaving the army, especially when he went to work for his foster father in the salt factory in 1858. He enjoyed army life and the camaraderie of the officers and enlisted men. He was a good soldier, even though he had not been in combat. Any brush with people in uniform sparked his old romance for the military. One of his several jobs prior to the banking fiasco was as a contractor for the army at Fort Riley, Kansas, where, like everyone else, he listened to the rumors about John Brown and the other raiders in the territory. Sherman worked with officers outdoors in checking munitions and supplies. He arrived early and stayed late, reveling in every minute he could spend with men in the army. He gushed to his wife that in that job especially, he really missed the service. Sherman told her that there was no more regret for him "than to meet my old comrades in the open field, just where I most like to be."[627]

Sherman's desire to get back into uniform consumed him and he made one last attempt by writing an officer he knew in the adjutant general's office, Don Carlos Buell, a classmate at West Point and one of the investors in his San Francisco bank whose money he had saved during the bank run. He asked Buell to recommend him for a job in the army paymaster's office. Sherman then enlisted his influential foster father to pressure President

Buchanan, with whom Ewing did not get along, to appoint him. Their combined influence did no good; both the army and the president turned Sherman down. His army days were apparently over. [628]

But there was one small sliver of hope in the winter of 1858–1859 for Sherman to get back into the military life, an opportunity neither he nor anyone else had anticipated. During the winter, a group of men in southern Louisiana began to raise funds to start a military school in Alexandria that they wanted to be the finest in the region, a Southern academy that could rival West Point. The school, the Louisiana Military Seminary, was seeking a superintendent. They wanted a retired army man who could offer the students military and academic training, and had some administrative experience to use in running the new institution. A plus would be a West Point graduate. A real plus would be a man with some fiscal background who could oversee the financial operations of the school.

They wrote letters to numerous men in the military seeking recommendations for the superintendent's post. One arrived on the desk of Colonel Buell, who immediately thought of his friend Sherman, who had protected his life savings in the San Francisco bank run. The Southerners might be alarmed that Cump Sherman's brother John had become one of the fiercest abolitionists in the House of Representatives, but if they indeed wanted a good administrator and genuine military talent, Buell assured them, his old army buddy seemed ideal for the job. [629]

Besides, Cump did not share his brother's views on slavery. William Sherman had never been very interested in the plight of blacks. In 1842, Cump Sherman had written of slaves in Charleston, South Carolina, "The Negroes are well dressed and behaved, never impudent or presuming and, so far as I can judge, feeling very light indeed the chains of bondage." He once wrote his wife, "All the Congresses on earth could not make the Negro anything else than what he was. He has to be the subject to the white man or he must amalgamate or be destroyed. The two races could not live in harmony save as master and slave." Later, at the end of the Civil War and in Reconstruction, he would often express the same sentiments. [630]

Unknown to him, at the same time that he was setting up his roadside business, friends had recommended him to be the superintendent of a new military academy. He was given that job in 1859 and soon became the much-praised leader of the academy, where he assumed a very fatherly attitude toward his student-cadets and renewed his own love of the military.

Chapter Fifteen

THE WHITE HOUSE

WINTER 1858: SWASHBUCKLING IN THE AMERICAS

The War Against Paraguay

Americans were startled to wake up on the morning of December 6, 1858, to read in their newspapers that President James Buchanan had launched what appeared to be a full-scale naval invasion of the South American nation of Paraguay. The president had sent a squadron of twenty-one warships carrying 187 cannon and nearly three thousand men to the harbor at Buenos Aires, in Argentina, a friendly nation to the United States, to prepare for an assault on Paraguay.

The president's war on Paraguay was triggered when national troops in a Paraguayan fortress fired on an American government ship, the *Water Witch*, engaged in a scientific survey. It was not clear if the *Water Witch*, either deliberately or mistakenly used an off-limits channel in the Paraguay River that ran in front of a military installation. The *Water Witch,* like all ships, was supposed to use a channel in mid-river. A Paraguayan officer at the fort hailed the *Water Witch* and told her captain to sail in the mid-river channel. The captain of the *Water Witch* claimed that he was not in the off-limits channel and that the nation of Paraguay could not claim ownership of the river, since the other side of it was in Argentina. The Paraguayan officer warned the *Water Witch* that she would be fired upon, but the American captain paid no attention to the warning and continued to sail upstream. Paraguayan artillerists then fired a shot near the American vessel as a signal to halt, but the shot was ignored. The Paraguayans then fired directly upon the *Water Witch*, damaging her and killing a sailor on board. The captain of the *Water Witch* fired back at the fort. Several volleys followed, in which no one was hurt. The American vessel eventually turned back.

Buchanan was furious and turned the unfortunate death of the sailor into a huge incident, branding the Paraguayans as unscrupulous international villains and charging that "the hostile attitude of the government of Paraguay towards the United States" was responsible for the entire episode. "That government had, upon frivolous and even insulting pretexts, refused to ratify the treaty of friendship, commerce, and navigation, concluded with it on the fourth of March, 1853, amended by the Senate, though this only a mere matter of form. It had seized and appropriated the property of American citizens residing in Paraguay, in a violent and arbitrary manner; and finally, by order of President Lopez, it had fired upon the United States steamer *Water Witch*…and killed the sailor at the helm, whilst she was peacefully employed in surveying the Parana River."[631]

Buchanan had long thirsted for American expansionism in Central and South America. Upon hearing the news, he dispatched the twenty-one-ship squadron that included the USS *Harriet Lane*, named after his niece and White House hostess. The ships rendezvoused in Buenos Aires harbor. They were to wait until a U.S. diplomat went upriver to meet with the president of Paraguay. The commissioner was going to demand an apology for the firing on the *Water Witch*, compensation to the manufacturers of the vessel, compensation to American property owners in Paraguay who claimed their assets had been seized by the Paraguayan government in recent months, the signing of a treaty negotiated with the United States in 1853 that had never been finalized, and the inking of a new treaty that granted access to all the rivers of Paraguay for American vessels. If the Paraguayan president did not agree to all of the demands, the ships were to proceed to the mouth of the Paraguay River and blockade it, crippling Paraguay's commerce. Understandably, the Paraguayans called the threatened blockade an act of war.[632]

James Buchanan, who had spent years in the diplomatic corps, not only believed in the Monroe Doctrine, in which all foreign nations were warned about undue influence in either North or South America, but was convinced that America had to annex parts of nations, entire republics, and Caribbean islands to fulfill its manifest destiny. Just as Polk had seen the war in Mexico, and its huge land acquisitions for the United States, as necessary for America, Buchanan saw action to acquire nations as part of the American dream.

Buchanan wanted to be the president who brought new states into the Union and made the United States one whole country from the Atlantic to the Pacific, connected by a transcontinental railroad. Moreover, he wanted to be known as the American president who acquired other countries' states and entire republics. He warned all nations that they risked war if they tried to stop the United States from its imperialistic course.

He was blunt about it, too, telling the world in his inaugural address that "no nation will have a right to interfere or to complain if...we shall still further extend our possession." And what would those possessions be? Everything the president could lay his hands on. "It is beyond question the destiny of our race to spread themselves over the continent of North America and this at no distant day... the tide of [U.S.] emigrants will flow to the South...if permitted to go there, peacefully, Central America will soon contain an American population which...will preserve the domestic peace, while the different transit routes across the Isthmus [of Panama]...will have assured protection."[633]

No other president would envision an American empire spreading through Mexico, Central and South America, and the Caribbean until the twentieth century, but James Buchanan was certain that he could establish one. His grand scheme had several components: 1. dislodging European governments that controlled Central and South America and the Caribbean islands, especially England, in return for U.S. protection of their citizens still living there; 2. the annexation of one or more of the northern states of Mexico; 3. new treaties with countries such as Paraguay and Brazil to make U.S. shipping more prosperous, to be enforced militarily; 4. the planning of some kind of waterway that could cut across the narrower sections of Central America in Honduras, Nicaragua, or Panama and save U.S. ships months on the dangerous trip around the southern tip of South America; 5. the purchase of Cuba and its annexation as a slave state; and 6. the rapid development of Honduras and Nicaragua as U.S. protectorates after, at his urging, thousands of Americans moved to those countries and peacefully took over their political and economic systems.

The president was careful in all of his public declarations and private correspondence to insist that all of this would be done through monetary purchase and political persuasion, not military might. He argued, too, that few American presidents had his long experience in foreign affairs as a congressman and ambassador to England. He selected Lewis Cass as secretary of state because Cass shared his imperialistic schemes. As soon as he was sworn in, the president set up a second presidential office at the State Department so he could work with Cass on his expansionist plans.

Under new treaties, the British, at his urging, had agreed to pull out of their Central American and Caribbean possessions, ceding their lands and forts to the local governments. They would not give up the Bay Islands, off the coast of Honduras and close to where Buchanan envisioned his cross-continent waterway. The president became enraged. He refused to honor the old treaty, and negotiations with England fell apart. A few months later talks resumed, and while the British did not formally agree with Buchanan's demands, they told him that they would not object to any interpretation of the treaties that he took. Buchanan, however, had to promise that he would not use any military action against the countries they had abandoned.

The president did so, certain that American immigration to these countries and islands would soon make the residents see that American business and governmental supervision were good for them. He also planned to ask Congress for hundreds of millions of dollars to buy up Mexican states and Caribbean islands. The president continually assured everyone that there would be no military invasions of these countries.

His promises fell apart in 1857 when, against his wishes, an American soldier of fortune, William Walker, took an expeditionary force to Nicaragua, intent on overthrowing the government there and setting up an independent, but pro-American, state. Following a congressional and media outcry, Buchanan dispatched a naval force to arrest Walker and his men. They did so, but Walker was not imprisoned. He returned to Central America on another jingoistic expedition later and was killed in an attempt to overthrow the government of Honduras.

Buchanan's actions in the Walker affair were questionable at best. Walker insisted that he had the secret blessing of the White House on his campaigns in Central America. Some scholars have suggested that while Buchanan publicly condemned Walker, he privately hoped that the adventurer would satisfy a dream of his by bringing Nicaragua under U.S. protection, thus permitting him to build a canal through it to connect the Atlantic and Pacific oceans. Many diplomats dismissed the president's criticism of Walker and viewed Buchanan's dreams about Nicaragua as sinister. British diplomat Charles Wyke wrote, "President Buchanan by word of mouth always condemned Walker's expeditions, and yet his government imbued with

Southern ideas, took no effectual means to prevent vessel after vessel crowded with armed men from leaving their ports."[634]

The president had an opportunity to use the army to seize large sections of northern Mexico in January 1858, when he was urged to do so by John Forsyth, the U.S. minister there. Several Americans had been killed in Mexico, including three doctors, as Mexico's government changed hands that month. Then the new head of state, General Felix Zuloaga, who had ousted the elected president, announced that he was taxing all of America's property and assets in Mexico.

Forsyth urged the president to attack Mexico and seize and annex one of its large northern states, Sonora, using the deaths of the Americans and the new taxes as a pretext. Wrote Forsyth, "You want Sonora? The American blood spilled near its line would justify you in seizing it…"[635]

Buchanan wanted to do just that, but for another reason, one that he thought the Congress and people would applaud. The legitimate government of Mexico, forced out by Zuloaga, had reconstituted itself at the city of Vera Cruz, with General Juarez, the former chief justice and second in line for the presidency under the Mexican Constitution, as its head. Buchanan told Congress that the two governments had made Mexico weak. He said the country was "a wreck upon the ocean, drifting about as she is impelled by different factions." That made her ripe for takeover by a foreign power, probably France, and that foreign power would pose a threat to the United States. Buchanan asked the Senate for permission to not only send the army to support the Juarez government, but take over northern Mexico. He told the senators that it was America's responsibility "to assume a temporary protectorate over the northern portions of Chihuahua and Sonora, and to establish military posts within the same." The Senate rejected his plea and would reject another suggestion in 1859 to send troops to Mexico to protect Americans living there and his 1860 plan to station troops in that country permanently to assist the government, whose officials claimed they faced a revolution.[636]

The president's actions to stop Walker upheld his direct military noninterference policy, but his naval action against Paraguay in December 1858 sent a signal to the nation and the world that perhaps he had changed his mind. The president certainly talked tough about his intentions in Paraguay. He told Congress, "Should our commissioner prove unsuccessful, after a sincere and earnest effort to accomplish the object of his mission, then no alternative will remain but the employment of force to obtain 'just satisfaction' from Paraguay."[637]

The Paraguayans understood the full meaning of his words in Washington and his warships in Buenos Aires. The Americans received everything they wanted in the ensuing talks with the government and the U.S. warships sailed home. The president used the incident to send several messages to his own country and the world. First, he wanted to gobble up as much of the world as he could; second, he would defend the Monroe Doctrine against any nation, ensuring American rights, and, third, he hoped his buccaneering in foreign affairs would somehow distract the attention of Americans at home from the slavery issue.

It did not.

ᶜᵡ₂

THE ATTEMPTED ANNEXATION OF CUBA

Cuba was a lush tropical island that sat just ninety miles off the southeastern tip of Florida and was, in 1858, a prosperous nation whose most successful industry was the raising of sugar cane—by tens of thousands of slave laborers. It was owned and governed by the Spanish crown and had been for years. The island enjoyed hot, tropical weather that was ideal for the production of sugar cane. It was a large island with several small cities, such as Havana, with harbors for seagoing ships. Sugar cane grown far from cities could also be loaded on to smaller boats that carried the crop out to ships anchored off the coast; those ships would then carry the cargo all over the world. Cuba was conveniently located geographically so its merchant ships could travel quickly to American ports, such as New Orleans, and ports in Mexico and South America.

James Buchanan had wanted to annex Cuba and make it another American state since 1848, when he worked in the State Department under President James Polk. He urged annexation of the island again in 1854, when he was minister to England and represented America in the talks that produced the Ostend Manifesto, a document that called for the purchase or annexation of Cuba by the United States and the outright seizure of it if Spain refused to sell the island. Cuba's sugar cane crop would add to the overall American economy and its slave status would make it another Southern slave state and one more state under the Democratic Party's control.

Buchanan publicly insisted on peaceful takeovers, but justified the use of force. Nowhere was that clearer than in an addendum to the Ostend Manifesto in 1854 when he wrote, "Our past history forbids that we should acquire the island of Cuba without the consent of Spain, unless justified by the great law of self-preservation." He added in a bizarre note that if Spain refused a fair monetary offer for Cuba, America could simply seize it, "upon the very same principle that would justify an individual in tearing down the burning house of his neighbor, if there were no other means of preventing the flames from destroying his own home."[638]

President Pierce had tried to purchase the island that year, at the suggestion of Buchanan and others, but failed. Pierce's secretary of state, William Marcy, wrote to the president, and to Buchanan in England, that he was certain the British government, which was opposed to slavery, would somehow send thousands of Africans to flood Cuba to disrupt the government there. They would then free the slaves on the island, who would turn on the Spaniards, butchering them. The United States would then have to send the Navy to Cuba to help put down the uprising, since the Spanish Navy was three thousand miles away. To avoid that bloodshed and gain Cuba, Marcy wanted to buy the island from Spain for $100 million. He engaged a French businessman from Louisiana, Pierre Soule, to negotiate a deal, but the Spanish government was still not interested and it fell through.[639]

A pro-U.S. rebel group had tried to recruit Colonel Robert E. Lee of the United States Army to lead an insurrectionist cabal against the Spanish government there that same year, but Lee declined after consulting his boss, then–Secretary of War Jefferson Davis. Numerous Southern politicians in office in 1858 lusted after Cuba. The Caribbean nation would be good for the country, good for the Democrats, and very good for President Buchanan. He knew there would be objections because of slavery in Cuba, but the country had annexed Texas, a slave territory, in 1845. What was the difference? Besides, if Buchanan could add Cuba to the United States, it would set a precedent for his plans to annex the northern states of Mexico and perhaps add the Central American countries of Nicaragua and Honduras, too. He needed some precedent to take over those countries after his previous efforts had failed; Cuba was the key.

The president considered himself an accomplished diplomat. He had contacts with governments all over the world. Yet so far his two years in office had resulted in nothing but foreign policy calamities. He had talked the British into vacating their positions of power in Central America, but his own government's efforts to acquire those nations through immigration and persuasion had failed. The attempts to seize Nicaragua and Honduras by William Walker, although opposed by the White House, had been international disasters that reflected badly on the whole country. If Buchanan could purchase Cuba it would not only be the huge international coup he had been seeking but, as the year 1858 was drawing to an end, would serve as an event that, like the attack on Paraguay, would distract the attention of the public from the issue of slavery, that grew as the year 1858 was coming to an end.

When he worked in the State Department, Buchanan advised the government to simply buy the island outright. He was certain that the king of Spain would sell because his country needed the money; the powerful Catholic clergy in Spain and Cuba would support the sale to prevent the king from continuing to sell church lands to raise funds. American bankers would benefit from the purchase of bonds in Cuba. But a rather badly organized conference to arrange the sale of the Caribbean island at that time ended in confusion.

Now that he was president, Buchanan was determined to annex Cuba by one means or another. He appealed to Christopher Fallon, a friend and Pennsylvania businessman who represented the interests of the Spanish Queen Mother. He insisted on "silence and discretion" from Fallon. He wrote him in December 1857, "The government of the United States is as willing now to obtain the island by fair purchase as it was in 1848. You are well-acquainted with the efforts made in that year to accomplish the object and the cause of their failure. It is now, I think, manifest that a transfer of the island to the United States for a reasonable and fair price would greatly promote the interest of both countries."[640]

Fallon warned Buchanan that convincing the Spanish crown to part with Cuba would prove very difficult politically, but he sailed off to Madrid in 1858 to attempt it. In Madrid, the intrepid Fallon worked behind the scenes toward his goal. He needed Buchanan to send a new Spanish minister over to facilitate the proceedings; the president agreed. The president also engaged his friend, Democrat Senator John Slidell, of Louisiana, to introduce a bill in Congress to provide $30 million to cover the costs of prepurchase negotiations and expenses to buy Cuba, a bill that would be introduced on New Year's Day 1859. The president even came up with a political slogan to bring about the annexation of Cuba that he was proud of, "We must have Cuba!"[641]

Buchanan gave Congress what he considered numerous reasons to buy Cuba in his annual message on December 6, 1858, as the dismal year ended. He enumerated a long list of transgressions by the governments of Cuba and Spain, highlighted by Cuba's refusal to pay back all of the debts it owed American businessmen and its role in the African slave trade. American citizens had suffered economic losses in Cuba that had not been addressed by the Cuban government, he said, and insisted that no real justice could be obtained because all claims had to go to Spain, not Havana, for resolution. After presenting an extended grievance list, Buchanan told Congress, "The truth is that Cuba, in its existing colonial condition, is a constant source of injury and annoyance to the American people."

The president said with firmness that the only solution was to buy it. At that point he backed off his previous belief that America should simply attack the Caribbean island and seize it by force. "We would not, if we could, acquire Cuba by any other means," the president told Congress, disregarding his jingoistic statements of earlier years. "This is due to our national character. All of the territory which we have acquired since the origin of the government has been by fair purchase from France, Spain, and Mexico or by the free and voluntary act of the independent state of Texas in blending her destinies with our own. This course we shall ever pursue unless circumstances should occur, which we do not now anticipate, rendering a departure from a clearly justifiable under the imperative and overruling law of self-preservation."[642]

Buchanan's insistence on the annexation of Cuba not only angered Northerners against slavery, but created yet another wave of speeches from Southerners calling for the reopening of the international slave trade, banned since 1808. This came about because, by putting the spotlight on Cuba, Buchanan inadvertently made people aware of the more than a dozen American ships that sailed out of Northern ports in the United States to Cuba and then engaged in the slave trade, carrying slaves between Cuba and Africa and Cuba and other Caribbean and South American countries. Some of these ships were stopped by U.S. Naval vessels, but many were not.

Angry Southerners accused Northerners of hypocrisy—on one hand they called for slavery's elimination, but on the other they privately made large sums of money engaging in the transportation of slaves. The British consul charged that in the late 1850s half of the fifty ships a year that stopped in Cuba on slave-trade expeditions sailed secretly out of New York City. Stephen Douglas charged a year later, in 1859, that clandestine American ships were carrying more than fifteen thousand slaves a year from Africa to America; he swore that he had himself seen three hundred new arrivals in Vicksburg, Mississippi.[643] The federal government had captured one slave ship trying to sneak into the United States through Carolina waters and detained the captain while the State Department decided whether he should be prosecuted by federal or state courts. Many Southern public officials used Cuba and the Northern slave ships in a new logic: if it was legal for a planter to buy slaves in Mississippi and transport them a thousand miles to his plantation in South Carolina, why was it illegal for a planter to buy slaves in Cuba and transport them ninety miles to Florida?[644]

Another group of Southerners argued that America's annexation of Cuba would end international slave trading, a mainstay at the island. Northerners, of course, argued that the Southern scenario then made Cuba a Southern state and permitted Cubans to send their slaves to other Southern states. It also permitted Southern planters to send slaves who were discipline problems to Cuba and to threaten slave families with deportation to the much hotter climate of the island.

The president, as usual, had grossly underestimated the opposition of the Republican Party and antislavery members of his own party. The Republicans opposed the purchase or annexation of Cuba because it would add yet another state to the "slave power" and open up a quasi-slave trade between Cuba and planters in Southern states, the principle they had denounced for so long in their successful opposition to the African slave trade.

The Republicans were also against it because many of them, particularly former members of the American and Know-Nothing parties, were anti-Catholic. They were opposed to the rapid spread of newly arrived Catholic immigrants throughout the country and any and all proposals for state governments to fund parochial schools, an issue that had become heated in large cities such as Boston and New York. Spain was the heart of Roman Catholicism, they believed, and they would do anything to curtail the power of the Catholic Spanish government; they would do even more to prevent the Spanish king and his bishops from lining their pockets with American money from the sale of a slave republic.[645]

The Republicans expressed their opposition to the annexation of Cuba as soon as the president began to discuss it. They were against the $30 million negotiation fund, against the $100 million purchase, and were sure they could defeat the measure. The president had a slogan, "We Must Have Cuba!" Sarcastic Republicans came up with one too, "We Must Have Slavery!"[646]

The president did not understand that this single goal of annexing Cuba would open a Pandora's box in Congress and that members would see it as an effort to open the door to the annexation of other islands and nations, the type of imperialistic land-grabbing that Congress, controlled by his own party, had turned down repeatedly during Buchanan's two years in office. In fact, as soon as the proposal was made, one Southern congressman insisted that America had to annex nations "from Alaska to Cape Horn." A congressman from Vermont joked that if the United States purchased Cuba, it should also purchase Jamaica, Santo Domingo, and the Bahamas.[647]

The proposal to purchase Cuba was debated extensively on the floor of the House of Representatives and at the same time the newspapers offered their opinions, positive in the South and negative in the North. It was soundly defeated. A nonplussed President Buchanan tried to convince Congress to approve it again in each of the years remaining in his term of office. Though he was determined to annex a nation, the Cuban idea never made it to the floor of the House for discussions again.

⁓

BUCHANAN'S LEGACY

Buchanan was alternately criticized and lampooned for his failed efforts at international diplomacy, whether it was sending the navy, with the *Harriet Lane*, threatening to get tough with Paraguay, annex states in Mexico, or buy Cuba. The editor of Washington's *National Intelligencer* was one of them.

He wrote at the end of 1858, "We must retrench the extravagant list of magnificent schemes which has received the sanction of the Executive... The great Napoleon himself, with all the resources of an empire at his sole command, never ventured the simultaneous accomplishment of so many daring projects. The acquisition of Cuba...the construction of a Pacific railroad…a Mexican protectorate; international preponderance in Central America, in spite of all the powers of Europe; the submission of distant South American states…the enlargement of the navy; a largely increased standing army…what government on earth could possibly meet all the exigencies of such a flood of innovation?"[648]

There were many others, though, who saw Buchanan's international swashbuckling as a pathetic cover for his unwillingness to address the great domestic crisis of the age, slavery. The presidents of the United States did not have enormous direct power in the middle of the nineteenth century, when Congress controlled most legislation, but Buchanan, like his predecessors and successors in that era, enjoyed as president enormous powers of persuasion to convince people to do what he thought was best for the nation. Not once did he use those powers.

In fact, he used the considerable powers of the president to engage in petty disputes, turning members of his own party against him. He could have called on his prestige as president to help candidates get elected, but instead he used it to defeat candidates of his own party, some of them among the best public officials in the nation's history, such as Stephen Douglas. He was unable to understand the thinking of anyone other than himself and did not realize that his feud with friend and newspaper editor John Forney would turn Forney against him and result in the defeat of numerous congressmen, including House Whip J. Glancy Jones, in the 1858 Pennsylvania elections. He made no effort as president and head of the Democratic Party to work with the party in the 1858 elections, which then turned into a disaster. He spent so much energy reviling William Seward that he spent no time studying other Republicans who might do harm to his party in the coming years, especially the relatively unknown Illinois legislator, Abraham Lincoln. In his efforts to destroy Douglas in Illinois he never considered that his efforts might accelerate the future rise of Lincoln.

The president dismissed the slavery issue in Kansas and elsewhere. He never understood the fury at the *Dred Scott* decision and the Fugitive Slave Act by millions of Americans, even though it was discussed daily in the newspapers in connection with the trial of the Oberlin rescuers, whom he continually tried to discredit. He underestimated the political strength of the abolitionists and did not see their growing influence with major figures, which he should have realized right away after William Seward's "irrepressible conflict" speech. He ignored the threat of John Brown, dismissing him as a fanatic. He paid no attention to the important Southern office holders and newspaper editors he held so dear. He completely ignored the ever more outrageous and inflammatory views of key Southern newspapers, such as Robert Rhett's *Charleston Mercury.* The national uproar over slavery, and talk of secession, was in the newspapers every day.

President James Buchanan began the year 1858 mingling with guests at a happy New Year's Day reception at the White House, discussing everything but slavery. He ended the year the same way. His very last official act of 1858 did not involve slavery at all, but his never-ending love of international diplomacy. That very last message of the year concerned an unimportant trade agreement between the United States and China. He began the year 1859 the same way. His first official act of the new year did not concern slavery, either, but the sending of documents to the House involving steamships accused of playing a role in an invasion of Nicaragua.[649]

The president ended 1858 the way that he began it, completely blind to the slavery issue that threatened to destroy the United States. He had ignored the abolitionists in all of the Northern states all year and now, at the very end of 1858, he would ignore the most dangerous abolitionist of all, John Brown, the fearless Kansas raider. Brown would return to the public eye once again in the waning days of the year in an audacious raid that would startle the entire nation.

TERRIBLE SWIFT SWORD: JOHN BROWN'S CHRISTMAS RAID INTO MISSOURI

John Brown, who had spouted verses from the Bible to anyone who would listen to him during his three years in Kansas, looked like a biblical figure by 1858. The abolitionist was a broad-shouldered man, six feet tall, 150 pounds in weight. He had a taut, strong body from years of labor as a farmer and tanner, and a face whose skin had deep seams, like tiny rivers, and all the wrinkles of a fifty-eight-year-old man. None of that impressed those who met Brown in the winter of 1858, though. What struck them was the foot-long, thick, white, Moses-like beard that he sported, his thatch of wavy white hair and his animated, bright sky blue eyes that seemed to flash in the night. He looked like "an Apostle," wrote one man when he met him.[650]

The striking features of his face were memorable. Frederick Douglass, who permitted him to board with him for several weeks in 1858, wrote, "His face…revealed a strong, square mouth, supported by a broad and prominent chin. His eyes were full of light and fire. When on the street, he moved with a long, spring racehorse step, absorbed by his own reflections, neither seeking or shunning observation."[651]

It was his dramatic physical appearance that drew the attention of all and that helped to make him a legend in the bloody wars between proslavery and antislavery militias and guerrilla bands that by 1858 had torn all of Kansas apart.

Those in his family described him as a kind and gentle man, a tough but fair parent who always inquired about their well-being in letters home when he was away or on the run from posses. His eldest son, John Jr., always rankled when he read descriptions of his father as a "cross and tyrannical" parent that appeared in books or journals. "While he was not exceptionally demonstrative in his affectional nature, and usually had an appearance of earnestness, not many I ever knew had deeper or warmer sympathies, and the children not only of his own family but the children of others always found a warm place in his heart," he said.[652]

His son Salmon remembered his father fondly and never forgot the family breakfasts when he was home. The family would finish eating and then Brown would read verses from the Bible to his children. Their mother would read, and then each child would read verses and sometimes entire chapters. Sometimes Brown, standing, read the Ten Commandments and a Catechism to his children. Those who knew him well later added that he often read poetry to them and maintained a fine sense of humor.[653]

His children also recalled that antislavery discussions figured prominently at meals. John Brown Jr. said that when he was eighteen he and several other teenage children were with Brown when he asked them who among them would join their father "to break the jaws of the wicked..." He asked each child in succession, "Are you Mary? Jason? Owen? John?" All answered yes and he told them to kneel with him.

Wrote John Jr., "After prayer, he asked us to raise our right hands and he then administered to us an oath, the exact terms of which I cannot recall, but in substance it bound us to secrecy and devotion to the purpose of fighting slavery, by force and arms, to the extent of our ability."[654]

That hatred of slavery and a desire to end it with arms was the trademark of Brown's entire life. He was the son of Owen Brown, a religious fanatic and antislavery advocate who ran a tannery in Hudson, Ohio. Following the death of his mother, Brown was greatly influenced by his father, who read the Bible to Brown and his siblings daily. John Brown was the father of twenty children by two wives. He was involved in his own tannery, in Pennsylvania, and then a succession of small businesses in several states. None were very successful. By 1854, at the age of fifty-four, he was financially destitute and living with his family on land given him by philanthropist and abolitionist leader Gerrit Smith in North Elba, New York. He resided there in a one-and-a-half story wood frame home surrounded by a white fence with a large barn at the rear.

Religious from childhood, Brown became a moral zealot as he aged. He was "a man of intense earnestness in all things," one of his sons said.[655] In his mid-thirties, Brown tried to start a school for black children and by 1839 was routinely denouncing slavery to anyone who would listen. In 1847, he first hatched a plan, never realized, to create an empire in the Allegheny Mountains for runaway slaves who would then, in raids, free slaves from Southern plantations. He said the mountain range that ran from New York south to Virginia, was "country admirably adapted in which to carry on guerrilla warfare."[656]

MISSOURI STRIKES FIRST

His life took a dramatic turn in 1855. Six of his sons had moved to the Kansas territory and its wind-swept plains where they would become farmers. The Kansas-Nebraska Act of the previous year had permitted residents of those territories to decide whether or not they desired slavery and this legislation had caused political turbulence that turned violent when proslavery supporters in neighboring Missouri began to stage raids on Kansas's antislavery residents. The Missourians also stuffed ballot boxes with illegal votes to swing elections to proslavery candidates in territorial campaigns.

The political situation deteriorated so quickly and so badly that by the time Brown arrived in 1855, the territory had two separate legislatures. Neither agreed with the other about anything. John Brown, distressed at the Kansas troubles that he read about with great regularity in the newspapers, and fearful for his sons' safety, loaded a wooden farm wagon with pistols and rifles, well-concealed under a canvas, and drove to Kansas to defend his family. When a neighbor asked where he was going with the heavy wagon, he looked directly at him and said, "I am going to Kansas to make it a free state."[657]

In Kansas, he was soon named the "captain" of an ad hoc militia company that was created to fight off the Missouri raiders. The troop was activated in the winter of 1855 when over a thousand Missourians arrived outside of the town of Lawrence, Kansas, intent on skirmishing with another thousand of Free-State defenders there. Brown's troop saw no action, though, because the territorial governor talked both sides out of a confrontation. A few months later, in the spring of 1856, Missouri raiders were back and this time attacked Lawrence. Eight hundred angry, armed Missourians rode into the town, left undefended by its residents for fear of legal reprisals. They fired on the Free-State Hotel with a small cannon, leveling much of it, wrecked the offices of the town's two newspapers, smashing their presses, tossing their type into a nearby river, and ripping up paper stock. They destroyed the home of the Free-Soil governor. The men, shouting and threatening any townspeople who tried to get in their way, ransacked private residences and stores, setting many on fire. Brown and his militia, on their way to Lawrence upon hearing the news, arrived too late to do anything except watch smoke rise from the charred buildings.[658]

The venom toward the Missouri raiders had been building in John Brown for months. The earlier murders of five Free-Soil men had gone unsolved. Proslavery settlers from Pottawatomie Creek had burned down the store of a Free-State man and now ruffians from Missouri, urged on by their fiery U.S. senator, David Atchison, had sacked Lawrence. The U.S. government did nothing to stop the Missouri proslavery assaults, Brown lamented, and neither did the territorial government of Kansas. If Kansas's law enforcement agencies would not avenge these illegal atrocities, John Brown would.

Gathering four of his sons, Brown staged a nighttime raid on the proslavery residents of the village of Pottawatomie. Five of the men were dragged from their homes and butchered with broadswords; their horses were stolen. The vicious, highly publicized attack was justified by Brown as necessary retaliation, but the proslavery settlers and their allies, and all the residents of the Southern states, saw it as murder. They gained revenge a few days later by burning down the community of Osawatomie, where Brown lived. The Pottawatomie massacre was the first bloody chapter in John Brown's war on slavery wherever he found it; there would be more.

Throughout the next two years, Brown and his sons rode with militia units in Kansas to fight the "border ruffians" who invaded the territory from Missouri; his son Frederick was killed in the wars. Their engagements were sometimes mere skirmishes and sometimes deadly. He also rode with the territory's leading guerilla commander, James Montgomery. Throughout those years, Brown vociferously defended his violent tactics, branding his victims as evil people. He explained to critics that he "had never killed an innocent man" and later told a crowd in Cleveland of his career in Kansas and Missouri that "he had never lifted a finger towards any whom he did not know was a violent persecutor of the Free-State men."[659] Charles Robinson, who appointed him a captain when he arrived, noted his "timely action against the invaders of our rights and the murderers of our citizens" and said that "history will pay homage to your heroism with the cause of God and humanity."

A Quaker in Kansas dismissed Brown's savage attack at Pottawatomie, too, and said that he "was a good man and he will be remembered for good in time long hence to come."[660]

Brown's guerrillas frightened Missourians and Kansans alike. One farmer in Kansas complained to territorial governor John Geary that Brown and his men plundered arms and pleaded with him for protection. He wrote the governor, "John Brown and his company, who were still marching through the country taking everything that they could get that they could make money out of…driving everybody back that did not suit their purposes and destroying crops."[661]

THE "SECRET SIX"

During those years, Brown traveled back and forth between his sons' farms in Kansas, his family home in North Elba, New York, and cities in New England where he became friendly with leading abolitionists. He pleaded with them for money to continue his crusade against slavery, just as he had begged other abolitionists, such as Frederick Douglass, for funds. Finally, he convinced a group of six prominent public figures in New England—Julia Howe, Gerrit Smith, Thomas Higginson, George Stearns, Theodore Parker, and F. B. Sanborn—to form a secret committee to raise money for his crusade and a slave insurrection in the South that he planned to organize.

Brown often wrote them from Kansas of his need for funds, always exaggerating his situation in order to obtain money. He was never discreet about pleading for contributions from the "Secret Six," as they were called. He wrote in the summer of 1858, as an example, that "a constant fear of new troubles seems to prevail on both sides of the line and on both sides of the companies of armed men. Any little affair may open the quarrel afresh…We shall soon be in *great want* of a small amount in a draft or drafts on New York to feed us. We cannot work for wages and provisions are not easily obtained on the frontier."[662]

He was often manipulative, asking for far more money than he needed, complaining when he received less than he requested, and threatening to make the financial support of his backers public.

The members of the "Secret Six" believed in Brown's cause, but worried about his means. They had given him money to buy arms in the Kansas wars, but how much further would he go? The six saw in him a man bold enough to take public risks in the war against slavery, but they also saw him as a man who might become too bold. They were not certain that the slaves of the South would rise up to free themselves either, as Brown promised. They were fearful, too, that if they did the slaves might turn against their former owners and families and produce unwanted bloodshed.[663]

Brown did not tell the Secret Six, or most, about his planned raid on Harper's Ferry, a federal arsenal in Virginia, but he did hint at it to Frederick Douglass, reminding him that "money and men, arms and ammunition, food and clothing were needed…not easily obtained."[664]

According to Martin Delaney, a black freedman who was one of his devoted followers, Brown had an alternate plan to send all of the slaves who fled the plantations to Kansas, where Brown planned to establish the Subterranean Passway, a final terminal for all of the Underground Railroads. The slaves would live in and be protected in a large fort Brown would build in the territory. The fort "would defy all the artillery that would be brought to bear against it," said Delaney. In time, Brown was going to establish an independent territory within Kansas, like an Indian nation, where the slaves would live. Delaney said Brown had spent much time on the state-within-a-state plan. He noted, "The whole matter had been well considered."

The amounts of money Brown raised were meager. His grand scheme, Brown told all, required a lot of money. These $50 contributions would help cover expenses, but not much else. He was usually disappointed in the amounts raised for him. In August of 1857, as an example, he expected $1,000 from supporters in Hartford, Connecticut, and another $7,000 from abolitionists in New Haven, Connecticut. All he received was $260 from Hartford and a paltry $25 from New Haven. He called the flimsy donations "disappointments."[665]

Abolitionists in Massachusetts conducted a subscription drive for Brown's wife and the remaining children that lived with her back East while Brown was in Kansas. "Family of Capt. John Brown of Osawatomie, have no means of support, owing to the oppression to which he has been subjected in Kansas Territory. It is proposed to put them [his wife and five children] in possession of the means of supporting themselves as far as is possible for persons in their situation, etc.," read one donor letter, with fifteen names written at the bottom and pledges of $1,000 for the Brown family.[666]

They purchased a farm in North Elba, in central New York, for the Brown family. One of them, F. B. Sanborn, wrote to the subscribers of Brown's wife and daughters, who would live there, "[They] are hardworking, self-denying, devoted women, fully sensible of the greatness of the struggle in which Capt. Brown is engaged, and willing to bear their part in it. I can assure the subscribers to the fund, that money was never better bestowed than in aiding these excellent women to maintain themselves."[667]

Brown always used religion to convince prospective contributors to give him money for his mission. The Second Great Awakening was sweeping the nation at that time; ministers in the North and the evangelical preachers who rode the circuit and brought the word of God to small villages in the Northeast and frontier towns on the prairies. They told congregations that it was not enough to simply go to church in order to find God. One had to be moral to find the Lord and to be moral one had to hate slavery. Brown and his men thought ministers were very effective. "[It] has its advantages," wrote John Kagi, one of his lieutenants. "Under its influence, people who are commonly barely unfavorable to slavery under religious excitement in meetings speak boldly against it."[668]

Brown ran ads in numerous newspapers to solicit funds for his nebulous operations. They all began: "To the Friends of Freedom." The ads told readers that his funds had been drained by his war in Kansas and he needed to replenish them, "anxious to continue his efforts, is induced to make this earnest appeal to the friends of freedom through the United States in the firm belief that his call will not go unheeded. I ask all lovers of liberty and human rights, both male and female, to hold up my hands by contributions of penury aid, either as counties, cities, towns, villages, societies, churches, or individuals…"[669]

With the money he obtained, whenever he was able to raise it, he purchased clothing and provisions for himself and his "army," that never consisted of more than fifteen men. The contributions were used to buy weapons, too, but his arsenal was never impressive and the men were never well equipped. Just as they relied upon supporters of "the cause" for cash to cover their expenses, they relied on those in the antislavery movement to supply them with guns. Weapons were expensive and there never seemed to be money to purchase enough of them, or to buy quality arms. Consequently, they operated as a hand-me-down army. In one letter lamenting his arsenal, Brown told a friend that he had "70 to 75 damaged U.S. army rifles" and "some powder," plus a field piece with "a damaged gun carriage." For his personal use, someone had sent him an old gun and a pair of pistols, all used, and four guns someone had manufactured as "an experiment," Brown noted.[670]

Madman or Prophet?

People either loved or hated John Brown; there was no middle ground. He was seen as an enlightened prophet or a dangerous madman.

No matter how they viewed him, all agreed that Brown was uncompromising, his opinions unshakable. He saw the government of the United States as unwilling to end slavery, an institution that he said violated the laws of God. He believed that peaceful means outside the government and courts had failed to do so and he did not have any faith that people opposed to slavery could, or would, abolish the institution. In his mind, therefore, only violence could end slavery, and since eliminating slavery was not only a proper course, but a course condoned by God, any violence was not only acceptable, but necessary.[671]

After he died, many referred to him as a larger-than-life, messianic savior of the blacks and the moral leader of an army determined to free the oppressed wherever they found them. Editor William Cullen Bryant of New York wrote that "history will record his name among those of its martyrs and heroes." Wendell Phillips wrote that, "Heroes of other days died for their own rights…John Brown died for a race in whose blood he had no share." Unitarian minister and abolitionist leader Rev. Theodore Parker of Boston called him "a saint." Henry David Thoreau of Massachusetts said he was a "crucified hero, an angel of light."[672]

Those who did not observe him from faraway New England but knew him personally during the Kansas wars agreed. James Emery met Brown in

1855, at the start of the bloody skirmishes there. "John Brown was a prophet of that early day, but he who associated with him daily did not know it… Brown found actual fighting to be done out here to save free soil from lapsing back and coming under the curse of a [slave] system that was abhorrent to his very soul," Emery wrote years later.[673]

Southerners, though, considered him a lunatic and madman who was determined to use violent means to end slavery and incite a black insurrection in which thousands of Southerners would be murdered.

Wrote Southerner Randolph Abbott Shotwell, "He was a rabid fanatic, naturally narrow-minded, and vindictive in his prejudices and fevered to furious hatred of the Southerners by the fruits of his own rashness and folly. It is probable he lacked from birth the balance of mind necessary to weight questions involving the control of his own likes and dislikes, and there was nothing in his early education, amid the bigotry-breeding atmosphere of a backwoods abolition village, to broaden his views, or restore his mental equipoise. Men of his turn are easily self-deluded into believing themselves special agents commissioned by Providence for 'a glorious work,' and having set out with this idea are apt, like a ship with a twisted rudder, to go wider and wider from the direct course as they advance until they are finally shipwrecked."[674]

ᐦ

THE CHRISTMAS RAID

John Brown wanted to attack and seize the federal arsenal at Harper's Ferry, Virginia, on the southern side of the Potomac River west of Washington, DC. Brown had targeted the area for over a year. He was certain that such a foray on a federal installation would rouse slaves throughout the South to insurrection and create havoc across the United States. Millions of slaves would rise up, throw off their chains and flee to freedom in the North. In December of 1857, when he and his band of nine volunteers were together at a snow-bound camp in Iowa, Brown told them that "our ultimate destination is Virginia." His followers were surprised and angry. They had dreamed of liberating Kansas, not Virginia, and argued with the old man, irritating him.

Two months later, in February 1858, while he was staying with Frederick Douglass in Rochester, New York, Brown again told people that he was formulating plans for some grand event, but he was not specific. In the autumn of 1858, in Kansas, he wrote F. B. Sanborn, one of his fundraisers, "I am most anxious about [the mission] and want you to name the earliest possible date when you can have your matters [funds] gathered up." He told his top confidante, John Kagi, that he wanted to attack Virginia soon, that "the hour is at hand." He wrote friends Wendell Phillips and Richard Hinton that time was running out and he wanted his mission to Virginia to begin with as much speed as possible. He dismissed Hinton's worry that he would never have enough men or arms, telling him that "a few men in the right and knowing they are right, can overturn a king."[675]

He wrote his wife from Rochester, "Courage, courage, courage! The great work of my life…I may yet see accomplished [God helping], and be permitted to return and 'rest at evening.'" He wrote the abolitionists who had been his financial and emotional backers, that he had "by far the most important undertaking of my whole life."[676]

A raid on Harper's Ferry, or any other slave-related assault, was not a spur-of-the moment decision. The idea of a violent raid to encourage the slaves into armed insurrection was already in the planning stages in the summer of 1858, when Brown outlined it to members of an antislavery convention in Chatham, Canada, without naming a target. A Chatham gun shop owner who thought the idea sheer folly vividly remembered Brown's determination to conduct organized raids. "We were discussing how the plans might fail. I think I had the floor at the time, and was telling the members how soon the slave power would surround them in their strongholds in the mountains… His general plan was to fortify some places in the mountains and call the slaves to his colors. I said to him that I was afraid he might be disappointed in the slaves," the merchant told a reporter years later. "I told him how utterly hopeless these plans would be if he persisted in making an attack with the few men at his command…ready to sacrifice their lives for the salvation of black men. While I was speaking, he was walking to and from, his hands behind, as was his custom when thinking of this, his favorite subject. He stopped suddenly and bringing down his hand with great force exclaimed, 'Did not my master, Jesus Christ, come down from heaven and sacrifice himself upon the altar for the salvation of the race? And should I, a worm, not worthy to crawl under His feet, refuse to sacrifice myself?'"[677]

There was no mistaking Brown's hatred of slavery in Chatham. In the Preamble of the new land's Provisional Constitution and Ordinances for the people of the United States, he wrote, "Slavery...is none other than the most barbaric, unprovoked, and unjustifiable war of one portion of citizens upon another."[678]

Some friends of Brown said the idea of a violent raid into a slave territory or state was in the back of Brown's mind for decades. Wrote Governor John Andrews of Massachusetts, "If I am rightly informed, he has cherished this scheme of liberating the slaves in Virginia for more than thirty years and laid his plans when he was a land surveyor in [Virginia]." Frederick Douglass remembered that in 1847 Brown had outlined his Allegheny slave empire to him. F. B. Sanborn said Brown wrote him of a general Southern invasion in December of 1839.[679]

Brown could not raise enough money and men, or procure enough weapons, for that Harper's Ferry assault, or any other attack in the spring of 1858, though. Wrote Luke Parsons, one of the men who rode with him, "Brown failed to find the money to carry on our plans so the [Harper's Ferry] raid was declared off for one year. Brown took three of the men back with him to Kansas."[680]

Kansas was relatively quiet in the spring of 1858 as most of the residents put down their guns to argue politics over the Lecompton Constitution. Brown made his reentry "with the utmost quiet," he said, and moved about Kansas under one of the several assumed names he used, such as Shubel Morgan. It was so quiet, in fact, that in the middle of October 1858, Brown thought about going back to New York, writing his wife that "I can now see no good reason why I should not be located nearer home."[681]

Illness may have caused him to return to his wife and family. His health had deteriorated during the past year. Throughout the autumn of 1858 he suffered from what he called an "ague" of some kind that caused trembling in his body. One week before Christmas, he wrote his wife that he felt a bit better. "My health is improving but still I get a 'shake' pretty often."[682]

He did not tell his wife that there was yet another bounty on his head, $500, for a non-violent November 13 raid with guerilla leader James Montgomery on the tiny community of Paris, Kansas, where Montgomery had been indicted for destroying ballot boxes in January elections there. The raiders wanted to confiscate the indictment document, but could not find it.

Locals were angrier at Brown than the governor. They saw the New Yorker as an outside agitator who had become a thorn in their side. Two weeks later, a sheriff and a posse of volunteers set a trap to capture Brown and Montgomery, but Brown was not with Montgomery and the latter's men fought off a poorly planned attack. As a result, Kansans' fear of the guerillas increased.[683]

In December 1858, Brown was told by Montgomery that he was planning to attack Fort Scott, ninety miles south of Kansas City, and rescue a Free-State man who was incarcerated there. Brown told Montgomery that his thinking was too limited, that they should burn the entire fort and all of its buildings; the total destruction of the fort was necessary to send both Kansans and Missourians a message. A shocked Montgomery disagreed. Brown sulked and had little to do with the raid on the fort, in which the captured man was freed but a pro-slaver who had once nearly slain Brown's disciple Kagi with a shotgun blast, was killed.

A few days later, by sheer luck, Brown's lieutenant, black freedman George Gill, met a mulatto from Missouri, Jim Daniels, who complained to him that his wife and children and another slave were going to be sold, their families broken up, by their owner, Harvey Hicklan. Daniels was desperate for help. Brown thought the man's plight offered a wonderful chance for a raid to liberate slaves and strike a blow for freedom. He was convinced that such a raid, and an eleven-hundred-mile exodus to free Canada, would garner substantial press attention. Despite the risks, such a raid would show the world what kind of man he was. "It is in times of difficulty that men show what they are. It is at such times that men mark themselves," he always said.[684]

George Gill, the black freedman, agreed. He wrote, "I am sure that Brown, in his mind, was just waiting for something to turn up; or, in his way of thinking, was expecting or hoping that 'God would provide him a basis of action.' When this came, he hailed it as heaven sent."

For Brown, it was an opportunity he could not ignore; he had always preached to his disciples that "God had created him to be the deliverer of the slaves, the same as Moses had delivered the children of Israel."[685]

His men believed that too, and would follow him anywhere. In Brown, they not only had a true believer in the antislavery cause, but a forceful leader with a resolute attitude. He got things done. Brown's near-dictatorial personality was evident to his children as they grew up. One of his sons described him as "a King against whom there is no rising up." Brown agreed, telling his son that he "habitually expected to succeed."

He was completely devoted to his cause. All who knew him, friends and foes, acknowledged that he pursued his goal of eradicating slavery with remarkable vigilance. Brown's soul "will be the inspiration of all men in the present and distant future who may revolt against tyranny and oppression," wrote Charles Robinson later. "He is the pure idealist, with no by-end of his own," added writer Ralph Waldo Emerson.

He dismissed any fears of his men that they would be captured, telling them that "the angel of the Lord will camp 'round me."

Brown was determined. Abolitionist Gerrit Smith wrote that once "our old friend has made up his mind, [he] cannot be turned from it." He possessed a steely will that always seemed to prevail in discussions with his raiders and supporters. "His arguments seemed to convince all…his appeals touched all and his will impressed all," wrote Frederick Douglass, who added that Brown had a mystical aura about him. "I never felt myself under a stronger religious influence than while in John Brown's house."

And there was no doubt of his willingness to use violence to achieve his means, frequently telling supporters and anyone who would listen by the winter of 1858 that "I am more than ever of the opinion that we must settle this question [slavery] in the old Anglo-Saxon way—by the sword."[686]

Brown should have realized the consequences of any raid in Missouri, though. The news that John Brown was back had infuriated Missourians. He wrote his son John Jr., "Having [me] on a conspicuous place and in full view for miles around in Missouri produced a ferment there which you can better imagine than I can describe. Which of the passions most predominated, fear or rage, I do not pretend to say."[687]

Late on the chilly night of December 20, just a few days before Christmas 1858, Brown and five men in his ten-man raider party rode into Missouri and attacked the farm of Harvey Hicklan. Hicklan was awakened by the sound of the hooves of a half-dozen horses in front of his tiny farmhouse on the prairie. Just as he walked into the main room from his small bedroom, the front door of the house flew open and there in front of him was the notorious abolitionist, John Brown. The intruder cut quite a dramatic figure as he stood in front of Hicklan, his long white beard flowing over his shirt, his rifle pointed directly at him.

Brown told Hicklan why he was there. "We have come after your Negroes and their property. Will you surrender or fight?" Hicklan, who feared for the safety of his family, did not resist and permitted Brown and his men to ride off with his six slaves.

Captain Brown sent five other men to the nearby farm of John Larue to liberate four slaves there. The Brown raiders confiscated the farmers' wagons and horses as well, plus clothing, bedding, food supplies, a pair of boots, and a shotgun and left just before dawn. He also took with him Larue and a friend as hostages with the suddenly free, and very nervous, slaves. The men with Brown could not resist the opportunity to loot the homes. "They ransacked the house in search of money and I suppose they would have taken it if they had found it," said Hicklan. Gill admitted that "watches and other articles were being taken; some of our number proved to be mere adventurers, ready to take from friend or foe as opportunity offered."[688]

A third group of Brown's men, led by Aaron Stevens, surprised David Cruise at his farmhouse in their rescue of a female slave there. Stevens saw Cruise move and assumed he was going for a weapon. A nervous Stevens fired at the farmer, killing him.[689]

The slaying of the much-respected Cruise turned the raid from just a rescue into an act that inflamed Kansans, Missourians, and Southerners and once again propelled John Brown into the national spotlight.[690] Newspapers in both Kansas and Missouri were appalled at the rescue, the death of Cruise, and the kidnapping of Larue and his friend. The *Harrisonville (Missouri) Democrat* said the raiders were murderers and begged authorities to do "something to protect our people." The editor of the *Wyandotte City Western Argus* wrote that Brown "will have a heavy account to settle some day—for surely a terrible retribution will come to them sooner or later."[691]

During the first week of January, 1859, a Kansas correspondent of the influential *St. Louis Missouri-Democrat* evoked the repulsion felt by many in both Kansas and Missouri by the Osawatomie raid, and the murder, in one of his stories. He called the raid and killing "of a nature so revolting that the mind grows dizzy with horror, and involuntarily inquires whether or not we are not relapsing into the barbarism of the middle ages. It is not probable that the killing of Cruise was premeditated, but finding himself attacked by robbers, he resisted, as remorselessly by the fiend who had attacked him. I have yet to see the first Free-State man of position in or around Osawatomie who does not condemn in the strongest terms any going into Missouri or committing depredations."[692]

The wagon Brown and his tiny army traveled in, and in which they transported the freed slaves, was one of the old Conestogas. Designed for long trips on the plains and used by those who traveled to the prairies with their families to start new lives, the wagons were slow moving, lumbering, and contained dozens of chains that hung from its sides to hold things that caused much noise as they banged against the wooden sides of the vehicle. That cold night, Brown led the large party of raiders and refugees, and their wagon, out of Missouri and thirty-five miles back into Kansas to a cabin near Osawatomie Creek, arriving at nightfall on Christmas Eve.

The raiders rode with their freed slaves and two captives toward the farm of Augustus Wattles, near Mound City, Kansas, constantly looking back over their shoulders to see if they were being followed by a posse. On the way, Brown surely told the captured farmers the same thing he told all of the proslavery Kansans and Missourians he captured or encountered in the territorial wars, alternately warning them to stay away from the free farmers of the area and threatening them.

"We wish no harm to you or your companions. Stay at home. Let us alone and we shall be friends," was his usual line of warning.

He often threatened captives, only to let them go. "I am the enemy of all evildoers. You came here to make this a slave state. You are fighting against liberty, which our revolutionary fathers fought to establish, when all men should be free and equal...you are a traitor to liberty and your country. You deserve to be hanged to the nearest tree."[693]

The raiders hoped to hide the slaves at the home of the Rev. Samuel Adair, who lived near Osawatomie Creek and who had harbored two of Brown's sons following the Pottawatomie massacre of 1856. The compact wagon train of fugitives and raiders arrived at the minister's home on Christmas Eve. At first he was uncertain whether or not he should cooperate because of the heated climate in the territory.

Adair wrote, "The fugitive slave law was still in force. I realized in some measure the responsibility of receiving them, consulted my wife, calling her attention to our responsibility, but would do as she said. She considered the subject for a few moments, then said: 'I cannot turn them away.' By this time, the team was in the road in front of the house. All were taken round to the backyard, and the colored people were brought into the back kitchen and kept there that night...”[694]

Even though they were happy to help, the Adairs did not want to house the freed blacks permanently. They suggested a vacant cabin nearby, owned by Charles Severn, a fellow abolitionist, on the banks of the Osawatomie. Severn had moved to Kansas a year before and was traveling. It was a small, nondescript home that had not been lived in for some time and might make a perfect hideout. The Adairs, and other friends in the area, would supply the refugees with food and clothing and protect them.

A man named Ambrose who lived near the Osawatomie was sound asleep when he heard a hard knocking on the front door of his cabin that night. Fearful of still more proslavery militants in the area, Ambrose did not open the door, but shouted through it to discover who was there.

“Samuel Mack,” said the visitor.

Ambrose let Mack, the local justice of the peace, into the cabin and shut the door. Mack informed him that John Brown and his men were harboring eleven slaves they had freed in Severn’s cabin, which could be seen from Ambrose’s farmhouse. The primitive cabin was constructed out of unhewn hickory poles and did not have a door, window or a wooden floor. It was in the middle of a wide, flat plain and could be observed for miles by anyone. Mack was there to alert Ambrose so he would not visit the cabin, attracting unwanted attention. “There were some men living in the neighborhood whom the old antislavery guard could not trust and a visit…might lead to the discovery of the fugitives,” Ambrose said.

Next, Mack rode to the home of Ambrose’s father-in-law, William Felton, who lived a half mile southwest of the cabin, and alerted him, too. Felton and his family were happy to help protect the fugitives. Ambrose said later, “They were all well pleased, and entered heartily into the business of assisting to provide for them during their stay, for they hated slavery with a holy hatred.”

Over the next few days, Ambrose and his father-in-law brought food and clothing to the runaways and raiders in Severn’s cabin. The runaways fixed the cabin, patched the holes between the hickory poles with dirt and grass, built a chimney and created a doorway that they covered over with a quilt. Ambrose rode regularly to the cabin at night with supplies and to warn the runaways if there was too much smoke coming out of the chimney that could be seen. He said, “I would…caution them about the great danger of being discovered.”

He was determined to help the freed slaves, but worried about himself, too, just as Rev. Adair had. "I felt a great anxiety about it. I was born in a slave state and knew the cursed spirit of slavery, and knew full well that if they were discovered so close to my habitation, all the hounds in the proslavery kennel would be turned loose upon me, under the law of the dark ages, the fugitive slave law."

Ambrose and anyone else involved in Brown's raid had good reason to worry. The proslavery forces in Kansas and Missouri were determined to hunt down and execute anyone involved in an effort to liberate slaves. U.S. Senator David Atchison, of Missouri, wrote a heated letter to Senator Jefferson Davis explaining, "In a public speech…I advised the squatters in Kansas and the people of Missouri to give a horse thief, robber or [murderer] a fair trial, but to hang a Negro thief and abolitionist, without judge or jury. This sentiment met with almost universal applause."[695]

One of the freed women was pregnant. She gave birth to a baby boy that she and her husband Jim immediately named John Brown out of gratitude to their liberator. The slaves had no time to gather up clothing, especially a baby's clothing, when they fled and the baby had no clothes. Mrs. Felton rode to Mrs. Ambrose's home and the two women made a toddler's suit and brought it, along with a gown and some blankets, to the Severn cabin, where the new mother thanked them profusely.

Mother and child, and the others, did not feel safe, though. The antislavery men in the area volunteered to spend nights in the Ambrose cabin keeping watch, rifles in their arms. They included Dr. Rufus Gillpatrick, Martin Ayers, David Harsha, Samuel Mack, James Fitton, Felton, and Ambrose. Two men deemed too old to engage in a gun battle if it broke out, James Blunt and Poindexter Maners, served as suppliers of food and clothing to the fugitives.

The slaves remained there for a month. None of the proslavery men in the area found them, but there were two close calls. Once Ambrose saw a well known pro-slaver walking past his home on a direct line toward the Severn cabin. Ambrose rushed outside to ask him where he was going.

"John Blunt's," he said.

Thinking quickly, Ambrose told him that he was on his way past Blunt's on an errand and he would drive him there in his wagon. The man said he could walk, but Ambrose insisted. The man jumped into his wagon and they drove off, taking a wide path away from the Severn cabin and then a long three miles to Blunt's.

On another occasion several of the men guarding the fugitives were with a proslavery man several miles from the Severn cabin. The pro-slaver was looking around the plains with a field glass and noticed a black man near the cabin.

"Who's that darky near the Severn place?" he asked no one in particular, putting the field glass down.

One of the guards, acting surprised, said, "Give me that field glass."

He then looked, saw the man, and handed the field glass to another, telling all, "I saw nothing."

The guards then passed the field glass back and forth and then, when the slave had disappeared into the cabin, handed it back to the pro-slaver, who looked through it again and saw no one. He shrugged his shoulders, put the field glass down and went about his business.[696]

These incidents, and the need to get the refugees to Canada, persuaded Brown, who visited the fugitives from time to time, to leave Kansas. He knew from conversations with his friends there, that even some of them objected to the murder of Cruise and the plundering. They would not support him. To them, he scoffed, "It is no pleasure to me, an old man, to be living in the saddle, away from home and family, exposing my life, and if the Free State men of Kansas feel that they no longer need me, I will be glad to go."[697]

Finally, on January 20, 1859, a month after the rescue, ready to depart, Brown rode to the Ambrose cabin and thanked the farmer for protecting the slaves. Ambrose told him it was his pleasure. "God bless you," he said to Brown. That last night was a magical moment for Ambrose. He was to describe him, "His gray hair and long, snow white beard gave him a venerable appearance and the tone of voice indicated that whosoever attempted to stop him would have to fight."

Ambrose proceeded to join Brown's raiders for the ride to the border. There, a grateful Brown told Ambrose that he no longer needed a local guide. He knew the roads out of the Osawatomie area to Lawrence, Kansas, and then to Iowa, his next stop on the road to Canada. Ambrose wrote proudly of his assistance to Brown, "Such a length of time in such weather may make the weak in the faith of the access of any enterprise that they might take hold of doubt; but no such Doubting Thomas has ever had anything to do with the work of the underground railroad, or they would not express such doubts."[698]

Officials of both Missouri and Kansas were livid. The Missouri General Assembly condemned Brown and the new governor of Kansas called the raid contemptible. Newspapers in both states criticized his actions and those throughout the Southern states demanded that federal, state, and local authorities join forces to capture and imprison him.

THE POWER OF THE PRESS

That was to be expected. What Brown was looking for was applause from the antislavery movement. To engender that response, he courted the press. To win press coverage of the raid, he invited a regional correspondent for the *New York Tribune,* William Hutchinson, to meet him at the Wattles home, in Moneka, Kansas, where he was hiding. He talked to Hutchinson in lengthy interviews that covered two days, December 30 and 31. The shrewd abolitionist leader then permitted the reporter to sit in on one of his "war councils" so he could observe Brown and the other raiders discussing their plans and, importantly, so he could see that they did not desire violence, just the liberation of slaves. Brown was so intent on garnering favorable coverage in the influential *Tribune* that at one point he turned to Hutchinson and asked what he thought the raiders should do. The young reporter, flattered, suggested more peaceful talks and no violence. The men agreed.

"I met with Brown and his boys about noon that day, Thursday," Hutchinson wrote. "We went to Wattles that night together and we were together all night and the next day, talking much with him and Wattles and others who called on us. They took special pains to have a war council on my account and appeared to have great confidence in 'the man from Lawrence,' as some termed me. I am so vain as to think my advice did have some good effect."

The reporter for the *Tribune* was one of the few people in the press to spend time with Brown during the raid and the liberators' eleven-hundred-mile trek to Canada. He remained with Brown at the Wattles home for nearly a week and observed Brown's intensity, writing that the raider was so fired up that he could barely sleep. Hutchinson wrote, "Our bed was a mattress made of hay, laid upon the floor of the second story. Sleep seemed to be a secondary matter with him. I am sure he talked on that night 'til the small hours, and his all-absorbing theme was 'my work,' 'my great duty,' 'my mission,' etc., meaning, of course, the liberation of the slaves. He seemed to have no other object in life, no other hope or ambition. The utmost sincerity pervaded his every thought and word."[699]

Writing in the *Tribune*, Hutchinson wrote that the raids were justifiable as retaliation for slave catchers stealing former slaves from their homes in the North. The *Tribune* story was balanced, but sympathetic to Brown. "Some bad may have grown out of the movement, but I have yet to see what it is. Much good has come of it. The bluster of Missouri has lessened. While hundreds of the non-slaveholding whites express great indignation at the invasion of their state, and boil over with patriotism in public, they privately laugh at the idea of their defending a species of property that is a curse to them, and rejoice that certain lordly slaveholders have 'come down to their level.'"[700]

Just before the raid, Brown had met with William Phillips, another Kansas reporter for the *New York Tribune*. Eager to alert the country to his mission through the press, Brown told Phillips (of slavery), "And now we have reached a point where nothing but war can settle the question. Had they [slavers] succeeded in Kansas, they would have gained a power that would have given them permanently the upper hand, and it would have been the death-knell of republicanism in America."

Brown told the reporter, too, that violence was necessary. "We are on the eve of one of the greatest wars in history… I drew my sword in Kansas when they attacked us, and I will never sheathe it until this war is over," he told Phillips in one of three meetings. He responded to the journalist's contention that the government had made up its mind about slavery, "I will remedy that."

All of this gave Phillips, and Hutchinson, too, a view of Brown as a man who accomplished his goals. Phillips wrote, "While others passed resolutions, he acted on them… The part of the evangelist that seemed to impress him most was the occasion of our Savior with whips of cords [driving] the money changers from the temple."[701]

Pleased with his success in persuading Hutchinson and Phillips to look favorably upon the Missouri raid and the harboring of the eleven fugitives, plus the newborn baby, Brown decided to conduct a press offensive to ensure the safety of his party. He needed all of the large city newspapers to approve of his work, not just the *New York Tribune.* To do that he decided to write a manifesto, called the *Parallels,* and mail it to the editors of the most important newspapers in the country, especially those in the Northeast, where he was not only seeking approval, but funds to further the cause.

In the *Parallels,* Brown argued that since proslavery men had murdered slaves and free men in Kansas, and slave catchers had snatched black freedmen in Kansas and in several Northern states, his Missouri raid was a "parallel" action. He cited an instance in which proslavery raiders killed eleven antislavery Kansas residents and compared that event to his Missouri raid. He wrote, "Now for a comparison. Eleven persons are forcibly restored to their natural, and inalienable rights, with but one man killed and all 'hell I stirred from beneath.' The marshal of Kansas is said to be collecting a posse of Missouri [not Kansas] men at West Point in Missouri a little town about ten miles distant, to 'enforce the laws' and all proslavery conservative Free-State, and Administration are filled with holy horror. Consider the two cases, and the action of the Administration party."[702]

His parallel analogy made sense to many in the North, and even in Missouri, where legislators demanded the cessation of all violence in Kansas, on both sides, for fear that "an eye for an eye" reprisals would continue. Many newspapers ran stories quoting the *Parallels* and Brown became a much-debated national figure as people wondered whether the elusive raider would make it to Canada.

There was some favorable reaction to the press coverage of Brown and his raiders. Montgomery, tired of the Kansas wars, surrendered himself on January 18 to authorities in Lawrence, who freed him on $4,000 bail pending his trial concerning the raid on the community. On January 20, Montgomery addressed an overflow crowd of three thousand at the Lawrence Congregational Church, speaking for three hours on the border strife and calling for an end to it. At the conclusion of his speech, as expected, there was applause for Montgomery. Then, completely unexpected, someone asked for a cheer for "Old John Brown" and the crowd erupted into frenzied applause and shouting.[703]

There was much opposition to Brown's raid in Kansas and Missouri, though. Farmers in Kansas feared yet more retaliation from Missourians for the attacks. One man told Brown that it was the residents of Kansas who would have to pay a heavy price if that happened, not Brown, who would disappear, as he always did. Even Wattles and Montgomery were angry with him because of the murder of Cruise. Brown did not understand their criticism. He argued that he had done precisely what he knew would cause freedom loving men everywhere to rise up. In fact, Brown told the pair, he had heard that farmers in western Missouri, hearing of the attacks, and fearing him, had fled into neighboring Arkansas.

Besides, he swore to them as he swore to everyone, he had not unjustly murdered anyone, in Missouri or in the Kansas wars of 1855 and 1856, as so many had charged, including eyewitnesses to the Pottawatomie massacre. His view had always been that the defenders of slavery were expendable. "I killed no innocent men," he told critics.[704]

Even many Republicans were mad at Brown. The editor of the moderate Republican *Lawrence Herald of Freedom* wrote, "Little did I think in 1856 that professedly free state men would be guilty of the same crime for which we denounced the proslavery men of that year and which raised such a storm throughout the nation."[705]

Sick of the criticism, Brown told Kansans, "You will have no more attacks from Missouri; I shall now leave Kansas, probably you will never see me again; I consider it my duty to draw the scene of the excitement to some other part of the country."[706]

If newspapers in Kansas and Missouri were not friendly, others were. Hutchinson's reports were followed by other positive stories about Brown and his daring raid in large city newspapers in the Midwest and the Northeast. The *New York Times* even wrote on January 11 that, "Brown especially has suffered wrongs enough at the hands of Missouri invaders to almost steel his heart against every sentiment of humanity. To avenge the death of his murdered son and the long list of outrages perpetrated upon him during the Kansas struggle he considers almost a religious duty."

The press coverage had helped convince his financial backers that he could succeed in a large raid and escape. Gerrit Smith wrote enthusiastically to his wife on January 10, "Do you hear the news from Kansas? Our dear John Brown is invading Missouri and pursuing the policy which he intended to pursue *elsewhere*." [707]

As he rode northward into Iowa, Brown had all of the press recognition that he sought. Would newspaper attention help him as he fled across the country toward Canada, though? He had to cover eleven hundred miles, traveling at night and during the day, in a brutal winter, and would have to move through farm villages and larger communities, always visible to those who wanted to capture him. He would have to rely on the assistance of the ordinary people of Iowa and other states on his way to Canada. He needed mayors and sheriffs to let him ride through on his way North, if not sympathetic to his cause then at least impressed enough with his bold raid to let him finish his journey. He needed abolitionists and friends to hide him and give him provisions, even though he was now a man wanted in both Kansas and Missouri, a man whose mere whereabouts would be worth $3,000 to any informer. Would they?

The first test came at Lawrence, Kansas, where his party, reduced for the time to just himself and George Gill and their eleven refugees and a baby, arrived at the home of supporter Major James Abbot late at night on January 24. The journey had been perilous and both Brown and Gill had nearly frozen limbs when they climbed off their horses at Abbott's home. There, to his relief, Brown discovered that Abbott and others were not only willing to help him, but eager. Working at night to avoid detection by Lawrence authorities, they loaded up his wagons with food and clothing and gave him fresh horses. They urged him to ride with Dr. John Doy, who had himself rescued several slaves and was intent on getting them out of Kansas. Brown refused, to his good fortune. Doy was captured by a posse, one of several looking for him and Brown, a few days later and imprisoned.

Brown and the raiders nearly met the same fate on their way to Topeka, Kansas. A severe storm that dumped several inches of snow on the landscape forced them to spend the night at a tavern in the village of Holton. News of their presence in the area spread quickly throughout the county. The next day they reached Spring Creek, where the rushing water was too high to permit a crossing of the wagon and the raiders on horseback. Brown felt trapped because the previous evening he was told that not only was a local posse waiting for him on the other side of Spring Creek, but that the governor of Missouri, told of his location, had sent troops—"several hundred," the story went—to capture him. Brown and the raiders slipped away in the morning, to Fuller's Crossing, but met another posse there.

The men in the large posse tracking them were near the other side of the creek, Brown was told, and warned not to continue. There were nearly a hundred of them, he was told, and they were armed. "What do you propose to do?" asked a frantic woman who lived there, certain he would turn back.

John Brown did not flinch. He looked directly at her and without hesitation said, "I propose to cross the creek and move north." He did, taking his men and the wagon through the surging waters to the other side. There, the twenty-two raiders and their freed slaves became engaged in a gun battle with eighty men in the posse. Acting boldly, the raiders charged the posse, forcing it back and eventually driving it out of the area following a flurry of gunshots. The men in the posse were so intent on retreating that many of their horses carried two men, both digging their boot spurs into their mounts.[708]

Brown and the raiders found themselves in the newspapers again the day after the battle, appropriately dubbed "the battle of the spurs," denounced by some and defended by others. The *Missouri Democrat* thought the entire affair amusing. "The chase was a merry one," its correspondent wrote, "and closed by Brown's taking off three of his pursuers as prisoners, with four horses, pistols, guns as legitimate plunder… Old Captain Brown is not to be taken by 'boys' and he cordially invites all proslavery men to try their hands at arresting him."[709]

Brown was relieved to be in a free state, writing his wife Mary, "I am once more in Iowa through the great mercy of God. Those with me and other friends are well. I hope soon to be at a point where I can learn of your welfare and perhaps send you something besides my good wishes."[710]

He soon reached Tabor, Iowa, where he had hidden out in the past. He was allowed to keep his slaves in a schoolhouse overnight and to remain with Gill, Kagi, Aaron Stevens, and a few others who had joined them in the exodus, but the raiders were not welcomed to stay more than one night because they had killed Cruise. The locals denounced him in a statement, "While we sympathize with the oppressed and will do all that we conscientiously can to help them in their efforts for freedom, nevertheless, we have no sympathy with those who go to slave states to entice away slaves and take property of life when necessary to attain that end."[711]

Unhappy, Brown left and headed east toward the much larger community of Des Moines, stopping for shelter along the way at Underground Railroad safe houses in several villages. He was disgusted with the citizens of Tabor, writing, "There are those who would sooner see me supplied with a good [noose] than anything else for my services [in Tabor]."[712]

Brown had nothing but praise for his raiders and all the men who had fought with him. "Strong, hearty farmers and mechanics, who had left their work and their homes [on hearing of an invasion] without even waiting to change their clothes; and were, as a whole, the most intelligent, sober, and orderly set of men I have ever seen collected…a set of determined men as I had no idea this Territory could boast of in any such numbers."[713]

The long trek and the close quarters the raiders and their liberated slaves maintained produced tension, though. Gill, at first a great admirer of Brown, later wrote that he was egocentric, could be vindictive, mean, and obstinate toward his own men, even petty, refusing to brew coffee for others when all he wanted was tea. He also seemed to want to hang everyone he thought betrayed his "cause" and was never intent on causing mere mischief when he could burn down an entire town or attack a settlement.[714]

Authorities in Des Moines were friendlier and the editor of the local newspaper, John Teesdale, an old acquaintance of both Brown and Kagi, gave him money to cover ferry tickets across the Des Moines river for his party. Brown later wrote Teesdale that he had no regrets about the murder of Cruise. "The most ready and effectual way to retrieve Kansas would be to meddle directly with the peculiar institution. Next, we had no means necessary of moving the rescued captives without taking a portion of their lawfully acquired earnings. All we took has been held sacred to that object and will be."[715]

The reception in Grinnell, Iowa, was far more gracious, as Brown hoped it would be. Joseph Grinnell, who founded the town, was the leading abolitionist in Iowa. Grinnell not only provided them with food, clothing, fresh horses, and several nights of accommodations, but arranged for two nightly meetings at the Congregational Church where he and three local ministers applauded the work of the raiders after Brown and Kagi gave speeches. "[We] were loudly cheered and full endorsed. [Ministers] all took part in justifying our course and in urging contributions in our behalf and there was no dissenting speaker present at either meeting," Brown wrote, adding that a few days later there was "last but not least, public Thanksgiving to Almighty God, offered up by Mr. Grinnell in the behalf of the whole company. [Thanks] for His great mercy and protecting care."[716]

The raiders moved on to Springdale, home to many antislavery Quakers, where they were treated as heroes during a three-week stay. Men from the community accompanied them east on March 9 to West Liberty, where they boarded a railroad box car that was hooked up to a train and transported them to Chicago. The locals were proud to have harbored the Missouri raiders, who by now had the attention of the entire nation through the published *Parallels* and newspaper accounts of their movements and gun battles, but they were also glad to be rid of them. They feared an attack by a large armed posse, rumored to be in the area.

In fact, Brown and Kagi were almost captured while at Springdale when they made an overnight visit to nearby Iowa City. There, a man carrying a rope tied into a hangman's noose confronted them in a tavern and threatened to hang "the nigger stealers of Kansas." The man left their table and rejoined a group of men in the street. Some of them remained outside the front door of the tavern and others surrounded the stable where Brown and Kagi's team of wagon horses were housed. The two men managed to leave the tavern and found refuge in a safe house outside of town. They slipped away unnoticed in the morning, fortunately not taking a road out of the area where a band of men with guns were taking target practice, telling a passerby that they were waiting to shoot "Old John Brown." If Brown, Kagi, Stevens, and Gill were trapped in Springdale, they told the residents there, they would shoot their way out, endangering the locals. "Just give me a house and I'll defend [it] against forty," bragged Stevens, the man who had killed David Cruise. One man "declared that he did actually see the sparks [of anger] flying from Stevens's eyes."[717]

ᏋᎧ

NORTH TO CANADA

Brown's exodus to Canada was not a happy one at first. Several posses in Kansas, and then in Iowa, were looking for him long after the Battle of the Spurs. He brooded over his disputes with Wattles and Montgomery and his demeanor was sour. Gill wrote that Brown had come to see himself as a messianic figure and was vindictive toward some, even his raiders and sons. That annoyed his followers, who were also tired from the raid, the hiding, and the march.[718]

Spirits had improved by the time they reached Chicago, though. The train had traveled through or stopped at numerous towns throughout Illinois, where Abraham Lincoln had just barely lost the election to the U.S. Senate to Stephen Douglas. No law enforcement officer or public official at any of those communities stopped the train to arrest Brown and the fugitives, although it would have been very easy to have done so.

The refugee train pulled quietly into Chicago at 3:30 a.m. on March 11, 1858, nearly three months after the rescue. Someone met Brown and his freed slaves at the empty train station and drove them in wagons through the dark streets of Chicago to the home of Allan Pinkerton, at the corner of Fifth Street and Franklin Street. Pinkerton was the head of a detective agency. He would later become Abraham Lincoln's personal bodyguard and, after the Civil War, his agency would become the nation's most famous. The refugees arrived at precisely 4:30 a.m. Pinkerton did not expect them and answered the knock on his door with a revolver in his hand. Surprised to see Brown and the party, Pinkerton let them all into his house, hugging Brown when he walked through the door. Pinkerton had used his home as a safe house on the Underground Railroad for years, and was happy to assist his most famous runaways. His wife, roused by the noise downstairs, took everyone into the kitchen and cooked them breakfast.

Brown told Pinkerton that he was out of money and needed clothing for himself and his party and about $500 to rent another railroad car to move on by rail to Detroit, where he planned to cross the Detroit River into Canada. Pinkerton hid Brown and his party in his home and in two other safe houses in the city over the next several days as he discreetly tried to gather clothes and cash. Pinkerton was frantic that he could not raise the money. The Chicago Judiciary Convention was meeting in town that week and the detective, a member, blurted out to a group of lawyers and judges on a committee that John Brown and his much-publicized refugees were hiding out in Chicago and needed funds to make it out of the country. There was a long pause and then one of the lawyers rose, walked to the head of the table, opened his wallet, and gave Pinkerton $50. Others followed and within just ten minutes the detective raised $600, more than he needed.

That night Pinkerton, his son at his side, put the slaves remaining at his house in a wagon and drove as noiselessly as they could throughout Chicago, picking up Brown, his men, and the rest of the slaves. Pinkerton took them to the railroad station, where they boarded a boxcar he had rented for them—unnoticed—and headed east toward Detroit. Before departing, Brown shook Pinkerton's hand warmly and thanked him for his help.

"Look well upon that man," Pinkerton said to his son as Brown boarded the train. "He is greater than Napoleon and as great as George Washington."[719]

The train took the slaves to a pier in Detroit where they boarded a ferry and crossed the Detroit River into Canada—and freedom. Their exhausted rescuer, John Brown, did not go with them. He bade the raiders farewell and watched the ferry slide out of its slip into the river and then left them. He turned south, toward Ohio, determined to sneak past jail guards to visit the Oberlin abolitionists.[720]

Brown was very proud of his fellow raiders, who had suffered greatly with him for "the cause." He praised them whenever he could for helping him "to further the cause of freedom in the U.S. and in all the world." He wrote of one volunteer, "He has contributed the entire service of two strong minor sons for two years and of himself for more than three years; during which time they have all endured great hardships, exposure of health and other privations…two [other] sons were made prisoners and subjected to most barbarous treatment. Two were severely wounded and one murdered."[721]

All of his men shared the zealousness of their leader and all were certain that their risky efforts would save Kansas from the slavers. Brown always pledged that, no matter how strong the opposition, "We will not give up the ship. Kansas, watered with the tears of the blood of our children, shall yet be free."[722]

They might have been proud, too, that following the Christmas raid, President Buchanan offered a reward of $250 for Brown, and that the governor of Missouri, far more eager for his apprehension, posted a hefty reward of $3,000.

The remarkable raid and eleven-hundred-mile flight to Canada in winter, that had taken eighty-eight days, produced many benefits for John Brown. It won him extensive and mostly positive press coverage in the Northern states and Canada and convinced his "Secret Six" contributors that Brown's fantastic crusade to abolish slavery just might succeed. They were all moved by the eleven-hundred-mile trek, his ability to protect his raiders and the runaways, and the rather lenient reaction of law enforcement toward him as he moved through snow and rainstorms across the plains to Canada. Gerrit Smith gushed over the raid. He wrote, "I was once doubtful in my own mind as to Captain Brown's course; I now approve of it heartily." Wendell Phillips, who publicly applauded the slave rescue, said that Brown was "the impersonator of God's law."[723]

Many in the public, too, were impressed and considered Brown a hero. A reporter in the *Boston Post*, a moderate Republican newspaper, wrote a line after Harper's Ferry that could have been applied to the Missouri raid. "John

Brown may be a lunatic, but if he is, then one-quarter of the people of Massachusetts are madmen."[724]

Abolitionists, important ones, were now finally convinced that he was the man to free those in bondage. Frederick Douglass wrote, "He had shown boundless energy and skill in dealing with the enemies of liberty in Kansas. With men so few, and means so small, and odds against him so great, no captain ever surpassed him. He went into the border of Missouri and liberated a dozen slaves in a single night and, in spite of slave laws and marshals, he brought these people through a half dozen states and landed them safely in Canada."[725]

John Brown was always proud of the Missouri raid and saw it as part of his religious mission. In a letter to his cousin, Rev. Luther Humphreys, before he was executed in 1859, the abolitionist defended his efforts to abolish slavery. He wrote the minister that the Almighty would not condemn him for his violent raids, but welcome him to heaven. "I humbly trust that no part [of my life] has been spent to better purpose. I would not say this boastingly but thanks be unto God who giveth us the victory through infinite grace. I have enjoyed much of life as it is, and have been remarkably prosperous, having early learned to regard the welfare and prosperity of others as my own."

After the raid, and the Harper Ferry's attack later, he expressed those same unremorseful sentiments about his devotion to the antislavery cause to many others, including his children.[726] He wrote, "As I trust my life has not been entirely thrown away, so I also humbly trust that my death shall not be in vain. God can make it to be of a thousand times more value…[for] his own cause than all the miserable service [at best] that I have rendered it during my life."[727]

He insisted later, too, that the violence that often occurred during his activities was not in his plans. "I intended certainly to have made a clean thing of that matter [free slaves], as I did last winter, when I went into Missouri and there took slaves without the snapping of a gun on either side, moved them through the country, and finally left them in Canada. I intended [in the future] to do the same thing, on a larger scale…I never did intend murder, or treason, or the destruction of property, or to excite or incite slaves to rebellion, or to make insurrection. I believe that to have interfered as I have done—as I have always freely admitted I have done—in behalf of his despised poor, was not wrong, but right."

Following the Missouri raid and the years of strife in Kansas, he predicted that the United States would be drenched "with the blood of millions in this slave country whose rights are disregarded by wicked, cruel and unjust enactments... So let it be done!" And later added, "I am now quite certain that the crimes of this guilty land will never be purged away but with blood."[728]

Brown was certain that the raid, while controversial at the time, would earn him a place in history. He wrote his wife, "Already dear friends at a distance with kindest sympathy are cheering me with the assurance that posterity at last will do me justice."[729]

The Christmas 1858 Missouri raid, added to Brown's previous years of violence in Kansas, naturally angered Southerners. They always accused Brown of being a homicidal maniac, and not a political agitator. Wrote one, "John Brown is an outstanding character in American history as a brutal, heartless, willful murderer. He committed willful and brutal murder in Kansas and, with malice aforethought, intended to see the Negroes of Virginia murder in endless numbers helpless women and innocent children."[730]

The editor of the *Wheeling* (now *West Virginia*) *Intelligencer* wrote of Brown's later raid at Harper's Ferry with the same contempt he felt toward his Missouri raid. "The idea of anything save a madhouse lunatic ever expecting to organize a widespread insurrection at the head of a raw, impoverished band of fifteen or twenty white men and five or ten Negroes on a public thoroughfare, easily accessible by telegraph and railroad to important and powerful military aid, is too wild and foolish for rational belief."[731] The Southerners' outrage was not directed just at Brown, but at the entire North. Southern leaders lumped Brown with all the Underground Railroad operators in the Northern states and all of the antislavery political leaders.

John Brown's actions were harshly criticized by many Northerners, too. The editor of *Harper's Weekly* magazine wrote after his death, "The South imagines that the Northern people sympathize with John Brown, and regard him as a martyr. It is a monstrous fallacy. The bulk of the Northern people have no sympathy whatever with John Brown. They regard him a man who broke his country's laws willfully, who caused the death of innocent men...this is the view taken by the great conservative body of the Northern people, including most of the merchants, farmers, mechanics, and citizens generally."[732]

President Buchanan agreed. He had put a bounty on Brown's head and condemned all of Brown's activities, accusing him of being insane. He wrote, "John Brown was a man violent, lawless, and fanatical. Amid the troubles in Kansas he had distinguished himself, both by word and deed, for boldness and cruelty." The president also said that Brown's raids persuaded Southerners that they were just the precursors of larger raids to come and that fear of continued assaults panicked them.[733] He reasoned that if slavery-hating Americans did this much for the rescue of eleven slaves in Missouri, imagine what kind of help they would extend to him on a larger, much more ambitious raid? In dozens—hundreds—of raids and in his drive to free all of the slaves in chains throughout the United States?

Perhaps William Allen White, the twentieth-century editor of the *Kansas City Star*, best described Brown's historical legacy when he wrote, "Every great movement needs an agitator. Every leader of spiritual ideals needs a John the Baptist."[734]

THE WHITE HOUSE

DECEMBER 1858

A happy President James Buchanan told the nation in his year-end message of 1858 that the slavery crisis that had divided America for years appeared to be over. "When we compare the condition of the country at the present day with what it was one year ago, we have much reason for gratitude to that Almighty Providence which has never failed to interpose for our relief at the most critical periods of our history. Much has been done, I am happy to say, towards the accomplishment of this object [defusing the slavery issue] during the last [year]."[735]

President Buchanan finished the turbulent year of 1858 in as much denial as he had begun it on that sunny, cold New Year's Day reception at the White House. He continued to ignore the slavery controversy at the end of the year just as he had ignored it during the previous eleven months. Midway through 1858, in July, he told William Reed with great confidence that the end of the Lecompton debate meant the end of the slavery debate. "The Kansas question as a national question is now at an end."[736]

The president had put the slavery issue behind him and was optimistic about his many new ventures to conquer or purchase enormous parcels of land for America, whether in Mexico, Central America, South America, or Cuba. He was so determined to forget slavery and champion his imperialistic policies that he devoted most of his annual message to foreign affairs.

The year 1859 would be just as successful as 1858 had been, the president believed. He would work hard to strengthen the Democratic Party in the upcoming fall elections and turn back the Republicans in the 1860 contests, making certain, though, that his Democratic successor as president was anyone but Stephen Douglas. The Republicans would surely nominate the abolitionist rabble-rouser that he detested, William Seward, but the end of the Kansas controversy, the continuing success of the *Dred Scott* decision, the public anger at violent agitators such as John Brown, and Democratic strength in the solid South would deny the White House to the "black Republican" Seward. The reversal of the Republican tide in 1860 would crush the new party, he thought, and he firmly believed all the eager Republicans who had been defeated in 1858, such as Abraham Lincoln of Illinois, would drift out of politics, never to be heard from again.

Buchanan had aged noticeably in his first two years in office. Richard Cobden, a British reformer who knew him in London in the early 1850s, visited him at the White House in 1859. He "found him looking much older and apparently out of spirits, and not so happy as when I knew him in London. Having attained the highest object of his worldly ambition, he is disappointed with the result."[737]

Buchanan never wavered in his defense of the South's constitutional right to sustain slavery, insisting on the eve of the Civil War in 1861 that it was right and proper in the Southern states. In the last days of his life, he told those who surrounded his deathbed that his policies as president, which created so much havoc and eventually resulted in a Civil War, were correct.

"He expressed to me his abiding conviction that the American people would, in due time, come to regard his course as the only one which at that time promised any hope of saving the nation from a bloody and devastating war and would recognize the integrity and wisdom of his course in administering the government for the good of the whole people, whether North or South. His conviction on this point was so genuine that he looked forward serenely to the future, and never seemed to entertain a misgiving or a doubt," said a friend, Dr. William Paxton of New York.

Buchanan told his niece, "Had I to pass through the same state of things again I do not see, before God, how I could act otherwise than as I did act." The president told friends that future generations would honor him. "Posterity will do me justice. I have always felt, and still feel, that I discharged every duty imposed on me conscientiously. I have no regret for any public act of my life and history will vindicate my memory from every unjust aspersion."[738]

History, however, has always viewed the fifteenth president as a spectacular failure. Buchanan spent the entire year of 1858, and all four years in the White House, ignoring the slavery controversy and becoming angry at anyone who brought it to his attention. Instead, he spent most of his time on Don Quixote-ish foreign policy adventures in a desire to create an American empire in North, South, and Central America, ignoring the wishes of the people who lived in countries he wanted to purchase, annex, or conquer. As president he made few efforts to bring the leaders of the slavery and antislavery factions together at the White House to attempt to discuss a resolution of the issue. He paid little attention to the views of newspaper editors. He was one of the least-effective heads of the Democratic Party in its history, doing little to help party members get elected during his administration, especially in 1858; thousands of Democratic Party members found his campaign to defeat Stephen Douglas deplorable.

His use of federal authority, especially his instructions to officials in Ohio to ignore any Ohio Supreme Court rulings concerning the Oberlin Rescuers, was a mockery of the Constitution. At the same time he tried to keep the Rescuers in jail, he did little beyond posting a tiny $300 bounty for John Brown, whose Christmas raiders had committed murder, violated the Fugitive Slave Act, the *Dred Scott* decision, inter-state commerce laws, and fired upon law enforcement officials.

President Buchanan's magical thinking that slavery would go away not only prevented him from addressing the most important issue in the nation's domestic history, but permitted firebrands on both sides of the issue, the John Browns as well as Southern radicals such as Charleston, South Carolina, newspaper editor Robert Rhett, to make slavery not just a political debate, but an all-consuming incendiary issue whose fires would shortly consume America.

In the waning days of his administration, following the election of Lincoln and the secession of seven Southern states, the President did made several efforts to salvage the country, appointing emergency congressional committees and issuing pleas to both North and South. These were too little and too late. None did any good and Buchanan was insulted by both sides, with Republican newspapers describing his speeches as "wretched drivel," his statements "brazen lies," and the president himself a "pharisaical old hypocrite."[739]

James Buchanan was certainly not the sole cause of the Civil War that erupted three years later, just one of many causes, but his ineffectiveness as chief executive dealt a crippling blow to the nation.

Buchanan had failed as a president and as the moral leader of the nation.

***

LINCOLN: THE SIXTEENTH PRESIDENT

On March 4, 1861, Buchanan's successor, Abraham Lincoln, was inaugurated as the nation's sixteenth president. The Capitol, where the next president would be sworn in following over a hundred threats on his life, was surrounded with soldiers, as were nearby buildings. Army sharpshooters took their places on the roofs of all the buildings overlooking the inaugural platform. The carriage carrying Lincoln to be sworn in stopped at the White House, by tradition, to pick up the outgoing president, Buchanan, to take him to the inauguration. Buchanan climbed into the carriage and faced the now-bearded Lincoln. He expected the incoming president, who would take office amid the threat of a Civil War, to ask him for his advice on how to run the country and avert the war.

Lincoln, whose tall, lanky body filled much of the carriage, ignored him. Ironically, all the incoming president told Buchanan as he looked at the soldiers on every block the carriage drove past was that he had no fear that he would ever be assassinated.[740]

Shortly after noon, Lincoln took the oath of office and was greeted by a long and loud roar of approval from an enormous crowd that had gathered to hear his inaugural address. At that moment, as he began his speech, President Abraham Lincoln swept into the history of the world as one of its most successful figures—and former president James Buchanan faded from it as one of its most colossal failures.

EPILOGUE

T he events of 1858 changed the lives of dozens of important people throughout the United States and, within a few short years, the history of the nation. These events, such as John Brown's raid and the Oberlin slave rescue, helped to dramatize slavery, which became one of the major underlying causes of the Civil War. Many of the people who suffered both triumph and defeat in their lives in 1858 became key players in that huge conflict, and all found themselves in important roles because of what happened to them in that troubled year.

❦

ROBERT E. LEE JOINS THE FIGHT

The inability of Colonel Robert E. Lee to make up his mind whether to resign from the United States Army and run Arlington House and the Custis family plantations in Virginia left him living in the gorgeous hilltop mansion overlooking Washington, DC, throughout 1858 and 1859. In October 1859, John Brown and a small band of raiders attacked Harper's Ferry, the U.S. military arsenal on the southern banks of the Potomac River in Virginia. The federal government was stunned by the raid and Southerners were panic-stricken that it was just the first of many abolitionist raids into Southern states to free slaves. President Buchanan immediately decided to send troops to Harper's Ferry to seize the facility, capture the raiders, and put down the insurrection that he and other national leaders feared would escalate into war.

Who to send to lead the troops? There were very few army officers in the nation's capital with any experience from America's last military engagement, the Mexican War of 1846. Then someone remembered Colonel Robert E. Lee. Lee was a longtime officer, West Point graduate, heralded veteran of the Mexican War, and cavalry leader. Lee was not only the perfect man for the job, but he was still on leave at Arlington House, right across the Potomac from the White House.

Lee was ordered to Harper's Ferry with a detachment of U.S. Marines and promptly ended the violent occupation, captured John Brown and his men, and supervised their hanging. In the raid and executions, Lee not only showed his considerable military experience, but admirable leadership and bravery. He exemplified the veteran officer who works well under intense pressure. Lee's actions at Harper's Ferry earned him enormous national publicity and, overnight, made him one of the most famous military figures in the country.

His newfound fame was such that when the Civil War began, Lee was offered the command of the Union Army, but turned it down to lead the forces of his native Virginia. Jefferson Davis, secretary of war when Lee was the superintendent at West Point, was the newly elected president of the Confederacy. Davis made Lee a general in the Confederate Army. In 1862, Lee was promoted to commander of the Army of Northern Virginia, the South's strongest force. General Lee went on to become the most notable general in the Confederate Army and, after the war, a genuine American hero. He remains so today.

The Union Army seized and occupied Arlington House and its grounds and used it as a camp throughout the war. The Lee family never lived there again. Later, Arlington House was turned into a museum, and today the lovely Lee and Custis family mansion overlooks Arlington National Cemetery, the burial ground for thousands of America's soldiers who died in its wars.

WILLIAM TECUMSEH SHERMAN REJOINS THE ARMY

Just as 1858 proved a pivotal year in the life of Lee, who became a legendary Southern commander in the Civil War, it was equally critical for Northerner William Tecumseh Sherman. He found himself lost at the end of 1858. His financial career had ended in shambles when his bank went out of business in the panic of 1857 and its aftermath; he had failed as a lawyer, too, and wound up the year running a roadside food stand in Kansas where he sold corn to prospectors.

His life settled down in 1859 after he became the head of a military academy in Louisiana. Sherman warned friends that Louisiana was making a mistake when it seceded from the Union in January 1861, to join the new Confederacy. He had seen the damage that splinter groups of any kind had caused when he confronted the vigilantes in San Francisco. The former United States army officer refused to have anything to do with the Confederacy, left the military academy, and traveled back to St. Louis, where he was given a job as president of a small railroad company.

Sherman quit his railroad post and joined the U.S. Army once again in April 1861, following Lincoln's call for seventy-five thousand troops to put down the rebellion. He was made a colonel and saw action in the summer of 1861. In 1862 he was reunited with Ulysses Grant, whom he had last seen selling firewood on a street corner in St. Louis. Grant made Sherman one of his top generals. Sherman, whom the army rejected in 1858, went on to distinguish himself at numerous battles. He and Grant were close friends throughout the war and continually defended each other against critics. Sherman said of Grant later, "He stood by me when I was crazy and I stood by him when he was drunk, and now we stand by each other always."[741]

When Lincoln named Grant to lead the entire U.S. Army, he named Sherman head of the army in the South. Starting in Chattanooga on May 7, 1864, Sherman's force of over ninety thousand men swept southward, earning a succession of victories, culminating with the capture of Atlanta and Savannah and the well-publicized "March to the Sea." These efforts were instrumental in the Union victory the following spring. General Grant was elected president in 1868 and the following year named Sherman the general-in-chief of the U.S. Army, a post he held for fourteen years. The man who desperately loved an army that had forsaken him in 1858 is remembered today as one of the nation's most remarkable military leaders.

◟

THE OBERLIN RESCUERS

It was the much-heralded rescue of fugitive slave John Price in Oberlin that, more than anything else, kept the antislavery campaign alive in 1858 and in the subsequent years. The Oberlin rescue had long-lasting political results. It enabled the Republicans to win the 1859 state elections there; in 1860, Republicans worked to produce one of the greatest electoral turnouts in U.S. history in Ohio. They voted for Republican Abraham Lincoln, who swept the state with nearly 66 percent of the popular ballots. If Lincoln had failed to carry Ohio, the presidential election would have been thrown into the House of Representatives, where Lincoln would have lost.

Ohio governor Brinkerhoff always directly connected the events. "Our victory in 1859 made a national victory possible in 1860 and its culminating result was the election of Abraham Lincoln as President."[742]

During the Civil War, more than 750 Oberlin College students and alumni fought in the Union Army; hundreds of men from Oberlin and Wellington joined them in the ranks. Twenty-one black residents of Oberlin joined the fabled Fifty-Fourth Massachusetts, one of the first black regiments. Six of the Oberlin Rescuers joined the army, too, including Charles Langston, who organized Ohio's first black regiment.

Professor Henry Peck, the leader of the Rescuers in prison, became one of the Union Army's most successful recruiters. He served as the editor of the *Lorain County News* toward the end of the Civil War and was later appointed U.S. minister to Haiti. John Mercer Langston, Charles's brother, became the acting president of Howard University in 1872 and in 1890 became the first African-American elected to Congress from Virginia. Lawyer Ralph Plumb moved to Illinois after the war and from 1885–1889 represented one of its districts in Congress.

Richard Winsor, the man who rode to Wellington in a buggy defiantly holding his rifles in the air, joined the army and was badly wounded at the battle of Winchester, Virginia, in 1862. He became a minister after the war and claimed all of his life that the emancipation of John Price and the Rescuers' ordeal in the jail was a major cause in the coming of the Civil War. He wrote, "No one could not see these thousands of noble men and women visiting us in that prison and notice the deep sadness in which they hung their heads for very shame for America's name without perceiving that hearts were moved in this nation as nothing heretofore had ever moved them, and that patriots were being made ready for the war that was so soon to follow."[743]

SEWARD LOSES THE PRESIDENTIAL NOMINATION

William Seward and his Svengali, political boss Thurlow Weed, were the two most overconfident men in America as the Republican Convention opened in Chicago in the summer of 1860. They believed that the "irrepressible conflict" speech at Rochester in October 1858, had locked up the presidential nomination for the New York senator. Seward had been so certain of it that he wasted eight months on a triumphal tour of Europe in 1859, spending no time politicking back home.

Both men were correct about one thing—the fiery Rochester campaign speech had made Seward the darling of the entire antislavery movement. They were wrong about Seward's political invincibility, though. Abraham Lincoln's men convinced the delegates at the convention that abolitionist Seward was, in fact, *too* popular. That was why Seward could not win the election and would bring down the party in his defeat.

The New Yorker would not capture the electoral votes of a single Southern state with his radical antislavery stand, they said. Douglas, the presumptive Democrat nominee, would defeat him throughout the South. Worse, using 1858 and 1859 election returns and public opinion polls, they argued that Seward could not carry the North either. He might sweep New England, New York, and Ohio, but could he take Illinois away from Douglas? Could he win New Jersey, where one-third of the state was below the Mason-Dixon Line and much of the crucial manufacturing trade of the Northern cities there was with the South? Could Seward capture the southernmost counties of Pennsylvania, which bordered on the slave states of Virginia and Maryland, where the close friends and relatives of the people in those conservative counties lived? Could he carry a border state like Maryland or Indiana? Could Seward, whose Rochester speech had hinted that a Civil War was inevitable, win the votes of the tens of thousands of moderates in every state who would vote against anybody who might lead the nation into such a conflict?

Lincoln's men did an admirable job and despite the seeming inevitability of his victory, William Seward lost the presidential nomination to Abraham Lincoln on the fourth ballot at the Chicago convention.

LINCOLN: THE GIANT KILLER

In his historic debates with Stephen Douglas in 1858, Lincoln had grown from a little-known former congressman and state legislator into a recognizable national figure. The *Chicago Press and Tribune* wrote just after the election that the debates and election "made for him a splendid national reputation" and that while he had a "reputation confined to his own state," he was now "a household word." Right after the 1858 election, the *Sandusky Ohio Commercial Register* became the first paper in the country to push for Lincoln's election as president. The editor of the *Peoria Daily Message* clearly understood what had happened in the 1858 Illinois senate race. He wrote, "Defeat works wonders with some men. It has made a hero of Abraham Lincoln," and went on to say that across the country there was a sudden movement to make Lincoln either president or vice president.[744]

The editor of the *Illinois State Journal* wrote of Lincoln, "All over the country his praises are on the lips of all good and true men. He has proved himself to be one of the foremost men of his party…his eloquent speeches…have not only brought him prominently forward before the people of the whole country, but contributed to make him a leader among leading men. [He is] a statesman for whom the Republicans throughout the Union can be proud of."[745]

The cheers for Lincoln, and predictions that he would be a national figure soon, came not merely from his friends in the Republican press in Illinois, but from all over America and even from the Democrats. The editor of the *Concord (New Hampshire) Independent Democrat* wrote, "In Abraham Lincoln, Stephen Douglas finds his equal and his superior, as a skillful debater and as an orator… Lincoln has excited enthusiasm among Republicans and displayed a degree of ability far exceeding the most sanguine expectations of those who expected most of him. He was the embodiment of the whole [1858] contest and [emerged] covered with honors."

Even Horace Greeley, who worked so hard to undermine Lincoln, was impressed. He wrote, "Mr. Lincoln's [1858] speeches justified the confidence and admiration of his supporters."[746]

Adroitly pulling back from his "house divided" speech at the start of the 1858 Senate campaign, Lincoln successfully assured the voters of Illinois that while he did not approve of slavery, he accepted it in the states where it existed. He may have been against the institution all of his adult life, but he had reminded listeners in the debates with Douglas and in other talks that he appeared to approve of its existence where it was and merely hoped that it would die out eventually. In that 1858 Senate race, he had served as his own campaign manager and could do so again in the presidential election. He was a moderate who might not win any Southern states, but could carry every one of the Northern states, especially his home state of Illinois, all of the northwestern states of his region, plus Pennsylvania and New Jersey.

And he could win. Abraham Lincoln's supporters continually reminded the delegates that he had actually beaten Douglas in the popular vote in the '58 race, although he lost the vote in the state legislature, which decided Senate seats at the time. If he beat Douglas once, he could do it again. They could not have made that claim if Douglas had won both the popular and legislative vote; ironically, Lincoln could thank the meddling of President Buchanan for that.

Douglas was confident that he would be president and never understood how much his defense of the territories' right to bar slavery if they so chose hurt him in the Southern states. He had given numerous speeches in the South after his legislative victory over Abraham Lincoln in the Senate race that placated few. He wrote a nineteen-page article in *Harper's Weekly* on that same territorial theme that further antagonized Southerners. Most Southerners felt betrayed and abandoned by the Little Giant. They believed that he had lost his soul to his soaring ambition. None said it clearer, and with more force, than Senator Judah Benjamin of Louisiana in a Senate speech in the spring of 1860.

"He [Douglas] went home and under the stress of a local election, his knees gave way; his whole person trembled," Benjamin said. "His adversary [Lincoln] stood upon principle and was beaten; and lo, he is the candidate for a mighty party for the Presidency of the United States. The senator from Illinois faltered. He got the prize for which he faltered; but lo, the grand prize of his ambition today slips from his grasp because of his faltering in his former contest; and his success in the canvass for the Senate, purchased for an ignoble price, has cost him the loss of the Presidency of the United States."[747]

There was a Southern mutiny against Douglas at the Democratic Convention in Charleston that ended in chaos. Douglas failed to win the nomination and the Southern delegates stormed out and nominated two other men to run for president, Vice President John Breckinridge on the new Southern Democrat ticket and Tennessee's John Bell on a Constitutional Union ticket, splitting the Democratic vote three ways. Douglas was finally nominated by the mostly Northern delegates of the Democratic Party, who met in Baltimore.

Douglas made history in the autumn of 1860 when he became the first presidential candidate to campaign across the country. He wasted much time campaigning in the South, where he had little support, and did not campaign long or hard enough in critical Northern states such as New York, Ohio, and his native Illinois. He faced an uphill struggle as Bell and Breckinridge solidified their hold on the electoral votes of the Southern states, winning almost all of the traditional Democratic votes between them.

Lincoln, perhaps fearful of verbal missteps in public speeches, did not personally campaign and followed the tradition of letting party leaders campaign for him. Back home in Springfield with his advisers, he devised a brilliant strategy in which he planned to carry just about all of the Northern states, targeting New York, Ohio, Indiana, Pennsylvania, and Illinois, and completely ignored the South. Those states alone would give him enough electoral votes to become president. On election day, Lincoln carried every Northern state except New Jersey, winning the election in New York where the strenuous campaigning of Seward and Weed brought him victory—and the White House.

Seward, so certain he was going to be president in 1858, became Lincoln's secretary of state. He served the president well and, in a key part of Union strategy to win the Civil War, convinced England to stay out of the conflict when they were wooed by the South. Seward was almost killed in the assassination plot against Lincoln in 1865.

Douglas, exhausted from the 1860 campaign, began yet another national campaign in the winter of 1861—this time to persuade Southerners who had seceded to rejoin the Union. His efforts failed, and so did his health. He died on June 3, 1861; his friend, President Abraham Lincoln, whom he had bested in their 1858 Senate race, had black drapes placed on White House windows and mourned his loss for days.

JEFFERSON DAVIS LEADS THE CONFEDERACY

While Lincoln led the United States from the White House in Washington, DC, Jefferson Davis led the Confederate States of America from the Southern White House in Richmond, Virginia. Davis, who survived a near fatal herpes/neuralgia attack in the spring of 1858 and later that year solidified his position as the leading secessionist in the country, was selected as the president of the Confederacy at a special convention in Alabama in February 1861. He was seen by Southerners as a military hero who could lead the South to victory in a Civil War, if one came, and as a national executive respected throughout the North, as evidenced by the warm reception accorded him on his trip to New England in the summer of 1858. His difficulty in working with anyone and short temper was not seen as a drawback—then.

EARNEST JOHN BROWN

None of the lives of the men involved in this book were affected more by events that transpired in 1858 than abolitionist John Brown. The radical antislavery leader, his flowing white beard now familiar throughout the North and South, became convinced during his Missouri raid that the federal government would not or could not stop him and that, eventually, thousands of like-minded abolitionists would join him in successive raids into the South to free slaves. That confidence led him and a band of twenty-two men—seventeen whites and five blacks, including two of the Oberlin Rescuers—to attack and seize Harper's Ferry in October of 1859, killing four townspeople in the process.

He expected thousands of abolitionists to join him at Harper's Ferry, but none did. A military detachment led by Colonel Robert E. Lee captured Brown in a shoot-out on October 18 in which one marine and seven raiders, including two of Brown's sons, were killed. Brown was tried, convicted, and hanged on December 2, 1859. Despite criticism of Brown and his Harper's Ferry raid by every leading federal official and many Republican leaders, including Abraham Lincoln, the abolitionist immediately became the martyred hero of the antislavery movement and numerous songs were written about him, including the fabled "John Brown's Body." Brown's raid gained him national acclaim, galvanized opposition to slavery in the North, and dramatically increased the Southern belief that the U.S. government would somehow eliminate slavery.

DAWN OF THE CIVIL WAR

And so, when Confederate guns opened up on Fort Sumter in Charleston's harbor at 4:30 a.m. on April 12, 1861, Abraham Lincoln was the president of the United States, William Seward was U.S. secretary of state, and Jefferson Davis was the president of the Confederacy. Robert E. Lee would shortly assume command of the Army of Northern Virginia and William Tecumseh Sherman would become one of the Union's most successful generals. By the time Southerners commenced their thirty-three hour bombardment of Fort Sumter just before dawn that morning, the antislavery movement in the United States had reached epic proportions, thanks to the Oberlin rescue and John Brown's 1858 Christmas raid into Missouri, just as fierce defense of slavery, and hatred of Northerners, had reached similarly titanic proportions in the South.

All of these people were in place because of events that occurred three years earlier, in 1858, a year when slavery became the overriding issue in the United States, and a year in which the president, James Buchanan, ignored it so he could spend time feuding with Stephen Douglas, threaten a war with Paraguay, try to annex Cuba, and open his niece's mail.

BIBLIOGRAPHY

HISTORICAL PAPERS

Papers of John Brown, Kansas State Historical Society

Papers of James Buchanan, Dickinson College

Papers of Howell Cobb, University of Georgia

Papers of Stephen Douglas, University of Chicago

Papers of Francis Hosford, Oberlin College

Papers of Robert E. Lee (Diary), Arlington House

Papers of Abraham Lincoln, Abraham Lincoln Presidential Library and Museum

Papers of William Porcher Miles, University of North Carolina

Papers of James Monroe, Oberlin College

Papers of Robert Rhett, South Carolina Historical Society

Papers of William Sherman, Rutgers University

JOURNALS

Andrew, J. Cutler. "The Confederate Press and Public Morale." *Journal of Southern History* (November 1966).

Barnard, Steiner. "The South Atlantic States in 1833, as Seen by a New Englander." *Maryland Historical Society Magazine* XIII (1918).

Brown, Salmon. "My Father, John Brown." *Outlook* (January 1913).

Burroughs, William. "Oberlin's Part in the Slavery Conflict." *Ohio Archaeological and Historical Publications*, Cleveland, Ohio (1911).

Cole, Arthur C. "Lincoln's Election an Immediate Menace to Slavery in the States?" *American Historical Review* (July 1931).

Ellis, Richard, and Aaron Wildavsky. "A Cultural Analysis of the Role of Abolitionists in the Coming Civil War." *Comparative Issues in Society and History* (January 1990).

Harrington, Frederick. "The First Northern Victory." *The Journal of Southern History* (May 1939).

Herndon, William. "Analysis of the Character of Abraham Lincoln." *Abraham Lincoln Quarterly* (December 1941).
Phillips, William. "Three Interviews with John Brown." *Atlantic Monthly,* Volume 28, 1879.
Smalley, E. V. "General Sherman." *Century Magazine* 5 (January 1884).
Steckel, Richard. "Migration in Political Conflicts: Precincts in the Midwest on the Eve of the Civil War." *Journal of Interdisciplinary History* (Spring 1998).
Updike, John. "Such a Sucker as Me." *New Yorker* (October 30, 1995).

BOOKS

Abels, Jules. *Man on Fire: John Brown and the Cause of Liberty.* New York: Macmillan Co., 1971.
Adams, Charles Francis, ed. *Memoirs of John Quincy Adams.* 12 vols. Philadelphia, 1876.
Angle, Paul. *Created Equal? The Complete Lincoln-Douglas Debates of 1858.* Chicago: University of Chicago Press, 1958.
Arlington House: The Robert E. Lee Memorial Cultural Landscape Report, Washington, D.C.: U.S. Department of the Interior, 2000.
Auer, Jeffrey, ed. *Anti-Slavery and Disunion, 1858–1861: Studies in the Rhetoric of Compromise and Conflict.* New York: Harper and Row, 1963.
Avery, Myrta. *Dixie After the War.* New York: Doubleday and Co., 1906.
Baker, George, ed. *The Works of William Seward.* 5 vols. Boston: Houghton-Mifflin Co., 1884.
Ballantine, W.G. *The Oberlin Jubilee: 1833–1883.* Oberlin, Ohio: E.J. Goodrich, 1883.
Bancroft, George. *The Life of William Henry Seward.* 2 vols. New York: Harper and Brothers, 1900.
Barton, William. *The Life of Abraham Lincoln.* 2 vols. Indianapolis: Bobbs-Merrill Co., 1925.
Bashford, Herbert, and Harr Wagner. *A Man Unbound: The Story of John C. Fremont.* San Francisco: Harr Wagner Publishing, 1927.
Basler, Roy. *The Collected Works of Abraham Lincoln.* 8 vols. New Brunswick: Rutgers University Press, 1953.
Baumann, Roland. *The 1858 Oberlin-Wellington Rescue: A Reappraisal.* Oberlin, Ohio: Oberlin College, 2003.
Beveridge, Albert. *Abraham Lincoln: 1809–1858.* 2 vols. New York: Houghton-Mifflin Co., 1928.
Birkner, Michael. *James Buchanan and the Political Crisis of the 1850s.* Selingsgrove, Pa.: Susquehanna University Press, 1996.
Blodi, Frederick, ed. *Herpes Simplex Infections of the Eye.* New York: Churchill Livingstone Company, 1984.
Blue, Fred. *Salmon Chase: A Life in Politics.* Kent, Ohio: Kent State University Press, 1987.
Boller, Paul. *Presidential Anecdotes.* New York: Oxford University Press, 1981.
Bonham, Jeremiah. *Fifty Years Recollections.* Peoria, Ill.: Franks Co., 1883.
Boyer, Richard. *The Legacy of John Brown: A Biography and History.* New York: Alfred Knopf, 1973.
Brady, David. *Critical Elections and Congressional Policy Making.* Stanford: Stanford University Press, 1988.
Brandt, Nat. *The Town That Started the Civil War.* Syracuse, N.Y.: Syracuse University Press, 1990.
Brigance, Henry, ed. *A History and Criticism of American Political Address.* New York: Russel and Russel Co., 1960.
Brinkerhoff, Roeliff. *Recollections of a Lifetime.* Cincinnati: Robert Clarke Company, 1900.
Brooks, William. *Lee of Virginia: A Biography.* Garden City, N.Y.: Garden City Press, 1932.
Brown, Bishop Robert. *"And Once Was A Soldier": The Spiritual Pilgrimage of Robert E. Lee.* Shippensburg, Pa.: White Maine Books, 1998.
Brown, John. *Provisional Constitutional Ordinances for the People of the United States.* St. Catharine's, Canada: William Day, printer, 1858.
Burnham, Dean. *Presidential Ballots: 1836–1892.* Baltimore: Johns Hopkins University Press, 1955.
Burton, Theodore. *John Sherman.* Boston: Houghton-Mifflin Co., 1906.
Canfield, Cass. *The Iron Will of Jefferson Davis.* New York: Harcourt, Brace, Jovanovich, 1978.
Carr, Clark. *Stephen Douglas,* Chicago: A.C. McClure and Co., 1909.
Chaney, William. *Duty Most Sublime: The Life of Robert E. Lee as Told Through the "Carter Letters."* Baltimore: Gateway Press, 1996.
Channin, Steven. *Crisis of Fear: Secession in South Carolina.* New York: Simon and Schuster, 1970.

Cochran, William. *The Western Reserve and the Fugitive Slave Law: A Prelude to the Civil War.* Cleveland: Western Reserve Historical Society, 1920.

Commager, Henry Steele. *Theodore Parker.* Boston: Little Brown and Co. 1936.

Congressional Quarterly Guide to United States Elections, 1799–1997, Official Results. Washington, D.C.: Congressional Quarterly Inc., 1975.

Connelly, Thomas. *The Marble Man: Robert E. Lee and His Image in American Society.* New York: Alfred Knopf, 1977.

Conrad, Earl. *The Governor and His Lady: The Story of William Henry Seward and His Wife Frances.* New York: G.P. Putnam's Sons, 1960.

Cooper, William, Jr. *Jefferson Davis: American.* New York: Alfred Knopf, Jr. 2002.

Coussons, John. *Thirty Years With Calhoun, Rhett, and the Charleston Mercury: A Chapter in South Carolina Politics.* Diss. Baton Rouge: Louisiana State University, 1971.

Cralle, Richard, ed. *John C. Calhoun, Works.* 6 vols. New York: D. Appleton and Co., 1883.

Craven, Avery, ed. *"To Markie": The Letters of Robert E. Lee to Martha Custis Lee.* Cambridge: Harvard University Press, 1933.

Crissey, Elwell. *Lincoln's Lost Speech.* New York: Hawthorn, 1969.

Curtis, George Ticknor. *The Life of James Buchanan, Fifteenth President of the United States.* Freeport, N.Y.: Books for Libraries Press, 1969.

Davis, Burke. *Gray Fox: Robert E. Lee and the Civil War.* New York: Rhinehart Co., 1956.

———. *Sherman's March.* New York: Random House, 1990.

Davis, Stanton. *Pennsylvania Politics, 1860–1863.* Cleveland: Western Reserve University Press, 1935.

Davis, Varina. *Jefferson Davis, Ex-President of the Confederate States of America: A Memoir.* 2 vols. New York: Belford Publishing, 1890.

Davis, William. *A Fire-Eater Remembers: The Confederate Memoir of Robert Barnwell Rhett.* Columbia, S.C.: University of South Carolina Press, 2000.

———. *Breckinridge: Statesman, Soldier, Symbol.* Baton Rouge: Louisiana State University Press, 1974.

———. *Robert Rhett: The Turbulent Life and Times of a Fire-Eater.* Columbia, S.C.: University of South Carolina Press, 2001.

———. *Jefferson Davis: The Man and His Hour.* New York: HarperCollins, 1991.

DeButts, Mary Custis, ed. *Growing Up in the 1850s: The Journal of Agnes Lee.* Chapel Hill: University of North Carolina Press, 1984.

Donald, David. *Charles Sumner and the Coming of the Civil War.* Chicago: University of Chicago Press, 1960.

———. *Lincoln.* New York: Simon and Schuster, 1995.

Douglass, Frederick. *The Life and Times of Frederick Douglass: His Early Life as a Slave, His Escape from Bondage, and His Complete History.* New York: Gramercy Books, 1993.

Dubin, Michael, ed. *United States Gubernatorial Elections, 1778–1860: The Official Results by State and County.* Jefferson, N.C.: McFarland Publishing, 2003.

DuBois, W. E. B. *John Brown.* Millwood, N.Y.: Kraus-Thomson Organization Limited, 1973.

Dubose, John. *The Life and Times of William Lowndes Yancey: A History of Political Parties in the United States, 1834–1864.* New York: Peter Smith Publishers, 1942.

Eaton, Clement. *Jefferson Davis.* New York: Free Press, 1977.

Ellett, Elizabeth. *Queens of American Society.* New York: Charles Scribner's Sons and Company, 1867.

Eyre, Alice. *The Famous Fremonts and Their America.* Boston: Christopher Publishing House, 1948.

Fehrenbacher, Don. *The Dred Scott Case: Its Significance in American Law and Politics.* New York: Oxford University Press, 1978.

———. *Prelude to Greatness: Lincoln in the 1850s.* Palo Alto, California: Stanford University Press, 1982.

Fellman, Michael. *The Making of Robert E. Lee.* New York: Random House, 2000.

Fletcher, Robert. *A History of Oberlin College.* 2 vols. Oberlin, Ohio: Oberlin College Press, 1943.

Flood, Charles. *Grant and Sherman: The Friendship That Won the Civil War.* New York: Farrar, Straus, and Giroux, 2005.

Foner, Eric. *Free Labor, Free Soil, Free Men: The Ideology of the Republican Party Before the Civil War.* New York: Oxford University Press, 1970.

Foote, Henry. *A Casket of Reminiscences.* Washington, D.C.: Chronicle Publishing, 1874.

Forney, John. *Anecdotes of Public Men.* 2 vols. New York: Harper and Brothers, 1881.

Fried, Albert. *John Brown's Journey: Notes and Reflections on His Journey and Mine.* Garden City, N.Y.: Doubleday Co., 1978.

Frothingham, Octavius. *Gerrit Smith: A Biography.* New York: G.P. Putnam's Sons, 1879.

Geary, Sister Theopain. *A History of Third Parties in Pennsylvania.* Washington, D.C.: Catholic University of America Press, 1938.

Gurley, A. R. *Morrison's Stranger's Guide to the City of Washington.* Washington, D.C.: William Morrison and Co., 1852.

Hale, Edward Everett. *William Seward.* Schenectady, N.Y.: Union College, 1951.

Hart, B. H. Liddell. *Sherman: Soldier, Realist, American.* New York: Praeger, 1960.

Hattaway, Herman, and Richard Berringer. *Jefferson Davis: Confederate President.* Lawrence, Kansas: University Press of Kansas, 1990.

Henes, Ernst. *Historic Wellington: Then and Now.* Lorain, Ohio: Southern Lorain County Historical Society, 1983.

Herndon, William, and Jesse Weik. *Abraham Lincoln: The True Story of a Great Life.* 3 vols. Chicago: Belford, Clarke, and Co., 1889.

———. *Life of Lincoln: The Historical and Personal Recollections of Abraham Lincoln as Originally Written by William Herndon and Jesse Weik, with Introduction and Notes by Paul Angle.* Cleveland: World Publishing, 1949.

Hirshorn, Stanley. *The White Tecumseh: A Biography of General William Tecumseh Sherman.* New York: John Wiley and Sons, 1997.

Holzer, Harold, ed. *The Lincoln-Douglas Debates.* New York: HarperCollins, 1993.

Horn, Stanley. *The Robert E. Lee Reader.* Indianapolis: Bobbs-Merill Co., 1949.

Howe, DeWolfe. *Home Letters of General Sherman.* New York: Charles Scribner's Sons, 1909.

Johannsen, Robert. *The Letters of Stephen A. Douglas.* Urbana, Ill.: University of Illinois Press, 1961.

———. *Stephen A. Douglas.* New York: Oxford University Press, 1973.

Jones, John William. *Life and Letters of Robert E. Lee, Soldier and Man.* New York: Neale Publishing Co., 1906.

Kennett, Lee. *Sherman: A Soldier's Life.* New York: HarperCollins, 2001.

Kimmel, Stanley. *Mr. Lincoln's Washington.* New York: Coward-McCann Inc., 1957.

King, Alvy. *Louis Wigfall: Southern Fire-Eater.* Baton Rouge: Louisiana State University Press, 1970.

Klein, Phillip. *President James Buchanan: A Biography.* University Park, Pa.: Pennsylvania State University Press, 1962.

Lee, Robert E. *Recollections and Letters of General Robert E. Lee.* Garden City, N.Y.: Doubleday and Co., 1974.

Lee, Robert, Jr. *Recollections and Letters of General Robert E. Lee.* Garden City, N.Y.: Garden City Press, 1926.

Lothrop, Thornton. *William Henry Seward.* Boston: Houghton-Mifflin Co., 1896.

Mackay, James. *Allan Pinkerton: The First Private Eye.* New York: John Wiley and Sons, 1996.

Malin, James. *John Brown and the Legend of Fifty-Six.* Philadelphia: American Philosophical Society, 1952.

Mapp, Alfred, Jr. *Frock Coats and Epaulets: The Men Who Led the Confederacy.* New York: Madison Books, 1982.

Marszalek, John. *Sherman: A Soldier's Passion for Order.* New York: Free Press, 1993.

McConnell, George. *Recollections of Stephen A. Douglas.* Springfield, Ill.: Illinois State Historical Society Transactions, 1900.

McElroy, Robert. *Jefferson Davis: The Unreal and the Real.* New York: Harper and Brothers, 1937.

Meade, Robert. *Judah Benjamin: Confederate Statesman.* New York: Oxford University Press, 1943.

Merrill, James. *William Tecumseh Sherman.* New York: Rand McNally, 1971.

Milton, George. *The Eve of Conflict: Stephen A. Douglas and the Needless War.* Boston: Houghton-Mifflin Co., 1934.

Moore, John, ed. *The Works of James Buchanan.* 12 vols. Philadelphia: J. B. Lippincott Company, 1908–1911.

Nelligan, Murray. *The Custis-Lee Mansion, the Robert E. Lee Memorial, Virginia.* Washington, D.C.: The U.S. Department of the Interior, 1962.

Nelson, Truman. *The Old Man: John Brown at Harper's Ferry.* New York: Holt, Rinehart, and Winston, 1973.

Nevins, Allan, ed. *The Diary of John Quincy Adams, 1794–1845*. New York: Longmans, Green, and Co., 1928.

Nevins, Allan. *The Emergence of Lincoln*. 2 vols. New York: Charles Scribner's Sons, 1950.

Newton, Joseph. *Lincoln and Herndon*. Cedar Rapids, Iowa: Torch Press, 1910.

Nichols, Franklin. *The Disruption of American Democracy*. New York: Macmillan Co., 1948.

Nicolay, John, and John Hay. *Abraham Lincoln: A History*. New York: The Century Co., 1890.

———. *The Complete Works of Abraham Lincoln*. 12 vols. New York: Frances Tandy Co., 1905.

Niven, John, ed. *Salmon P. Chase Papers: Correspondence, 1858–1863*. 4 vols. Kent, Ohio: Kent State University Press, 1996.

———. *Samuel Chase: A Biography*. New York: Oxford University Press, 1995.

Nolan, Alan. *Lee Considered: Robert E. Lee and Civil War History*. Chapel Hill: University of North Carolina Press, 1991.

Oates, Stephen. *To Purge This Land of Blood: A Biography of John Brown*. New York: Harper and Row, 1970.

Oliphant, Mary, Alfred Odell, and T. C. Eaves, eds. *The Letters of William Gilmore Sims*. 5 vols. Columbia: University of South Carolina Press, 1956.

Palmer, Beverly, ed. *The Selected Letters of Charles Sumner*. 2 vols. Boston: Northeastern University Press, 1990.

Perritt, Henry. *Robert Rhett: South Carolina Secession Spokesman*. PhD diss. Gainesville: University of Florida Press, 1954.

Phillips, Wendell. *Speeches, Lectures, and Letters*. Boston: J. Redpath,1863.

Pollard, Edward. *Life of Jefferson Davis with a Secret History of the Southern Confederacy Gathered "Behind the Scenes in Richmond."* Philadelphia: National Publishing Company, 1869.

Putnam, George. *Abraham Lincoln*. New York: G.P. Putnam's Sons, 1909.

Quarles, Benjamin. *Allies for Freedom: Blacks and John Brown*. New York: Oxford University Press, 1974.

Redpath, James. *The Public Life of Captain John Brown*. Boston: Thayer and Eldridge, 1860.

Renehan, Edward Jr. *The Secret Six: The True Tale of the Men Who Conspired with John Brown*. New York: Crown Publishers, 1995.

Rhodes, James. *History of the United States from the Compromise of 1850*. 2 vols. New York: Macmillan Co., 1902.

Rice, Allen, ed. *Reminiscences of Abraham Lincoln by Distinguished Men of His Time*. New York: North American Review Publishing, 1886.

Richards, Leonard. *The Slave Power: The Free North and Southern Domination, 1780–1860*. Baton Rouge: Louisiana State University Press, 2000.

Robbins, John. *Confederate Nationalism: Politics and Government in the Confederate South*. PhD diss., Rice University, 1964.

Roland, Charles. *Reflections on Lee: An Historian's Assessment*. Mechanicsburg, Pa.: Stackpole Books, 1995.

Ross, Isabel. *The First Lady of the South: The Life of Mrs. Jefferson Davis*. New York: Harper and Brothers, 1958.

Rossbach, Jeffrey. *Ambivalent Conspirators: John Brown, the Secret Six, and a Theory of Slave Violence*. Philadelphia: University of Pennsylvania Press, 1962.

Roswenc, Edwin, ed. *The Causes of the American Civil War*. Boston: Heath and Co., 1961.

Rowan, Richard. *The Pinkertons: A Detective Dynasty*. Boston: Little Brown and Co., 1931.

Rowland, Dunbar, ed. *Jefferson Davis, Constitutionalist: His Letters, Papers, and Speeches*. 10 vols. Jackson, Miss.: Mississippi Department of Archives and History, 1923.

Ruchames, Louis. *A John Brown Reader*. New York: Abelard-Schuman Co., 1959.

Russo, Peggy, and Paul Finkelman, eds. *Terrible Swift Sword: The Legacy of John Brown*. Athens, Ohio: University Press, 1905.

Sanborn, Margaret. *Robert E. Lee: A Portrait*. Moose, Wyo.: Homestead Publishing, 1966.

Sandburg, Carl, and Frederick Meserve. *The Photographs of Abraham Lincoln*. New York: Harcourt, Brace and Company, 1944.

Sandburg, Carl. *Abraham Lincoln: The Prairie Years*. 2 vols. New York: Harcourt, Brace, and Company, 1926.

Scarborough, William, ed. *Diary of Edmund Ruffin*. Baton Rouge: Louisiana State University Press, 1973.

Scheidenhelm, Richard. *The Response to John Brown*. Belmont, Calif.: Wadsworth Publishing Co., 1972.

Schurz, Carl. *Reminiscences*. 3 vols. New York: McClure and Co., 1909.

Seitz, Don. *Horace Greeley: Founder of the New York Tribune*. Indianapolis: Bobbs-Merrill Co., 1926.

Seward, Frederick. *Autobiography of William H. Seward: from 1801 to 1834: With a Memoir of His Life, and Selections from His Letters from 1831 to 1846*. New York: D. Appleton and Co., 1877.

———. *William H. Seward at Washington as Senator and Secretary of State: A Memoir of His Life, with Selections from His Letters*. 2 vols. New York: Derby and Miller, 1898.

Sheahan, James. *The Life of Stephen Douglas*. New York: Harper Bros., 1860.

Sherman, William. *Memoirs*. 2 vols. New York: D. Appleton and Co., 1875.

Shipherd, Jacob. *History of the Wellington-Oberlin Rescue*. Boston: J. P. Jewett Co., 1859.

Siebert, William. *The Underground Railroad from Slavery to Freedom*. New York: Russell and Russell, 1898.

Sigelschiffer, Saul. *The American Conscience: The Drama of the Lincoln-Douglas Debates*. New York: Horizon Press, 1973.

Simms, Henry. *A Decade of Sectional Controversy*. Chapel Hill: University of North Carolina Press, 1942.

Simon, John, ed. *The Papers of Ulysses S. Grant, 1837–1861*. 26 vols. Carbondale, Ill.: Southern Illinois University Press, 1967.

Simpson, Harold, ed. *Robert E. Lee by Jefferson Davis and Alexander Stephens*. Hillsboro, Tex.: Hill Junior College, 1983.

Smith, Elbert. *The Presidency of James Buchanan*. Lawrence, Kan.: University Press of Kansas, 1975.

Sparks, Edwin. *The Lincoln-Douglas Debates,* vol. 3, in *Lincoln Series*, vol. 1. Collections of the Illinois State Historical Society Library. Springfield, Ill.: Illinois State Historical Society, 1908.

Stampp, Kenneth. *America in 1857: Nation on the Brink*. New York: Oxford University Press, 1990.

Sterling, Ada, ed. *A Belle of the Fifties, Memoir of Mrs. Clay of Alabama, Covering Social and Political Life in Washington and in the South, 1853–1866*. New York: Doubleday, Page and Co., 1905.

Stewart, James. *Wendell Phillips: Liberty's Hero*. Baton Rouge: Louisiana State University Press, 1986.

Strode, Hudson. *Jefferson Davis: American Patriot*. 3 vols. New York: Harcourt, Brace, and World Inc., 1955.

———. *Private Letters of Jefferson Davis*. New York: Harcourt, Brace, and World, 1966.

Sundquist, James. *Dynamics of the Party System: Alignment and Re-Alignment of Political Parties in the United States*. Washington, D.C.: Brookings Institute, 1983.

Sydnor, Charles. *The Development of Southern Sectionalism*. Baton Rouge: Louisiana State University Press, 1948.

Taylor, John. *William Seward: Lincoln's Right Hand*. New York: HarperCollins, 1991.

Taylor, Walter. *General Lee: His Campaign in Virginia, 1861–1865, with Personal Reminiscences*. Lincoln: University of Nebraska Press, 1974.

Teeter, Dwight Jr., and Jean Folkerts. *Voices of a Nation: A History of Mass Media in the United States*. Third ed. Boston: Allyn and Bacon Co., 1998.

Thomas, Emory. *Robert E. Lee: A Biography*. New York: W.W. Norton and Co., 1995.

Thomas, Hugh. *The Slave Trade: The Story of the Atlantic Slave Trade, 1440–1870*. New York: Simon and Schuster, 1997.

Van Der Heuvel, Gerry. *Crowns of Thorns and Glory, Mary Todd Lincoln and Varina Howell Davis: The Two First Ladies of the Civil War*. New York: E. P. Dutton, 1988.

Van Deusen, Glyndon. *Thurlow Weed: Wizard of the Lobby*. Boston: Little, Brown and Co., 1947.

———. *William Henry Seward*. New York: Harcourt, Brace, Jovanovich, 1978.

Villard, Henry. *Memoirs of Henry Villard, Journalist and Financier, 1835–1900*. 2 vols. Boston: Houghton-Mifflin Co., 1904.

Villard, Oswald. *John Brown, 1800–1859: A Biography Fifty Years After*. New York: Alfred Knopf, 1943.

Wallace, David. *History of South Carolina*. 3 vols. New York, 1934.

Waugh, John. *On the Brink of Civil War: The Compromise of 1850 and How It Changed the Course of American History*. Wilmington, Del.: SR Books, 2003.

Weed, Harriet, ed. *Thurlow Weed: Life of Thurlow Weed, including his autobiography and a memoir, embellished in Portraits, and other illustrations*. 2 vols. Boston: Houghton-Mifflin Co., 1884.

Wellman, Paul. *The House Divides*. Garden City, N.Y.: Doubleday Co., 1966.

Wells, Damon. *Stephen Douglas: The Last Years, 1857–1861*. Austin: University of Texas Press, 1971.

White, Laura. *Robert Barnwell Rhett: Father of Secession*. Gloucester, Mass.: Peter Smith Co. 1965.

Wilson, Edmund. *Patriotic Gore*. New York: Oxford University Press, 1952.

Wiltse, Charles. *John C. Calhoun, Sectionalist, 1840–1850*. Indianapolis: Bobbs-Merrill Co., 1951.

Windle, Mary. *Life in Washington and Life Here and There*. Philadelphia: 1859.

Winkley, J. W. *John Brown: The Hero*. Boston: James West Co., 1905.

Woldman, A. A. *Lincoln and the Russians*. Cleveland: World Publishing, 1952.

Woodworth, Steven. *Jefferson Davis and His Generals: the Failure of Confederate Command in the West*. Lawrence, Kansas: University Press of Kansas, 1990.

Young, Mary, ed. *John Young, Men and Memories: Personal Reminiscences*. 2nd ed. New York: 1901.

Zarefsky, David. *Lincoln, Douglas, and Slavery: In the Crucible of Public Debate*. Chicago: University of Chicago Press, 1990.

NEWSPAPERS

Akron (Ohio) Beacon

Albany Evening Journal, 1854–58

Border City Star, 1923

Boston Daily Advertiser, 1858

Boston Post, 1858, 1859

Buffalo Republican, 1858

Centreville (Ind.) True Republican, 1858

Charleston Courier

Charleston Mercury, 1858–1861

Chatham (Canada) Daily News, 1923

Chicago Democrat, 1858

Chicago Press and Tribune, 1854–1860

Chicago Times, 1854–1858

Cincinnati Commercial, 1858

Cincinnati Daily Gazette, 1859

Cleveland Herald, 1858

Cleveland Leader

Cleveland Plain Dealer, 1858–1860

Columbia Telegraph, 1858–1860

Concord (N.H.) Independent Democrat, 1858

Congressional Globe, 1844–1861

Daily Pantagraph, 1858

Des Moines (Iowa) Sunday Register

Dubuque (Iowa) Express, 1858

Eastern (Me.) Argus, 1858

Evansville (Ind.) Journal, 1885

Frank Leslie's Newspaper, 1881

Freeport Weekly Bulletin, 1858

Galesburg (Ill.) Democrat, 1858

Harper's Weekly, 1858–59

Harrisburg Telegraph, 1858

Harrisonville (Kans.) Democrat, 1859

Hornellville National American, 1858

Illinois Journal, 1854–59

Illinois State Register, 1857–58

Jackson (Miss.) Observer and State Gazette, 1858

Jackson Mississippian

Jacksonville (Ill.) Sentinel, 1858

Jonesboro (Ill.) Gazette, 1858

Kansas Herald, 1859

Lafayette (La.) Statesman, 1850

Lancaster (Pa.) Intelligencer, 1858
Lawrence (Kans.) Daily Journal World, 1943
Little Rock Star Gazette and Democrat
Louisville Democrat, 1857–58
Lowell (Mass.) Journal and Courier, 1858
Macon (Ga.) Jeffersonian, 1844
Memphis Commercial Appeal, 1912
Missouri Democrat, 1859, 1959
Monroe Democrat, 1851
Montgomery (Ala.) Confederation, 1858
National Intelligencer, 1857–58
National Slavery Standard, 1858–1860
New Orleans Crescent, 1858
New York Evening Post, 1858
New York Herald, 1858
New York Times, 1854–1860
New York Tribune, 1858
Norwalk (Ohio) Reflector, 1859
Oberlin (Ohio) News, 1859
Oberlin Evangelist, 1859
Ohio Commercial Register, 1858
Ohio Statesman, 1859
Overland Monthly, 1891
Oxford (Miss.) Mercury, 1858
Pennsylvania Public Ledger, 1858
Peoria (Ill.) Transcript, 1858
Philadelphia Evening Bulletin, 1858
Philadelphia North American, 1858
Philadelphia Press, 1858
Portland (Me.) Transcript, 1858
Portland (Ore.) Telegram, 1906
Quincy (Ill.) Daily Herald, 1858
Quincy (Ill.) Herald, 1858
Rochester Democrat and American, 1858
Rockford (Ill.) Republican, 1858
Sangamon Journal, 1840
Spartanburg (S.C.) Spartan
Springfield Sunday Republican
St. Louis Globe-Democrat, 1888
Summit Beacon, 1855
Sumter (S.C.) Watchman
Vicksburg (Miss.) Sentinel, 1846
Vincennes Sun, 1858
Warrenton (Va.) Index, 1858
Washington Star, 1858
Washington Union, 1858
Weekly North-Western Gazette, 1858
Wheeling (Va.) Intelligencer, 1859
Wyandotte Western Argus, 1859

ENDNOTES

1. *National Intelligencer*, January 2, 1858.

2. James McPherson, *The Battle Cry of Freedom: The Civil War Era* (New York: Oxford University Press, 1990), 190–191.

3. Letter of anonymous army officer, November 3, 1857, in the *National Intelligencer*, December 9, 1857.

4. *New York Herald Tribune*, January 1, 1858; Phillip Klein, *President James Buchanan: A Biography* (University Park, Pennsylvania: Pennsylvania State University Press, 1962), 316.

5. *National Intelligencer*, December 3, 1857.

6. *Chicago Press and Tribune*, January 4, 1858.

7. McPherson, *The Battle Cry of Freedom: The Civil War Era*, 156–157; Michael Holt, "Another Look at the Election of 1856," in Michael Birkner, *James Buchanan and the Political Crisis of the 1850s* (Selingsgrove, Pa: Susquehanna University Press, 1996), 46–49.

8. Kenneth Stampp, *America in 1857: A Nation on the Brink* (New York: Oxford University Press, 1990), 47.

9. Paul Boller, *Presidential Anecdotes* (New York: Oxford University Press, 1981), 118.

10. James Buchanan to John Reynolds, February 22, 1821, Dickinsoniana, D.C., in Phillip Klein, *President James Buchanan: A Biography* (University Park, Pennsylvania: Pennsylvania State University Press, 1962), 141.

11. Klein, 140. Klein was one of the few biographers of Buchanan who had a positive view of him. Most considered him inept and historian Michael Birkner called him "a disaster."

12. Comments of Elbert Smith in a conference at Franklin and Marshall College, September 21, 1991, "The Presidency of James Buchanan, A Reassessment," in Michael Birkner, *James Buchanan and the Political Crisis of the 1850s*, 173.

13. William Scarborough, ed., *Diary of Edmund Ruffin* (Baton Rouge: Louisiana State University Press, 1973), entry of February 17, 1857.

14. Franklin Nichols, *The Disruption of American Democracy* (New York: Macmillan Co., 1948), 68–69.

15. Kenneth Stampp's comments in the Franklin and Marshall symposium, "The Presidency of James Buchanan, a Reassessment," in Birkner, *James Buchanan and the Political Crisis of the 1850s* (Selingsgrove, Pennsylvania: Susquehanna University Press, 1996), 174–175.

16. Buchanan to Lewis Cass, February 21, 1857, Buchanan Papers, Firestone Library, Princeton University, microfilm.

17. Buchanan to Henry Wise, December 2, 1856, Buchanan Papers.

18. John Forney, *Anecdotes of Public Men* (New York: Harper and Brothers, 1881), 2 vols., 1:74.

19. Jeremiah Black to Howell Cobb, April 30, 1857, Cobb Papers, University of Georgia, in Klein, 285.

20. Michael Birkner, *James Buchanan and the Political Crisis of the 1850s* (Selingsgrove, Pennsylvania: Susquehanna University Press, 1996), 21.

21. John Forney, *Anecdotes of Public Men* (New York: Harper and Brothers, 1881), 2 vols., 1: 65, 62.

22. James Buchanan to Lord Clarendon, March 27, 1858, John Moore, ed., *The Works of James Buchanan*, 12 vols., (Philadelphia: J.B. Lippincott Company, 1908–1911), 10:199–200.

23. James Buchanan to Arnold Plumer, Buchanan Papers, Princeton University.

24. Annie Buchanan's letter on the president's death, George Ticknor Curtis, *The Life of James Buchanan, Fifteenth President of the United States* (Freeport, N.Y.: Books for Libraries Press, 1969), II: 676.

25. William C. Davis, *Breckinridge: Statesman, Soldier, Symbol* (Baton Rouge: Louisiana State University Press, 1974), 181.

26. Stanley Kimmel, *Mr. Lincoln's Washington* (New York: Coward-McCann Inc., 1957), 173; Franklin Nichols, *The Disruption of American Democracy* (New York: MacMillan Co., 1948) 52–77.

27. James Buchanan to William Marcy, February 15, 1856, Moore, *Works*, 10:49.

28. James Sundquist, *Dynamics of the Party System: Alignment and Re-Alignment of Political Parties in the United States* (Washington, D.C.: Brookings Institute, 1983), 52–53; James Buchanan, speech at Wheatland, November 6, 1856, Moore, *Works*, 10: 96–98.

29. James Buchanan to Joshua Bates, November 6, 1856, Moore, *Works* 10: 98–99.

30. Ibid.; Nichols, 73.

31. A. A. Woldman, *Lincoln and the Russians* (Cleveland: World Publishing, 1952), 18.

32. *National Intelligencer*, December 7, 1857.

33. *National Intelligencer*, December 25, 1857.

34. *National Intelligencer*, December 28, 1857.

35. *New York Herald Tribune*, January 5, 1858.

36. Elbert Smith, *The Presidency of James Buchanan* (Lawrence, Kansas: University Press of Kansas, 1975), 14–15.

37. Ibid., 302.

38. James Buchanan to James Denver, March 27, 1858, Moore, *Works*, X: 200–202.

39. Alexander Stephens to Thomas Thomas, June 16, 1856, "Correspondence of Robert Toombs, Alexander Stephens and Howell Cobb," Annual report of the American Historical Association (1911), 2:372.

40. Klein, 296–299.

41. Elbert Smith, *The Presidency of James Buchanan* (Lawrence, Kansas: University Press of Kansas, 1975), 95.

42. James Denver letter in the *National Intelligencer*, January 1, 1858.

43. *New York Herald Tribune*, March 15, 1858; Leonard Richards, *The Slave Power: The Free North and Southern Domination, 1780–1860* (Baton Rouge: Louisiana University Press, 2000), 204.

44. Moore, *Works*, X: 145–151.

45. Buchanan to James Denver, March 27, 1858, *Works*, X: 339–370.

46. *National Intelligencer*, December 9, 1857.

47. Charles Sumner to Salmon Chase, September 18, 1857, Beverly Palmer, ed., *The Selected Letters of Charles Sumner*, 2 vols. (Boston: Northeastern University Press, 1990), 1:481–482.

48. Charles Sumner to the Duchess of Arguyll, ibid., 1:497–498; David Donald, *Lincoln* (New York: Simon & Schuster, 1995), 203.

49. Thaddeus Stevens quoted in the *Lancaster Intelligencer*, August 31, 1858.

50. Salmon Chase to Gerrit Smith, March 30, 1858, John Niven, ed., *Salmon P. Chase Papers: Correspondence, 1858–1863*, 4 vols. (Kent, Ohio: Kent State University Press, 1996), 1: 8–10.

51. Richards, *The Slave Power*, 208.

52. James Buchanan to Joseph Baker, January 11, 1858, Moore, *Works*, X:176–177.

53. Dunbar Rowland, ed., *Jefferson Davis, Constitutionalist: His Letters, Papers and Speeches*, 10 vols., (Jackson, Mississippi: Mississippi Department of Archives and History 1923) 3: 167–175.

54. Smith, 38–40.

55. *National Intelligencer*, January 16, 1858.

56. *National Intelligencer*, 1858: December 6, 8, 28, 31.

57. William Sherman to Ellen Sherman, September 25, 1858, Sherman Papers, Rutgers University.

58. *National Intelligencer*, December 30, 1857.

59. Leonard Richards, *The Slave Power: The Free North and Southern Domination, 1780–1860* (Baton Rouge, Louisiana: Louisiana State University Press, 2000), 1.

60. Ada Sterling, ed., *A Belle of the Fifties, Memoir of Mrs. Clay of Alabama, Covering Social and Political Life in Washington and in the South, 1853–1866* (New York, Doubleday, Page and Co., 1905, reprinted by DeCapo Press, 1969), 68.

61. Clement Eaton, *Jefferson Davis* (New York: Free Press, 1977), 102–103.

62. Dunbar Rowland, ed., *Jefferson Davis, Constitutionalist: His Letters, Papers and Speeches*, 10 vols., (Jackson, Mississippi: Mississippi Department of Archives and History 1923) 2:337.

63. Edward Pollard, *Life of Jefferson Davis with a Secret History of the Southern Confederacy Gathered "Behind the Scenes in Richmond"* (Philadelphia: National Publishing Company, 1869), 33.

64. Robert McElroy, *Jefferson Davis: The Unreal and the Real* (New York: Harper and Brothers, 1937), 178.

65. *Macon Jeffersonian*, August 2, 1844.

66. Hudson Strode, *Jefferson Davis: American Patriot*, 3 vols. (New York: Harcourt, Brace and World, Inc., 1955), I: 301.

67. Hudson Strode, *Jefferson Davis, American Patriot*, 1: 104.

68. Jefferson Davis to William Howell, April 18, 1859, Rowland, 6: 246.

69. *Sewanee Review*, 16 (1908), 412.

70. Varina Howell Davis, *Jefferson Davis, Ex-President of the Confederate States of America: A Memoir*, 2 vols. (New York: Belford Publishing, 1890), 1: 176–177

71. *Sewanee Review* 16 (1908), 408.

72. Rowland, 2:336.

73. Jefferson Davis to Varina Howell, March 8, 1844, Hudson Strode, *Private Letters of Jefferson Davis* (New York: Harcourt, Brace and World, 1966), 18.

74. Jefferson Davis to Varina Howell, Rowland, 2:705.

75. Isabel Ross, *The First Lady of the South: The Life of Mrs. Jefferson Davis* (New York: Harper and Brothers, 1958), 6–12.

76. Varina Davis, *Memoir*, I: 199.

77. Eron Rowland, 346.

78. David Donald, *Charles Sumner and the Coming of the Civil War* (Chicago: University of Chicago Press, 1960), 211.

79. Elizabeth Ellett, *Queens of American Society* (New York: Charles Scribner's and Company, 1867), 81.

80. Gerry Van Der Heuvel, *Crowns of Thorns and Glory, Mary Todd Lincoln and Varina Howell Davis: the Two First Ladies of the Civil War* (New York: E.P. Dutton, 1988), 72.

81. Ada Sterling, ed., *A Belle of the Fifties: Memoirs of Mrs. Clay of Alabama* (New York: Doubleday, Page and Company, 1904), 134.

82. *Vicksburg Sentinel*, July 21, 1846.

83. *Lafayette (La.) Statesman*, June 26, 1850.

84. Davis speech to Confederate Congress, April 29, 1861, in Edwin Roswenc, ed., *The Causes of the American Civil War* (Boston: D.C. Heath and Co., 1961), 32; Davis speech in the Senate, February 13 and 14, 1850, Rowland, 1:286.

85. Rowland 4: 61–88.

86. William Davis, *Jefferson Davis: The Man and His Hour* (New York: HarperCollins, 1991), 280.

87. *Monroe Democrat*, May 30, 1851.

88. Ibid., 266.

89. Jefferson Davis speech in the Senate, February 13 and 14, 1850, Rowland, 1:265.

90. Ibid.

91. Jefferson Davis to David Yulee, July 18, 1851, Rowland, 4:218.

92. John Robbins, *Confederate Nationalism: Politics and Government in the Confederate South* (PhD dissertation, Rice University, 1964), 10.

93. Jefferson Davis to Horatio Harris, April 17, 1851, Rowland, 4:179.

94. Rowland, 2: 72–80.

95. Frederick Blodi, ed., *Herpes Simplex Infections of the Eye* (New York: Churchill Livingstone Company, 1984), 4–11.

96. Varina Howell to Mrs. William Howell, January 30, 1846, Museum of the Confederacy Library.

97. Ross, *The First Lady of the South*, 64–68.

98. Franklin Pierce to Jefferson Davis, September 7, 1852, Rowland, 4:307–308.

99. Jefferson Davis to Sam Cartwright, September 23, 1851, Rowland, 4:225.

100. Robert McElroy, *Jefferson Davis: The Unreal and the Real* (New York, Harper and Brothers, 1937), 179.

101. Alfred J. Mapp Jr., *Frock Coats and Epaulets: The Men Who Led the Confederacy* (New York: Madison Books, 1982), 58.

102. William Cooper Jr., *Jefferson Davis: American* (New York: Alfred Knopf Jr., 2002), 288.

103. Varina Davis, *Memoir* I: 575–576, William Davis, *Jefferson Davis: The Man and His Hour*, 261.

104. Eron Rowland, 342.

105. Nichols, *The Disruption of American Democracy*, 172–173.

106. Davis in the *Congressional Globe*, 36th Congress, 1st session, 917.

107. William Davis, *Jefferson Davis: The Man and His Hour*, 261.

108. Seward friend and later enemy Horace Greeley always said he practiced "dexterity," a phrase the *New York Tribune* editor enjoyed using, Richards, 5; Eron Rowland, 346.

109. Glyndon Van Deusen, *William Henry Seward* (New York: Oxford University Press, 1967), 260.

110. Ross, 85.

111. Gerry Van Der Heuvel, *Crown of Thorns and Glory: Mary Todd Lincoln and Varina Howell Davis: The Two First Ladies of the Civil War* (New York: E.P. Dutton, 1988), 75.

112. Strode, *Jefferson Davis*, 1:301–303.

113. John Taylor, *William Henry Seward: Lincoln's Right Hand* (New York: HarperCollins, 1991), 122.

114. Jefferson Davis to Franklin Pierce, April 1, 1858, Strode, *Jefferson Davis*, 1: 304.

115. Strode, *Jefferson Davis*, 1:388.

116. Ibid., 1:304.

117. *Jackson (Mississippi) Observer and State Gazette*, June 9, 1858.

118. Cass Canfield, *The Iron Will of Jefferson Davis* (New York: Harcourt, Brace, Jovanovich, 1978), 34.

119. Steven Woodworth, *Jefferson Davis and His Generals: the Failure of Confederate Command in the West* (Lawrence, Kansas: University Press of Kansas, 1990), 14–15; Herman Hattaway and Richard Beringer, *Jefferson Davis: Confederate President* (Lawrence, Kansas: University Press of Kansas, 1990), 22.

120. Edward Pollard, *Life of Jefferson Davis, with a Secret History of the Southern Confederacy, Gathered "Behind the Scenes in Richmond"* (Philadelphia: National Publishing Company, 1869), 33.

121. Strode, *Private Letters of Jefferson Davis*, 48.

122. Robert Meade, *Judah P. Benjamin: Confederate Statesman* (New York: Oxford University Press, 1943), 115–117.

123. William Davis, *Jefferson Davis: The Man and His Hour* (New York: HarperCollins, 1991), 171–172.

124. Cass Canfield, *The Iron Will of Jefferson Davis* (New York: Harcourt, Brace, Jovanovich, 1978), 34–35.

125. Rowland, 3:274–281.

126. Jefferson Davis to Independence Day Committee of Philadelphia, July 1, 1858, Rowland 3: 270–271.

127. *Boston Post*, July 5, 1858, Rowland, 3: 271–274.

128. Speech of Jefferson Davis to the Portland Convention, August 24, 1858, Rowland 3: 284–288.

129. Speech of Jefferson Davis at Belfast Encampment, Rowland 3: 288–289.

130. *Eastern (Maine) Argus*, September 29, 1858, Rowland 3: 305–315.

131. William Cooper, *Jefferson Davis: American* (New York, Alfred Knopf, Jr., 2002), 292.

132. Eron Rowland, 353.

133. Ross, 85–86; Eron Rowland, 353–354.

134. Ibid., 86–87; Varina Davis, *Memoir*, I:593–594.

135. Davis's speech at the Palace Gardens, New York, Oct. 19, 1858, Rowland, 3: 332–339.

136. Ralph Richardson, "Jefferson Davis: Sectional Diplomat," in Jeffrey Auer, ed., *Anti-Slavery and Disunion, 1858–1861, Studies in the Rhetoric of Compromise and Conflict* (New York: Harper and Row, 1963), 52.

137. McElroy, *Jefferson Davis: The Unreal and Real*, 186.

138. *Charleston Mercury*, July 30, October 16, 1858.

139. Letter to Davis from a Mr. Campbell, November 25, 1858, Rowland 3: 360–62.

140. *Jackson Mississippian*, November 17, 1858.

141. Davis speech in Vicksburg, November 16, 1858, Rowland 3: 339–360.

142. *Montgomery Confederation*, December 22, 1858, *Oxford Mercury*, quoted in the *Jackson Mississippian*, December 1, 1858, Richardson, in Auer, 67–68.

143. Buchanan Papers, Don Fehrenbacher, *The Dred Scott Case: Its Significance in American Law and Politics* (New York: Oxford University Press, 1978), 312.

144. Kenneth Stampp, *America in 1857: A Nation on the Brink* (New York: Oxford University Press, 1990), 92–94.

145. Report of the Decision of the Supreme Court of the United States in the Case of Dred Scott versus Sandford (New York: DeCapo Press, 1970), 13; Smith, 24–29.

146. Klein, 269–271; Michael Birkner, ed., *James Buchanan and the Political Crisis of the 1850s*, 115–116; Phillip Auchampaugh, *James Buchanan and His Cabinet on the Eve of Secession* (Lancaster, Pennsylvania: Privately printed, 1926), 30–31.

147. Klein, 47.

148. Fehrenbacher, 417–419; Stampp, 101.

149. Fehrenbacher, 515; Stampp, 104.

150. Abraham Lincoln senatorial nomination acceptance speech, June 16, 1858, 461–467, Lincoln speech at Galesburg, Ill., October 7, 1858, III: 27, 230–231, in McPherson, *The Battle Cry of Freedom*, 179–180.

151. McPherson, 180.

152. *Congressional Record*, 35th Congress, 1st Session, 941.

153. Buchanan's third message to Congress, December 17, 1859, Buchanan Papers.

154. Douglas Southall Freeman, *Lee: A Biography*, 4 vols. (New York: Charles Scribner's Sons, 1934–1935), 1:380n, from Lee's 1858 diary, Virginia Historical Society, entries February 4, 8.

155. Freeman, 1:82; Emory Thomas, *Robert E. Lee: A Biography* (New York: W.W. Norton, 1995), 145, 65; Walter Taylor, *General Lee: His Campaign in Virginia, 1861–1865, With Personal Reminiscences* (Lincoln: University of Nebraska Press, 1994), 21–22; Paul Haynes description in Jones, 359.

156. Robert E. Lee to Anna Fitzhugh, November 22, 1857, Lee Family Papers, Duke University.

157. Lee Diary, November 11, 1857.

158. Michael Fellman, *The Making of Robert E. Lee* (New York: Random House, 2000), 24–25.

159. Freeman, 1:379.

160. Margaret Sanborn, *Robert E. Lee: A Portrait* (Moose, Wyoming: Homestead Publishing, 1966), 193; Robert E. Lee to Anna Fitzhugh, November 27, 1857, Lee Family Papers.

161. Robert E. Lee, *Recollections and Letters of General Robert E. Lee* (Garden City, N.Y.: Doubleday, 1904), 20–21; Emory Thomas, *Robert E. Lee: A Biography* (New York: W.W. Norton and Co., 1995), 175.

162. Margaret Sanborn, *Robert E. Lee: A Portrait* (Moose, Wyoming: Homestead Publishing, 1966), 164; Mary Lee to Martha Custis, August 28, 1831, Lee Family Papers; Thomas Connelly, *The Marble Man: Robert E. Lee and His Image in American Society* (New York: Alfred Knopf, 1977), 35.

163. Mary Custis Lee DeButts, ed., *Growing Up in the 1850s: The Journal of Agnes Lee* (Chapel Hill: University of North Carolina Press, 1984), 116, 63.

164. Murray Nelligan, *The Custis-Lee Mansion, the Robert E. Lee Memorial, Virginia* (Washington, D.C.: U.S. Department of the Interior, National Park Service, 1962), 16–18.

165. Elizabeth Calvert Diary, Lee Family Papers.

166. Nelligan, *The Custis-Lee Mansion*, 22.

167. From an obituary of George Washington Parke Custis, *Harper's Weekly*, October 24, 1857.

168. Mildred Lee, entry of July 20, 1890, in sister Agnes's journal, in DeButts, *Growing Up in the 1850s: the Journal of Agnes Lee.*

169. Elizabeth Calvert, "Childhood Days at Arlington," Mss., Arlington House Archives.

170. A. R. Gurley, *Morrison's Stranger's Guide to the City of Washington* (Washington, DC: William H. Morrison and Co., 1852), 33–34.

171. Arlington House, *The Robert E. Lee Memorial, Cultural Landscape Report*, vol.1, History (Washington, DC Department of the Interior, National Parks Service, National Central Region, Cultural Landscape Program, 2001), 21.

172. Mildred Lee, in Mary Custis Lee DeButts, *Growing Up in the 1850s: The Journal of Agnes Lee*, 117–118.

173. Mary Lee to Robert E. Lee, May 9, 1861, Ely-DeButts collection, Arlington House Archives.

174. Robert E. Lee to Colonel Andrew Talcott, May 5, 1836, Lee Family Papers.

175. DeButts, 97–98, 101.

176. Charles Roland, *Reflections on Lee: An Historian's Assessment* (Mechanicsburg, Pa.: Stackpole Books, 1995), 16.

177. Colonel Harold Simpson, ed., *Robert E. Lee by Jefferson Davis and Alexander Stephens* (Hillsboro, Texas: Hill Junior College, 1983), 1.

178. William Chaney, *Duty Most Sublime: The Life of Robert E. Lee as Told Through the "Carter Letters"* (Baltimore: Gateway Press, 1996), 31–32, 45; Bishop Robert Brown, *"And Once Was A Soldier": The Spiritual Pilgrimage of Robert E. Lee* (Shippensburg, Pa.: White Maine Books, 1998), 70–71.

179. Jefferson Davis, Robert E. Lee, *North American Review* 150, January 1890, Robert E. Lee to Joseph Totten, January 29, 1855, Superintendent's letter book, USMA, Thomas, 157.

180. *Warrenton (Va.) Index*, in Jones, 286–287.

181. DeButts, 72.

182. Robert E. Lee to his wife Mary, December 1856, in J. William Jones, *Life and Letters of Robert E. Lee, Soldier and Man* (New York: Neale Publishing, 1906), 374–375.

183. G. W. P. Custis will, Ms. Records, Alexandria County, Virginia, December 7, 1857, Freeman 1:380.

184. Lee Diary, April 9, 1858; Thomas, *Robert E. Lee: A Biography*, 175–177.

185. J. William Jones, *Life and Letters of Robert E. Lee, Soldier and Man* (New York: Neale Publishing, 1906), 90–91.

186. Robert E. Lee to Mary Lee, December 27, 1856, Lee Family Papers.

187. Alan Nolan, *Lee Considered: General Robert E. Lee and Civil War History* (Chapel Hill: University of North Carolina Press, 1991), 24.

188. Robert Lee Jr., *Recollections and Letters of General Robert E. Lee*, reprint (Garden City, N.Y.: Garden City Press, 1926), 226–234.

189. Freeman, 4:401.

190. Myrta Avery, *Dixie after the War* (New York: Doubleday, 1906), 72.

191. Robert E. Lee to Mary Lee, ibid.; William Brooks, *Lee of Virginia: A Biography* (Garden City, N.Y.: Garden City Publishing Company, 1932), 62–63.

192. Fellman, *The Making of Robert E. Lee*, 69.

193. Lee Jr., *Lee*, 306.

194. Robert E. Lee to Mary Lee, April 24, 1832, Lee Family Papers; Thomas 72–73.

195. Robert E. Lee to Mary Lee, April 20, 1839, DeButts and Ely Papers.

196. Robert E. Lee to Thomas Carter, May 1865, in Lee, *Recollections and Letters of General Robert E. Lee*, 168.

197. Robert E. Lee to Rep. Andrew Hunter, January 11, 1865, in Nolan, 175–177.

198. Robert E. Lee letter, July 8, 1858, Lee Family Papers.

199. Thomas, 177.

200. Robert E. Lee to Rooney Lee, May 30, 1858, Lee Family Papers.

201. Robert E. Lee to Rooney Lee, March 12, 1860, Lee Family Papers.

202. Mary Lee to W. G. Webster, February 17, 1858, Museum of the Confederacy Library, to Custis Lee, January 17, 1858, Lee Family Papers.

203. Burke Davis, *Gray Fox: Robert E. Lee and the Civil War* (New York: Rhinehart Co., 1956), 7.

204. Avery Craven, ed., *"To Markie": The Letters of Robert E. Lee to Martha Custis Lee* (Cambridge: Harvard University Press, 1933), 58–59.

205. Robert E. Lee to his son Custis Lee, January 23, 1861, Jones, 136–137.

206. Robert E. Lee to Custis Lee, January 23, 1861, in Freeman 1:420–421.

207. Robert E. Lee to Mary Lee, December 27, 1856, Lee Family Papers.

208. Connelly, 9.

209. Robert E. Lee to Jack Mackay, June 27, 1838, Lee Family Papers.

210. Stanley Horn, *The Robert E. Lee Reader* (Indianapolis: Bobbs-Merrill Company, 1949), 84.

211. Sanborn, 194.

212. Robert E. Lee to Custis Lee, July 4, 1860, Lee Family Papers.

213. Robert E. Lee to Adjutant General Irvin McDowell, Freeman, 386–387.

214. *Missouri Democrat*, September 30, 1858.

215. Nichols, 63.

216. Saul Sigelschiffer, *The American Conscience: The Drama of the Lincoln-Douglas Debates* (New York: Horizon Press, 1973), 81; *Chicago Times*, September 4, 1854; *Illinois Journal*, September 4, 1858.

217. Klein, 303; *Chicago Press and Tribune*, December 4, 1857.

218. Robert Johannsen, *Stephen A. Douglas* (New York: Oxford University Press, 1973), 584–588.

219. *New York Times*, December 3, 1857.

220. Elbert Smith comments on the Buchanan-Douglas feud, Birkner, 188.

221. Stephen Douglas to Charles Lamphier, December 6, 1857, Robert Johannsen, *The Letters of Stephen A. Douglas* (Urbana, Ill.: University of Illinois Press, 1961), 405.

222. Anonymous letter, February 11, 1858, Johannsen, *Letters*, 411–412.

223. Clark Carr, *Stephen Douglas* (Chicago: A.C. McClurg and Co., 1909), 41–42.

224. *Louisville Democrat*, November 18, 1858; *New York Evening Post*, August 27, 1858; Carl Schurz, *Reminiscences*, 3 vols. (New York: McClure Co., 1907–08), 2:94 *Quincy (Ill.) Herald*, November 4, 1858.

225. *Illinois Journal*, October 10, 1854; *Illinois State Register*, June 4, 1857; *Newburyport Herald*, in the *Illinois State Register*, September 28, 1857; Mary Windle, *Life in Washington and Life Here and There*, (Philadelphia, 1859), 65–66.

226. *New York Herald*, December 11, 1857.

227. Daniel Morton to Douglas, February 22, 1858, Douglas Papers.

228. Smith, 84–85.

229. Buchanan, 84.

230. Buchanan, 52–53.

231. Buchanan to Arnold Plumer, February 14, 1858, Buchanan Papers.

232. Buchanan to George Wharton, October 16, 1858; Buchanan to C. Zarley, July 22, 1858, Buchanan Papers.

233. Johannsen, 599–604.

234. *New York Times*, January 30, 1858.

235. Stephen Douglas to John Forney, February 15, 1858, Douglas to John McClernand, February 21, 1858, Johannsen, *Letters*, 413, 417.

236. Johanssen, 515.

237. *Congressional Globe*, 35ᵗʰ Congress, 1ˢᵗ session, 50, 10, 121, 140, Johannsen, 596–597.

238. Stephen Douglas to Samuel Treat, February 26, 1858, Johannsen, *Letters*, 418.

239. Johanssen, 620–621.

240. *Chicago Democrat*, May 10, 1858.

241. Linder to Douglas, May 15, 1858, Douglas Papers.

242. Howell Cobb to Alexander Stephens, September 8, 1858, "Correspondence of Toombs, Stephens and Cobb," American Historical Association, *Annual Report* (1911), II 443.

243. Henry Wise to James Buchanan, October 12, 1858, Buchanan Papers.

244. *Dubuque (Iowa) Express*, September 26, 1858.

245. *Cleveland Plain Dealer*, September 26, 1858.

246. "St. Louis Republican," in the *Cleveland Plain Dealer*, September 24, 1858.

247. *Washington Union*, December 27, 1858.

248. George Milton, *The Eve of Conflict: Stephen A. Douglas and the Needless War* (Boston: Houghton Mifflin Co., 1934), 279.

249. Johannsen, 63; Milton, 313–314; *Chicago Times*, July 10, 1858; *Chicago Tribune*, July 10, 12, 1858.

250. Baker, 3:341.

251. William Herndon, "Analysis of the Character of Abraham Lincoln," *Abraham Lincoln Quarterly*, December 1941, 410–411.

252. Roy Basler, *The Collected Works of Abraham Lincoln*, 8 vols. (New Brunswick: Rutgers University Press, 1953), 2:461–462; Fehrenbacher, 82; *Missouri Republican*, June 24, 1858.

253. Sigelschiffer, 16.

254. Edmund Wilson, *Patriotic Gore* (New York: Oxford University Press, 1962), 110.

255. Abraham Lincoln to Joshua Speed, August 24, 1855, Basler, ed., *The Collected Works of Abraham Lincoln*, 2:320–323.

256. Basler, 2:265.

257. Elwell Crissey, *Lincoln's Lost Speech* (New York: Hawthorn, 1969), 178; Albert Beveridge *Abraham Lincoln: 1809–1858* (New York: Houghton Mifflin Co., 1928), 2 vols., 2:679;

fragment of speech at Galena, Ill., July 23, 1856, Basler, 2:3; fragment of speech sometime in 1858, Basler 2:222.

258. Lincoln speech in Peoria, Illinois, October 16, 1854, Basler 2:247–248.

259. Sigelschiffer, *The American Conscience: The Drama of the Lincoln-Douglas Debates*, 211; *Chicago Times* in Paul Angle, *Created Equal? The Complete Lincoln-Douglas Debates of 1858* (Chicago: University of Chicago Press, 1958), 90.

260. *Galesburg Democrat*, October 13, 1858.

261. Harold Holzer, ed., *The Lincoln-Douglas Debates* (New York: HarperCollins Co., 1993), 2; Angle, *Created Equal? The Complete Lincoln-Douglas Debates of 1858*, xxiv-xxv.

262. David Zarefsky, *Lincoln, Douglas and Slavery: In the Crucible of Public Debate* (Chicago: University of Chicago Press, 1990), 28; Richard Steckel, "Migration in Political Conflicts: Precincts in the Midwest on the Eve of the Civil War," *Journal of Interdisciplinary History*, (Spring 1998), 586.

263. Burnham, 368; Hansen, 84.

264. *Cleveland Plain Dealer*, September 24, 1858, *Chicago Daily Democrat*, June 18, 1858.

265. Hansen, 204; Dwight Teeter Jr. and Jean Folkerts, *Voices of a Nation: A History of Mass Media in the United States*, 3rd ed. (Boston: Allyn and Bacon Co., 1998), 179.

266. Edwin Sparks, ed., *The Lincoln Douglas Debates*, vol. 3, in *Lincoln Series*, vol. 1, Collections of the Illinois State Historical Society Library (Springfield: Illinois State Historical Library, 1908), 3:20–24; Abraham Lincoln to W. H. Wells, January 8, 1859, Basler, 3:349; Lincoln to Salmon Chase, April 30, 1859, Basler, 3:378, Donald, 204; Lincoln to Joseph Gillespie, July 25, 1858, Basler, 3:192–193; Don Fehrenbacher, *Prelude to Greatness: Lincoln in the 1850s* (Palo Alto, Calif.: Stanford University Press, 1982).

267. *Illinois State Journal*, October 27, 1858, *New York Evening Post*, October 21, 1858.

268. *Cincinnati Commercial*, July 12, 1858.

269. *New York Herald*, July 27, 1858, Beveridge 1:628.

270. Basler, 3:186–188; *Weekly North-Western Gazette*, August 21, 1858.

271. Beveridge, 1:570; *Quincy Whig*, June 3, 1858, Abraham Lincoln to Theodore Canisius, May 17, 1859, Lincoln Papers.

272. Angle, xvii.

273. Lincoln to Gustave Koerner, July 15, 1858, Basler, 2:502.

274. Zarefsky, *Lincoln, Douglas, and Slavery: In the Crucible of Public Debate*, 24; Angle, x.

275. Donald, 211.

276. Angle, xii, xvi.

277. John Updike, "Such a Sucker as Me," *New Yorker*, October 30, 1995.

278. Basler, 2:247–248.

279. Basler, 1:382–383.

280. Basler, 2:551–553.

281. Abraham Lincoln speech of December 26, 1839, Basler, 1:177.

282. Carl Sandburg, *Abraham Lincoln: The Prairie Years*, 2 vols. (New York: Harcourt Brace and Company, 1926), vol. I & II combined, 2:126.

283. *Illinois State Journal*, June 3, 1856; Horace White, in William Herndon and Jesse Weik, *Life of Lincoln: The Historical and Personal Recollections of Abraham Lincoln as Originally Written by William Herndon and Jesse Weik, with Introduction and Notes by Paul Angle* (Cleveland: World Publishing, 1949), 10–22.

284. *Sangamon Journal*, January 3, 1840; *Boston Daily Advertiser*, September 12, 1848.

285. James Putnam to Leonard Swett, July 20, 1860, Abraham Lincoln Papers.

286. Zarefsky, 35–36; Mildred Berry, "Abraham Lincoln," in Henry Brigance, ed., *A History and Criticism of American Political Address* (New York: Russel and Russel Co., 1960), 829, 850; Jeremiah Bonham, *Fifty Years Recollections* (Peoria, Illinois: Franks Co., 1883), 159–160.

287. Herndon and Weik, II:294–297, Allen Rice, ed., *Reminiscences of Abraham Lincoln by Distinguished Men of His Time* (New York: North American Review Publishing, 1886), 479–480.

288. *New York Evening Post*, August 27, 1858.

289. Frederick Meserve and Carl Sandburg, *The Photographs of Abraham Lincoln* (New York: Harcourt Brace and Co., 1944), 6; Herndon and Weik, I:xxvi.

290. Sigelschiffer, 152.

291. Basler, 3:84, Sigelschiffer, 203.

292. *Illinois State Register*, September 10, 1858.

293. *Lowell Journal and Courier*, August 24, 1858.

294. *Illinois State Register*, August 2, 1858.

295. *Illinois State Journal*, August 3, 1858; *Illinois State Register*, July 31, 1858.

296. Stephen Douglas to Abraham Lincoln, July 30, 1858, Sparks 3:70, Sparks, 3:59–60.

297. *New York Evening Post*, quoted in the *Rockford Republican*, September 9, 1858, Angle, xxviii, *Chicago Times*, July 11, 1858.

298. Milton, 312.

299. Beveridge, 596–598.

300. Milton, 317.

301. Zarefsky, 30; Herndon and Weik, 2:73, 93–94.

302. Zarefsky, 29.

303. Beveridge, 1:592; Johanssen, 643.

304. *Washington Union*, July 20, 27, May 27, August 3, 8, 17, September 3, 15, 1858, in Johannsen, 646; Milton, 294–295, *Quincy Daily Whig*, July 21, 1858.

305. Zarefsky, 13–15; Thomas Harris to Charles Lamphier, May 21, 1858; Milton, 301–302.

306. Johanssen, 649.

307. Jeremiah Black to J. W. Davidson, August 1, 1858, *House Reports*, 36th Congressional 1st Session, No. 648, 323–324; *Jonesboro Gazette*, Oct. 23, 1858, in Johanssen, 647.

308. *New York Post*, August 18, 1858; *Philadelphia North American*, August 25, 1858; *Philadelphia Press*, November 4, 1858; *New York Herald*, November 5, 1858.

309. Don Fehrenbacher, *Prelude to Greatness: Lincoln in the 1850s* (Stanford: Stanford University Press, 1962), 112–113; Milton, 328.

310. *Illinois State Journal*, August 6, 1858; *Philadelphia Evening Bulletin*, August 5, 1858.

311. Stephen Douglas to Usher Linder, August 1858, Johannsen, *Letters*, 427.

312. Angle, *Created Equal* ?, 90.

313. Abraham Lincoln to Alexander Sympson, October 24, 1858, Basler 3:332, Milton, 329.

314. Johannsen, 652; *New Orleans Crescent*, reprinted in the *Buffalo Republican*, October 26, 1858.

315. John Forney to Stephen Douglas, February 14, 1858, February 16, 1858, Douglas Papers.

316. John McClernand to Stephen Douglas, February 17, 1858, *Letters*, 417n.

317. *Cleveland Plain Dealer*, from Illinois reports, November 1, 1858.

318. J.A. de Carteret to Douglas, October 12, 1858, Douglas Papers.

319. *New York Evening Post*, August 24, 1858.

320. Holzer, 1.

321. *Chicago Press and Tribune*, August 23, 26, 1858; *Chicago Times*, August 22, 1858.

322. Basler, 2:541; Angle, 13–14; Holzer, 268.

323. Herndon and Weik, 2:74–77.

324. George Putnam, *Abraham Lincoln* (New York: G. P. Putnam's Sons, Knickerbocker Press, 1909), 44–45.

325. Henry Villard, *Memoirs of Henry Villard, Journalist and Financier, 1835–1900*, 2 vols. (Boston: Houghton-Mifflin Co., 1904), 1:92–93.

326. Holzer, 16–17; Nicolay and Hay, 1:108, 303.

327. Sigelschiffer, 160–161; James Rhodes, *History of the United States from the Compromise of 1850*, 2 vols. (New York: Macmillan Co., 1902), 2:128; George McConnell, *Recollections of Stephen A. Douglas* (Springfield, Illinois: State Historical Society Transactions, 1900), 41; *Louisville Democrat*, September 5, 1858.

328. Allan Nevins, ed., *The Diary of John Quincy Adams, 1794–1845* (New York: Longmans, Green and Co., 1928), 566; Schurz, *Reminiscences*, 2:95.

329. Stephen Douglas to Samuel Treat, February 28, 1858, Johannsen, *Letters of Stephen Douglas*, 418; Douglas to Abraham Lincoln, July 24, 1858, Johannsen, *Letters*, 423–424.

330. *Centreville (Indiana) True Republican*, September 2, 1858.

331. *Chicago Press and Tribune*, August 23, 1858.

332. McPherson, 186–187; Angle, 117.

333. *Freeport Weekly Bulletin*, August 26, 1858; *Chicago Press and Tribune*, August 26, 1858; *Daily Pantagraph*, August 24, 1858; *Jacksonville (Ill.) Sentinel*, August 27, 1858.

334. *New York Evening Post*, September 9, 1858; *New York Tribune*, September 27, 1858.

335. *Peoria (Ill.) Transcript*, August 24, 1858.

336. Joseph Newton, *Lincoln and Herndon* (Cedar Rapids, Iowa: Torch Press, 1910), 208.

337. Angle, 180–181.

338. *Rockford Republican*, September 2, 1858; *Illinois State Journal*, August 30, September 1, 1858; Holzer, 88.

339. James Sheahan, *The Life of Stephen Douglas* (New York: Harper Bros., 1860), 169; Beveridge, 1:617.

340. *Congressional Globe*, December 23, 1851, 32nd Congress, 1st session, 66.

341. John Nicolay and John Hay, 160.

342. Sparks, *The Lincoln-Douglas Debates*, 145.

343. *Galesburg Semi-Weekly Democrat*, September 1, 1858; *Alton Weekly Courier*, September 2, 1858.

344. *Illinois State Journal*, August 30, 1858.

345. Lincoln speech at Charleston, Basler 3:145–146.

346. Sandburg, 159.

347. Lincoln's Alton speech, October 15, 1858, Basler, 3:315.

348. Basler, 3:146; *Illinois State Journal*, November 1, 1858.

349. Abraham Lincoln to Norman Judd, October 20, 1858, in John Nicolay and John Hay, *The Complete Works of Abraham Lincoln* (New York: Frances D. Tandy Co., 1905), 12 vols., 3:329–330; *Mississippian*, September 14, 1858.

350. *Portland (Me.) Transcript*, October 23, 1858.

351. James Buchanan to John Forney, September 30, 1853, Buchanan Papers.

352. Nichols, 55–56.

353. James Buchanan to John Forney, February 28, 1857, Moore, 10:104; John Forney to Buchanan, March 6, 1857, Ibid., notes.

354. Letters to and from John Forney and Jeremiah Black, May 15 and June 15, 1857, in Klein, 281–282; Nichols, 80–63; Kenneth Stamp on Forney; Birkner, 178.

355. Klein, 264–266.

356. James Buchanan to Joseph Baker, January 11, 1858, Moore, X: 175–177.

357. Forney, 2:237.

358. Forney, 2:247–248.

359. Forney, 2:364.

360. *Boston Daily Advertiser*, November 6, 1858.

361. Nat Brandt, *The Town That Started the Civil War* (Syracuse, N.Y.: Syracuse University Press, 1990), 48–49.

362. W. G. Ballantine, *The Oberlin Jubilee: 1833–1883* (Oberlin, Ohio: E. J. Goodrich, 1883), 20–21, 50–51.

363. Roland Baumann, *The 1858 Oberlin-Wellington Rescue: A Reappraisal* (Oberlin, Ohio: Oberlin College, 2003), 8.

364. Ernst Henes, *Historic Wellington: Then and Now* (Lorain, Ohio: Southern Lorain County Historical Society, 1983).

365. Brandt, *The Town That Started the Civil War*, 62–64; *Cleveland Plain Dealer*, April 8, 1859.

366. Artemas Halbert trial testimony, in Jacob Shipherd, *History of the Wellington-Oberlin Rescue* (Boston: J.P. Jewett and Co., 1859), 22.

367. *New York Daily Tribune*, September 19, 1858; trial testimony of Seth Bartholomew, *Cleveland Plain Dealer*, April 6, 1859.

368. Richard Winsor, "How John Price Was Rescued," W. G. Ballantine, *The Oberlin Jubilee: 1833–1883* (Oberlin: E.G. Goodrich, 1883), 252.

369. Owl, June 6, 1896.

370. Baumann, *The 1858 Oberlin-Wellington Rescue: A Reappraisal*, 14; Norris Wood trial testimony, in Shipherd, *History of the Wellington-Oberlin Rescue*, 24.

371. *Oberlin News*, March 3, 1899.

372. Fugitive slave law guidelines in Wilbur Siebert, *The Underground Railroad from Slavery to Freedom* (New York: Russell & Russell, 1898), 28.

373. Trial testimony of Isaac Bennett, *Cleveland Plain Dealer*, April 8, 1859.

374. Owl, June 6, 1896.

375. Jennings trial testimony, in Shipherd, 20.

376. Jacob Wheeler's trial testimony, in Shipherd, 22.

377. Chauncey Wack and Noah Woods's testimony, in Shipherd, 33.

378. Shipherd, *History of the Wellington-Oberlin Rescue*, 123.

379. Winsor account of rescue in Ballantine, 254.

380. Brandt, 101–104.

381. Jennings trial testimony, in Shipherd, 21.

382. Brandt, 106.

383. *Cleveland Plain Dealer*, September 24, 1858.

384. William Cochran, *The Western Reserve and the Fugitive Slave Law: A Prelude to the Civil War*, publication no. 101, Collections (Cleveland: Western Reserve Historical Society, 1920), 134,

in Jeffrey Auer, ed., *Anti-Slavery and Disunion, 1858–1861: Studies in the Rhetoric of Compromise and Conflict* (New York: Harper and Row Publishers, 1963), notes.

385. Richard Ellis and Aaron Wildavsky, "A Cultural Analysis of the Role of Abolitionists in the Coming Civil War," *Comparative Issues in Society and History*, January 1990, 91.

386. Baumann, x.

387. *Cleveland Plain Dealer*, December 7, 1858.

388. Shipherd, 4; *Cleveland Plain Dealer*, December 8, 1858.

389. Brandt, 127–130.

390. *Daily Cleveland Herald*, January 15, 1859.

391. Brandt, 134–135.

392. *Cleveland Herald*, April 5, 1859; Brandt, 145.

393. *Cleveland Plain Dealer*, April 25, 1859, December 7, 1858, May 24, 1859, January 19, 1859.

394. Seth Gates to Rep. Joshua Giddings, May 26, 1859, Boyd Stutler Collection of Papers on John Brown, Ohio Historical Society, copies at Princeton University.

395. Shipherd, 274.

396. Cochran, *The Western Reserve and the Fugitive Slave Law*, 133.

397. Shipherd, 141.

398. Shipherd, 144.

399. Riddle's trial summation, in Shipherd, 55.

400. Warren Guthrie, "The Oberlin-Wellington Rescue Case, 1859," in Auer, ed., *Antislavery and Disunion, 1858–1861*, 90.

401. Shipherd, 88–89.

402. Ibid., 181.

403. Brandt, 196.

404. *Oberlin Evangelist*, April 27, 1859.

405. Shipherd, 90, 92.

406. Shipherd, 91–92.

407. William Lincoln, "Wellington Rescue," Palmer Collection, Western Reserve Historical Society, in Brandt, 200.

408. *Oberlin Evangelist*, May 25, 1859.

409. *Cleveland Plain Dealer*, April 18, 1859.

410. Charles Galbreath, *History of Ohio*, 2 vols. (Chicago: American Historical Society, Inc., 1928–29), 2:228.

411. Brandt, 175.

412. Brandt, 188.

413. Charles Langston testimony, in Shipherd, 178.

414. *Norwalk (Ohio) Reflector*, May 17, 1859.

415. Shipherd, 220–221.

416. Brandt, 188–189.

417. Brandt, 176–177.

418. Jules Abels, *Man on Fire: John Brown and the Cause of Liberty* (New York: Macmillan and Co., 1971), 233.

419. Ibid., 203–204; *Cleveland Plain Dealer*, May 24, 1858.

420. Shipherd, 258.

421. Salmon Chase to Charles Sumner, May 23, 1856, in Sumner Papers, Harvard University, in Fred Blue, *Salmon Chase: A Life in Politics* (Kent, Ohio: Kent State Press, 1987), 106.

422. *Ohio Statesman*, May 28, 1859.

423. Salmon Chase to Abraham Lincoln, May 15, 1859, John Niven, ed., *Salmon P. Chase Papers: Correspondence, 1858–1863*, 4 vols. (Kent, Ohio: Kent State University, 1993), 2:14–15.

424. Joseph Medill to Salmon Chase, Niven, 2:10–11.

425. John Niven, *Salmon P. Chase: A Biography* (New York: Oxford University Press, 1995), 207–209.

426. Salmon Chase to John Sherman, March 3, 1866, Sherman Papers, Ohio State Historical Society.

427. *New York Times* editorial reprinted in the *Cincinnati Daily Gazette*, June 3, 1859.

428. *Cleveland Plain Dealer*, May 24, 1858.

429. Ex Parte Bushnell, 9 Ohio State Reports 198, 1859, in Auer, notes.

430. *Cleveland Plain Dealer*, May 31, 1859.

431. Brandt, 213.

432. Douglas to Robert Scott, Robert Johannsen, *Letters of Stephen A. Douglas*, 247–248; Fred Harvey Harrington, "The First Northern Victory," *Journal of Southern History*, May 1939, 186.

433. Abraham Lincoln to Samuel Chase, June 9, 1859, Basler, 3:384.

434. Abraham Lincoln to Samuel Galloway, July 28, 1859, Basler, 3:394.

435. Shipherd, 264–265.

436. Robert Fletcher, *A History of Oberlin College*, 2 vols. (Oberlin, Ohio, 1943), 1:410; Shipherd, 265.

437. Shipherd, 265–275. James Fitch, "Wellington Rescue Case in 1858," Frances Hosford Papers, Oberlin College Library, in Brandt, 236–237.

438. Wilbur Burroughs, "Oberlin's Part in the Slavery Conflict," *Ohio Archaeological and Historical Publications*, Cleveland, Ohio (1911), 20:300.

439. William Lloyd Garrison to James Monroe, April 22, 1859, Monroe Papers, Oberlin College Library.

440. James Buchanan to J. B. Baker, August 17, 1858, Buchanan Papers. This attitude was prevalent in letters throughout the campaign.

441. Isaac Sturgeon to James Buchanan, October 1, 1858, Buchanan Papers.

442. Isaac Sturgeon to Buchanan, October 13, 1858, Buchanan Papers.

443. Isaac Sturgeon to James Buchanan, October 2, 1858, Buchanan Papers.

444. Isaac Sturgeon to James Buchanan, October 1, 1858, Buchanan Papers.

445. Ibid.

446. *New York Herald*, October 5, 1858, Buchanan Papers.

447. James Hughes to Isaac Sturgeon, sent on to James Buchanan, October 7, 1858, Buchanan Papers.

448. *New York Tribune*, October 26, 1858.

449. Thornton Lothrop, *William Henry Seward* (Boston: Houghton-Mifflin Co., 1896), 59.

450. Earl Conrad, *The Governor and His Lady: The Story of William Henry Seward and His Wife Frances* (New York: G.P. Putnam's Sons, 1960), 320–321.

451. *Rochester Democrat and American*, October 25, 1858.

452. Robert Oliver, "William Seward on the 'Irrepressible Conflict,'" October 25, 1858, in Auer, 30–31.

453. William Seward to Theodore Parker, July 1858, Seward Papers.

454. Frederick Seward, *William H. Seward at Washington as Senator and Secretary of State: A Memoir of His Life, with Selections from his Letters*, 2 vols. (New York: Derby and Miller, 1891), 2:350.

455. Edward Everett Hale on Seward, *William Seward*, (Schenectady: Union College, 1951 reprint), 9.

456. May Young, ed., *Men and Memories: Personal Reminiscences*, 2d ed. (New York: F.T. Neely, 1901), 60, in John Waugh, *On the Brink of the Civil War: The Compromise of 1850 and How It Changed the Course of American History* (Wilmington, Delaware : SR Books, 2003), 111; Oliver, 37.

457. Frederick Seward, *William H. Seward at Washington as Senator and Secretary of State*, 352.

458. William Seward speech in Buffalo, October 19, 1855, George Baker, ed., *The Works of William Seward*, 5 vols. (Boston: Houghton-Mifflin Co., 1884), 4:248.

459. Speech at Albany rally, 1855.

460. Senator John Wilson, *New York Tribune*, November 9, 1858.

461. *William Seward*, Union College pamphlet, 8.

462. Murat Halstead's physical description of Seward from his notes from covering the 1860 presidential campaign, in John Waugh, *On the Brink of Civil War: The Compromise of 1850 and How It Changed the Course of American History* (Wilmington, Del.: SR Books, 2003).

463. *Albany Evening Journal*, October 26, 1858; *New York Times*, October 26, 1858.

464. Harriet Weed, ed., *Thurlow Weed: Life of Thurlow Weed, including his autobiography and a memoir, embellished in Portraits, and other illustrations*, 2 vols. (Boston: Houghton Mifflin Co., 1884), 2:468.

465. Don Seitz, *Horace Greeley, Founder of the New York Tribune* (Indianapolis: Bobbs-Merrill Co., 1926), 168.

466. Weed, 423.

467. Glyndon Van Deusen, *Thurlow Weed: Wizard of the Lobby* (Boston: Little, Brown and Co., 1947), 236–238.

468. Van Deusen, *Thurlow Weed: Wizard of the Lobby*, 88–89.

469. Conrad, *The Governor and His Lady: The Story of William Henry Seward and His Wife, Frances*, 268–269.

470. *New York Tribune*, September 25, 1848.

471. William Seward to James Watson Webb, February 1, 1849, Baker, ed., *The Works of William Seward*, 3:415.

472. Van Deusen, 110–111.

473. Elihu Nott to Seward, February 14, 1849, Frederick Seward, 376.

474. *New York Tribune*, February 9, 1849.

475. Foner, 65; Frederick Seward, ed., *Autobiography of William H. Seward, from 1801 to 1834: With a Memoir of His Life, and Selections from His Letters from 1831 to 1846* (New York: D. Appleton and Co., 1877), 268.

476. Van Deusen, 117.

477. William Seward to Hamilton Fish, Van Deusen, 118.

478. William Seward to the Orleans County Whig Meeting, August 21, 1848, Baker, *Works*, 3:411.

479. Bancroft, 287.

480. Baker, 4:249.

481. Van Deusen, 205.

482. Davis, *Breckinridge*, 181.

483. Henry Foote, *A Casket of Reminiscences* (Washington, DC: Chronicle Publishing, 1874), 130–131.

484. John Dubose, *The Life and Times of William Lowndes Yancey: A History of Political Parties in the United States, 1834–1864* (New York: Peter Smith Publishers, 1942), 383.

485. Paul Wellman, *The House Divides* (Garden City, N.Y., Doubleday, 1966), 328.

486. William Seward to George Patterson, February 9, 1850, Seward Papers.

487. Henry Simms, *A Decade of Sectional Controversy* (Chapel Hill, University of North Carolina Press, 1942), 53.

488. Taylor, *William Henry Seward, Lincoln's Right Hand*, 90.

489. Ibid., 84–86.

490. Seward's "higher law" speech, *Congressional Globe*, 31st Congress, 1st session, 260–269.

491. Hale in *Congressional Globe*, 31st Congress, 1st session, Appendix, 1065.

492. F. A. Seward to William Seward, June 2, 1850, Seward Papers.

493. *New York Tribune*, March 19, 1850.

494. Lothrop, *William Henry Seward*, 83; John Waugh, *On the Brink of Civil War: The Compromise of 1850 and How It Changed the Course of American History* (Wilmington, Del.: SR Books, 2003), 155.

495. *Charleston Courier*, March 23, 1850.

496. Van Deusen, 124–125.

497. Van Deusen, 128.

498. George Bancroft, *The Life of William Henry Seward*, 2 vols. (New York: Harper and Brothers, 1900), 280–290.

499. Eric Foner, *Free Labor, Free Soil, Free Men: The Ideology of the Republican Party Before the Civil War* (New York: Oxford University Press, 1970), 303; William Seward to Gerrit Smith, May, 1845, Baker, 3:439.

500. McPherson, *Battle Cry of Freedom*, 145.

501. Baker, 4:517; *New York Times*, February 7, 1855.

502. Hale, 237; *New York Tribune*, February 1, 1855.

503. Van Deusen, *Thurlow Weed: Wizard of the Lobby*, 206–207.

504. Seward speech at a Republican rally in Albany, N.Y., on October 12, 1855, Baker, 4:240.

505. *Charleston Mercury*, June 2, 1858.

506. Van Deusen, *Thurlow Weed: Wizard of the Lobby*, 202–203.

507. Klein, 259.

508. Alice Eyre, *The Famous Fremonts and Their America* (Boston: Christopher Publishing House, 1948), 273–276; Lothrop, *William Henry Seward*, 140–145; McPherson, 155–157.

509. William Seward to Frances Seward, June 6, 1856; John Schoolcraft to Seward, June 14, 1858 (from Seward letter to George Baker on June 17, 1856), Seward Papers.

510. Frederick Seward, 278.

511. Klein, 257.

512. McPherson, 160–161.

513. Richard Rowan, *The Pinkertons: A Detective Dynasty* (Boston: Little, Brown and Co., 1931), 133.

514. Alvy King, *Louis T. Wigfall: Southern Fire-Eater* (Baton Rouge: Louisiana State University Press, 1970), 61.

515. Herbert Bashford and Harr Wagner, *A Man Unbound: the Story of John C. Fremont* (San Francisco: Harr Wagner Publishing, 1927), 362–363.

516. Seward journal entries of December 10, 1857, January 1, 1858, in Frederick Seward, *Autobiography of William H. Seward, from 1801 to 1834: With a Memoir of His Life, and Selections from His Letters from 1831 to 1846.*

517. John Dubose, *The Life and Times of William Lowndes Yancey: A History of Political Parties in the United States, 1834–1864*, 385; Albert Richardson, of Lawrence, Kansas, to William Seward, January 1, 1858, Seward Papers.

518. Buchanan, 45; *National Intelligencer*, December 30, 1857, through the spring; George Baker to William Seward, January 12, 1858, Seward Papers.

519. Nichols, *Disruption*, 54.

520. Foner, 126; *Congressional Globe*, 35th Congress, 1st session, 939–945, 959–962.

521. Ibid.

522. Van Deusen, 190.

523. Michael Dubin, ed., *United States Gubernatorial Elections, 1776–1860: The Official Results by State and County* (Jefferson, N.C.: McFarland Publishing, 2003), 179–180.

524. *Albany Evening Journal*, October 28, 1858.

525. *Albany Evening Journal*, October 27, 1858.

526. *Hornellsville National American* editorial, quoted in the *Albany Evening Journal*, October 26, 1858.

527. *Albany Evening Journal*, November 3, 1858.

528. *Albany Evening Journal*, October 27, 1858.

529. Wendell Phillips, *Speeches, Lectures and Letters* (Boston: J.Redpath, 1863), 353.

530. Cornelius Baker to William Seward, January 19, 1858, Seward Papers.

531. J. F. Brown to William Seward, January 18, 1858, Seward Papers.

532. Baker, 4:289–302; Rozwenc, *The Causes of the American Civil War*, 11–20.

533. Seward speech at Rome, N.Y., October 29, 1858, in *Albany Evening Journal*, November 2, 1858.

534. *Rochester Democrat and American*, November 4, 1858.

535. Hobart Berrian to William Seward, November 9, 1858, Seward Papers.

536. George Palmer to William Seward, November 12, 1858, George Harris to Seward, November 12, 1858, Chester Harding to Seward, November 5, 1858, Seward Papers.

537. George Baker to William Seward, November 4, 1858, Seward Papers; *New York Tribune*, December 1, 1858.

538. Frederick Seward, 251.

539. *Little Rock State Gazette and Democrat*, November 12, 1858; Davis, *Breckinridge*, 207.

540. Buchanan, 57–58.

541. Ibid., 58.

542. *New York Times*, October 28, 1858.

543. Foner, *Free Soil, Free Labor, Free Men: the Ideology of the Republican Party Before the Civil War*, 69–70; Simms, 150.

544. Frederick Seward, 353.

545. Dubin, *United States Gubernatorial Elections, 1776–1860: The Official Results by State and County*, 179–180.

546. *New York Tribune*, November 4, 1858.

547. *Albany Evening Journal*, November 3, 1858.

548. Waugh, 122.

549. Comments of political leaders on Seward, Baker, 4:681–687.

550. *New York Times*, November 2, 1858; *Rochester Union and Advertiser*, November 3, 1858.

551. "Sewardism" might have been first used in the *New York Atlas and Argus* newspaper, October 29, 1858, reprinted in the *Albany Evening Journal*, October 30, 1858.

552. T.C. Leland to William Seward, November 1, 1858, Seward Papers.

553. John Hasbrouck to William Seward, January 18, 1858, Seward Papers.

554. Edward Everett Hale Jr., *William Henry Seward* (Philadelphia: George Jacobs and Co., 1910), 237–241.

555. Conrad, 321–322.

556. Frederick Seward, 353.

557. *Cincinnati Gazette*, October 25, 1858.

558. W. Dean Burnham, *Presidential Ballots, 1836–1892* (Baltimore: Johns Hopkins University Press, 1955), 704; *National Intelligencer*, October 25, 1858; Brady, 28–29, 37.

559. Milo Holcomb to Abraham Lincoln, July 19, 1860, Abraham Lincoln Papers, Princeton University.

560. Stanton Davis, *Pennsylvania Politics, 1860–1863* (Cleveland: Western Reserve University Press, 1935), 29.

561. *Pennsylvania Public Ledger*, February 28, 1856.

562. Sister Theopain Geary, *A History of Third Parties in Pennsylvania* (Washington, DC: Catholic University of America Press, 1938), 226.

563. *Harrisburg Telegraph*, October 27, 1858.

564. *Philadelphia Press*, October 25, 1858.

565. James Buchanan to Harriet Lane, October 15, 1858; Moore, 10:229; Milton, 307; *American Volunteer*, November 27, 1856.

566. Dubin, *United States Congressional Elections, 1788–1997, Official Results*, 181–184; *Congressional Quarterly Guide to United States Elections* (Washington, DC: Congressional Quarterly Inc., 1975), 604–605.

567. Nichols, *Disruption*, 219–221.

568. *Cleveland Plain Dealer*, November 4, 1858; *Buffalo Register and Times*, November 6, 1858; *Philadelphia Press*, November 6, 1858; *Daily Chicago Times*, November 8, 1858; *National Slavery Standard*, November 13, 1858; *New York Evening Post*, November 5, 1858; *Philadelphia Press*, November 4, 1858.

569. Nichols, 223–224.

570. William Herndon and Jesse Weik, *Abraham Lincoln: The True Story of a Great Life*, 3 vols. (Chicago: Belford, Clarke and Co., 1889), 2:127; Basler, 3:335; William Barton, *The Life of Abraham Lincoln*, 2 vols. (Indianapolis: Bobbs-Merrill Co, 1925), 1:403; Basler, 3:346.

571. Damon Wells, *Stephen Douglas: The Last Years, 1857–1861* (Austin: University of Texas Press, 1971), 132–133; Zarefsky, 207; *Illinois State Journal*, November 3, 1858.

572. Beveridge, 2:697n; Zarefsky, 205; Holzer, 373.

573. David Brady, *Critical Elections and Congressional Policy Making* (Stanford: Stanford University Press, 1988), 22.

574. Nichols, 21–40.

575. Brady, 38–39.

576. Brady, 40.

577. James Sundquist, *Dynamics of the Party System* (Washington, DC: The Brookings Institute, 1983), 78–79.

578. Sundquist, 82–83.

579. *Washington Star*, September 25, 1858; Buchanan to Harriet Lane, October 15, 1858, Moore, 10:229–230.

580. William Sherman to Ellen Sherman, April 15, 1859, Sherman Papers; John F. Marszalek, *Sherman: A Soldier's Passion for Order* (New York: Free Press, 1993), 119.

581. Pawn shop slip, December 23, 1857, with January 23, 1858, expiration date, John Simon, ed., *The Papers of Ulysses S Grant, 1837–1861*, vol. 1 of 26 vols. (Carbondale, Illinois: Southern Illinois University Press, 1967), 1:339.

582. U.S. Grant to his sister Mary, March 21, 1858, John Simon, ed., *The Papers of Ulysses S. Grant, 1837–1861*, 1:340–341.

583. U.S. Grant to his sister, Simon, 1:339.

584. *New York Times*, September 10, 1885.

585. B. H. Liddell Hart, *Sherman: Soldier, Realist, American* (New York: Praeger Publishing, 1960), 46–47.

586. James Merrill, *William Tecumseh Sherman* (New York: Rand McNally, 1971), 96.

587. William Sherman to Thomas Ewing, January 3, 1857, Sherman Papers, Princeton University Archives.

588. William Sherman to Thomas Ewing, January 1, 1857, Sherman Papers.

589. Marszalek, 20–24.

590. E. V. Smalley, "General Sherman," *Century Magazine* 5 (January 1884), 453.

591. William Sherman to Ellen Ewing, August 21, 1839, Sherman Papers.

592. William Sherman to Ellen Sherman, November 10, 1847, February 3, 1848, Sherman Papers.

651. Frederick Douglass, *Life and Times of Frederick Douglass: His Early Life as a Slave, His Escape from Bondage and His Complete History* (New York: Gramercy Books, 1993), 260–261.

652. *Akron (Ohio) Beacon*, June 1881.

653. Salmon Brown, "Personal Recollections of My Father," *Portland (Oregon) Telegram*, October 20, 1906; Salmon Brown, "My Father, John Brown," *Outlook*, January 25, 1913, 142–150; *New York Evening Post*, October 23, 1909.

654. John Brown Jr. to a friend, December 12, 1890, Stutler Collection.

655. Salmon Brown, "My Father, John Brown," *Outlook*, January 1913, 142–150.

656. W. E. B. DuBois, *John Brown* (Millwood, N.Y.: Kraus-Thomson Organization, Limited, 1973), 71.

657. Richard Boyer, *The Legacy of John Brown: A Biography and History* (New York: Alfred Knopf, 1973), 560.

658. McPherson, 148–149.

659. Brown speech, March 22, 1859, Redpath, 239–240.

660. Charles Robinson to John Brown, September 14, 1856, J. W. Winkley, *John Brown: The Hero* (Boston: James West Co., 1905), 14, 16.

661. James Malin, *John Brown and the Legend of Fifty-Six* (Philadelphia: American Philosophical Society, 1942), 648.

662. John Brown to F. B. Sanborn, August 5, 1858, Edward Renehan Jr., *The Secret Six: The True Tale of the Men Who Conspired with John Brown* (New York: Crown Publishers, 1995), 171–172.

663. Henry Steele Commager, *Theodore Parker* (Boston: Little, Brown and Co., 1936), 199; Jeffery Rossbach, *Ambivalent Conspirators: John Brown, the Secret Six and a Theory of Slave Violence* (Philadelphia, University of Pennsylvania Press, 1982), 148–153.

664. Truman Nelson, *The Old Man: John Brown at Harper's Ferry* (New York: Holt, Rinehart and Winston, 1973), 28.

665. John Brown to Owen Brown, February 5, 1858, Brown to George Hearns, August 8, 1857, Stutler Collection.

666. Subscription list, undated, Stutler Collection.

667. F. B. Sanborn to George Stearns, Amos Lawrence, and other subscribers, August 25, 1857, Stutler Collection.

668. John Kagi to John Brown Jr., October 10, 1859, Stutler Collection.

669. The ads ran in dozens of newspapers and were quoted in many diaries, including Randolph Abbott Shotwell, in unpublished notes.

670. Anonymous letter, undated, Stutler Collection.

671. Peggy Russo and Paul Finkelman, eds. *Terrible Swift Sword: The Legacy of John Brown* (Athens, Ohio: Ohio University Press, 2005), 111.

672. Richard Scheidenhelm, *The Response to John Brown* (Belmont, California: Wadsworth Publishing Co., 1972), 57, 63; McPherson, 210–211.

673. From paper written by James Emery in 1896, in the *Lawrence (Ks.) Daily Journal-World*, May 31, 1943.

674. From unpublished notes of Randolph Abbott Shotwell, J. G. de R. Hamilton, ed., *The Papers of Randolph Abbott Shotwell* (Raleigh, N.C.: North Carolina Historical Commission, 1929), Stutler Collection.

675. Jules Abels, *Man on Fire: John Brown and the Cause of Liberty* (New York: Macmillan Co., 1971), 212–213.

676. John Brown to his wife, January 30, 1858, Sanborn, *Life and Letters of John Brown*, 440–441; John Brown to Thomas Higginson, February 2, 1858, Higginson Papers, Boston Public Library; Stephen Oates, *To Purge This Land of Blood: A Biography of John Brown* (New York: Harper and Row, 1970), 225.

677. *Cleveland (Ohio) Leader*, August 10, no yearly date.

678. John Brown, *Provisional Constitutional Ordinances for the People of the United States* (St. Catharine's, Canada: William Day, printer, 1858), preamble.

679. F. B. Sanborn letter, December 12, 1890, Stutler Collection.

680. *Weston Independent*, 1920 issue.

681. John Brown to Ellen Brown, October 11, 1858, Stutler Collection.

682. John Brown to Ellen Brown, December 17, 1858, Sutler Collection.

683. Oswald Villard, *John Brown, 1800–1859: A Biography Fifty Years After* (New York: Alfred Knopf, 1943), 364–365.

684. John Brown to Owen Brown, May 21, 1858, Stutler Collection.

685. Stephen Oates, *To Purge This Land of Blood: A Biography of John Brown*, 220.

686. Richard Boyer, *The Legend of John Brown: A Biography and History* (New York: Alfred Knopf, 1973), 188, 122; *New York Tribune*, September 1, 1872; James Redpath, *The Public Life of Captain John Brown* (Boston: Thayer and Eldridge, 1860), 48; Octavius Frothingham, *Gerrit Smith: A Biography* (New York: G.P. Putnam's Sons, 1879), 239; Fried, 157.

687. Abels, *Man on Fire: John Brown and the Cause of Liberty*, 210.

688. "John Brown's Raids," *St. Louis Globe-Democrat*, April 15, 1888.

689. Villard, 369; Abels, 217.

690. Villard, 369.

691. *Harrisonville Democrat*, quoted in the *Kansas Herald*, January 8, 1859; *Wyandotte Western Argus*, January 15, 1859.

692. *Missouri Democrat*, January 5, 1859.

693. Winkley, 60, 79–80.

694. Rev. S. L. Adair to James Hanway, February 2, 1878, Hanway Papers, Kansas Historical Society, in Villard, 372.

695. David Atchison to Jefferson Davis, September 24, 1854, Stutler Collection.

696. Villard, 370–379.

697. Abels, 220.

698. Newspaper account by Ambrose published February 28, 1878, in *The Commonwealth* (community unknown).

699. Hutchinson letters, Kansas Historical Society Collection, in Villard, 373.

700. Abels, 227.

701. Boyer, 128; William Phillips, "Three Interviews With John Brown," *Atlantic Monthly* 28 (1879), 738–744.

702. Kansas Historical Society collections.

703. Villard, 377–378.

704. Nelson, 42.

705. Warren, 200.

706. Wattles testimony to Congress, U.S. Senate Committee Reports, 1859–1860, 2:223.

707. Abels, 226.

708. Warren, 306; Abels, 224–225.

709. *Missouri Democrat*, February 8, 1859.

710. John Brown to Ellen Brown, February 10, 1859, Stutler Collection.

711. Villard, 285.

712. Warren, 308.

713. John Brown to the editor of the *Summit Beacon*, December 20, 1855.

714. George Gill to Richard Hinton, July 7, 1893.

715. Kansas Historical Society.

716. Brown diary notes, Kansas Historical Society collections.

717. Villard, 387–393; Gill mss., Kansas Historical Society.

718. Gill, in the Hinton Papers, Oates, 264. For other accounts of the raid and exodus, see Warren, 298–310; Benjamin Quarles, *Allies for Freedom: Blacks and John Brown* (New York: Oxford University Press, 1974), 54–59.

719. James Mackay, *Allan Pinkerton: The First Private Eye* (New York: John Wiley and Sons, 1996), 82–85.

720. Oates, 264–265.

721. John Brown to a friend, April 1858, Stutler Collection.

722. John Brown to a friend, October 3, 1857, Stutler Collection.

723. Octavius Frothingham, *Gerrit Smith: A Biography*, 237–238, James Stewart, *Wendell Phillips: Liberty's Hero* (Baton Rouge: Louisiana State University Press, 1986), 200–201, 158–159.

724. *Boston Post*, December 1859, in Stewart, 201.

725. Frederick Douglass address on John Brown, May 30, 1881, in Louis Ruchames, ed., *A John Brown Reader* (New York: Abelard-Schuman Co., 1959), 318.

726. John Brown to Rev. Luther Humphrey, November 19, 1859, Stutler Collection.

727. John Brown to his children, November 22, 1859, Stutler Collection.

728. John Brown speech at Harper's Ferry sentencing, November 2, 1859, John Brown to Lora Case, December 2, 1859, Stutler Collection.

729. John Brown to his wife, October 21, 1859, Stutler Collection.

730. W. E. Doyle, "Fanaticism a Virtue," *Confederate Veteran*, August 1924.

731. *Wheeling (Virginia) Intelligencer*, October 19, 1859.

732. *Harper's Weekly*, December 17, 1859.

733. Buchanan, *Mr. Buchanan's Administration on the Eve of Rebellion*, 84–85.

734. News clippings, Kansas State Historical Society, Petersen, 79.

735. Buchanan, *On the Eve of the Rebellion*, 46.

736. James Buchanan to William Reed, July 31, 1858, Moore, *Works,* 10:224–225.

737. Quoted in Allan Nevins, *The Emergence of Lincoln*, 2 vols. (New York: Charles Scribner's Sons, 1950), 1:432.

738. Dr. William Paxton to Curtis, April 11, 1883, in Curtis, *The Life of James Buchanan: Fifteenth President of the United States*, 2:674; Annie Buchanan to a friend, in Curtis, 2:582.

739. McPherson, 251.

740. Curtis, 1:506.

741. Flood, *Grant and Sherman: The Friendship That Won the Civil War*, frontispiece.

742. Roeliff Brinkerhoff, *Recollections of a Lifetime* (Cincinnati: Robert Clarke Company, 1900), 117.

743. Richard Winsor's account of the rescue, Ballantine, 255.

744. *Chicago Press and Tribune*, October 29, 1858; Sandusky, *Ohio Commercial Register*, November 6, 1858; "Peoria Daily Message," quoted in the *Quincy Daily Herald*, November 25, 1858.

745. *Rochester (N.Y.) Democrat*, November 10, 1858; *Illinois State Journal*, November 12, 1858.

746. *Concord Independent Democrat*, quoted in the *Illinois State Journal*, November 3, 1858; *New York Tribune*, November 9, 1858.

747. *National Intelligencer*, May 23, 1860; Robert Meade, *Judah Benjamin: Confederate Statesman* (New York: Oxford University Press, 1943), 137.

INDEX

Emery, James, 262–63
Ewing, Ellen. *See* Sherman, Ellen Ewing
Ewing, Thomas, 222–28
Ewing, Thomas Jr., 234

F
Fairchild, Calvin, 151, 152
Fallon, Christopher, 248
Farragut, David, 233
Felton, William, 270, 271
Filmore, Millard, 3
Fish, Hamilton, 185
Fitch, Jacob, 162
Fitch, James, 144, 154, 166–67, 170
Fitton, James, 271
Fitzhugh, Anna, 55
Floyd, John, 6
Foote, Henry, 4, 38, 178, 186, 189
Forney, John
    Buchanan and, 8, 212, 217, 252
    Douglas and, 118
    in Pennsylvania, 211
Forsyth, John, 245
Freeport debate, 128–31
Freeport Doctrine, 131
Fremont, John C., 3, 9, 82, 102, 194–95
Fugitive Slave Act, 2–3, 11, 48–49, 126, 127, 130, 146, 157, 164–68, 187, 252

G
Galloway, Samuel, 168
Garrison, William Lloyd, 171
Gates, Seth, 157
Geary, John, 259
Geyer, Henry, 47
Giddings, Joshua, 157, 162, 165, 167
Gill, George, 266, 268, 277, 278
Gillpatrick, Rufus, 271